M000314395

International Management Behavior

Global and Sustainable Leadership

Eighth Edition

Now in its eighth edition, this is the textbook for current and future global leaders wanting to lead competently and sustainably in their business practices.

Fully updated, the authors build on their forty years of teaching, researching, and working with managers worldwide to bring students the latest developments in global business practice.

Now including end-of-chapter reflection questions to guide topic comprehension, and directed further resources to assist individual research, this edition also sees the return of Ivey Business School, and IMD cases in the book.

This edition also includes a new conception of mindful global leadership as the integrating framework for execution of global strategy, highlighting the importance of a holistic approach to working across cultures and distance.

Combining a wealth of theoretical knowledge with real-world examples from diverse cultures, countries, and industry sectors, the practical guidance and well-chosen examples throughout the book bring key concepts to life.

Dr. Henry Lane is Professor of International Business & Strategy, D'Amore-McKim School of Business, Northeastern University (Boston). His research and teaching interests include executing global strategy, cross-cultural management, organizational learning, and managing change. His Doctorate in Organizational Behavior is from the Harvard Business School. He serves as a faculty member for university and corporate courses globally. In 2009 he received the Academy of Management, International Management Division's Outstanding Educator Award for continuous excellence and innovation in teaching international management; and also the 2009 Academy of Management Review Decade Award for the co-authored article "An Organizational Learning Framework: From Intuition to Institution."

Dr. Martha Maznevski is Professor of Organizational Behaviour and Faculty Co-Director for Executive Education at Ivey Business School (Canada). Dr. Maznevski completed her PhD at Ivey with research on multicultural teams, and is an expert on global teams, global leadership, culture and identity, and empowering individual differences. She has published widely on these topics in academic and management arenas. She works closely with leaders and their organizations around the world on innovative approaches to achieving sustainable performance across levels, industries, and organizational types in today's highly complex global environment.

International Management Behavior

Global and Sustainable Leadership

EIGHTH EDITION

Henry W. Lane
D'Amore-McKim School of Business, Northeastern University

Martha L. Maznevski
Richard Ivey School of Business, Western University

CAMBRIDGE
UNIVERSITY PRESS

CAMBRIDGE
UNIVERSITY PRESS

University Printing House, Cambridge CB2 8BS, United Kingdom

One Liberty Plaza, 20th Floor, New York, NY 10006, USA

477 Williamstown Road, Port Melbourne, VIC 3207, Australia

314–321, 3rd Floor, Plot 3, Splendor Forum, Jasola District Centre, New Delhi – 110025, India

79 Anson Road, #06–04/06, Singapore 079906

Cambridge University Press is part of the University of Cambridge.

It furthers the University's mission by disseminating knowledge in the pursuit of
education, learning, and research at the highest international levels of excellence.

www.cambridge.org
Information on this title: www.cambridge.org/9781108473286
DOI: 10.1017/9781108637152

© Henry W. Lane and Martha L. Maznevski 2019

This publication is in copyright. Subject to statutory exception
and to the provisions of relevant collective licensing agreements,
no reproduction of any part may take place without the written
permission of Cambridge University Press.

First published 2019

Printed in the United States of America by Sheridan Books, Inc.

A catalogue record for this publication is available from the British Library.

Library of Congress Cataloging-in-Publication Data
Names: Lane, Henry W., 1942– author. | Maznevski, Martha L., author.
Title: International management behavior : global and sustainable leadership / Henry W. Lane,
Northeastern University, Boston, Martha L. Maznevski, Western University.
Description: 8th edition. | Cambridge, United Kingdom ; New York, NY : Cambridge University Press,
2019. | Includes index.
Identifiers: LCCN 2018018890 | ISBN 9781108473286 (hbk)
Subjects: LCSH: International business enterprises – Management. | Organizational behavior. | Culture.
Classification: LCC HD62.4 .L36 2019 | DDC 658/.049–dc23
LC record available at https://lccn.loc.gov/2018018890

ISBN 978-1-108-47328-6 Hardback
ISBN 978-1-108-46114-6 Paperback

Cambridge University Press has no responsibility for the persistence or accuracy
of URLs for external or third-party internet websites referred to in this publication
and does not guarantee that any content on such websites is, or will remain,
accurate or appropriate.

To all the friends who have helped me learn about their cultures, and my own.
Henry (Harry) W. Lane

To Julianna, Katie, Andrea, Arielle and Alexander, to help them inspire the next generation.
Martha L. Maznevski

Contents

Preface

> The real voyage of discovery consists not in seeking new landscapes,
> but in having new eyes.
>
> Marcel Proust

Welcome to the eighth edition!

International management has evolved since we published the seventh edition in 2014, and we've crafted this edition with a fresh look. We've revised and updated the content significantly, adding new chapters, concepts, and examples to illuminate the complexity of today's environment. Most importantly, we've woven a thread of mindfulness – situation awareness and a process orientation – throughout the book. We have also brought teaching cases back into the book, to facilitate its use as a textbook in courses on international or cross-cultural management.

Developing Global Leaders: Research-Grounded, Pragmatically Tested

We have developed, refined, and tested the perspectives in this book for over forty years with undergraduates, graduate students, and practicing executives of all levels around the world. By combining conceptual knowledge and contextually based skill-building, this book provides an effective learning package. In addition to drawing on the up-to-date research of experts in the business and management fields, we have conducted our own research on the issues and skills relevant to international management, and also on how best to train global managers.

Management Focus

In this book we take the perspective of a practicing manager, someone faced with situations and who needs to act. We therefore provide a problem-solving approach to international business. International business activities are complex situations in which both business factors and cultural factors are simultaneously embedded, and need to be managed together. The skills needed to cross boundaries cannot be isolated from management realities, and appreciating various and multiple influences on behavior can make a difference in outcome and performance.

Behavioral Focus

This book emphasizes that the human element in managing effectively across cultures is just as important as, and sometimes more important than, the technical or functional elements. However, most managers develop stronger technical or business skills than the behavioral boundary-spanning, interpersonal and cultural skills. They need to complement these strong technical backgrounds with behavioral skills; if they don't, they may never get the opportunity to use the business or technical skills.

Process Focus

Related to the behavioral focus is the process focus – behaving, interacting, learning, and moving forward to meet objectives. This perspective is an important contributor to success in a global market. In other words, leading well in an international setting is not just about having the right characteristics or competences; it's about the dynamics of knowing how to adapt quickly and effectively. Often, good international management is less about "finding a solution or making a decision" and more about "identifying and embarking on a process."

Intercultural Focus

The material in this textbook focuses on the interaction between people of different cultures in work settings. This intercultural orientation is distinct from a comparative approach, in which management practices of individual countries or cultures are examined and compared. While we do often report on cultural comparisons, we focus on what happens at the intersection. This is the boundary that provides both the greatest challenges and the most interesting opportunities.

Culture-General Focus

This book is intended for a wide variety of managers and international staff who must function effectively in a global environment; therefore, we do not concentrate deeply on particular cultures, countries, or regions. A culture-general perspective provides a framework within which country-specific learning can take place more rapidly as necessary. It helps to know what questions to ask and how to interpret the answers received when conducting business globally or helping others to do the same. It helps the learner become more effective at learning and adapting to other cultures. We do provide specific examples of cultures, countries, and regions: not enough to take the place of in-depth culture-specific training for people who are assigned to a particular place, but enough to enhance the impact of that training.

Outline of the Book: Following the Challenges and Opportunities

The four parts of this book follow the main categories of challenges and opportunities we see international managers experiencing most frequently. Each part closes with a series of teaching cases that apply the concepts of the section to management practice.

Part I looks at "The New Global Context" of international management behavior. The first chapter, "Global Leaders in the Twenty-First Century," looks carefully at the business and leadership context of today's globalization, and identifies general leadership competences needed for leading in this complexity. Chapter 2 examines the importance of "Mindful Global Leadership." This chapter explores the role of people who manage others in a global environment, and what makes this different from "regular" management. It introduces the concepts of mindfulness, global mindset, a global leadership competences model, and a set of principles for leading. These concepts set the organizing framework for the rest of the book. In Chapter 3, "Understanding Culture," we identify why culture is such an important element of the international management context, and develop a set of tools for describing and comparing cultures.

Part II consists of three chapters that look at "Leading People across Contexts." Chapter 4, "Interpersonal Skills for International Management," provides a model for interacting effectively across cultures and illustrates it with many examples. Chapter 5 looks at "Leading Global Teams," including virtual teams and broader networks of teams. "Talent Management" is the subject of Chapter 6, where we look at how organizations select, prepare, and support global leaders.

In Part III, we turn to the relationship between management behavior and company performance. Chapter 7, "Executing Global Strategy: Foundations," discusses the principles of organizational design, drawing on a model of organizational alignment. The framework explains how aligned organizations are more likely to execute strategy effectively and perform well. Chapter 8, "Executing Global Strategy: Applications," illustrates a repertoire of organizational types from large, matrixed multinational enterprises to small born-global start-ups. Because global leaders are almost constantly involved in influencing organizational change, Chapter 9 provides guidance for "Leading Change in Global Organizations."

Part IV, "Integrity and Sustainable Performance," looks at the relationship between leaders, their organizations, and society. Chapter 10 focuses on "Competing with Integrity" as individual decision-makers with "Personal Integrity." Chapter 11 takes this to the organizational level with "Corporate Sustainability."

Chapter 12 provides a conclusion for the book, with our reflections about global leadership journeys.

The chapters combine our own research and experience and that of many others. While we do not provide a review of all the research in the field (other resources do that well), we focus on the research and frameworks that provide the most immediate practical guidance for managers, and present it in ways that have proven to be helpful for practice. We provide many examples throughout the book to help readers see how others have applied the lessons, and generate ideas for applying the ideas and behaviors themselves. Most of our examples come directly from the experience of managers we've worked closely with, and we've tried to capture the flavor, feeling, and tempo of these people and the places in which they live and work. They may not be recognized as leaders who capture headlines in the press, but through their experiences we are able we provide more behavioral and reflective insights. We find they are great role models.

Acknowledgments

The eighth edition of this book is a major revision of material from previous editions and includes many new changes.

We start by acknowledging Joseph J. DiStefano's historical contribution to this book and to our careers by including his name on the cover. In 1975, Professor DiStefano interviewed Professor Lane who was doctoral candidate at the Harvard Business School, and recruited him to Canada. He became a colleague, co-author, and friend. Professor DiStefano started one of the first cross-cultural courses anywhere in 1974 at the Ivey Business School (at the time the Western Business School) which was the genesis of this book. Professor DiStefano was the Chair of Professor Maznevski's PhD thesis committee. In January 2000, Professor DiStefano joined IMD in Lausanne, Switzerland, and recruited Professor Maznevski to IMD in 2001. In 2016 Professor Maznevski returned to the Ivey Business School where this book has its roots.

Another person at the University of Western Ontario (now Western University) who became a colleague, co-author, and friend, Professor Don Simpson, deserves special recognition for introducing Professor Lane to Africa and helping him begin his "voyage of discovery" into the reality of functioning in other cultures and doing business internationally.

We have appreciated the support for our work on international business shown by our colleagues and research associates over the years at the Ivey Business School, Northeastern University, University of Virginia, and IMD.

Both of us owe a special debt to our professors, colleagues, and friends who shaped our interests and knowledge at Ivey. We are grateful to: Deans J. J. (Jack) Wettlaufer, C. B. (Bud) Johnston, Adrian Ryans, and Larry Tapp; Professors Jim Hatch, Terry Deutscher, and Ken Hardy; the directors of Research and Publications at the Ivey Business School; and especially the donors of the Donald F. Hunter professorship (a Maclean Hunter endowment) and the Royal Bank professorship, which provided extra time for Professors Lane and DiStefano to undertake much of the initial work in developing this text. We all recognize the special contribution and mentorship of the late Professor Al Mikalachki who taught us so much about change.

In 1994, Professor Lane assumed responsibility for Ivey's Americas Program and that same year he began working with IPADE in Mexico and is very appreciative of the wonderful colleagues and friends he has made there over twenty years who not only have contributed to his education about Mexico and Latin America, but also made it enjoyable to spend time there learning. In September 1999, Professor Lane moved to the D'Amore-McKim School of Business at Northeastern University as the Darla and Frederick Brodsky Trustee Professor in Global Business. Professor Lane is grateful for their support and friendship.

In 1994, Professor Maznevski moved from Ivey to the McIntire School of Commerce at the University of Virginia. She thanks her colleagues there, in particular Dean Carl Zeithaml. The commitment of the school to making its programs global provided substantial support for her involvement in developing material for this book. Dean Zeithaml sponsored, both financially and with his enthusiasm, the first ION conferences and the genesis of a great network of colleagues which still influences our work and the field today.

In 2001, Professor Maznevski moved to IMD, and her learning and this book have been greatly influenced by her experiences there. She thanks her colleagues for their collaboration and learning adventures. As Program Director of large general management programs, the full-time MBA, and many programs for companies, she worked with senior executives from around the world, and accompanied them on their global development journeys.

To this list of acknowledgments we need to add a large number of people and institutions from around the world who have broadened and informed our experience: managers in both the public and private sectors; colleagues at other universities and institutes; companies who have provided access to their operations for the purpose of writing cases; and a number of former students and research assistants who worked with us to develop material for this and previous editions. Among the former research assistants, a special note of thanks is due to Professor Bill Blake of Queen's University and to Professor Lorna Wright of York University. We would like to thank David Ager, Dan Campbell, Celia Chui, Karsten Jonsen, and David Wesley for their substantial contributions. Other previous doctoral students who contributed to the intellectual tradition in international business at Ivey and to our learning include Paul Beamish, Neil Abramson, Shawna O'Grady, Terry Hildebrand, Iris Berdrow, Sing Chee Ling, and Jonathan Calof. As the newest additions to the research assistant team, Ali Beres and Gena Zheng provided strong support on this edition.

The restructuring that has taken place in the publishing industry adds considerably to this list of acknowledgments. A series of acquisitions and reorganizations has led to experience with six publishers and nine editors during the writing of the eight editions. All were strong believers in, and advocates for, this book and we value our relationship with all of them. Sincere thanks go to all those who helped along the way and particularly to Rosemary Nixon at Blackwell then Wiley. A major change with this edition is a new publisher, Cambridge University Press and new editor, Valerie Appleby, who has worked hard to make the eighth edition a reality. We want to recognize Jane Adams and Lisa Pinto of CUP's Textbook Development Department for their work preparing the book for publishing, and we look forward to a continuing and productive relationship with them. And in this context, we thank Professor Paul Beamish at Ivey and Professor Bert Spector at the D'Amore-McKim School of Business at Northeastern University for introducing us to Valerie and to Cambridge University Press.

We also express our appreciation to colleagues who have provided the publishers, and us, with helpful critiques. To Nick Athanassiou, Bert Spector, Chris Robertson, Jeanne McNett and Andy Savitz we say a special thanks for the reviews, suggestions, and editing which shaped this, and earlier, editions. We thank Professor Joerg Dietz for his contribution as a co-author of the sixth edition.

Students and managers who have worked with our materials, and colleagues who have adopted the book and have written to us with thanks and suggestions, all have helped us and others learn. To them we add our gratitude. Professor Lane would acknowledge, in particular, Professors Nick Athanassiou, Sheila Puffer, Alexandra Roth, David Wesley, and Tricia McConville who have used this book at Northeastern and the executives who have shared their experiences with us or have facilitated access to case situations: Ken Clark, Gail Ellement, Ted English, Charles Forsgard, Astrid Nielsen, Philipp Röh, and Ron Zitlow. Professor Maznevski thanks all the many executives in programs at IMD who have shared their stories and challenges, and new colleagues and students at Ivey who have pilot tested the development of new ideas and materials. We thank the reviewers for the eighth edition whose helpful comments are reflected in these pages.

We both warmly thank our friends and colleagues at ION, the International Organizations Network. This group has greatly facilitated and inspired our work, helped us make new friends and create new knowledge, and is always fun.

Last, but hardly least, we thank our families who have supported our learning and the publishing of what we have learned. This has meant time away from home, time spent alone writing, and time and energy devoted to the many visitors and friends from around the world who have shared our homes. All have been critical to our development. Our spouses, Anne and Brian, have been more than patient; they have contributed significantly to our understanding and commitment, as have our children and grandchildren. We thank them all for their love and assistance.

Notwithstanding this lengthy list of personal acknowledgments, we close with the usual caveat that we alone remain responsible for the contents of this book.

Introduction

This book is for managers like Rachna, an Indian now in Europe globally sourcing service contracts for a US-based multinational; like Jonatas, a Brazilian now in Singapore, optimizing a supply chain for a specialty chemicals firm created from a European–Middle Eastern joint venture; like Rich, a Canadian who returned to his home country after working abroad, to innovate new practices in the oil industry; like Frances, a young Chinese leader developing as a global leader; and like Jaclyn, just starting her career, intrigued about international management and eager to learn what it entails.

This book is for managers like Jan, a senior German manager who has worked and lived in many countries, and is now CEO of a large multinational firm and working with his teams to develop and implement global strategies; like Magdi, a senior Lebanese manager who has also worked and lived in many countries, and now in charge of global production for a large multinational firm; and like Amy, an American senior manager in Silicon Valley with a great track record in new product development and marketing in innovative firms around the world. It is for people like Eivind, Mads, Kirsi, and other leaders in Human Resources responsible for attracting, assessing, developing, and enabling all the people who manage their organizations internationally.

It's also for people like Jemilah, Ed, Teo, Feena, and Dermot: senior leaders in global non-governmental organizations (NGOs) who are actively trying to help the world while simultaneously revolutionizing their industry to make aid more effective. And it is for Jesper, Mahoto, and Liesbeth, managers creating innovative ways to combine aid, development, and entrepreneurship to help people help themselves in countries with developing economies.

This book is not just a book about global business. It is about *people who conduct business – and manage other types of organizations – in a global environment.* It discusses and explores typical situations that managers encounter: the problems and opportunities; the frustrations and rewards; the successes and failures; the decisions they must make and the actions they must take.

Bird and Mendenhall (2016) have pointed out that there is ambiguity in the terminology used by management scholars when talking about management outside the strictly domestic context. They consider "international management" to be the broadest classification incorporating international strategy, talent management, and other aspects of managing an organization. It also includes understanding and practicing cross-cultural management. You will find all these activities and skills discussed in this book.

International management is not an impersonal activity, and it should not be studied solely in an impersonal way. It is important to understand trade theories; to be able to weigh the pros and cons of exporting versus licensing; or to understand the advantages of a joint venture versus a wholly-owned subsidiary. But eventually, theory must give way to practice; strategizing and debating alternatives must give way to action. Working globally means interacting with colleagues, customers, and suppliers from other countries to achieve a specific outcome. We focus on these interactions, on getting things done with and through other people in an international context.

Globalization means that one does not have to travel to another country to be exposed to situations of cultural diversity. For example, consider a manager in Boston who worked for Genzyme, which is one of the world's leading biotech companies. This company was founded in Boston in 1981 and was acquired by Sanofi SA from France in 2011. Now the American manager may travel to France frequently or interact with French mangers when they come to Boston. This same manager possibly interacts with a number of other local Boston companies that are also now foreign-owned. He or she may have an account with Citizen's Bank (owned by the Royal Bank of Scotland Group) or Sovereign Bank (owned by Santander from Spain); purchase insurance from John Hancock (owned by Manulife Financial of Canada); and buy groceries from Stop & Shop (owned by Ahold Delhaize of the Netherlands). And managers from these companies also are likely to be experiencing working with their Scottish, Canadian, Spanish, and Dutch counterparts.

In countries with long histories of immigration, such as Canada, the USA, and Brazil, there is considerable diversity within the domestic workforce and many managers experience working with cultural diversity as part of their daily routine. Managers in all of these countries find the material in this book is also useful in these situations, and they can apply it without their ever having to leave their home base.

Focus on the Voyage

This book is based on the philosophy that learning is a lifelong, continuous process. Although the book contains many recommendations about how to interact and manage in other cultures, rather than simply provide what appear to be the "answers" about the way to act in global management situations and an illusion of mastery, we hope it stimulates and facilitates even more learning about other cultures and how to work effectively with others. For some readers, the material in this book may represent a first encounter with different cultures. Other readers may have been exposed to different cultures through previous courses or personal experience. For those with prior exposure to other people and places, the journey continues with a new level of insight. For those without prior experiences, welcome to an interesting journey!

Bibliography

Bird, A., & Mendenhall, M. E. (2016). From Cross-Cultural Management to Global
    Leadership: Evolution and Adaptation. *Journal of World Business*, 51, 115–126.

PART I
The New Global Context

1 Global Leaders in the Twenty-First Century

> It's a dangerous business, Frodo, going out your door. You step onto the road, and if you don't keep your feet, there's no knowing where you might be swept off to.
>
> J. R. R. Tolkien, *The Lord of the Rings*

Globalization: That Was Then, This Is Now

The phrase "That Was Then, This Is Now" comes from the book of that title by S. E. Hinton (first published in 1971), and it has become a popular expression indicating that things change.

Change is the only constant. After the Uruguay Round of the General Agreement on Tariffs and Trade (GATT) in the late 1980s led to major reductions in tariffs and created the World Trade Organization, companies hastened to become global. However, according to *The Economist*, the global company is now in retreat. "The biggest business idea of the past three decades, is in deep trouble," it noted. "Companies became obsessed with internationalizing their customers, production, capital and management ... Such a spree could not last forever; an increasing body of evidence suggests that it has now ended" (The Economist, 2017). What happened?

"**Globalization**" became one of the biggest buzzwords in business and in business schools. Proponents of globalization saw it reducing poverty and bringing the world closer together. Opponents saw it as a vehicle for continued Western or American economic and cultural domination.

Until recently, business schools made two implicit assumptions in discussions about globalization. The first was that globalization and **global organizations** were recent phenomena. However, by some accounts globalization began when our ancestors started moving out of Africa; one only needs to read about trade routes such as the Silk Road, the Spice Route, and the Triangle Trade to realize that globalization has been an ongoing process. And as one of the oldest religious institutions, the Catholic Church may have been the world's first global organization. Recent economic globalization has been propelled by **trade liberalization, deregulation**, and reduced transportation costs. Modern communication technologies and channels, such as the Internet and mobile phones, have made the process manageable and more visible, and today social media facilitates commentary and discussion both positive and pejorative.

The second assumption was that globalization primarily focused on economic considerations. It is true that trade liberalization opened borders across which capital and products moved more easily, particularly in Europe, where cross-border restrictions of goods are nearly non-existent. However, globalization has also been propelled by other factors. Airline travel and reliable, inexpensive communication have effectively reduced distances and minimized the impact of physical boundaries so that corporations can manage far-flung operations. Alliances and networks blur the lines of organizational boundaries. The forces of deregulation, industry consolidation, and technology have reshaped corporate and social landscapes. Companies globalized by both responding to and feeding the trend of boundary erosion.

In 1983, economist Theodore Levitt contributed to popularizing the concept of economic globalization. He stated that technology and globalization were shaping the world and that they would converge resulting in "global corporations, offering everyone simultaneously high-quality, more or less standardized products at optimally low prices" (Levitt, 1983). To many academics and executives, globalization became primarily about the production and distribution of products.

In 1987, Christopher Bartlett and Sumantra Ghoshal were writing about the need to develop **transnational** capabilities. In so doing, they popularized the concept of the **transnational corporation** (Bartlett and Ghoshal, 1987, 2002). Corporations increasingly began thinking of themselves as global, transnational organizations. In 2006, Sam Palmisano, the former CEO of IBM, characterized the modern global company as a globally integrated enterprise that "fashions its strategy, its management, and its operations in pursuit of a new goal: the integration of production and value delivery worldwide. State borders define less and less the boundaries of corporate thinking or practice" (Palmisano, 2006; The Economist, 2008).

The increasing global reach of companies, as discussed in business schools, is usually considered from narrow perspectives, such as the number of markets served, the global reach of the supply chain and sources of supplies, where parts of the company's value chain are located, and alliances, or mergers and acquisitions, to source intellectual capital (knowledge). These market-oriented and technology-oriented perspectives describe only a part of the reality of globalization. They also tend to focus on external factors, such as trade and investment flows or the percentage of international sales to total sales while ignoring organizational and human considerations.

A basic feature of globalization is that people, countries, and organizations worldwide have become more economically interdependent. However, the erosion of national and company boundaries has led to concern over control of national boundaries and the influx of immigrants. **Brexit**, the rise of **populism, economic nationalism**, concern about immigration, the 2016 election of Donald Trump as President of the USA, and the increased popularity of right-wing parties in Europe have all contributed to what Bob Moritz, Global Chairman of PwC (PricewaterhouseCoopers), refers to as a "new phase of globalization" (Moritz, 2017) while Larry Summers (2016) calls it "responsible nationalism" (see also Girod, 2017).

There have been positive and negative effects from globalization. On the positive side, globalization has increased wealth in the world overall, reduced poverty, improved living standards, and spread innovations. However, the distribution of those gains has been uneven.

Economist Branko Milanovic, a leading scholar on income inequality and author of *Global Inequality: A New Approach for the Age of Globalization* (Milanovic, 2016), in a speech at the World Bank (October 2013) said, "Globalization has benefited an emerging 'global middle class,' mainly people in places such as China, India, Indonesia, and Brazil, along with the world's top 1 percent. But people at the very bottom of the income ladder, as well as the lower-middle class of rich countries, lost out." In addition to a greater distortion in the distribution of wealth from globalization, we have witnessed the appearance of a dark side to globalization as pollution, terror, and criminal enterprises globalized and cyber security became a major concern. Therefore, we must be specific when we discuss globalization – the globalization of what and to the benefit of whom?

Executives such as Bob Moritz (2017) believe that the benefits of globalization outweigh the harms. He said:

For those of us who share that view – that globalisation's pros outweigh its cons – it's time to get in the game. Although keeping immigrants and imports out may sound like a quick fix to workers struggling to keep up in the global, high-tech marketplace, it's important to seek alternate solutions. We are now at the inflection point where the idea of making globalisation work for more people needs to be supported with action.

Much of the observation and writing about the new phase of globalization and its slowdown reflects a North American and Western European orientation and must be understood from that perspective. The location of globalization drivers such as technology, cost structures, growth rates, population trends, and consumers appears to be shifting away from the North Atlantic region (Europe and the USA) to an Asian one (China, India). Jeffery Sachs (Sachs, 2017) believes that,

The dominance of the North Atlantic was a phase of world history that is now closing … the so-called American century has now run its course. The United States remains strong and rich, but no longer dominant.

The key word in his opinion is "dominant." As Sachs suggests, we are not necessarily moving to a China Century or to an India Century, but perhaps a "World Century" characterized by greater economic and technological equality.

What does this all mean for US, Canadian, or EU companies? Their rush to expand globally may slow but they will not simply abandon their international operations and crawl back into their domestic shells. The Economist (2017) sees three operating modes in the future of global business. First, **multinational corporations** (MNCs) will increase their local footprints (production, supply chain, management) to reduce government criticism and nationalistic concerns. Second, technology companies will use more franchising to grow internationally. Finally, companies with e-commerce platforms will continue to grow globally.

The need for executives who can function effectively in this new era of globalization and who are able to manage complex internal and external networks will not disappear. In this book, we focus primarily on the business and management dimensions of globalization and on organizations that attempt to integrate their global activities.

When we examine the processes of companies that globalize, sterile statistics give way to people who create and manage the processes. The picture that emerges at the operational level is often less glamorous than the one provided by macro-level descriptions. The road to globalization has been littered with the debris of ill-considered mergers, acquisitions, and new market entry attempts. In other words, globalization is easy to talk about, but difficult to do.

What is a Global Company?

What exactly is a global company? Is it a company that has plants and subsidiaries in many countries? Is it a company that sells its products and services around the world? Or is it a company that derives more of its revenue from international sales than from domestic sales? Those are some of the characteristics of a global company but we don't believe a company is truly global until the management and employees develop a global mindset. Jack Welch, former CEO of General Electric, said "the real challenge is to globalize the mind of the organization ... Until you globalize intellect, you haven't really globalized the company" (Rohwer, 2000).

Just because a company operates in multiple locations around the world, sells its products in many countries, and derives revenue from international sales does not necessarily make it a global company. It simply means that it functions in a lot of countries. Global strategy is executed by, and global operations are managed by, people from one country interacting with people from another country. They are the managers who interface with the suppliers, alliance partners, and government officials. They are also the people who manage the plants and workforces around the world.

You don't globalize companies unless you globalize people. For example, think of a Japanese company that operates in many countries but whose top managers all have Japanese passports. This is a Japanese company operating in many countries – but not necessarily a company that has been truly globalized. A global company will have a cadre of managers who have global mindsets and understand how to operate in the modern world of economic, political, and cultural interdependence.

In 1990, C. K. Prahalad characterized the world of global business:

A world where variety, complex interaction patterns among various subunits, host governments, and customers, pressures for change and stability, and the need to reassert individual identity in a complex web of organizational relationships are the norm.

This world is one beset with ambiguity and stress. Facts, emotions, anxieties, power and dependence, competition and collaboration, individual and team efforts are all present ... Managers have to deal with these often conflicting demands simultaneously.

Although Prahalad did not use the term "**complexity**," he described this characteristic of globalization accurately. Rather than considering globalization as the proportion of trade conducted across national borders, or by some other economic or social measure, we argue that we should talk about it as a manifestation of complexity that requires new ways of thinking and managing.

Managing Globalization = Managing Complexity

The sixth edition of this book was written just as the global economic crisis was unfolding in 2008. We fully expected that by the time we wrote the seventh edition, the crisis would have been resolved and we would be describing the opportunities and lessons from recovery. Yet as we write the eighth edition, the economic and geopolitical conditions that managers face may have become more demanding. Some writers describe this "new normal" as VUCA – volatile, uncertain, complex, and ambiguous – a term originally used by the US military to describe the post-Cold War situation.

As part of our research for *The Blackwell Handbook of Global Management: A Guide to Managing Complexity* (Lane et al., 2004a) we were trying to learn from managers what globalization meant to them. Economists tended to define globalization in terms of flows of goods or money or people across borders but we sensed that managers experienced it differently in their day-to-day roles. We spoke with managers who were working both outside and inside their home countries, traveling a lot or a little. When we asked them, "What is the effect of globalization on your management role?" their answer surprised us. They all responded: "It's exhausting."

When we probed further, we found that whatever level of cross-border transactions a single manager dealt with, the effect of a more globalized economy and society meant increased complexity. This increased complexity, in turn, meant that the traditional way of managing – often one learned in business school – was not adequate. Managers were working harder to understand complex forces in order to plan and execute with some predictability. The result was a feeling of being overwhelmed and exhausted. Our experience with managers today suggests that this trend continues. Although it may represent the "new normal," many managers have not yet developed the mindset or skills to manage effectively within it.

Interdependence: Increased Connections

What gave rise to the VUCA business environment? First, globalization of trade increased the **interdependence** between countries and people in those countries. We are all more connected than we used to be. The fall (or at least permeability) of barriers to the cross-border flow of people, goods, and money means that events and decisions in one company or in one part of the world impact others who may be distant and seemingly unconnected to those events. In 2008, for example, a **subprime mortgage crash** in the USA triggered the global financial crisis. Subsequently, China's hunger for basic resources such as steel and wood influenced the price of those commodities globally. This impacted the environment and created social conflicts in countries where natural resources were sourced. With such high levels of interdependence around the world, it is impossible for a manager to predict the impact of a specific action, making effective managerial decision-making extremely difficult.

Variety and Ambiguity: Increased Variables and Options but Decreased Clarity

Executives face more **variety** than ever before. In many countries, the domestic workforce is becoming more diverse. For example, in metropolitan Toronto, Canada, approximately 200 languages are spoken and in the 2011 census only 55 percent of the people identified English as their mother tongue. But workforce diversity is just one aspect of the increased variety that managers face today. With modern media and technology, businesses and consumers have become more discerning, forcing companies to better define customer segments. Competitors offer more variety in products and services. In voice communications, companies such as Nokia and Motorola found it difficult to respond to challenges from Apple and Samsung, even as Skype and other Voice over Internet Protocol (VOIP) software challenged traditional methods of telecommunications. Companies that operate in many countries face numerous economic, legal, and regulatory environments. Developing consistent compensation policies in a global company is almost impossible. Making decisions and taking action are much more complicated with so many variables to consider.

Along with increased variety came more **ambiguity**, or lack of clarity. Interconnectedness and variety make it much more difficult to see cause–effect relations. Simple cause and effect are difficult to establish. Although we have more information available to us today than at any time in the past, the reliability of this information is not always clear or meaningful. Financial analysts give us ratings of companies – how do we know what information they've based those ratings on, and what should we do with the information? Customers complain through websites – how representative are they of all customers? How much impact will public complaints have on potential new customers? Recently, the ambiguity of available information and news has been exacerbated during and after the 2016 US presidential election with the appearance of "fake news" on social media websites. Again, decision-making and action are much more challenging when information is ambiguous, when we are not sure about the **cause–effect relations** or the clarity of our information.

The Multiplier Effect: Dynamic Complexity and Flux

Peter Senge distinguished detail complexity arising from many variables from dynamic complexity which equals Variety × Interdependence × Ambiguity (Senge, 2006). Tightly linked, complex global organizations operating in a tightly coupled global environment potentially become more vulnerable as interdependence increases (Weick and Van Orden, 1990). For example, a single email sent simultaneously to several locations in the world can be interpreted differently and forwarded to several other destinations, each generating varied interpretations and possible actions. The increase in complexity leads to a decrease in buffers, slack resources, and autonomy of units. There also is less time to contemplate corrective action. All this makes problem diagnosis and action planning difficult. Problems appear and must be resolved. "Now" has become the primary unit of time in the world of global managers.

As if that weren't enough, the configuration of our complex environment is always shifting and changing. Even if you could take a snapshot today of the interdependence, variety, and information available and study it enough to understand and make clear decisions, tomorrow will likely be different. Decisions you made yesterday may no longer be valid. We refer to this as **flux** because it represents rapid unpredictable change in many directions, not predictable change in a few dimensions.

It is no wonder that managers feel overwhelmed, whether or not they are directly involved in cross-border transactions! This environmental complexity is depicted in Figure 1.1.

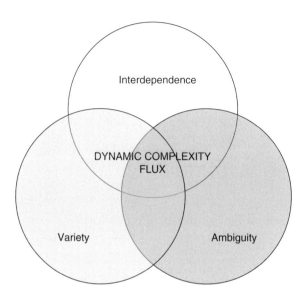

Figure 1.1 The complexity of globalization

Managing Complexity

How do you manage this level of complexity in the environment? The traditional way taught in business schools encourages the use of data, comparison, measurement, categorization, analysis, planning, and maybe **stretch goals** before taking action. However, this **command and control** mode may not be sufficient to respond to globalization pressures since not everything is under our control and change is constant. The management of people in a complex setting like globalization presents much more of a challenge; however, as we have seen in our research on complexity, it is absolutely critical to the success of organizations today.

The way to manage the complexity of globalization is by using the capacity that is in people to manage it themselves. The most complex thing in any organization is people: human brains and the relationships among people. When managers simplify a few key control processes, such as the organizational structure, the company values, goals and strategy, and some key performance indicators, they can develop a more **facilitative** and **collaborative** style to "let go" and empower people to manage the complexity. This more facilitative and process-oriented **mindful global leadership** style, using a flexible mode of operating, will make dealing with complexity more manageable and will be discussed in detail in Chapter 2.

Global Leadership: Leading People across Boundaries

What is the role of a global (or international) manager (or leader) who must function in this complex international environment? What makes it different from someone doing the same job in a single country? We explore the tasks an international manager is responsible for, and consider some basic definitions.

Manager or Leader? International or Global?

Rather than one or the other, we use manager and leader, and international and global as complementary definitions, not antagonistic roles or situations.

The debate about management versus leadership is an important one conceptually. When it was first raised by Abraham Zaleznik of the Harvard Business School in 1977 it was helpful to identify the importance of taking responsibility, setting direction, and inspiring people (**leadership**) in addition to executing organizational mandates (**management**) (Zaleznik, 2004). This debate generated an acknowledgment that those who lead businesses should include values, motivation, and other aspects of non-rational leadership in their agendas. Bennis and Nanus put it simply, "Managers do things right, leaders do the right things" (Bennis and Nanus, 1985). However, as Mintzberg pointed out twenty years later, we cannot lose sight of the fact that even leaders need to get things done, responsible leaders do it well, and this requires good management (Mintzberg, 2005).

In reality, the person who is responsible for mandates across international borders must both lead and manage, often at the same time. We therefore use the terms manager and leader interchangeably, and when it is important to specify which competences or perspectives are important for which aspects of the role, we do so carefully.

The distinction between **global** and **international** has also been the subject of much conceptual debate, both in the literature and within companies. In global strategy, the terms differentiate an approach of having the same product or services everywhere (global) from one that is highly adapted to local conditions (multi-domestic or international). This is often reflected in structures that are highly centralized or coordinated (global) versus ones that are more decentralized (international, multi-domestic).

For the purposes of our discussion, it is more important to define global as complexity, and identify different levels of "global" or complexity by the type of task and extent of global context. It is less important to distinguish global from international. The focus of this book is the perspective of the *person* in the *role* of being responsible for mandates across borders, situations involving the crossing of boundaries, and the interpersonal and organizational dynamics encountered.

Global Leaders

Although clearly most managers' jobs have become more global, some jobs are more global than others. The more global a job or mandate, the more it requires global leadership and the kinds of management competences and perspectives addressed in the following chapters.

A leader's role can be more global to the extent that it requires (Caligiuri, 2006; Caligiuri and Tarique, 2009):

- Working with colleagues from other countries
- Interacting with external clients from other countries
- Interacting with internal clients from other countries
- Speaking a language other than one's mother tongue at work
- Supervising employees who are of different nationalities
- Developing a strategic business plan on a worldwide basis
- Managing a budget on a worldwide basis
- Negotiating in other countries or with people from other countries
- Managing foreign suppliers or vendors
- Managing risk on a worldwide basis

Using the characterization of global as complexity discussed earlier, Reiche et al. defined global leadership as:

the processes and actions through which an individual influences a range of internal and external constituents from multiple national cultures and jurisdictions in a context characterized by significant levels of task and relationship complexity. (Reiche et al., 2017)

From this definition they created a typology of four global leadership roles that they termed **incremental** or **connective** based on low task complexity and either low or high relationship complexity; and **operational** or **integrative** based on high task complexity and either low or high relationship complexity. Their typology is shown in Figure 1.2.

High

CONNECTIVE Global Leadership	INTEGRATIVE Global Leadership
• **Task:** Low levels of variety and flux • **Relationship:** High number & variation of boundaries and high levels of interdependence *Example role:* • Leader of globally distributed team that handles firm's back office *Example role behaviors:* • Learn nuances of distinct interaction contexts • Continuously adapt and respond to different exchange partners' behaviors (code-switching) • Build interaction frequency and intensity through virtual communication and frequent travel • Leverage social frictions for problem solving	• **Task:** High levels of variety and flux • **Relationship:** High number & variation of boundaries and high levels of interdependence *Example role:* • Senior executive of global multi-unit firm *Example role behaviors:* • Recognize and handle trade-offs and paradoxes across both task and relationship domains • Develop synergistic solutions • Engage in regular coordination and integration activities across tasks and constituent groups • Contextualize change implementation processes • Engage in distributive leadership processes
INCREMENTAL Global Leadership	OPERATIONAL Global Leadership
• **Task:** Low levels of variety and flux • **Relationship:** Low number & variation of boundaries, and low levels of interdependence *Example role:* • Export director in firm that operates internationally through licensing *Example role behaviors:* • Lead incremental change efforts • Focus on technical innovation • Create visions that are narrow in scope • Use routinized and standardized forms of communication	• **Task:** High levels of variety and flux • **Relationship:** Low number & variation of boundaries and low levels of interdependence *Example role:* • Leader of product development in firm that provides financial services to global customers *Example role behaviors:* • Locally adapt task prioritization, allocation of resources, problem solving processes • Scan, process. attend to and continuously analyze disparate operational information • Lead varying operational changes at local levels

Relationship Complexity

Low   Task Complexity   High

Figure 1.2 Global leadership typology

Superheroes or Ordinary Humans?

Research on global leadership has skyrocketed in recent years, and many studies have been published identifying the skills that global leaders need.

With lists of required competences reaching as high as 250, it seems that only a superhero can be a global leader. However, there are ways of sorting out the most important criteria, and the following framework best captures key capabilities. The Pyramid Model of Global Leadership developed by Bird and Osland (Bird and Osland, 2004) (Figure 1.3) summarizes the most important skills and knowledge, and illustrates how they build on each other. In their view, global managerial expertise is a constellation of traits, attitudes, and skills or what

Figure 1.3 Global competences model

they call "**global competences.**" Each level presumes and builds on the level below, and the more global a job is, the more it requires sophisticated competences in the higher levels of the pyramid.

The foundational level is "Global Business Knowledge." This is deep knowledge about the manager's business and how that business creates value. It also includes knowledge about the political, economic, social, and technical environment. This foundational knowledge is necessary before any of the next steps.

The next level identifies "Threshold Traits." Knowledge will lie dormant without the personal predisposition to use it. Among the myriad personality traits associated with effectiveness, four stand out as differentiating people who are effective in global settings from those who are less effective: integrity, humility, inquisitiveness, and resilience. Integrity is having a firm set of values associated with honesty and transparency, and being true to those values. Humility is recognizing that knowledge and skills are widely distributed, and that others know and can do things that you, yourself, may not. Inquisitiveness is active motivation to know things one does not already know. While humility creates openness, inquisitiveness drives action to learn more, and to experiment with different ways of creating value. Finally, resilience is the ability to persevere in the face of challenges and difficulties. This resides partly in the manager's own personality, and partly in the extent to which the manager has a support network of family, friends, and/or colleagues.

The next level of the pyramid is an important set of "Attitudes and Orientations" – ways of seeing the world and the task of international management. The basic traits suggest potential within an individual; attitudes and orientations guide that potential so the individual sees opportunities. The most important is a **global mindset**, or the tendency and ability to see and understand the world differently than one has been conditioned to see and understand it. In other words, it is a view from outside of one's own borders. Two attitudes and orientations contribute to developing a global mindset. **Cognitive complexity** is an ability to see a situation from multiple perspectives, to see connections among the perspectives, and to build new connections with existing and new information. **Cosmopolitanism** is having a positive attitude toward people, things, and viewpoints from other parts of the world. For example, people who are cosmopolitan are more likely to have close friends who are from countries other than their own. Chapter 2 will focus on ways one can develop a global mindset.

The three most important "Interpersonal Skills" for global leaders are **mindful communication**, building trust, and multicultural teaming. Mindful communication is paying attention to how you communicate with others, especially those who are different, and adapting your communication as necessary to ensure that meaning is transmitted the way you intend. This includes both sending messages (speaking, writing, and non-verbal acts) and receiving them (listening, reading, and observing the behavior of others). Building trust is creating a relationship where all parties believe that the other will act with good intentions for the relationship, and can make decisions on each other's behalf. **Multicultural teaming** is working effectively with people from different cultures on joint deliverables.

Armed with these skills, leaders are better equipped to work with others to develop and implement ideas. Many other interpersonal skills are of course important to global leadership effectiveness, such as negotiation and conflict resolution. However, if a manager is adept at mindful communication, building trust, and multicultural teaming, then generally these other skills will follow. The reverse is not necessarily true – one can negotiate solutions and resolve conflicts without increasing trust, for example.

Finally, a set of six "Systems Skills" are critical for global leaders: spanning boundaries, building community, leading change, architecting, influencing stakeholders, and ethical decision-making. Boundary-spanning is working effectively across countries, organizations, divisions within organizations, and so on. It involves using all the skills and attitudes identified in lower parts of the model to create insights and **synergies** across different perspectives. Building community is creating a sense of identity and joint commitment among a group of people distributed across different countries and units. Leading change effectively is about helping an organization through diverse ways of doing things, while creating capabilities for adapting to further change. **Architecting** is designing and implementing organizational structures and systems that facilitate the organization. Influencing stakeholders, which is an important part of any leadership role, becomes more complex in a global role, where stakeholder variety reflects different interests in different contexts. Ethical decision-making is about making and implementing decisions that consider the long-term benefit of individuals and society.

We believe these systems skills are an extremely important part of global leadership, recognizing that they rest on the levels below. But international managers find much less guidance for these systems skills. We take a systems approach throughout this book, and later chapters address them specifically. Table 1.1 presents a summary of the global competences.

You most likely have a certain level of global business knowledge and are developing more knowledge and skill. So, we assume that the basic traits are given. Therefore we focus on the bottom rows of Table 1.1.

In this chapter, we have acknowledged that today's business environment is highly complex, and the trends creating the complexity are accelerating. Success in such an environment means leading people to achieve results. Global leaders must have the knowledge and skills to create openness to new ways of thinking and acting about personal and business effectiveness. Global leaders must also have a set of competences, including interpersonal and systems skills. The remaining chapters of this book help to develop these global leadership skills.

Table 1.1 **Global leadership competences descriptions**

Level	Competency	Description
Threshold traits	Integrity	Adherence to moral and ethical principles; soundness of moral character; honesty
	Humility	A willingness to learn from others and not assume that one has all the answers
	Inquisitiveness	An interest in learning; questioning; curious about other people and cultures
	Resilience	Capable of surviving under unfavorable conditions; resistance to stress; emotionally resilient
Attitudes & orientations: Global mindset	Cognitive complexity	Ability to balance contradictions and ambiguities; ability to view a situation from many ways and with many connections
	Cosmopolitanism	External orientation; free from local, provincial, or national ideas or prejudices; at home everywhere
Interpersonal skills	Mindful communication	Culturally appropriate and skillful communication
	Create and build trust	Ability to inspire confidence in the certainty of future actions
	Multicultural teaming	Ability to lead and work effectively in multicultural teams, including geographically distributed teams
Systems skills	Build community	Ability to bring the members of heterogeneous groups together to act in concert
	Span boundaries	Creating and maintaining linkages that integrate and coordinate across organizational boundaries
	Architect	Build organizational structures and processes that facilitate effective global interactions
	Lead change	Lead individuals, teams, and organizations to new ways of doing things, build capacity to learn and adapt
	Influence stakeholders	Consider multiple, often conflicting stakeholder needs; make decisions taking them into account; influence them toward alignment
	Making ethical decisions	Adhere to accepted standards of behavior; identify a clear and strong set of values and act according to them

Reflection Questions

Our reflection questions at the end of each chapter are intended to help you apply the ideas and frameworks from the chapter to your own experiences and to companies and situations you are interested in, to develop your global mindset, and to practice mindful global leadership. We hope you'll see the questions as a starting point, and use them to find and pursue other questions that are interesting to you.

1. In your own experience, what are the ways you and your community have been affected by globalization of trade, people, and information? How has it made things better? Worse?
2. We've described globalization by the level of complexity in the business environment: interdependence, variety and ambiguity, and dynamic flux. Think about a company or other organization you're very familiar with. How has the organization responded to the current complexity? Has it found opportunities in the complexity, such as new customer offerings or knowledge bases?
3. How would you assess your current level of global leadership capabilities? Looking at the leadership competence pyramid in Figure 1.3 on p. 19, think about your threshold traits, global mindset, interpersonal skills, and systems skills. What are your strengths, and what do you want to develop further?
4. Think of people you know with strong global leadership capabilities – it could be different people with different strengths. What can you learn from these people to help your own leadership? How could you build a mentoring relationship with them?

Further Resources

There are many books and articles tracing the history of globalization, and the scholarly references from this chapter point to the ones that have shaped our thinking the most. It's helpful to read about globalization as a narrative, and these are three books we think are particularly insightful, told in very compelling ways:

Garten, J. E. (2016). *From Silk to Silicon: The Story of Globalization through Ten Extraordinary Lives.* HarperCollins.

Issenberg, S. (2008). *The Sushi Economy: Globalization and the Making of a Modern Delicacy.* Avery.

Rivoli, P. (2009). *The Travels of a T-Shirt in the Global Economy: An Economist Examines the Markets, Power and Politics of the World Trade*, 2nd edn. Wiley.

Bibliography

Bartlett, C. A., & Ghoshal, S. (1987).
Managing across Borders: New Strategic
Requirements. *MIT Sloan Management
Review*, 28, 7–17.

Bartlett, C. A., & Ghoshal, S. (2002).
*Managing across Borders: The
Transnational Solution*. Harvard
Business Press.

Bennis, W., & Nanus, B. (1985). *Leaders: The
Strategies for Taking Charge*. Harper &
Row.

Bird, A., & Osland, J. (2004). Global
Competencies. In H. W. Lane, M. L.
Maznevski, M. Mendenhall, & J. M.
McNett (eds.), *The Blackwell Handbook
of Global Management: A Guide to
Managing Complexity*. Blackwell.

Bremmer, I. (2014). The New Rules of
Globalization. *Harvard Business Review*
(January–February).

Caligiuri, P. M. (2006). Developing Global
Leaders. *Human Resource Management
Review*, 16, 219–228.

Caligiuri, P., & Tarique, I. (2009). Predicting
Effectiveness in Global Leadership
Activities. *Journal of World Business*, 44,
336–346.

Girod, S. (2017). *The New Rules of
Globalization*, April 18. Retrieved
October 2017 from Global Network
Perspectives: http://gnp.advanced
management.net/article/2017/04/
future-globalization-new-phase

Lane, H. W., Maznevski, M. L., Mendenhall,
M., & McNett, J. (eds.) (2004a).
*The Blackwell Handbook of Global
Management: A Guide to Managing
Complexity*. Blackwell.

Lane, H. W., Maznevski, M. L., Mendenhall,
M., & McNett, J. M. (2004b).
Globalization: Hercules Meets Buddha.
In H. W. Lane, M. L. Maznevski, M.
Mendenhall, & J. M. McNett (eds.),
*The Blackwell Handbook of Global
Management: A Guide to Managing
Complexity*. Blackwell.

Levitt, T. (1983). The Globalization of
Markets. *Harvard Business Review*, 61,
92–102.

Mendenhall, M. E., Osland, J. S., Bird, A.,
Oddou, G. R., Maznevski, M. L., Stevens,
M. J., & Stahl, G. K. (2013). *Global
Leadership*. Routledge.

Milanovic, B. (2013). *The Winners and
Losers of Globalization: Finding a
Path to Shared Prosperity*, October 25.
Retrieved October 2017 from The World
Bank: www.worldbank.org/en/news/
feature/2013/10/25/The-Winners-and-
Losers-of-Globalization-Finding-a-Path-
to-Shared-Prosperity

Milanovic, B. (2016). *Global Inequality:
A New Approach for the Age of
Globalization*. Harvard University Press.

Mintzberg, H. (2005). *Managers Not
MBAs: A Hard Look at the Soft
Practice of Managing and Management
Development*. Berett-Koehler
Publishers.

Moritz, B. (2017). *Understanding the
New Phase of Globalisation*. Retrieved
October 2017 *from PwC Global: www
.pwc.com/gx/en/ceo-agenda/pwc-at-
davos/blogs/2017/understanding-the-
new-phase-of-globalisation.html*

Palmisano, S. (2006). The Globally
Integrated Enterprise. *Foreign Affairs*,
85, 127–136.

Prahalad, C. K. (1990). Globalization: The
Intellectual and Managerial Challenges.
Human Resource Management, 29, 27–37.

Reiche, S. B., Bird, A., Mendenhall, M. E.,
& Osland, J. S. (2017). Conceptualizing
Leadership: A Typology of Global
Leadership. *Journal of International
Business Studies*, 48, 552–572.

Rohwer, J. (2000). GE Digs Into Asia.
Fortune, 142, 178.

Sachs, J. (2017). *The Shifting Global Landscape*, October 17. Retrieved October 2017 from Center for Sustainable Development: http://csd.columbia.edu/2017/01/22/the-shifting-global-landscape/

Senge, P. M. (2006). *The Fifth Discipline: The Art & Practice of the Learning Organization*, revised edn. Doubleday.

Summers, L. (2016). *Voters Deserve Responsible Nationalism Not Reflex Globalism*, July 10. Retrieved October 2016, from The Financial Times: www.ft.com/content/15598db8-4456-11e6-9b66-0712b3873ae1

The Economist (2008). A Bigger World: A Special Report on Globalization. *The Economist,* September 20.

The Economist (2017). The Retreat of the Global Company. *The Economist,* January 28.

Weick, K. E., & Van Orden, P. (1990). Organizing on a Global Scale: A Research and Teaching Agenda. *Human Resource Management*, 29, 49–61.

Zaleznik, A. (2004). Managers and Leaders: Are They Different? *Harvard Business Review* (January). Reprinted in *"Best of HBR"* for 2004, 74–81.

2

Mindful Global Leadership

Mindfulness can encourage creativity when the focus is on the process and not the product.

If something is presented as an accepted truth, alternative ways of thinking do not even come up for consideration.

Ellen J. Langer, *Mindfulness*

Mindful Global Leadership: What Is It?

In the previous chapter we provided examples of managers at different levels of the hierarchy and what they do as global leaders. You know that managers today are facing a complex global environment and that their roles vary by the task and relationship complexity that they face. But what does it really mean to be a *mindful* global leader?[1]

Introduction

Ellen Langer, a psychology professor at Harvard University, wrote a book called *Mindfulness* which describes what it means to be a mindful leader and what happens when you are not (Langer, 1989, 2014). In the book she recounts the story of Napoleon's ill-fated attempt to conquer Russia. The outcome is well known. In June 1812, Napoleon entered Russia with 422,000 troops and in December 1812 he limped out of Russia with 10,000 – a devastating defeat.

---

[1] An earlier version of this chapter was published in ISTMO, December 2016, a publication of Instituto Panamericano de Alta Dirección de Empresa (IPADE), Mexico City.

Professor Langer suggests that Napoleon was not "mindful." The opposite of mindful is "mindless" which means following pre-existing routines and doing things the same old way while processing information without questioning it and assuming that it is context free.

Napoleon was an extremely successful general. He had conquered most of Europe and defeated his enemies though the use of firepower and maneuver. He was fixated on conquering Russia and destroying the Russian army. However, success often breeds complacency and a culture of arrogance, which can lead to "mindless" action and failure. After all, why change a formula that works so well? The answer is because the *context* may be different.

As he advanced rapidly, the Russian army continually retreated destroying anything that Napoleon's troops could use. Soon Napoleon had outrun his supply line. His troops could not be resupplied nor were they able to forage and live off the land since the withdrawing Russians had destroyed everything. Napoleon's interpretation of this rapid advance was that he was "winning" and the Russians, in retreat, were "losing." However, the Russian general, Kutuzov, had a different perspective, which was to lay a trap in the context of the coming Russian winter.

In this brief description we see the dimensions of Napoleon's ascribed "mindlessness." First, he apparently had a narrow category width and couldn't break loose from previously created categories of events, such as that rapid advance signifies winning and retreat signifies the opposite, losing. Second, he apparently did not question the information he was receiving about the Russian retreat. Third, he had a limited perspective, which was that conquest was capturing terrain and eventually, Moscow, and not a broader perspective like Kutuzov's of creating a trap in the context of the approaching winter.

In addition to being able to break old categories and create new ones and being able to engage different perspectives, Langer says that mindfulness involves being **context sensitive** and **process oriented**, not simply goal and outcome fixated.

Mindful Categorization

What does this tale have to do with business today? As we thought about the characteristics of mindfulness and mindlessness, we realized that it was an organizing framework for describing what we have been teaching in Canada, the USA, Mexico, Europe, Asia, and Africa during our careers. We have been intrigued by the failures of many well-known companies that tried to enter markets outside their home countries. They took business models that worked well at home into a new market only to see them fail. They tried to transfer policies and procedures that worked well at home only to see them fail as well. Executives gave a lot of thought to their business model, their strategy, and the goals they wanted to achieve, but did not plan the implementation process sufficiently to reach those outcomes. They had established ways of doing business that had been successful and they presumed they would work anywhere.

As an example consider Wal-Mart's experience in Germany in 2006. It had a successful "formula" that it used in the USA: everyday low prices, tight inventory control, and a wide array of products in its stores. It was (and is) an exceptional and successful retailer, but "hubris" may have partially contributed to its failure in Germany and the sale of its Superstores to a competitor. Germany had its own discount chains, but Wal-Mart must have thought that its everyday low price formula and way of operating would differentiate it from the competition. It was locked into its formula. Successful "formulas" can be powerful and difficult to break away from. Wal-Mart left Germany in 2006 but in 2014 its formula was apparently still giving it trouble in another country, Brazil. Its everyday low pricing was failing to win over customers there who, unconvinced it had the lowest prices, continued their normal routine of comparison shopping and searching for the lowest prices. Its expansion plans did not sufficiently take into account the impact of existing discount retailers or people with different shopping habits.

Category range or width refers to the number of different events, activities, behaviors, situations, places, and so on that one sees as equivalent. Napoleon, apparently trapped in his formula, could only see the retreat of the Russian army as "losing" rather than as an alternative, a "trap." Bruner, Goodnow, and Austin defined categorization as "classifying a variety of stimuli as forms of the same thing" and stated, "To categorize is to render discriminably different things equivalent, to group the objects and events and people around us into classes, and to respond to them in terms of their class membership rather than their uniqueness" (Bruner, Goodnow, and Austin, 1956).

Another categorization example comes from the early days of online grocery home-delivery business. Webvan, an early entrant into this business in the USA, was founded in the late 1990s and became one of the textbook failures of the dotcom era. It filed for bankruptcy in July 2001. Peter Relan, the founding head of technology at Webvan from 1998 to 2000, said the company made some big mistakes – its target audience segmentation and pricing model; its complex infrastructure mode; and a grow big fast mentality accompanied by spending too much money too fast. It cost US$50 million to start up in each city. Part of the infrastructure model was to build warehouses from which deliveries would be made. Relan said, "We touted our 26-city expansion plan, signing a $1 billion Bechtel contract to build several state-of-the-art warehouses worth more than $30 million each." With high start-up costs, high initial capital expenditures, and a low margin business, the company was never profitable.

In contrast, Peapod started in the grocery delivery business in Illinois in 1989. However, it avoided the big capital expenditure mistake of building separate warehouses by choosing to partner with existing supermarket chains in its target markets. The online model also was being explored in the UK around the same time by companies such as Tesco. There was a big difference, however, between the online channel development in the USA and the UK. In the UK:

the established grocery retailers, with extensive history in the traditional store based business, were driving the development of online. In the US the start-ups entering the grocery retail industry with purely online based business models were the active players and the traditional grocery retailers remained sceptical about the new channel. (Kivilahti, 2013)

As Tesco executives developed their "brick and click" model, like Peapod, they realized that existing supermarkets were essentially warehouses. These executives were able to see supermarkets and warehouses as equivalents and avoid the expensive mistake that Webvan made.

Many of the companies that failed in their attempts to globalize also exhibited a lack of context sensitivity. Executives did not understand the unique characteristics of the new country or the culture. They could not understand their new market or their business model from the perspective of the people in the host country. They had a limited world-view based on experience in their home countries rather than a larger, cosmopolitan world-view, or what we call a global mindset. The inability to interpret differences correctly usually resulted in insufficiently detailed implementation plans. A lesson that Wal-Mart learned was that acquiring local retailers with specific market knowledge and not necessarily re-branding them could be a successful entry strategy.

Mindful global leaders are executives who possesses a global mindset so that he or she can see and understand different perspectives; are context sensitive to their own administrative heritage and corporate culture as well as to the culture of the host country; and have a process orientation that becomes reflected in a realistic implementation process.

Mindfulness: Introspective or Context Responsive? Individual or Collective?

There are differing interpretations of the concepts of mindfulness. We think it important to make clear how we interpret and use these concepts, not as a claim that ours are better, but rather to avoid creating confusion.

Mindfulness has become a popular topic in academia and practice in business. However, the term is commonly conflated with meditation and people often think they are the same thing. Although mindfulness as we use it does draw on the concepts of the religious tradition, it has been adapted and made different from that root and when applied to methods of global leadership. There are multiple definitions of mindfulness and some common characteristics from these include being fully present; a heightened state of awareness; active attention; or not being on auto-pilot.

Langer's pragmatic orientation brings awareness and active thinking into clear relationship with the external world or "context" and action or "process" (Langer, 1989, 2014). We revert to Langer for her definition:

Mindfulness is ... best understood as the process of drawing novel distinctions ... Actively drawing these distinctions keeps us situated in the present ... makes us more aware of the context and perspective of our actions than if we rely upon distinctions and categories drawn in the past. Under this latter situation, rules and routines are more likely to govern our behavior, irrespective of the current circumstances, and this can be construed as "mindless" behavior.

Langer and Moldoveanu enumerate the results of mindfulness over **mindlessness** as: "a greater sensitivity to one's environment; more openness to new information; the creation of new categories for structuring perception; and enhanced awareness of multiple perspectives in problem solving" (Langer and Moldoveanu, 2000).

One theory of mindfulness that we do not engage with in this book is that of Karl Weick (Weick and Sutcliffe, 2007; Weick, Sutcliffe, and Obstfeld, 1999). He based his conception of mindfulness on Langer's concept, but transfigured it from the individual level to an organizational or collective way of understanding and applied it to the realm of organizational safety in his research on high reliability organizations (HROs). In that context, mindfulness permits adaptive learning and high or "reliable performance" and it also has a process orientation. In this sense it is consistent with Langer's and with our use of mindfulness.

Our application of the term "mindful," like Langer's, is at an individual level when we are applying it to international business and global leadership – it is a competency for leaders, not processes for whole organizations. This is different from Weick's collective concept applied to reliability. Learning and the ability to create knowledge come from being able to notice, understand, and classify differences. Adaptive learning comes from the ability to be sensitive to differing contexts (cultural context which requires a global mindset) as well as alertness to differing physical and organizational contexts. Often organizations are guilty of over-simplifying the similarity of contexts (home and abroad) and assume things can be done the same way as at home.

Mindful Global Leadership Starts with a Global Mindset

Global managers must learn how to function as effectively in other contexts as they do in their own country, and to build bridges across the world. In the broadest terms, this means reorganizing the way they think as managers.

As one executive put it, "to think globally really requires an alteration of our mindset." At the heart of the global mindset is the ability to see and understand the world differently than one has been conditioned to see and understand it. It is a meta-capability that permits an individual to function successfully in new and unknown situations and to integrate this new understanding with other existing skills and knowledge bases. In other words, it is the ability to "have new eyes" and to be able to understand context from multiple perspectives.

Academics have shown considerable interest in the concept of global mindset in recent years. Based on research by the Global Mindset Project at Thunderbird, Mansour Javidan and colleagues say that leaders who have a high level of global mindset are more likely to succeed in working with people from other cultures (Javidan and Bowen, 2013). They define global mindset as

The set of individual qualities and attributes that help a manager influence individuals, groups and organizations who are from other parts of the world.

According to Javidan and Bowen, a global mindset entails three core elements (Javidan and Bowen, 2013):

- **Intellectual capital:** Global business savvy, cognitive complexity, cosmopolitan outlook.

- **Psychological capital**: Passion for diversity, quest for adventure, self-assurance.
- **Social capital**: Intercultural empathy, interpersonal impact, diplomacy.

Those core elements tend to be at the individual level as identified in Chapter 1 in the discussion of Bird and Osland's global competences model. We agree that a mindful global leader will display those traits; however, as important as a global mindset is, mindfulness is about the process of using those traits in management situations.

Mindful global leaders are executives who possess a global mindset so that they can see and understand **different perspectives**. They also are **context sensitive** to their own administrative heritage, organizational context, and corporate culture as well as to the culture of the host country; and have a **process orientation** that becomes reflected in a realistic implementation process. Mindful global leadership, as we define it, anchors the concept in management roles and not only in terms of culture and personal traits.

A global mindset enables an executive to adapt to the changing needs of global business. It is a way of organizing a set of attitudes and skills for developing and acting on knowledge in a dynamic world. A global mindset incorporates knowledge and openness about working across cultures, and about implementing business across strategic complexity. We define a global mindset like this:

A global mindset is the capacity to analyze situations and develop criteria for personal and business performance that are independent from the assumptions of a single country, culture, or context; and to implement those criteria appropriately in different countries, cultures, and contexts.

For example, a company was implementing self-managed teams throughout the organization for its new modular-based production facilities. In its dynamic and interdependent environment, the company believed it was important to place decision-making authority with the people who had the most immediate information to make the decisions, and who had to implement the decisions. The company developed a model of how self-managed teams should work; pilot-tested it in their home country; then rolled out the new structure around the world. However, it met with resistance. In many parts of the world, the idea of teams managing themselves, without a specific boss to lead them, is completely unheard of. Some plant managers pushed through the self-managed teams program to greater and greater dissatisfaction; others gave up and just kept the more rigid and hierarchical teams.

Some managers, however, did something a bit different. They looked at the two most important criteria for identifying who should make a decision in this new manufacturing context: the people who have the information, and the people who have to implement it. They also realized that manufacturing would not achieve its potential unless there was more interdependence among the various parts of the process. Then they questioned whether the only way to accomplish this was the self-managed team model that headquarters dictated. They met with their managers and teams, and developed a way to achieve the required working relationships and decision processes that fit with the local teams' preferences and context. In some cases, this solution had more hierarchy, in others it had fewer specific roles and more fluidity, and still others had more individual responsibility. In all cases, it achieved the performance goals.

These managers were working with a global mindset. They were able to separate performance criteria, like "people with the information make the decisions," from culturally influenced contextual preferences, like "self-managed teams." Then they found a way to achieve the performance criteria in different contexts.

Components and Domains of a Global Mindset

The crux of developing a global mindset is achieving self-awareness and other-awareness including the relationship between context and characteristics of the self and others. How much of my behavior is "me" and how much of it is influenced by my context? Or, more appropriately, when and how is my behavior more or less influenced by my context? When and how is this the case for others? In business, we need this understanding both about ourselves and others as individuals, and ourselves and others in social groups, especially organizations.

Two orientations that characterize a global mindset are cognitive complexity and cosmopolitanism (Boyacigiller et al., 2004). These orientations help to develop four types of knowledge in the domains in which a global mindset operates, shown in Table 2.1.

Type 1: Knowledge about Self. A global mindset incorporates a concept of self, both as an individual and as part of an organization. We need to acknowledge and understand what it is about our mindset that has been shaped by our own context. Both national culture and organizational culture are critical parts of context that influence self. A global mindset should include sophisticated knowledge about these cultures.

Table 2.1 **Domains of a global mindset**

	Individual	Organizational
Self	**Type 1: Myself** Understand myself and how who I am is associated with my culture and the context I am in.	**Type 3: My own organization** Understand my own organization and how its characteristics, organizational culture, and effectiveness are associated with the context and national culture it is in.
Other	**Type 2: Others** Understand how characteristics of people from other countries and cultures are associated with the contexts they are in.	**Type 4: Other organizations** Understand how characteristics, cultures, and effectiveness of organizations from other countries and national cultures are associated with the contexts they are in.

Culture is an implicit agreement among a group of people concerning what people's actions mean. It is their list of shoulds and oughts for life or, as Hofstede (1980) described it, the collective programming of the mind that distinguishes one group from another. Brannen has pointed out that we should not use "nation as a cognate for culture" (Brannen, 1999; Tung, 1999). Gender, age, religion, or region of a country, for example, can be considered cultures, and a person can be a member of many cultures simultaneously. Culture is often hidden from members of the culture: we rarely examine our own values or context in the normal course of doing things – it is there, taken for granted as the foundation. To paraphrase Edward T. Hall, culture is like air to us, all around and necessary for survival but usually not noticed (Hall, 1959, 1973). Hall observed:

[Culture] is a mold in which we are all cast, and it controls our daily lives in many unsuspected ways ... Culture hides much more than it reveals, and strangely enough what it hides, it hides most effectively from its own participants. Years of study have convinced me that the real job is not to understand foreign culture but to understand our own. (Hall, 1959, 1973)

Becoming aware of the influence of culture on one's self can be both uncomfortable and difficult. But the ability to "see" it and to examine it is critical to developing an effective global mindset.

   Type 2: Knowledge about Others. Of course, different contexts create different assumptions and value systems. This is the more obvious part about cultural differences. It is easy to see that people from different cultures perceive the same situation differently, interpret what they notice differently, evaluate the situation differently, and take different actions. A global mindset means going beyond these superficial observations and understanding the deeper nature and impact of these differences.

Type 3: Knowledge about Own Organization. A global mindset also requires understanding how the organizations of which we are a part (families, peer groups, institutions, companies) are influenced by their context. Most companies have a particular administrative heritage or organizational culture that has evolved in their home countries. This means that a potential cultural bias may exist in their strategy, systems, and practices – "the way things are done in the headquarters' home country."

Hofstede observed that "theories reflect the cultural environment in which they were written" (Hofstede, 1980). Management concepts and practices are explained by theories regarding organization, motivation, and leadership. Therefore, theories of management systems and management practices may work well in the culture that developed them because they are based on local cultural assumptions and paradigms about the right way to manage.

Type 4: Knowledge about Other Organizations. Knowledge about other organizations and the relationship with their context allows a manager to adapt continually to business and contextual contingencies. This is what helps the manager identify criteria for performance that can be universally applied, and then adapt them to different contexts. For example, a human resource system that provides collective performance bonuses in Mexico and individual performance bonuses in the USA might fit with cultural preferences in those countries and encourage high performance today. However, a human resource system dedicated to motivating all employees to perform well, whatever their background or preferences, will always be subject to adaptation and will encourage high performance into the future.

Developing Global Mindsets in Theory and Practice

A global mindset is not something innate, it can be developed. However, it cannot be developed by simply reading a book on an airplane or by being lectured about it in a classroom. It has to be actively shaped, which implies changes have to take place.

A global mindset is a specific type of mental framework, or cognitive **schema**, for organizing information; in other words, a world-view or mindset. Schemas influence what we notice and what meaning we attribute to perceptions and guide our actions in the world around us. Schemas are simple at first and become more complex with greater experience. The development of more complex schemas allows a person to process enormous amounts of information and to see patterns without getting lost in the detail. There is a difference in the way that expert and novice global managers think, as shown by Bird and Osland:

When entering into a new situation [experts] notice more and different types of cues, they interpret those cues differently, they choose from a different, wider range of appropriate actions than do novices, and then they execute/implement their chosen course of action at higher levels than do novices. In the case of global managers, these differences between novices and experts are magnified ...

[As] they become more competent, experts recognize complexity and a larger set of cues. They are able to discern which cues are the most important and are able to move beyond strict adherence to rules and to think in terms of trade-offs. On attaining the expert stage, they can read situations without rational thought – they diagnose the situation unconsciously and respond intuitively because over the years they have developed the holistic recognition or mental maps that allow for effortless framing and reframing of strategies and quick adaptation. (Bird and Osland, 2004)

Once a schema exists, it changes through one of two processes – **assimilation** or **accommodation** (Furth, 1970). In assimilation, new information is seen to be consistent with the schema and is incorporated readily, perhaps refining the details of the schema. In accommodation, new information contradicts the schema to the extent that the schema itself is changed. In organizational learning, these processes have been referred to as **single-loop** and **double-loop** learning (Argyris and Schön, 1978) and **evolutionary** and **revolutionary** change (Gersick, 1991). Good learning maximizes both processes.

Assimilation is the easier of these two processes. When perceptions are consistent with assumptions, people don't need to question assumptions, they can simply "bolt on" new knowledge. For example, Jack, a manager in a US consumer products firm, learned that people are motivated by individual monetary incentives such as bonus schemes and commissions. He implemented incentives to influence his salespeople's focus on specific products in the portfolio – one shampoo brand this season, a shower gel product next season. The results were immediate, sales in the right categories went up, and his knowledge was reinforced through assimilation.

Accommodation is a much more difficult and uncomfortable process. When people encounter something that contradicts existing assumptions, they experience "cognitive dissonance," a feeling of imbalance. People try to reduce the imbalance to achieve consistency again either by changing perceptions of the evidence to match the assumptions (call into question the subject of the contradiction), or by changing assumptions to match the evidence (call into question ourselves). People are more inclined to invoke the first method than the second; it requires a great deal less energy, is reinforced by others who hold the same assumptions, and is less confusing. The other option, altering one's own assumptions, unfortunately is usually a less chosen alternative.

After several years of success, Jack moved to his company's Norwegian subsidiary. But when he implemented his trusted incentive schemes and bonuses, he did not see corresponding increases in sales of the desired products. Why not?

At first I thought there was something wrong with the salespeople. I knew the incentive schemes and bonuses always work, so it must have been the local salespeople that created the problem. I started to think about how to fix that – maybe I had the wrong staff? Then I started to wonder maybe, just maybe, they motivated salespeople differently here. I began asking my Norwegian colleagues how they influenced salespeople to change their focus in their portfolios.

The sales managers told me that they just talk with them, ask them questions, and then sales change to the right things. This sounded crazy to me, but they were getting results, so I started sitting in on the discussions to see what was going on. I saw what I thought was a very complex process of managers discussing the market with each salesperson, and combining the salesperson's advice with the manager's own expertise, to kind of emerge to an agreement about what to sell. It seemed that the Norwegian salespeople – in our company at least – were more motivated to change by having their expertise valued, than by financial incentives. It took me a while, but I learned to work with my salespeople in this way, and then I began to wonder if this approach would also work back in the US. I'll sure try combining it with traditional methods when I go back.

Jack's response is an accommodation response – questioning your assumptions and adjusting the schema itself.

To learn through accommodation, managers must be able to articulate their current schema accurately. They must realize that a current schema exists to shape information processing; only with this knowledge can they identify its limits and address them with a new structure.

Feedback is critical for learning through accommodation. A learner can best judge the appropriateness of a schema if its impact is clearly seen (Argyris and Schön, 1978). This is why experiential learning is much more effective than passive knowledge acquisition: the experience provides immediate feedback (Kolb, 1983).

Developing Your Own Global Mindset

First, developing your own global mindset requires active learning. You have to engage problems where you must assess the situation, see options, make decisions, implement actions, and experience feedback. Second, it requires paying close attention to your own reactions and to what is happening in the environment.

You will become aware of how your assumptions and frameworks shape perceptions, values, and behavior as you confront the different sets of assumptions guiding the views and practices of others. If you are exposed to new experiences under the right circumstances, part of your response may include an examination of your own guiding values and theories of management – the beginning of developing a global mindset. You may find that your existing frameworks are incomplete or are disconfirmed because you did not see the whole picture or could only see it from a narrow point of view. The use of case studies, experiential exercises, and the debriefing of personal experiences in class or group settings are useful tools and techniques. The educational experience is richer and can have a greater impact if it includes a diverse set of participants.

As you go through the material in this book, focus both on building awareness of yourself in your own context, as well as learning about others in their contexts. Question your assumptions and those of others, and test the application of your knowledge in different contexts. Ask people you work with questions – questions you may not have thought of before. Pay attention to surprises, both as you read the book and as you ask questions and engage with others. Surprise is an indicator that you had hidden assumptions, and provides an opportunity to identify them. These actions will help you build a global mindset. They will extend your repertoire of behaviors and enrich your personal experience of the world.

Today's business environment is highly complex, and the trends creating the complexity are accelerating. Success in such an environment means leading people to achieve results. Global leaders must have a global mindset – a way of organizing knowledge to create openness to new ways of thinking and acting about personal and business effectiveness. They also need to be context sensitive.

Context Awareness: Culture

Two expressions of culture that repeatedly cause complications for executives not fully aware of them are the culture of the host country and their own organizational culture – a company's administrative heritage including its strategy, structure, systems, practices, and management style.

National Culture

Business is conducted globally with people from various countries and cultural backgrounds. Culture has a pervasive and often hidden influence on behavior including management behavior. Cultural differences, if not understood, can be barriers to the implementation and success of a business venture. Culture is the set of assumptions and values shared by a group of people that guide interactions; that identify what should be done and what shouldn't; what is to be prioritized; and how people should behave. Culture is easily seen in norms and practices, such as language, clothing, and behavior; however, its meaning and important influence are much deeper than these surface manifestations. These beliefs and values are taught to us so early and so unobtrusively that we are usually unaware of their influence so they are easy to overlook.

It may sound trivial to say that all groups have cultures. However, experience has taught us that because culture is often invisible to the executives who share a culture, they often think that only the "others" have a culture and, therefore, overlook the impact of their own culture on their own behavior. Additionally, they often think of culture only as it relates to people's behavior and don't see how it has an impact on the company's strategy, systems, and procedures.

Can managers be expected to know the nuances of the multiple cultures in which their companies are doing business? Understanding all of them at any one time might be too much to ask of any executive. However, there are tools available to help executives learn about and understand the cultural contexts of many countries. Chapter 3 will focus on national cultures in depth and Chapter 4 will develop the Map–Bridge–Integrate framework (MBI) for using this information in practice.

Even with these tools that increase our understanding the question always arises about how to operate in another culture. Do we do it their way, our way, or a third way? Do we adapt to the local norms and culture or do they adapt to us? Paula Caligiuri helps to answer that question with her concept of cultural agility (Caligiuri, 2012). The mindful global leader is culturally agile, meaning that he or she succeeds in accomplishing their objectives in contexts of "unfamiliar sets of cultural norms or multiple sets of them." They have a grounded understanding of their context and a broad repertoire of behaviors that allows multiple response paths. When it is necessary that the home culture approach to business is used they may choose "cultural minimization," which is doing it "our way." This could include issues such as health and safety, bribery, brand management, elements of strategy, or the business model. Where those considerations are not present, they may choose "cultural adaptation" which is adapting to the local way of doing things such as marketing, government relations, local manufacturing operations, or some HR policies, for example. Finally, there is the possibility of finding a new way, perhaps one that is a synthesis of "our way" and "their way" – or even a totally different way of operating.

Organizational Culture

Organizations also have cultures of shared assumptions, beliefs, and values as reflected in a set of systems, practices, management style, and norms about ways of operating. Often it is described simply as "the way we do things around here." Robert Richman, a culture strategist, says that after you strip away all the words, culture boils down to a feeling created by experiences with people in an organization (Richman, 2015). But can an organization's culture really affect employees' behavior? The answer would appear to be "yes." Organizational culture can be either a positive force or a negative one and there have been a number of highly public negative examples as we write this eighth edition.

The Wells Fargo sales scandal which was revealed in 2016 shows the impact that a negative culture can have. Susan M. Ochs, writing in the *Harvard Business Review* says, "the high-pressure sales environment drove employees to create as many as two million fake accounts. Former employees have alleged a 'soul-crushing' culture of fear and daily intimidation by managers, where they were pressured to reach extreme sales goals, some by breaking the law." The former head of the community bank unit used daily and monthly "Motivator" reports that people "lived and died by" as well as retail scorecards to keep the pressure on and track performance. Eventually the bank fired over 5,300 employees; the CEO resigned and had US$28 million clawed back by the Board of Directors; and the community bank unit head was fired.

Wells Fargo is not the only company having a dysfunctional culture. Other recent examples have included VW and Uber. In January 2017, the *Financial Times* printed an article entitled, "The Volkswagen scandal shows that corporate culture matters," stating that you had to look beyond economics to understand why VW developed cheating software to beat emissions tests on their diesel cars. The article placed the blame on the firm's governance and concluded that, "culture is there and it matters. And if we ignore it there will be more dieselgates in the future" (Armstrong, 2017).

Uber was founded in 2009 in San Francisco and quickly became the dominant ride-sharing company, disrupting the taxi industry worldwide. In 2017, it was operating in 632 cities around the world. In that short period of time, not only did it become one of the most successful technology start-ups, with a valuation in the US$50–68 billion range, but it also became the "poster child" for companies with business-limiting, dysfunctional cultures. In February 2017, Susan Fowler, a former employee, described a culture where performance was the only thing that mattered; a culture where infighting, back-stabbing, sexual harassment, and undermining direct supervisors to take their jobs were commonplace. The Board brought in former US Attorney General Eric Holder to lead an internal investigation into the situation. In June 2017, after more scandals, defections of executives, and under pressure from large investors and shareholders, Travis Kalanick, founder and CEO, resigned. Board member Arianna Huffington, claimed a "new Uber" would be different and that there would be "no room for brilliant jerks."

We don't want to imply that toxic cultures like Uber and Wells Fargo are the norm, but when they make the headlines they become very visible. At the same time, there are many companies with positive organizational cultures. Examples can be found in numerous business-oriented magazines and media sites such as *Fortune, Forbes, Entrepreneur, Fast Company*, and *Business Insider* that publish lists of the best companies to work for, the most admired companies, or companies that are doing well by doing good.

One of the important insights regarding corporate culture is that your organization either already has a culture or it will have one. It may emerge on its own, unguided, from the independent interactions of employees and managerial decisions. It may be positive, negative, or even toxic. It may even threaten the existence of the organization. A corporate culture also can be consciously created and nurtured. As an executive, you can play a role in shaping the culture you want to have. We will look at organizational culture in more depth in Chapter 8.

Organizational Context: Strategy, Structure, and Systems

Executives don't always understand their own organizational context or how the administrative systems create alignment between employees, the tasks they perform, and the organization's strategy. Three important questions to answer in developing a strategy include:

- Who is your target market?
- What is your product or service?
- How do you develop and deliver your product or service?

If you decide to serve a new category of customers or change from a product offering to a service offering, the "how" used to deliver your product may not work for your new service and may have to change. Many of the firm's organizational arrangements, such as its structure and systems, may have to be realigned to the new strategy.

There are a number of companies that have changed their strategy from a best product strategy to a customer solutions strategy. Customer-centricity, or what Galbraith (2001) refers to as the rise of the customer dimension, has been brought about by the globalization of customers; their preference for partnerships or relationships; their desire for solutions and not simply products or services; the increase in their power vis-à-vis producers; and e-commerce. Faced with competitors' equally high-quality products or services, companies have turned to providing "solutions" as a differentiator to create loyalty and drive growth. This means no longer competing on the basis of product economics or features either through low cost or differentiation and instead building a relationship with customers that redefines their experience with the product or service and focuses on customers' profitability.

However, this does not always work as seamlessly as anticipated. Many executives talk about customer-centricity but they fail to "walk the talk." They don't fully understand or appreciate their administrative heritage or organizational context. They don't understand the significant changes that might have to be made internally to their structures, evaluation, and reward or control systems to really be customer-centric.

The mindful global leader understands his or her strategy, administrative systems, and policies and organizational culture in relation to the context of its current customers and the international market to be entered. Strategy is embedded in a context when it is developed in the home country and it is embedded in a context when it is implemented in a host country – it is not context free.

However, most failures are not the result of a poor strategy but rather the result of poor implementation. Execution is often hindered by corporate culture and a lack of process understanding or change management skills. Executives tend to pay attention to only half the challenge, which is strategy formulation, the big picture, and the end result, without spending as much time and attention on planning the execution – the on-the-ground reality and details. They have a tendency to focus on the "visible" inputs such as legal, financial, and market data rather than the "invisible" things like relationships and culture – both national and organizational. The visible issues are necessary but are not sufficient for success.

Organizations have to be strategically and organizationally aligned to execute strategy successfully. Questions that often go unasked are: Will our evaluation and reward systems that we use at home work in the host country? Will existing policies and procedures work? Have the right people been selected to do the implementation? If you are engaged in a merger or acquisition you also need to make sure that your organizational cultures or "the way we do things" are compatible. Often companies spend more time looking for a compatible business opportunity and not enough time looking for compatible partners.

Organizational and strategic alignment will be addressed in Chapter 7.

Context: Beyond Culture

Culture is not the only element of context that it is important to consider. There can be institutional and regulatory peculiarities or, as Napoleon discovered, important physical characteristics of the host country. Executives at headquarters, distant from direct contact or experience with the market, may create unworkable plans and schedules because they don't have a direct and profound understanding of the new environment.

Take, for example, a company that installed communication infrastructure in countries around the world. Executives responsible for the installation in an African country telephoned headquarters to say that their arrival at the site and implementation would be delayed. There was only one small ferry across a lake that they had to traverse with the equipment and the traffic was backed up a long distance to the ferry. People at headquarters thought they were crazy and told them that they were looking at a map and there was no lake there. However, it was the rainy season and the torrential rains created a "lake" that became a barrier. Alfred Korzybski remarked that, "the map is not the territory." There is no substitute for direct knowledge of context and it is important not to confuse representations like plans and spreadsheets for reality. Often the people at headquarters who develop strategy don't understand that there may be a "lake" as a barrier to their success.

Jesús Sotomayor, a serial entrepreneur in Mexico, former visiting professor at IPADE Business School in Mexico and occasional student in classes that one of the authors taught offered this advice in class, "Nobody ever lost money on a spreadsheet." However, it happens all the time; companies overestimate the benefits of a project or market entry and underestimate costs. He also offered this corollary, "If you torture the numbers long enough, they will confess." You can make any project look good with enough assumptions and sufficient data manipulation. Unfortunately, managers often confuse the map with the territory.

Process

Simply having targets or stretch goals will not guarantee a successful project or market entry. Although specifying a desirable end result is a good idea, remember that it will take a journey to reach that destination. Success depends on having a well thought out implementation plan and process to reach the desired destination. Choosing the right change agent or agents is key and they need to be mindful and have a process orientation.

What does it mean to have a process orientation? Leading mindfully is not just about having the right personal characteristics or competences, although these are important. It also means paying attention to the "verbs" of management such as interact, negotiate, partner, learn, understand, relate, train – the dynamics of knowing how to adapt quickly and effectively to move forward to meet objectives. Mindful leaders understand that this may mean interacting with colleagues, customers, suppliers, and officials from other countries to achieve the desired outcome. Success comes from getting the job done with and through other people. Mindful global leadership often is less about making a decision and more about identifying and embarking on a process.

A process perspective is the "currency" of implementation. Richard Pascale contrasted the Japanese "proceeding" with a typical American "deciding" mentality (Pascale, 1978). He said, "The process of 'proceeding' generates further information; you move toward your goal through a sequence of steps rather than bold-stroke actions. The distinction is between having enough data to decide and having enough data to proceed." An end result focus may obscure the need to get more or better information in order to make progress to the desired result. Changing strategies or conducting business in other countries and cultures is an activity filled with ambiguity and uncertainty and "proceeding" may be the appropriate mode of operation. Information must be collected to put pieces of a puzzle together. This is usually accomplished through "process," or a series of interactions with other people. This process of leading change will be examined closely in Chapter 9.

An organization does not need to be operating globally for its executives to manage mindfully. All organizations need mindful leaders to cope with the complexity inherent in the world today and to adapt to changing market conditions.

Reflection Questions

As we discussed in this chapter, mindfulness is about being context sensitive and process-oriented. In global leadership, mindfulness requires developing a global mindset – an awareness of the relationship between people and organizations and their context, including your own. This chapter's reflection questions are intended to explore mindfulness actively.

1. Try an exercise in active mindfulness. The next time you go somewhere outside your home – shopping, office, school, transit, anywhere – pay attention to the other people around you, and how they are interacting with others and with things in the environment. What patterns do you see? What individual differences do you see? Which ways of interacting are more like the way you would do it? What do these observations tell you about yourself? Can you question any of your own assumptions about what is "natural" or "normal"?

2. Consider trying the same exercise together with someone who is likely to see the world quite differently from you. Share your observations with each other, and explore the ways in which your observations are similar and different. Pay particular attention to how you and the other person categorize objects, behaviors, and emotions. What do you see as going together, or as being different from each other?

3. Think of an example from your own experience of a company, organization, or leader failing because they weren't mindful about a process or a context. It could even be you. What was the impact of the mindlessness? Why do you think the context or process was missed? What could have been done to increase mindfulness?

4. To develop mindfulness about the process of your own learning, create a list or mind map of questions and ideas you have related to leading people in international settings. Refer to the list as you go through this book/course, identifying answers and adding more questions to explore.

Further Resources

Anyone interested in mindfulness as situation awareness and process orientation should read Ellen Langer's important book *Mindfulness* (1989, 2014).

It is fascinating to track Napoleon's ill-fated campaign in Russia. Dominic Lieven's *Russia against Napoleon* (New York: Viking, 2010) is excellent in this regard. The famous map of Napoleon's campaign drawn by Charles Minard can be found at http://scimaps.org/mapdetail/napoleons_march_to_m_9

We find that several business news sites offer excellent articles that illustrate the importance of mindfulness and a global mindset. These include

- *Business Insider*, www.businessinsider.com/
- *Entrepreneur*, www.entrepreneur.com/magazine
- *Fortune Magazine*, http://fortune.com/
- *Forbes*, www.forbes.com/#6da9cd342254
- *Fast Company*, www.fastcompany.com/

Bibliography

Argyris, C., & Schön, D. (1978). *Organizational Learning: A Theory of Action Perspective*. Addison-Wesley.

Armstrong, R. (2017). *The Volkswagen scandal shows that corporate culture matters. Financial Times*, January 13. Retrieved October 2017 from: www.ft.com/content/263c811c-d8e4-11e6-944b-e7eb37a6aa8e

Bird, A., & Osland, J. (2004). Global Competencies. In H. W. Lane, M. L. Maznevski, M. Mendenhall, & J. M. McNett (eds.), *The Blackwell Handbook of Global Management: A Guide to Managing Complexity*. Blackwell.

Boyacigiller, N., Beechler, S., Taylor, S., & Levy, O. (2004). The Crucial Yet Illusive Global Mindset. In H. W. Lane, M. L. Maznevski, M. Mendenhall, & J. M. McNett (eds.), *The Blackwell Handbook of Global Management: A Guide to Managing Complexity*. Blackwell.

Brannen, M. Y. (1999). The Many Faces of Cultural Data. *AIB Newsletter*, first quarter.

Bruner, J., Goodnow, J., & Austin, G. (1956). *A Study of Thinking*. Wiley.

Caligiuri, P. (2012). *Cultural Agility*. Jossey-Bass.

Furth, H. (1970). *Piaget for Teachers*. Prentice-Hall.

Galbraith, J. (2001). Building Organizations around the Global Customer. *The Ivey Business Journal*, September–October.

Gersick, C. (1991). Revolutionary Change Theories: A Multi-Level Exploration of the Punctuated Equilibrium Paradigm. *Academy of Management Review*, 16, 10–36.

Hall, E. (1959, 1973). *The Silent Language.* Doubleday.

Hofstede, G. (1980). *Culture's Consequences: International Differences in Work Related Values.* Sage Publications, 2nd edn. 2001.

Javidan, M., & Bowen, D. (2013). The "Global Mindset" of Managers: What It Is, Why It Matters, and How to Develop It. *Organizational Dynamics*, 42, 145–155.

Kivilahti, A. (2013). *Evolution of Online Groceries*, November 28. Retrieved October 2017 from Digital Foodie: www.digitalfoodie.com/evolution-of-online-groceries/

Kolb, D. (1983). *Experiential Learning: Experience as the Source of Learning and Development.* Prentice-Hall.

Korzybski, A. (1931). A Non-Aristotelian System and Its Necessity for Rigour in Mathematics and Physics. Reprinted (1933) in his *Science and Sanity.* International Non-Aristotelian Library.

Langer, E. J. (1989, 2014). *Mindfulness* (25th Anniversary Edition). Da Capo Press and Addison-Wesley.

Langer, E. J., & Moldoveanu, M. (2000). The Construct of Mindfulness. *Journal of Social Science*, 56, 1–9.

Ochs, S. M. (2016). The Leadership Blind Spots at Wells Fargo. *Harvard Business Review*, October 6. Available at: https://hbr.org/2016/10/the-leadership-blind-spots-at-wells-fargo

Pascale, R. (1978). Zen and the Art of Management. *Harvard Business Review*, 56.

Relan, P. (2013). *Where Webvan Failed and How Home Delivery 2.0 Could Succeed*, September 28. Available at: https://techcrunch.com/2013/09/27/why-webvan-failed-and-how-home-delivery-2-0-is-addressing-the-problems/

Richman, R. (2015). *The Culture Blueprint* (Version 1.5). Licenses under a Creative Commons Attribution-Share Alike 4.0 International License.

Tung, R. L. (1999). The Cross-Cultural Research Imperative: The Need to Balance Cross-National and Intra-National Diversity. *Journal of International Business Studies*, 39, 41–46.

Weick, K. E., & Sutcliffe, K. M. (2007). *Managing the Unexpected: Resilient Performance in an Age of Uncertainty.* San Francisco: Jossey-Bass.

Weick, K. E., Sutcliffe, K. M., & Obstfeld, D. (1999). Organizing for High Reliability: Processes of Collective Mindfulness. In R. S. Sutton & B. M. Staw (eds.), *Research in Organizational Behaviour*, vol. 1. JAI Press.

3 Understanding Culture: Through the Looking Glass

"I don't understand you," said Alice. "It's dreadfully confusing." "That's the effect of living backwards," the Queen said kindly, "it always makes one a little giddy at first."

Lewis Carroll, *Alice through the Looking-Glass,*
and What Alice Found There

International management is about leading people and implementing mandates with people across cultural borders. The starting point for effective international management behavior, therefore, must be a deep understanding of culture. In a world of global media, tourism, and story-telling, most people are highly aware of the basic notion of culture: people do things differently in different places. In Japan, business cards are given and received with two hands. In many European countries, such as France, Switzerland, Belgium, and Spain, people categorize themselves based on the number of kisses used in greetings among friends. In the USA, handshakes should be strong and firm. It is important to know these differences, and most businesspeople have funny (or not-so-funny) stories about making mistakes with these behaviors. But in fact it is much more important to see what is behind these surface-level behaviors. Just like Alice, when we go through the looking glass we see an alternate world where things seem different or even backwards, and where we begin to question our assumptions of culture. It is these assumptions that provide both the **barriers** to communication and the opportunities for **synergy**.

Consider this interchange between two technology developers in Dubai: Jan, a Dutch expatriate, who had a strong record of effectiveness and had lived in many countries before coming to Dubai, and Ahmed, an Emirati. They were talking about a deal that Ahmed and his team had been working on with a potential foreign partner:

Ahmed: I couldn't believe how rude that guy was. He refused my coffee, he handed papers to me with his left hand, he showed the sole of his shoe. He was completely ignorant of our culture. I can tell you, we won't be doing business with him!

Jan: (laughing) Yeah, I've seen a lot of that. It's amazing how oblivious some people are. But tell me, Ahmed, really. You're a smart businessman. Is that really why you wouldn't do a deal with him? Just because he handed papers to you the wrong way?

Ahmed: (thoughtfully) Well, no, now that you mention it. Those were just the tip of the iceberg. What was really frustrating was that he didn't seem to care about us. He didn't want to tell us anything about why doing business with us was important to him. He wasn't interested in why we developed our technology, or the history of our company. He treated my boss like he was an assistant. And when we tried to show him our way, he just ignored us. It's easy to laugh at how stupid he was with some of our customs. But it was these other things that told us we couldn't develop trust with him.

The potential partner in this situation missed the deeper importance of relationships and hierarchy in the Emirati culture. This created barriers with Ahmed and his team, and also prevented the possibility of, for example, long-term technological development that could combine different perspectives.

Developing Mindful Awareness of Culture

Culture is an important context for people's behavior, but most people, most of the time, are unaware of culture. We often use Edward Hall's analogy that culture is to people like water is to fish. Water is all around the fish and is critical to a fish's survival, but the fish does not notice it or know what water is. It is simply the context in which the fish lives. Most of the time, we experience culture as a set of unquestioned assumptions that create a context for our interactions together – the implicit "rules of the game" or "the way we do things." Often people become much more aware of their own cultures when they visit other cultures. However it is gained, mindful awareness of culture is critical to leading effectively in an international context and overcoming the "fish out of water" syndrome.

Some people begin a journey of mindful cultural awareness through experiencing variety. Gena grew up in a Chinese immigrant family in Toronto. Perhaps because she learned to navigate her family and new country cultures early, she developed a curiosity for learning about other cultures. She went on work and school exchanges to Europe, Southeast Asia, and Africa, and always explored local life beyond her immediate assignment. Rather than become confident that she understood global culture, she continued to expand her horizons to explore more variety. She found that each new cultural exploration helped her appreciate variation and reflect on universals of human existence, and also discover practices that would benefit people back "home." Eventually she realized that her global adventures were helping her confront and appreciate her own identity as a second-generation immigrant. This mindfulness unlocked a new set of insights that helped her both to develop individually and to contribute more meaningfully to global organizations.

Other people are mindful through depth in their experience; always noticing the cultural context they are in, and how it evolves. Kathryn, an American working in senior roles in Japan for over two decades, described how she evolved over time to deeply understand and navigate some of the nuances of the culture, beyond learning the language. For example, she experienced the complexities and benefit of building trust in a culture that is highly indirect and values high levels of interdependence. She observed how the younger generation was challenging some traditional norms about how trust can be built, by relying on different kinds of relationships and networks. She also saw how new media and social patterns were bridging deep cultural needs with the demand for global value chains, allowing people to build relationships in new ways. With this cultural mindfulness, she helped Japanese companies meet challenges about creating relationships in fast-moving global business partnerships without losing their traditional strengths.

In this chapter, we start by defining culture, identifying its influence, and discussing why it is so important for global leaders to be mindful of culture. We then provide some important frameworks for comparing cultures, helpful ways to understand new situations and enter new cultures effectively. On these two foundations, we'll build a discussion on the richness of international and multicultural situations, such as multicultural individuals, cultural change, and culture related to other aspects of the environment.

Culture: What It Is, How It Influences

Think about the following examples of cultures: Nigerian, Japanese, Québécois, soccer (football) fans, golfers, snowboarders, wine connoisseurs, Generation Y, engineers, artists, Nestlé Corporation, and Toyota. What other examples have you come across? What do they have in common? What makes each a culture? As we saw in Chapter 2:

Culture is the set of deep beliefs and underlying values that are shared by a group of people, to guide that group of people's interactions with each other. The beliefs and values are taught to successive generations as truths, and are often so implicit that group members are unaware of the beliefs and values. These beliefs and values are manifested in norms and artifacts that are common in the culture.

Culture is most readily seen in norms and practices, such as language, clothing, and behavior; however, its meaning and influence are much deeper than these surface manifestations. Speaking French and eating poutine do not make one automatically Québécois; watching the World Cup and wearing a football jersey do not make one automatically part of the football (soccer) culture. A new employee at either Nestlé or Toyota becomes part of the culture slowly.

The assumptions and values that define culture – the ones that are held by members of the culture – are those that identify what is successful and what isn't, what is to be prioritized, and how people should behave in the world and toward each other. These assumptions and values are learned by passing them on from one generation to the next in both formal ways, such as school or orientation programs, and informal ways, such as story-telling and social reinforcement.

Groups Need Cultures for Efficiency and Identity

Culture serves two important functions for groups. First, it makes action more simple and efficient. When people know what to prioritize and how to interact with each other, business and social interactions take place quickly and easily. There is no need to question each action. Members of the Japanese culture can produce and interpret each level of bowing without conscious thought; engineers can easily proceed together using standardized work methods and mathematics.

Think about the last time you were in a new culture, working or as a tourist. How did you feel at the end of the first day? Some people say excited or exhilarated, some say frustrated, but most people say they were exhausted. This exhaustion comes from spending the day wondering what is meaningful and what is not. Should I tip the driver? How much? The receptionist didn't smile at me. Is that normal or was I rude? Or was the receptionist rude? Which side of the sidewalk should I walk on? What are others doing? Oops I just used my left hand – is that impolite here, or is it okay? Or should I have used both hands? Even if you have read all the guidebooks, questions like these arise. When you are interacting across cultures, you lose the efficiency that comes from shared meaning and values within a culture.

Second, culture provides an important source of social identity for its members. Humans have a basic need to belong to social groups. Belonging to a culture – as demonstrated by acting in accordance with the norms and values – brings safety and security from the group, and separates the group from outsiders who are different and perhaps even threatening. Interestingly, most people feel this identity even more strongly when they are outside their own culture than when they are in it. Foreign students or expatriates from the same country often choose to socialize together more closely than the same individuals might when in their own country.

Culture and individuals interact in many ways. Culture is a characteristic of groups, and is defined in terms of what group members share. However, individuals within the culture are all different and subscribe to the culture's assumptions and values to a greater or lesser degree. We are all members of many cultures – cultures related to our national, regional, professional, organizational, age, gender, hobby, and other identities (Maalouf, 2000). The culture we identify with most closely in a given situation influences which set of assumptions and values we prioritize in that situation. When a Nigerian oil engineer is working at the company's Norwegian headquarters as an internal consultant, she may identify most closely with her professional and corporate cultures and act with the priorities and assumptions of a corporate engineer. When she is working in her home country on the oil rig supervising local employees, she may identify more with her national culture and interpret events and act according to Nigerian cultural assumptions (Gibson, Maznevski, and Kirkman, 2009).

Is Culture Becoming Less Important?

Working across cultures is one of the two fundamental characteristics that distinguish international management from "normal" domestic management (strategic complexity is the other). Many people argue that this perspective is misleading. They assert that cultures around the world are converging, that business is business everywhere. Of course, there is some truth to this. People around the world wear jeans and carry European bags and pens, eat at McDonald's, talk on Samsung phones, work on iPads, and play games and DVDs on their Nintendo or Sony devices. Currencies are traded globally every moment, and there are global infrastructures and norms for conducting business. Accounting standards are becoming more and more global. Everyone has the same basic physiological and psychological needs.

However, take another look at the converging cultures examples. We think McDonald's is an interesting example to analyze. Yes, the golden arches and basic format are recognizable everywhere. Kids all over the world love the Happy Meal, and McDonald's is the world's single largest toy distributor. The Big Mac is such a universal item that the magazine *The Economist* bases its **purchasing power parity** (PPP) index on the price of a Big Mac in different countries (The Economist, 2017), assuming that a Big Mac would have approximately the same meaning in each country.

Now look a bit deeper: McDonald's has different menu items in different countries. Beer is served in Germany, a McArabia is on the menu in the Middle East, and there is no beef in Indian McDonald's. Corn is an alternative to fries in many Asian countries, and it is hard to find a VeggieMac in Italy. Look a bit deeper still: watch the people, learn to see the norms about McDonald's. In North America, a large proportion of revenue comes from drive-through. This proportion is increasing elsewhere, but nowhere else does it reach the same level as in North America. What might this indicate about North American culture? The importance of efficiency, of being on the go, of moving from one place to another? The unimportance of eating as a social event, where people sit down for a meal together? In Delhi, India, outside the expatriate areas McDonald's is frequented by small, wealthy families. It is more of a luxury family experience than a commodity eating experience. In Saudi Arabia, McDonald's has two sections which are completely separated starting at the front door and continuing to the service to the eating areas: one for singles (men), the other for "families," defined as women or mixed groups of men with women. In the family section, the booths can be closed with a curtain so women can eat in privacy and remove their veils if they choose. In southern Norway, McDonald's is the place families go on rainy Sunday afternoons. Why? It has the only indoor playground in town, and both family time and activity are important in Norwegian culture. In Malaysia and some other predominantly Muslim countries, McDonald's has an all-you-can-eat event during Ramadan. Ramadan is the traditional month of fasting in the Islamic calendar, and adherents must fast during the day but may eat in the evening. More and more people in Kuala Lumpur take advantage of McDonald's one price evening ticket. This creates some controversy in the city, with some appreciating McDonald's adaptation to their culture, and others decrying a degeneration of Ramadan that focuses on consumerism rather than discipline.

In short, McDonald's, one of the icons of globalization, represents the complexities of culture and the debate on cultural convergence and divergence. Cultures are both converging and diverging. The convergence allows us to do business together. It allows mergers and acquisitions to be negotiated, money and goods to be traded, and employees to stay briefly in foreign countries. It allows us to work together, at least on the surface. However, deeper level differences become apparent when people have to interact more intensively with each other on a day-to-day basis. Naïve assumptions about convergence can cause problems or disappointments.

Managers must understand the context of the people they are working with in order to lead them well, and one of the most important elements of context is culture. As long as people live and work in groups, managers will need to work effectively across cultures.

Why Focus on Country Cultures?

Although we defined culture as the set of values and assumptions shared by any group of people, in international management we tend to focus on the role of **country cultures**. Within a country, the institutions that carry culture tend to be very powerful and consistent. For example, most countries have one official language which is the language of most families, is taught in all state schools, is the language of regional- and country-level government, and is the language of official and most unofficial media. Most countries have a single basic legal system (e.g., constitutional or civil or Islamic law), a system of government that is relatively consistent across regions (e.g., representative democracy in different states or cantons, or a monarchy that reigns throughout the country), a single relationship between church and state (e.g., there is a strong relationship or there is officially no relationship). These practices and relationships are often different from those in the country next door. The beliefs and values associated with these institutions are taught to people early and implicitly through family norms and institutional practices, such that most people are unaware of their influence.

There are some important exceptions, such as Canada, Belgium, Switzerland, and India, which have two or more official languages, legal systems, and other institutions. However, the generalization is true for most countries. Country is therefore a very important type of culture to account for in international business. For most of this chapter, and indeed the book, we will focus, therefore, on country-based cultures. However, toward the end of the chapter we turn to some important caveats around this notion, and throughout the book we will acknowledge the important influence of other cultures.

Culture Affects Individual Perceptions and Behavior

To understand culture's influence, first we need to understand the basic role of **assumptions** and **perceptions** in influencing our thoughts and actions. This allows us to see our own culture's influence on us, and why cross-cultural encounters are both so difficult to understand and so interesting (Erez and Earley, 1993).

An assumption is an unquestioned, taken-for-granted belief about the world and how it works. Assumptions help create our world-view, or the cognitive environment in which we operate. They come in many different varieties. Some are so deeply ingrained and unquestioned that it is difficult ever to surface them; even when surfaced, they are not testable. "Human nature is essentially good" is an assumption of this type. Other assumptions are learned at various stages of our lives, and, once learned, are taken for granted without further questioning. In the first few years of life, a child learns to take so much for granted: day and night follow each other; manipulating switches makes things work; things that move are either alive or powered by something; when in doubt, Google. As we develop through life, we learn more and more sets of assumptions. A financial analyst valuing companies takes for granted certain assumptions about efficient markets and develops analyses that affect companies' ability to obtain resources. An advertising account manager takes for granted certain assumptions about human motivations and produces advertising campaigns that play to those motivations and invoke them.

Assumptions influence the process of perception, or what we notice and how we interpret events and behaviors. The financial analyst focuses on financial ratios, earnings growth, or dividends, but may not notice programs with long lead-times that may enhance the company's reputation for social responsibility. If she did notice this information, she may interpret it as something admirable but nothing that should influence the ability to borrow money today. The advertising account manager may only notice product features that fit into his framework of assumptions about motivation for the target audience and miss other implications of those features.

Assumptions are necessary. Without assumptions, we would be paralyzed by the constant need to inquire about the meaning of events and the motives of others. The more others share our assumptions, the more easily we can interact and communicate effectively with each other. It is not surprising that our assumptions are generally effective when we operate within our own culture.

A simple way to remember this process of social perception is captured by the acronym DIE, which stands for Describe–Interpret–Evaluate. We observe something and take note of its characteristics, or describe it. In describing something we stay with the objective facts. What we are inclined to notice is influenced in part by our assumptions of what is important. We then interpret those facts, or give them meaning, again based on our assumptions. Finally, we evaluate the facts and take action based upon our evaluation.

For example, when selecting a potential supplier for specialty chemicals, a purchasing agent may notice that different companies offer different prices for the same grade of chemical. The purchasing agent will build a table comparing the suppliers, describing their price ranges. The purchasing agent may not notice that the suppliers offer different types of technical assistance or compound customization, because his assumptions about priorities may not include this. Although price is sometimes an indicator of quality, the purchasing agent may interpret the chemical grade as the quality information. As long as prices are identified for the same chemical grade, the purchasing agent interprets that he is comparing them on an equal basis. Finally, the purchasing agent evaluates the lowest price compound as good for the company. He takes action and buys this compound.

Just like the purchasing agent, we all act based on the world we perceive, the world we see through the DIE sequence. Since the sequence builds so heavily on our assumptions of the world and how it works, those assumptions end up influencing our own actions and what we think of others' actions. There is a tendency, however, to jump quickly to interpretation and then to evaluation before adequately "describing" or understanding.

Culture Influences our Perceptual Lenses

Figure 3.1 shows the influence pattern of culture on assumptions, perceptions, and management behavior, and demonstrates why culture and assumptions play such a large role in cross-cultural encounters.

Culture is not deterministic: we are not mechanically driven to think or behave according to the expectations of our culture, and individuals within culture vary enormously. At the same time, when we do behave according to our culture (following the flow illustrated in Figure 3.1), we're able to be more efficient and we're seen as more effective. We also get the emotional satisfaction of feeling a sense of fit or belonging (Dorfman et al., 2012). So although it is not deterministic, culture is a very strong influence on our thoughts and behaviors.

When Cultures Meet: Question the Other or Question Ourselves?

What happens when people from two or more different cultures meet or work together? Their assumptions and value systems (cultures) may direct them to perceive the same situation differently, interpret what they notice differently, evaluate the situation differently, and take different actions. Here's a very short exchange:

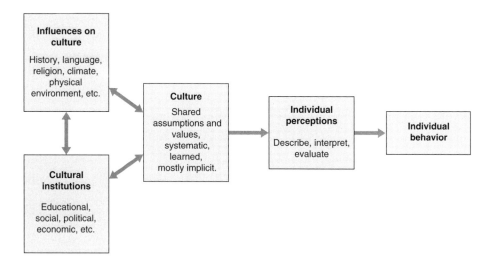

Figure 3.1 Culture's influence on individual behavior

Susan (British, new expatriate in Chile): Pablo, the company has decided to transfer you
    to the regional headquarters in São Paulo.
Pablo (Chilean): That will be very difficult. I'd prefer to stay here.

There is an awkward pause. What are they both thinking? The same situation –
transferring Pablo from Santiago to São Paulo – may be interpreted and evaluated differently by each of them. Susan, from a low interdependence culture, is
probably wondering whether Pablo is really interested in developing his career:
"A transfer to regional headquarters is an important promotion. Very strange he
would not want that." Pablo, from a high interdependence culture, may wonder
why Susan or the company would transfer him: "My family, my young children
and elderly parents, are here. I don't even speak Portuguese. When my children
are older I could go."

    Cross-cultural interactions like this set up a potential conflict situation. From
"my" point of view, "you" are thinking and behaving in a way that doesn't fit
with my assumptions about the world (assumptions I am not conscious of holding). I experience this conflict as dissonance and I want to reduce it, to make the
interpretation consistent with my assumptions.

    The easiest and most common way for me to reduce dissonance is to keep
my own assumptions while revising my perception of the other person. Susan
could change her positive perception of Pablo's career potential, and "realize" he is not as ambitious as she thought; Pablo could change his positive
perception of the company, and "realize" they don't care about him. With this
interpretation, both people make assumptions about the other's motivations
and values, based on their own assumption set: an ethnocentric error. We all
have a strong tendency to use our own group's assumptions as the benchmark
when viewing other groups. Ethnocentrism is carrying that one step further and
using that benchmark to evaluate "us" as better and "them" as worse (Shultz,
Hartshorn, and Kaznatcheev, 2009). Susan's thoughts may continue with, "No
wonder the Chilean economy is still struggling." Pablo might think, "This is just
another example of Anglo values colonizing the rest of the world." Reducing
dissonance by maintaining your own assumptions often leads to conflict in
cross-cultural encounters.

    The other way to reduce dissonance is to change assumptions. This requires
active mindfulness. Susan may wonder whether managers have different
typical career paths in Latin America than in the UK, and develop a broader
understanding of human motivation and leadership development in different

contexts. Pablo may wonder whether UK firms look after employees differently, and develop a broader understanding of human capital in multinational firms. Reducing dissonance by questioning and changing your assumptions often leads to positive synergies in cross-cultural encounters.

The dynamics of what happens when individuals from different cultures meet are shown in Figure 3.2. The same perceptual process occurs as described earlier and shown in Figure 3.1, but in this case two different people are acting based on two different sets of cultural assumptions. The resulting different decisions or behaviors set up the conditions for conflict or synergy.

In global leadership, our aim is to decrease negative aspects of conflict and increase potential for positive synergy. To the extent that we're more mindful to anticipate cultural differences, we're more likely to observe, interpret, and evaluate others objectively. We turn next to some tools and frameworks for increasing cultural mindfulness.

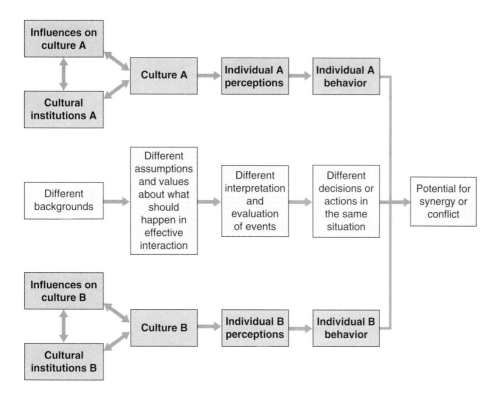

Figure 3.2 When individuals from different cultures interact

Mapping Cultures

In Chapter 2, we described the importance of mindful categorization: having a broad range and depth of categories for understanding a set of situations (page 27). With mindful categorization, when you encounter new situations you're able to connect and make sense of them effectively, rather than "pigeon-holing" everything into a small set of less-comprehensive categories. In this section we discuss tools for mapping cultures – for comparing cultures with each other, and for developing expectations about how to work with people from different cultures. These tools are invaluable to increase mindful categorization when working across cultures, especially when the cultures are also complex and changing.

We use the metaphor of mapping quite deliberately. A map is a picture for navigating in a new territory. The map is useful to the extent that it is accurate, provides just the right level of detail and scale, and shows reference points. Features are not inherently good or bad in themselves; they must always be interpreted in context. A good map should help you develop a guess about how to get from one place to another. A "you are here" point makes a map even more practical.

Maps of social features are less common than maps of geographical ones, and mapping social features of groups is difficult because it is hard to verify the data against an objective, unchanging reality. However, social maps that are carefully constructed help people enter new cultural territories mindfully as much as geographical maps help people enter new physical territories.

Choosing a Map

Just as a geographer uses different types of maps for different purposes, an international manager has access to several cultural maps. Each map shows different dimensions of culture, and allows different types of cultural comparisons. For example, Hall wrote several books and articles describing elements of culture that are relevant to business. In his classic article, "The Silent Language in Overseas Business," he describes cultural differences and their impact on international behavior, relating to the five dimensions of Time, Space, Things, Friendships, and Agreements (Hall, 1960).

Cultural mapping started in the field of anthropology. Parsons and Shils developed some of the earliest dimensions (Parsons and Shils, 1951). Kluckhohn and Strodtbeck built on their work and created the first comparative maps: the

Cultural Orientations Framework (Kluckhohn and Strodtbeck, 1961).They analyzed hundreds of ethnographic descriptions of cultures from around the world, and identified six problems or challenges that all societies throughout recorded history face: Relation to the Environment, Relationships among People, Mode of Normal Activity, Orientation to Time, Belief about Basic Human Nature, and Use of Space.

Applying this to the business context, Hofstede developed an extensively researched cultural map, which has contributed importantly to research and practice (Hofstede, 1997, 2001). By analyzing the satisfaction surveys of employees in a large multinational enterprise, he identified four basic value patterns of cultures around the world: Individualism, Power Distance, Uncertainty Avoidance, and Masculinity (Hofstede, 1980a, 1980b). He also linked these dimensions to management theories and practice. Later, with his colleague Michael Bond, he identified a fifth value of Confucian Dynamism, or Long-Term Orientation (Chinese Culture Connection, 1987; Hofstede, 1997).

In the ambitious and important GLOBE project (Global Leadership and Organizational Behavior Effectiveness), House and colleagues extended Hofstede's framework across multiple organizations and countries (Javidan et al., 2004). They included nine dimensions: Uncertainty Avoidance, Power Distance, Societal Collectivism, In-Group Collectivism, Gender Egalitarianism, Assertiveness, Future Orientation, Performance Orientation, and Humane Orientation. This study also examined differences and universals for leadership effectiveness. Everywhere, they found, followers expect their leaders to develop a vision, inspire others, and create high-performing teams. On the other hand, cultures differ dramatically in terms of valuing leaders who are status conscious, autonomous, or face-saving (Dorfman et al., 2012).

Schwartz and colleagues developed a framework of values, specifically focusing on the values that are related to an individual's interaction with society (Sagiv and Schwartz, 2000; Schwartz, 1994, 1999). Schwartz found that cultures differ in terms of valuing mastery over versus harmony with the environment, embedded versus autonomous relations, and hierarchical versus egalitarian control.

All of these mapping tools have different strengths. Hofstede's, for example, provided the earliest comprehensive set of data and has been used extensively to guide interactions and research since its publication in 1980. GLOBE's in-depth analysis of leadership values and behaviors helps guide research in these fields. Schwartz's dimensions allow a translation from country to individual level values.

When we map cultures for mindful international management, we find the GlobeSmart tool provides the best combination of validity and practical application. GlobeSmart maps five dimensions: Task vs. Relationship, Independent vs. Interdependent, Egalitarian vs. Status, Direct vs. Indirect, and Risk vs. Certainty. The five dimensions help compare cultures, and the "you are here" survey gives individuals an easy way to compare themselves with each other and with different cultural profiles

Mapping with GlobeSmart Dimensions[1]

The first GlobeSmart dimension is about the primary focus of interaction. The next three compare cultures on different aspects of how people work together, while the final one is related to people's approach to the tasks they're working on. For each dimension, we provide scores from a sample of seventeen countries that cross different cultural patterns and geographic regions: Brazil, People's Republic of China, Canada, France, Germany, India, Japan, Kenya, Malaysia, Mexico, Poland, Russia, Spain, Sweden, UK, USA, and United Arab Emirates (UAE).

The Core of the Interaction: Task versus Relationship

All groups of people need to coordinate how they get things done together. This requires taking care of both tasks (what gets done) and relationships (the connections among people who coordinate their efforts). Different cultures have different agreements or preferences, though, for which they prioritize first in order to build the other: Tasks or Relationships. The seventeen countries' scores are shown in Figure 3.3, from most task-oriented to most relationship-oriented.

In Task-oriented cultures, people prefer to move quickly to the work to be done, and then build relationships through the actual work. This is assumed to be most efficient, and the work is a common goal around which to form the relationships. People are valued and respected for what they contribute to the task, whether it's expertise, skills, or resources. This respect can build over time to deeper trust. Anglo, Nordic, and Germanic cultures tend to focus first on task. In these cultures, a new group working together likely dives straight in to agreeing

---

[1]   GlobeSmart data and framework used with permission from Aperian Global.

Relationships

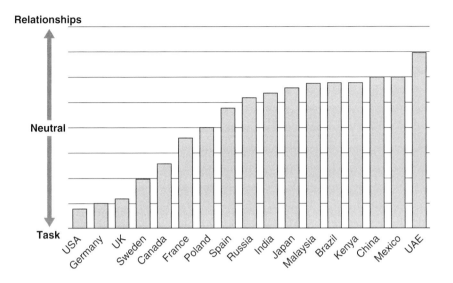

Neutral

Task

USA Germany UK Sweden Canada France Poland Spain Russia India Japan Malaysia Brazil Kenya China Mexico UAE

Figure 3.3 GlobeSmart profiles: Task vs. Relationship

on a common goal and identifying a work plan. Teams measure progress by how many milestones they have achieved. They get a sense of cohesion from accomplishing parts of the task together, and this accomplishment may inspire them to get to know each other and build stronger relationships. It's quite common for colleagues from these cultures to have little or no knowledge of each other's hobbies, values, or personal lives, at least until they've worked together for a while. Task-oriented cultures tend to be efficient and productive, especially at the start. People value each other for hard work and discipline, so the work tends to be steady. On the other hand, work colleagues may be slower to build deep trust with each other, which is critical for implementing in complex situations.

In Relationship-oriented cultures, people prefer to build the relationship first, then to work together. It is assumed that whatever the task, once people know and understand each other coordination will be smoother with greater understanding and cooperation. People are valued for their ability to build relationships, and for how connected and respected they are. Most country cultures are more Relationship focused. Relationship-oriented cultures tend to be able to innovate and implement big initiatives well and quickly based on trust, and accomplish tasks through ambiguity by relying on the relationship. On the other hand, they may be slower to get to the task in the first place, and can miss opportunities.

A Canadian executive in a global program reflected on the moment he deeply realized the difference between Task and Relationship cultures:

We had Mexicans in our class, so naturally, we discussed the Mexican culture. We spoke about their tendency to socialize first, business second, in order to build a relationship. We even saw a video of an American trying to do business when the Mexican host (obviously) wanted to speak about his family and his city. We laughed at the foolish American.

Later, we asked the Mexicans in our study team if they ever ran across people like that "for real." And one of the Mexicans put up his hand and said, "I am uncomfortable discussing these things with complete strangers. Could we introduce ourselves around the table before we continue, please? I am sorry to interrupt."

An embarrassed silence hung in the air. Here we were, discussing the concept while completely ignoring the concept. That single event had a tremendous impact on my perception of "culture." It's really there. Our culture is so ingrained, it's really hard to put it aside, even for a moment. I didn't feel a need to know more about our guests now, that would come later, at dinner, and after a few drinks. I was perfectly willing to work with someone for an hour, a day, without knowing much about them or their families. I expect the Mexicans think that we are quite shallow people.

Which is better as a core focus for interaction, Task or Relationship? Phrased this way the answer is obvious: neither is inherently better or worse. As stated earlier, all cultures engage both the Task and Relationships. Organizations that perform well sustainably in complex environments have systems and organizational cultures that direct people to take care of both tasks and relationships. Moreover, individuals tend to have their own personal preferences to focus on tasks or relationships first. At the same time, *cultures differ in the extent to which they prefer one or the other as the starting point for interaction*. Within a culture, whatever people's individual preferences are, they tend to work with others according to the assumptions of their own culture.

Moreover, because people tend to act most of the time according to the norms of their own culture, cross-cultural interactions offer the opportunity for synergy. For example, a team with mindful members who come from both Task and Relationship cultural norms can balance those two priorities without neglecting either. It may take more effort from the team members, but the payoffs are clear for high performance.

How We Interact with Each Other: Independent versus Interdependent

In every society, complex work tasks must be done by people working together. Different cultures have different agreements and preferences about how to coordinate work and interact with each other around work. The seventeen countries' scores are shown in Figure 3.4, from most Independent to most Interdependent.

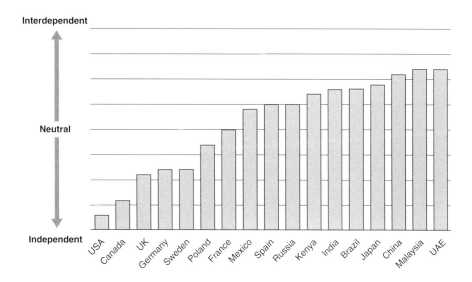

Figure 3.4 GlobeSmart profiles: Independent vs. Interdependent

In Independent cultures, people are expected to work as much as possible on their own, on clearly separated parts of a task. People who take individual initiative are highly valued, young people are taught to look after themselves, and individual achievements are emphasized. Anglo cultures tend to value and prefer high levels of Independence. In many companies from Anglo cultures, we see Independence assumptions in Human Resources (HR) practices. For example, companies such as GE and Google expect employees to drive their own careers and take initiative to direct their own progress. Someone who can move things ahead without relying on others is considered to be a great performer.

In Interdependent cultures, people are expected to work as much as possible by coordinating with and helping each other, on tasks that are related to one another. People who work well with others are highly valued, young people are taught to adapt to others, and group membership is emphasized. East Asian cultures tend to value and prefer high levels of Interdependence. In many companies from East Asian cultures, we see these assumptions in Human Resources practices. For example, companies in Japan such as Mitsubishi and Dentsu tend to hire managers based on their pre-work networks, and they rotate managers frequently so they develop networks and perspectives that help them see the whole company. Someone who contributes to the company wherever and however needed is considered to be a great performer.

Independent and Interdependent cultures both value teams, but they tend to engage in teamwork differently. In Independent cultures, team members tend to work on their own (even if in the same room) to accomplish their own part of the task. Roles must be clear so that accountability is also clear – team members must be able to track actions for both praise and blame. A good team leader coordinates the work of the team and brings the outputs together. Teams that work this way can be innovative and productive. In Interdependent cultures, team members tend to work with frequent interaction and member coordination as the task evolves. Roles are more fluid, with team members reaching out to help each other as task needs shift. Team members feel accountable for the output together, and find it difficult to articulate the contribution of each member. A good team leader facilitates interaction among team members. Teams that work this way tend to be adaptable and good at implementing as conditions change.

Both Independent and Interdependent social interactions are important for different types of performance. In fact, all cultures interact with both Independence and Interdependence, and high-performing organizations draw on both in different situations. Individuals, personally, have different preferences for independent or interdependent work, even within the same culture. At the same time, *cultures differ in the extent to which they prefer one or the other as the starting point for interaction.* Within a culture, whatever people's individual preferences are, they tend to work according to the assumptions of their own culture. As we emphasized above, this provides both efficiency and identity.

If they have people familiar with both Independent and Interdependent ways of working, cross-cultural interactions offer the opportunity for synergy. For example, a team with mindful members who come from both Independent and Interdependent cultural norms can learn to draw on both, and achieve all of innovation and adaptability, productivity and the ability to implement well over time.

How We Distribute Power and Responsibility: Egalitarian versus Status

Every society must develop agreements around how power and responsibility are allocated and distributed. There seems to be a universal principle that power and responsibility ought to go hand-in-hand: those with more power over others also have more responsibility for the performance and well-being of others. But cultures vary widely in their preferences for the extent to which power is shared. The seventeen countries' scores are shown in Figure 3.5, ranging from most Egalitarian to most Status.

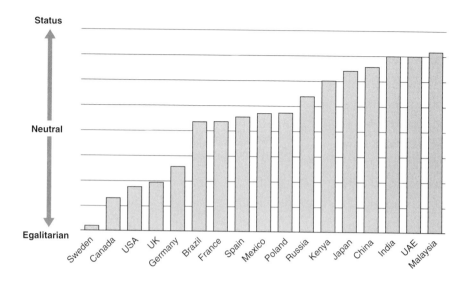

Figure 3.5 GlobeSmart profiles: Egalitarian vs. Status

Egalitarian cultures tend to assume that power and responsibility should be distributed broadly and as equally as possible. Decisions should be made by consensus, and everyone has permission (and obligation, even) to contribute to the decision process. In these cultures, a leader's role is to empower and facilitate decisions and performance, not to direct. Scandinavian cultures tend to be strongly egalitarian. In Swedish companies, such as Volvo Trucks and Ericsson, the hierarchy is very flat and employees are encouraged to go directly to people at different levels and in different parts of the organization to get information and to influence implementation. Volvo was the first large company to implement self-managed work teams throughout its production. These teams decide their own recruitment, performance management, compensation, and other practices, within a framework of company goals. Egalitarian cultures tend to maximize employee engagement and commitment. They tend to make high quality decisions, especially in situations where different inputs are needed. On the other hand, decision-making can be slow, and ambiguity on roles can lead to either gaps or redundancies.

Status cultures tend to assume that power and responsibility should be distributed more vertically, with some people having more (even much more) power and responsibility than others. Decisions should be made by leaders at the top. They may get input from others, but it's clear that the leader is responsible for making the decision and cascading it down. A good leader has a clear picture of the whole situation, is able to fit the different parts together, makes good decisions, and determines who is responsible for implementing what. A leader's role is also to take responsibility for ensuring performance and other outcomes; whether things go well or badly, the leader is accountable. Indian culture tends to be very hierarchical, and this plays out in Indian organizations such as Tata and Reliance Industries. Roles throughout the hierarchy are clear. Information may flow in multiple directions, but authority follows a clear pattern of cascading. Many Status-oriented cultures are also very patriarchal, and this tends also to be true in India. The boss looks after his or her employees, by supporting their careers, their families, and their communities. Status cultures tend to maximize efficiency in executing, especially when the situation is relatively clear. Employees tend to feel supported, and know where to go in the organization for what they need. On the other hand, innovation and initiative can be low, and communication across different parts of the hierarchy can be slow.

Which is better, Egalitarian or Status distribution of power and responsibility? Again, the answer is obvious: neither is inherently better or worse, the two ends of this spectrum enable different types of performance. It's important to realize that all cultures have mechanisms for involvement from everyone, *and* for enacting hierarchies of power. For example, quality circles in Japan and bottom-up processes ensure that everyone contributes and has voice for continuous improvement, while the vertical hierarchy enforces direction and responsibility. In Sweden, the consensus works more efficiently over time with a boss who directs it actively, and takes responsibility for the team's outcomes. Within cultures, individuals vary in their preference for Egalitarian or Status, often in ways related to family or professional background. Even though both orientations are present in all cultures, cultures differ in the extent to which they prefer one or the other as the starting point for distribution of power and responsibility. Within a culture, people tend to work according to those assumptions as the default – when in doubt, go with the cultural norm – and adapt or add variations in specific situations.

For this dimension, too, cross-cultural interactions offer opportunities for synergy. A team with mindful members who come from both Egalitarian and Status cultural norms can learn to draw on both at the same time. In new product or service teams, for example, the different stages of development and implementation benefit from Egalitarian (ideas from everywhere, broadening the scope) and Status (executing in an aligned way by a certain timeline for customers) modes.

How We Consider Others in Communication: Direct versus Indirect

In every culture, social interaction has norms about how to show consideration for the people you're communicating with. Effective communication is transmitting meaning from a sender to a receiver, as it was intended by the sender. This means communication requires commitment to the interaction from both the sender and the receiver. Different cultures have different social agreements about how people signal their commitment to communicating effectively together. The seventeen countries' scores are shown in Figure 3.6, ranging from most direct to most indirect in their communication norms.

In Direct cultures, people confront difficult topics openly, and value being concise, concrete, and to the point. They tend to separate the person from the message, the emotion from the facts. In Germany, for example, people tend to explain that it is respectful to others to value their time and their need for exact understanding so they can take precise action; therefore, it is important to be clear and direct in communications. This includes saying difficult things, such as disagreements or criticisms, directly. In Holland, people often say that it's so important to be respectful of the other person's need for information to act on, that there's no need to discuss what is good. It's more important to focus on what needs to be changed. These cultures are also sometimes referred to as low

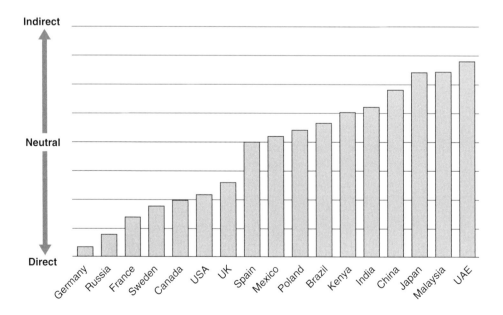

Figure 3.6 GlobeSmart profiles: Direct vs. Indirect

context – there is no need to understand anything about the context in order to understand the communication, all the meaning is in the words themselves. In cultures with a preference for Direct communication, meetings and conversations tend to be quick and to the point. Written minutes or transcripts of meetings capture all the meaning. Written communication, including email or texting, can substitute fairly easily for face-to-face contact. Direct communication styles tend to be efficient and clear, leaving little ambiguity. They provide everyone with clarity around what they should deliver, when, how, and why. On the other hand, they may miss nuances of the situation that could inform quality or adaptability, and they may miss exploring deeper reasons for current situations.

In Indirect cultures, people assume that others in the conversation may have different views, which should be considered or taken care of by avoiding apparent disagreement. These are often called **high context** cultures, because both speakers and listeners take into account the context when they communicate, often relying on contextual cues – even pauses and silences – to deliver part of the message. In Malaysia and Thailand, a manager may provide feedback to an under-performing subordinate by pointing out that the task may have been too challenging for the employee, and acknowledging that the employee has a lot of potential and could succeed with hard work. The Malaysian or Thai employee would know clearly that this is an indication they need to perform better, but the relationship has been preserved by the boss's indirect communication. When Indirect cultures are also Status cultures, which is often the case, there is a strong prohibition against disagreeing with the boss. At the same time, effective managers know how to ask the questions to save face. For example, a Malaysian boss may not ask "do you understand?" because a subordinate would not directly say "no" in order to avoid implying that the manager has not explained correctly. Instead, a Malaysian boss may ask something like "when you explain this to your own subordinates, what questions do you think they may have?" This allows the manager's subordinate to articulate his or her own questions while contextualizing them in a situation that maintains face for both the manager and subordinate. In Indirect cultures, communication tends to be holistic and comprehensive, exploring the situation and the contexts of the people involved in the communication. It also tends to maintain relationships among people, so they are motivated and committed to reaching out to each other. On the other hand, it can be slow, and it often leaves room for ambiguity about what should happen next.

Both Direct and Indirect communication preferences have strengths and complications. In all cultures, good communicators' intentions are to look after the relationship and to ensure the clarity of the message sent and received. Even in Direct cultures, people recognize that face-to-face communication facilitates non-verbal signals about how a message is being received, and ensures that the person and emotion are "looked after" even if the facts are difficult. In Indirect cultures, there are many sanctioned "off the record" mechanisms, such as social interactions after work (think about golf courses, karaoke restaurants), that create an environment for direct messages to be delivered without disrupting work relationships. Within cultures, individuals vary in their preference for Direct or Indirect, as personality differences. Even though both orientations are present in all cultures, cultures differ in the extent to which they prefer one or the other as the starting point for effective communication. Within a culture, people tend to work according to those assumptions as the norm, and compensate for its weaknesses in other ways and situations.

As for the other dimensions, cross-cultural interactions offer opportunities for synergy. For example, a team with mindful members who come from both Direct and Indirect cultural norms rely on some members to clarify ambiguity for analysis and action, and others to highlight nuances in the context for deeper understanding. Over time, all team members are likely to broaden their repertoire to be flexible in their communication norms according to the situation.

How Much Information We Need before Action: Risk versus Certainty

People in all groups must coordinate planning and action, and that means also having an implicit agreement about the relationship between planning and action: how much certainty do we need about the outcomes of an action, before taking the action? Different cultures agree on different levels of certainty required, with implications for how they engage in the action itself. The seventeen countries' scores are shown in Figure 3.7, ranging from most risk-oriented to most certainty-oriented.

In Risk-oriented cultures, people focus on the importance of demonstrating quick results. They tend to value flexibility and speed, and make decisions to take action with just enough information to indicate a direction. There's a general belief that waiting too long may risk losing an opportunity. Once people

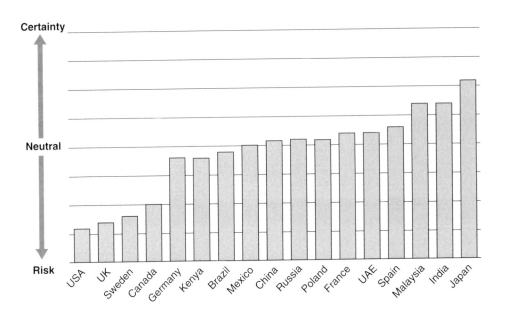

Figure 3.7 GlobeSmart profiles: Risk vs. Certainty

make a decision to go ahead with something, they tend to monitor feedback to get more information, and adapt as they go along. American innovation firms, such as Ideo, are extreme examples of the US affinity toward the Risk end of this dimension. Ideo, a well-respected and award-winning design firm, is famous for its passion to "Fail often to succeed sooner." Experimenting, pilot testing, fast prototyping – these are all common ways for American companies to launch new products, services, and markets. Risk cultures tend to be highly innovative and fast in taking action, and adaptable in implementation. On the other hand, they can develop redundancies or miss implications for larger systems, sometimes sub-optimizing quality or long-term results.

In Certainty-oriented cultures, people focus on the importance of getting it right the first time. Before committing to action, they gather extensive information and analysis and develop strong contingency plans. Once they launch action they monitor for variation from plan, and act to bring results back to the planned path. French and Spanish cultures tend to be more on the Certainty end of this dimension. In both French and Spanish companies, such as Société Générale and Banco Santander, strategic planning processes are highly structured with extensive requirements for background information and analysis. Planning across the entire company is carefully coordinated so all the pieces fit together in a logical way, with consistency and alignment built into the process. Once the plan is approved, managers expect it will be implemented with the expected results, and they monitor indicators for deviance. Certainty cultures tend to have strongly aligned and consistent systems, reliable results, and coordination for quality across multiple measures. On the other hand, they tend to be less innovative, and find it hard to adapt to changes in the environment.

Good managers in all cultures are strong at both planning and taking action, balancing risk and certainty. In Risk cultures, various mechanisms provide a foundation for Certainty. For example, the bankruptcy protection laws in the USA allow entrepreneurs and companies to take business risks without as much fear of shutting down the company in case of negative outcomes, compared with entrepreneurs and companies in many other countries. In Japan, a high Certainty culture, there is strong agreement that sometimes you need to take action without full information, and the plan becomes a series of small, specific experiments. Within cultures, individuals vary in their preference for Risk or Certainty, often from personality differences. These individual differences may translate to career choices or industry choices within the culture. Even though both orientations are present in all cultures, cultures differ in the extent to which they prefer one or the other as the starting point for determining a course for the future. Within a culture, people tend to prioritize those preferences, and balance with the other orientation in the implementation process.

Again, cross-cultural interactions offer opportunities for synergy. For example, a team with mindful members who come from both Risk and Certainty cultural norms can draw on these different values and practices to maximize both planning and learning from action.

The Discipline of Cartography: Cultural Mixes, Changes, and other Complexities

Being able to map involves more than knowledge about the dimensions. It requires using the dimensions to understand, explain, and predict others' attitudes and behavior. Mapping creates awareness and appreciation of differences and their implications in a structured and consistent way. It begins a conversation about similarities and differences using a common language and framework, and allows the conversation to move quickly and constructively to individual and situational differences. Like cartographers, managers need to combine various sources of information to create their own dynamic maps and use them to navigate complex territories. Just like any other skill, managers can practice mapping and improve their ability to map.

The Limits of Maps

Mapping is a good first step to cross-cultural understanding, but it is important to recognize its limits.

First, individuals do not always conform to their cultures. Variety and unpredictability are both the beauty and the complexity of human nature. We are all different, and we do not always behave as predicted! Within cultures, some people hold more strongly to the cultural norms than others. Personality and environmental factors influence individual behavior. Brannen and Salk described three broad categories of people that exist simultaneously in each culture and who display mainstream cultural attributes to varying degrees – probably depending on the context: cultural-normals (the typical or "average" person of that culture); hyper-normals (people who believe and follow very strongly the espoused values of a culture); and marginals (those who believe less strongly or differently) (Brannen and Salk, 2000). Even people who are strong proponents of their culture's values do not always behave in a way that is consistent with those values. This limitation is called the **ecological fallacy**: by knowing the culture (ecological level) you cannot always predict individuals; by knowing an individual, you cannot automatically predict the culture. Think about yourself: are you more or less typical of the cultural group you identify yourself with?

Not surprisingly, some countries are more culturally diverse than others. Our research showed some interesting results when we looked at within-country homogeneity or diversity, as shown in Table 3.1. Countries like Brazil and Canada are diverse due to patterns of immigration, while China and Russia are diverse due to ideological shifts in the country, with younger generations preferring different ways of working than older generations. Anthropologists propose that within-culture diversity is important for cultural change and adaptation. Japan's cultural homogeneity was seen as a key factor for creating initial growth through efficiency in alignment, but now may be associated with less growth from innovation.

Second, all individuals belong to multiple cultures, and types of cultures, simultaneously. Tan Sri Dr. Jemilah Mahmood, a prominent humanitarian, considers herself part of the Malaysian, Malay, Chinese, medical doctor, Muslim, female, mother, humanitarian aid, and global business cultures, and she articulates clearly what it means to be part of each of those cultures. Which culture she draws upon to guide her perceptions and behaviors depends on her context. She is always guided by her religious culture, covering her hair with a scarf in public, observing prayers and other disciplines, and reflecting in her behavior

Table 3.1 **Countries categorized by within-culture variance**				
High cultural homogeneity	Moderate cultural homogeneity	Mixed	Moderate cultural diversity	High cultural diversity
Belgium	Austria	Australia	Greece	Brazil
Japan	Finland	Denmark	India	Canada
South Korea	France	Hong Kong	Ireland	China
Saudi Arabia	Germany	Italy	Switzerland	Philippines
Singapore		Malaysia	UK	Romania
Taiwan		Mexico	USA	Russia
Thailand		Netherlands		South Africa
		New Zealand		
		Nigeria		
		Norway		
		Spain		
		Sweden		

the lessons of the Prophet and the Koran. She is proud of her Malaysian culture and is a strong advocate of Malaysians worldwide. She also celebrates Chinese holidays and traditions, and has close ties with her Chinese family. When delivering babies at the hospital, she behaves according to the norms and values of the medical doctor culture. When providing medical aid in an emergency situation, such as after natural disasters in Indonesia or Myanmar or as a result of conflict in Iraq or Gaza, she disregards some of the procedures typical of the hospital culture and behaves according to the emergency (for example, doing surgery outside her area of specialization), consistent with the humanitarian aid culture. When negotiating for resources with corporate sponsors for the humanitarian organization she founded, Mercy Malaysia, or when gaining access to emergency situations in her role at the International Federation of the Red Cross and Red Crescent Societies, she acts according to the global business culture, and she is well-respected as a tough player. She does not always choose to act according to a single culture, because she carries all these cultures in her, and often uses several at the same time to guide her behavior. For example, when trying to get emergency supplies to a conflict site, she uses both the humanitarian aid and the global business culture, and leverages her identity and expertise as a doctor to establish her credibility.

Mahmood's set of cultural identities is more complex than most people's. She is one of a growing minority of people in the world who are considered bicultural (or *n*-cultural) by having two (or more) ethnic cultures. Research on biculturalism shows that people who grow up with two or more cultures, such as children of immigrants or children whose parents come from two cultures, face unique challenges in developing their identity but also can develop advantages such as flexibility and cognitive complexity (Brannen, 1992; Brannen et al., 2008; Cheng, Lee, and Benet-Martinez, 2006; Fitzsimmons, 2009, 2013; Leu, Benet-Martinez, and Lee, 2000; Thomas, 2008). They manage these identities in different ways, for example they may prioritize one identity over another, they may separate them and draw on each in different situations, or they may combine them in various ways. Although Mahmood is an extreme example, it is important to remember that the pattern is common to everyone, and we all identify with multiple cultures.

Finally, cultures are dynamic, always changing. Cultures must change or they will stagnate and die, and that change is made possible by the variation of individuals within cultures and the existence of subcultures (Kluckhohn and Strodtbeck, 1961). Usually change is quite slow, but sometimes external and internal events combine to create fast change. For example, our research shows that in some emerging markets – notably China, India, and Russia – the preference for Interdependence over Independence is much less pronounced now than it was four years ago. This suggests the possibility that economic growth is somehow associated (cause or effect?) with a shift away from strong Interdependence. However, we see the same shift toward lower relative preference for Interdependence in France and Greece, where growth has slowed or even reversed. What are the causes and effects there? We will leave it to you to speculate. Our point here is that maps may show a misleadingly static picture. Those who use maps must remember that cultures shift and take care to ensure that they reflect current realities.

The Map is Not the Territory

Maps are critical tools for navigation, but it is important to remember that the map is not the territory. In its most basic form, mapping is sophisticated stereotyping. Sophisticated stereotyping is describing cultures using objective, non-evaluative data to predict thinking and behavior patterns of the culture's members (Adler, 2008; Bird and Osland, 2000). As we illustrated above, sophisticated stereotyping is extremely helpful when we enter new situations or try to understand unexpected events. People who go into new countries and cultures without sophisticated stereotypes, saying "I have no expectations, I have an open mind," are really assuming "I think they will be like me." This is due to the basic human processes related to the assumptions and perceptions described earlier in this chapter. When people go into a new situation with a map of expectations concerning how the others are likely to be different from oneself – sophisticated stereotypes – they are more prepared for differences in thinking and behavior, and they manage those differences much better.

Mapping is About Efficiency, But Don't Forget Identity

In this discussion on mapping cultures, we have focused mostly on the cognitive aspect of culture: our shared values and assumptions influence how we perceive the world and the people in it, how we make choices, and how we act. For the mechanics of doing business, this cognitive aspect is important. Furthermore, it is often misinterpreted, leading to conflict more often than synergy in intercultural interactions.

It is equally important to respect the identity that culture provides. Managers have a tendency to downplay cultural identity: "We are all part of a global business culture." But remember that identity becomes more important to the extent that it is threatened. If you disrespect identity – for example by behaving in a way that is considered rude in the culture, by serving food that is unacceptable in the country, by not accommodating requirements of the culture – you set up a situation in which the other people become more locked into their cultural identity in order to defend it. This makes conflict more likely, and makes it more difficult to achieve synergies.

Culture is the Core Context of International Management

Knowledge about culture is one of the most important foundations of mindful global leadership. Culture is the context in which international management is conducted. Culture provides guidance for how people interact, decide, and behave, and provides an important source of identity for its members. It is possible to ignore cultural difference for a short time or for basic transactions – that is, to operate without being mindful about culture – especially if you have power or other resources. However, high performance and sustainable performance in a multinational business world are only possible with strong mindfulness about culture, and an ability to draw on the strengths of different cultures in different situations. Moreover, all international managers we know agree that cultural differences create the most interesting, dynamic, and ever-enjoyable canvas possible on which to paint a management journey.

Reflection Questions

Reflection questions for this chapter encourage you to think carefully about your own cultural profile and identity, and your cross-cultural experiences.

1. Go online to www.globesmart.com (see below in "Further Resources") and map your own cultural profile on the five dimensions outlined here. How do you compare with these countries? How do your own personal preferences align with the culture(s) you identify with? An interesting survey should raise at least as many questions as it does answers: What questions about your own culture(s) arise from mapping yourself?

2. Reflect on experiences you've had in different cultures, whether working or on vacation, whether traveling or different types of culture where you live. Think particularly about the first few days of interactions. How did you learn the new culture? How did you become comfortable with the new norms? In what ways did you become more aware of your own culture through this process?

3. Think about an interaction you've had in your own culture, with someone whose cultural background is different. Try to remember one that was at least somewhat confusing to you: maybe it left you a bit uncertain. Applying the perception-behavior analysis illustrated in Figure 3.2, try to identify what you and the other person might have been going through in your interaction. How does this analysis explain the interaction and the outcome?

4. All of us are multicultural; we all hold many cultures inside, as well as additional sources of identity. What are your main sources of identity? Think about three main categories of identity:

   • individual characteristics of yourself as a person (e.g., height, coloring, personality, skill strengths ...)
   • groups you belong to, either by your life circumstances (e.g., birth citizenship, ethnicity, religion from your family, community you grew up in) or by your own choices and actions (e.g., hobbies, graduate education, sports teams you follow, religion you chose)

- roles you hold – formal or informal positions you are in, that have specific responsibilities toward other people, e.g., mother, son, boss, employee, engineer ...

Don't worry about which category a particular source of identity falls into (e.g., "professor" could fit into role, group, or even individual characteristics). The categories are there to help you raise awareness about different aspects of your identity, even ones you may not think about every day.

To what extent do you integrate versus separate different elements of your identity? Do you combine them all the time, or do you separate them and draw on them in different contexts? How important are your sources of cultural identity, compared with other sources of identity for you? What strengths do you bring to work tasks, related to your identities?

Further Resources

GlobeSmart and Aperian Global

GlobeSmart (www.globesmart.com) is an online cultural inventory and knowledge base developed by Aperian Global (www.aperianglobal.com). It focuses on the work cultures of different countries. The GlobeSmart Profile allows you to identify your own preferences on the five dimensions of Task versus Relationships, Independent versus Interdependent, Egalitarian versus Status, Direct versus Indirect, and Risk versus Uncertainty. This knowledge provides the "you are here" point for mapping yourself compared with different country profiles. The basic profiling tool is free, with a fee for accessing comparison profiles. The GlobeSmart knowledge base provides very helpful country profiles for over ninety countries, based on more than one million registered users around the world. The knowledge base includes country profiles, descriptions of the cultures, advice for working in the cultures, and training modules for working in different cultures. The knowledge base is available for individual or corporate subscription. Instructors who adopt this textbook for a course will have free access to some of the GlobeSmart resources for their class.

Other Resources

For those who would like to dig more deeply into other maps of culture, the following resources will be helpful. Hofstede's seminal study, *Culture's Consequences*, is available in a second edition (Hofstede, 2001). The Hofstede Centre (https://geert-hofstede.com/national-culture.html) provides information on cultural dimensions and data allowing a comparison of countries. The main report of the GLOBE study is Javidan et al.'s

Culture, Leadership, and Organizations (2004). Hall's book *Beyond Culture* (1989) is a classic on understanding non-verbal aspects of culture such as high- and low-context communication.

For culture's impact on perception and behavior, Erez and Earley's book *Culture, Self-Identity, and Work* (1993) provides a strong foundation.

More on bi- and multicultural individuals can be found in Fitzsimmons's work alone and with colleagues. A good starting point is Fitzsimmons's (2013) article "Multicultural Employees: A Framework for Understanding How They Contribute to Organizations."

A website that provides information about etiquette and manners in different countries is Cyborlink (www.cyborlink.com/). The tool we use in our courses is GlobeSmart (www.aperianglobal.com/learning-solutions/online-learning-tools/globesmart/). This is an online tool developed by Aperian Global for developing one's global business knowledge.

Bibliography

Adler, N. J. (2008). *International Dimensions of Organizational Behaviour*, 5th edn. Thomson South-Western.

Bird, A., & Osland, J. (2000). Beyond Sophisticated Stereotyping: Cultural Sense-Making in Context. *Academy of Management Executive*, 14, 65–79.

Brannen, M. (1992). Organizational Culture in a Bi-National Context: A Model of Negotiated Culture. *Anthropology of Work Review*, 18, 6–17.

Brannen, M., & Salk, J. (2000). Partnering across Borders: Negotiating Organizational Culture in a German–Japanese Joint Venture. *Human Relations*, 53, 451–487.

Brannen, T. M., Roth, D., Cheng, K., Locke, G., Garcia, D., Lee, F., & Fitzsimmons, S. (2008). Biculturalism in the Global Marketplace: Integrating Research and Practice. Paper presented at the Academy of Management Meetings (BII) and Valence of Cultural Cues. Anaheim, CA.

Cheng, C., Lee, F., & Benet-Martinez, V. (2006). Assimilation and Contrast Effects in Cultural Frame Switching (CFS): Bicultural Identity Integration (BII) and Valence of Cultural Cues.

Journal of Cross Cultural Psychology, 37, 1–19.

Chinese Culture Connection (1987). Chinese Values and the Search for Culture-Free Dimensions of Culture. *Journal of Cross-Cultural Psychology*, 18, 143–164.

Dorfman, P., Javidan, M., Hanges, P., Dastmalchian, A., & House, R. (2012). GLOBE: A Twenty Year Journey into the Intriguing World of Culture and Leadership. *Journal of World Business*, 47, 504–518.

Erez, M., & Earley, P. (1993). *Culture, Self-Identity, and Work*. Oxford University Press.

Fitzsimmons, S. R. (2009). Multiple Modes of Biculturalism: Antecedents and Outcomes. Dissertation, Simon Fraser University, Canada.

Fitzsimmons, S. R. (2013). Multicultural Employees: A Framework for Understanding How They Contribute to Organizations. *Academy of Management Review*, 38, 525–549.

Gibson, B., Maznevski, M., & Kirkman, B. L. (2009). When Does Culture Matter? In R. Bhagat & R. Steers (eds.), *Handbook of Culture, Organizations, and Work*. Cambridge University Press.

Hall, E. T. (1960). The Silent Language in Overseas Business. *Harvard Business Review*, 38, 87–96.

Hall, E. T. (1989). *Beyond Culture*, 2nd edn. Random House.

Hofstede, G. (1980a). *Culture's Consequences: International Differences in Work Related Values*. Sage Publications.

Hofstede, G. (1980b). Motivation, Leadership and Organization: Do American Theories Apply Abroad? *Organizational Dynamics*, 9, 42–63.

Hofstede, G. (1997). *Cultures and Organizations: Software of the Mind*. McGraw-Hill.

Hofstede, G. (2001). *Culture's Consequences: Comparing Values, Behaviours, Institutions, and Organizations across Nations*, 2nd edn. Sage Publications.

Javidan, M., Gupta, V., House, R. J., Hanges, P. J., & Dorfman, P. W. (2004). *Culture, Leadership, and Organizations: The GLOBE Study of 62 Societies*. Sage Publications.

Kluckhohn, R., & Strodtbeck, F. (1961). *Variations in Value Orientations*. Row, Peterson.

Leu, J., Benet-Martinez, V., & Lee, F. (2000). Bicultural Identities: Dynamics, Individual Differences, and Socio-Cognitive Correlates. *International Journal of Psychology*, 35, 105.

Maalouf, A. (2000). *In the Name of Identity*. Penguin Books.

Parsons, T., & Shils, E. (1951). *Toward a General Theory of Action*. Harvard University Press.

Sagiv, L., & Schwartz, S. H. (2000). A New Look at National Culture: Illustrative Applications to Role Stress and Managerial Behavior. In N. M. Ashkanasy, C. P. M. Wilderom, & M. F. Peterson (eds.), *The Handbook of Organizational Culture and Climate*. Sage Publications.

Schwartz, S. H. (1994). Beyond Individualism/Collectivism: New Cultural Dimensions of Values. In U. Kim, H. Triandis, C. Kagitcibasi, S. Choi, & G. Yoon (eds.), *Individualism and Collectivism: Theory, Method, and Applications*. Sage Publications.

Schwartz, S. H. (1999). A Theory of Cultural Values and Some Implications for Work. *Applied Psychology: An International Review/Psychologie Appliquée: Revue Internationale*, 48, 23–47.

Shultz, T. R., Hartshorn, M., & Kaznatcheev, A. (2009). Why is Ethnocentrism More Common than Humanitarianism? In N. Taatgen & H. van Rijn (eds.), *Proceedings of the 31st Annual Conference of the Cognitive Science Society (Austin, TX)*.

The Economist (2017). *The Big Mac Index*, July 13. Retrieved April 2013 from: www.economist.com/blogs/graphicdetail/2013/01/daily-chart-18

Thomas, D. C. (2008). Biculturalism Pays. *National Post*, November 11.

⚕ IVEY | Publishing

HAZELTON INTERNATIONAL

Henry W. Lane and Lorna L. Wright wrote this case solely to provide material for class discussion. The authors do not intend to illustrate either effective or ineffective handling of a managerial situation. The authors may have disguised certain names and other identifying information to protect confidentiality.

This publication may not be transmitted, photocopied, digitized or otherwise reproduced in any form or by any means without the permission of the copyright holder. Reproduction of this material is not covered under authorization by any reproduction rights organization. To order copies or request permission to reproduce materials, contact Ivey Publishing, Ivey Business School, Western University, London, Ontario, Canada, N6G 0N1; (t) 519.661.3208; (e) cases@ivey.ca; www.iveycases.com.

Copyright © 1984, Richard Ivey School of Business Foundation

Version: 2018-05-07

Dan Simpson was both anxious and excited as he drove with John Anderson in their jeep up the rutted road to the river where they would wait for the ferry. John was the current project manager of the Maralinga-Ladawan Highway Project and was taking Dan, his replacement, on a three-day site check of the project. During this trip John was also going to brief Dan on the history of the project and the problems he might encounter. Dan was anxious about the project because he had heard there were a number of messy problems, but was excited about the management challenge involved.

Hazelton, a Canadian consulting engineering firm, was an adviser on the project and had little success so far in getting the client to heed its advice. After two years of operation, only 17 kilometers of the 245-kilometer highway were under reconstruction.

Background

Since 1995 Hazelton had successfully completed assignments in 46 countries across Africa, Asia, Europe, South and Central America, and the Caribbean region. A large proportion of the projects had been in Africa but the company was now turning its attention to developing its Asian operations. Hazelton had done only 10 projects in Asia – less than 10 per cent of all projects completed.

Hazelton provided consulting services in transportation, housing and urban development, structural engineering, and municipal and environmental engineering, to both government and corporate clients around the world. Specific services included technical and economic feasibility studies, financing, planning, architecture, preliminary and final engineering design, maintenance programming, construction supervision, project management, and equipment procurement.

Projects ranged from extremely large (building an international airport) to very small, requiring the skill of only a single expert (advising on a housing project in Malaysia). The majority of these projects were funded by international lending agencies (ILAs) such as World Bank, African Development Bank, and aid agencies like the U.S. Agency for International Development (USAID) and the Canadian International

Exhibit 1: Map of Soronga

Exhibit 1: Map of Soronga
             (not to scale)

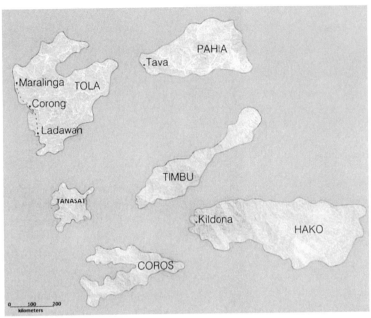

Development Agency (CIDA).[1] The previous year, Hazelton's worldwide annual fee volume had exceeded US$80 million.

Hazelton staffed its overseas projects with senior members of its permanent staff. In addition, outside experts with international experience and capabilities in the applicable language were used whenever possible. Both these principles had been adhered to in the Maralinga-Ladawan Project.

Maralinga-Ladawan Highway Project

Soronga was a nation of islands in the Pacific Ocean. The Maralinga-Ladawan project required design and construction supervision services for the reconstruction of a 245-kilometer highway along the western

coast of the island of Tola from Maralinga in the north to Ladawan in the south (see Exhibit 1). Sections of the highway past Ladawan were being reconstructed by other firms funded by aid agencies from Japan and Australia. In addition to supervising the project, Hazelton was responsible for a major training program for Sorongan engineers, mechanics, operators, and administrative staff.

This was the fifth largest project ($3.26 million in fees) Hazelton had ever undertaken (see Exhibit 2). It was a joint venture with two other firms, Beauval Ltd. and Thomaston Brothers Limited (TBL), whom Hazelton involved to strengthen its proposal. Hazelton acted as the lead firm on behalf of the consortium and assumed overall responsibility for the work. Over the life of the project, the three firms would send 22 expatriates, including highway designers, engineers, mechanics, and operators.

TBL was involved because it was a contractor and Hazelton felt it might need those

---

[1] In 2013 the Canadian International Development Agency (CIDA) was merged into the Department of Foreign Affairs, which in 2015 was renamed for public purposes (but not legally) Global Affairs Canada.

Exhibit 2: Hazelton's Six Largest Projects

Project	Location	Fee
1. International airport	Africa	$8 million
2. Highway supervision	South America	$6.8 million
3. Highway feasibility	South America	$4.5 million
4. Highway design	South America	$4.5 million
5. Highway betterment	Soronga	$3.26 million
6. Secondary roads: graveling	Africa	$3.26 million

types of skills when dealing with a "force account" project. Usually, Hazelton supervised their project and left the actual construction to experienced contractors. This project was different. Force account meant that the construction workers would be government employees who would not be experienced in construction work.

Beauval had been working in Asia for 17 years and had established a base of operations in Kildona. It had done several projects on the island of Hako, but this would be the first on the island of Tola. This local experience helped the proposal gain acceptance both in the eyes of the financing agency, and the client, the Sorongan Highway Department (SHD).

The financing agency provided a combination loan and grant for the project and played a significant role in the selection of the winning proposal. The grant portion paid for the salaries of the expatriates working on the project while the loan funds were for necessary equipment.

Under the contract's terms of reference, Hazelton personnel were sent as advisers on the techniques of road construction and equipment maintenance. The training component was to be the major part of the project with the actual construction being the training vehicle. The project was to last five years with Hazelton phasing out its experts in about four years. By that point the Sorongans would be trained to take over

the project themselves. The training program would use formal classroom instruction and a system of counterparts. Each expatriate engineer or manager would have a counterpart Sorongan engineer or manager who worked closely with him in order for their expertise to be passed on. At the mechanic and operator levels, training programs would be set up involving both in-class instruction and on-the-job training.

SHD's responsibilities included providing counterpart staff, ensuring that there was housing built for the expatriates, and providing fuel and spare parts for the equipment that would be coming from Canada.

It was thought that a force account project – with government staff doing the work – would be the best way to marry the financial agency's objective of training with the Sorongan government's aim of building a road. It was one of the few times that SHD had found itself in the role of contractor.

Hazelton was in the position of supervising one arm of the organization on behalf of another arm. It was working for the client as a supervising engineer, but the client also ran the construction. Hazelton was in the middle.

In Soronga's development plans, this project was part of the emphasis on developing the transportation and communications sector. It was classed as a betterment project, meaning that Soronga did not want undue resources going toward a "perfect" road in engineering terms; merely one that was better than the present one and that would last. Another important objective was to provide employment in Tola and permit easier access to the rest of Soronga, because the province was a politically sensitive area and isolated from the rest of the country.

Tola

Tola was the most westerly island of the Sorongan archipelago. It was isolated from the rest of the country because of rough terrain and poor roads. It was a socially conservative province and fundamentalist in religion. The majority of Tolanese were very strict Muslims. The ulamas (Moslem religious leaders) played an important role in Tolanese society, perhaps more so than in any other part of Soronga.

Economically, the province lagged behind Hako, the main island. The economy was still dominated by labor-intensive agriculture. Large-scale industry was a very recent development with timbering providing the biggest share of exports. A liquefied natural gas plant and a cement factory were two new operations begun within the past two years.

From its earliest history, Tola had enjoyed a high degree of autonomy. In 1851, it signed a treaty with a European country guaranteeing its autonomy in commerce. This was revoked in 1901 when that European country signed a treaty with another European colonial power, recognizing the latter's sovereignty over the whole of Soronga. The Tolanese understood the implications of this treaty and tried to negotiate with their new masters to retain Tola's autonomous standing. Neither side was willing to compromise, however, and in 1903 the European country declared war on Tola. This war continued for 50 years, and the fierce resistance of the Tolanese against colonization became a model for Soronga's own subsequent fight for independence. Even after the Tolanese officially surrendered, this did not mean peace. Guerrilla warfare continued, led by the ulamas. With the advent of the Second World War and the arrival of the Japanese, resistance to foreigners intensified. At the end of the war, the Japanese were expelled, and the European colonizers returned to Soronga, but not to Tola.

With the independence of Soronga, Tola theoretically formed part of the new nation, but in practice, it retained its regional social, economic, and political control. In 1991, however, the central government in Kildona dissolved the province of Tola and incorporated its territory into the region of West Pahia under a governor in Tava. Dissatisfaction with this move was so intense that the Tolanese proclaimed an independent Islamic Republic in 1993. This rebellion lasted until 2001, when the central government sought a political solution by giving back provincial status to Tola. In 2007, Kildona granted special status to the province in the areas of religion, culture, and education.

Tola's long periods of turmoil had left their mark on the province and on its relations with the rest of the country. Tolanese were deeply suspicious of outsiders (particularly those from Hako, since that was the seat of the central government), strongly independent and fiercely proud of their heritage and ethnic identity. Although all Tolanese could speak Sorongan because that was the only language used in the schools, they preferred to use their native language, Tolanese, amongst themselves. The central government in Kildona had recently become concerned about giving the province priority in development projects to strengthen the ties between the province and the rest of the country.

Progress of the Project

The First Year

Negotiations on the project took longer than expected, and the project actually began almost a year after it was originally scheduled to start. Hazelton selected its personnel carefully. The project manager, Frank Kennedy, had been successful in a similar position in Central America and had also successfully cleaned up a problem situation in Lesotho. In September, Frank and an administrator arrived in Soronga, followed a month later by the major design team, bringing the total expatriate contingent to 10 families. They spent a month learning the Sorongan language but had to stay in Kildona until December because there was no housing in Maralinga. The houses had not been finished; before they could be, an earthquake had destroyed the complex. Eventually, housing was rented from Australian expatriates working for another company who were moving to a complex of their own.

Hazelton was anxious to begin work, but no Sorongan project manager had been specified, and the vehicles did not arrive until late December. When the vehicles did arrive, the fuel tanks were empty and there was no fuel available. Neither was there provision in SHD's budget to buy fuel or lubricants that year. The project would have to wait to have money allotted to it until the new fiscal year began on April 1.

The Second Year

By the beginning of the year, the equipment was on site, but the Sorongan counterpart staff were not. Hazelton had no control over SHD staff, since it had no line responsibility. When the SHD project manager finally arrived, he was reluctant to confront the local staff. Senior SHD people on the project were Hakonese, whereas most of the people at the operator level were local Tolanese. There was not only the Hakonese-Tolanese animosity but an unwillingness on the part of the senior staff to do anything that would stir up this politically volatile area.

Frank was having a difficult time. He was a construction man. There were 245 kilometers of road to build and nothing was being done. It galled him to have to report no progress month after month. If the construction could start, the training would quickly follow. On top of the project problems, Frank's wife was pregnant and had to stay in Singapore, where the medical facilities were better. As his frustration increased, he began confronting the Sorongan project manager, demanding action. His behavior became counter-productive to the point that he had to be replaced. The person chosen as his replacement was John Anderson.

John Anderson

John Anderson was a civil engineer who had worked for Hazelton for 15 years. He had a wealth of international experience in countries as diverse as Thailand, Nigeria, Tanzania, and Kenya. He liked the overseas environment for a variety of reasons, not the least of which was the sense of adventure that went with working abroad. "You meet people who stand out from the average. You get interesting points of view."

Professionally, it was also an adventure. "You run across many different types of engineering and different ways of approaching it." This lent an air of excitement and interest to jobs that was lacking in domestic work. The challenge was also greater because one didn't have access to the same skills and tools available at home: as John said, "You have to make do."

Even though he enjoyed overseas work, John had returned to headquarters as office manager for Hazelton. His family was a major factor in this decision. As his two children reached high school age, it became increasingly important for them to be settled and to receive schooling that would allow them to enter a good university. John had no intention of going overseas in the near future; however, when it became evident that a new project manager was needed for Soronga, loyalty prompted him to accept without hesitation when the company called.

John had been the manager of a similar project similar to the Maralinga-Ladawan Highway Project in Nigeria and had done a superlative job. He had a placid, easy-going temperament and a preference for operating by subtle suggestions rather than direct demands. Hazelton's top management felt that if anyone could make a success of this project, John could.

John's Perception of the Project

From the description of Maralinga in the original project document, John knew he would face problems from the beginning. However, when he arrived on site, it wasn't as bad as he'd expected. People were friendly, the housing was adequate, and there was access to an international school run by the Australians.

The work situation was different. The equipment that had come from Canada could not be used. Bridges to the construction sites had not been built and the existing ones could not support the weight of the machines. The bridge work would have to be done before the road project started. Roads had to be widened to take the construction equipment, but no provisions had been made to expropriate the needed land. Instructions were that the road must remain within the existing right-of-way. Technically, SHD could lay claim to 15 meters, but they had to pay compensation for any crops lost, even though those crops were planted on state land. Because of these problems, the biggest pieces of machinery, such as the crusher plant, had to be taken apart and moved piece by piece. Stripping a machine down for transportation took time, money, and labor – all in short supply.

The budgeting process presented another problem. It was done on an annual basis rather than for the entire project period. It was also done in meticulous detail. Every litre of fuel and every nut and bolt had to be included. The budget was also extremely inflexible. Money allocated for fuel could not be used for spare parts if the need arose.

When the project was initially planned, there was plenty of money, but in the years following the 2008 global financial crisis, the Sorongan economy was hit hard by declining foreign aid, foreign direct investment and remittances. As a result, restrictions on all projects were quickly instituted. Budgets were cut in half and the money originally planned was no longer available for the project. Further problems arose because the project was a force account. The government bureaucracy could not react quickly, and in construction fast reactions were important. Revisions needed to be approved quickly, but by the time the government approved a change, it was often too late.

The training component of the project had more than its share of problems. Counterpart training was difficult because Sorongan managers would arbitrarily reassign workers to other jobs. Other counterparts would leave for more lucrative jobs elsewhere. Among the mechanics, poor supervision compounded the problems. Those who showed initiative were not encouraged and any spark soon died.

John's Arrival on Site

John arrived in Soronga in March. SHD budgets were due soon after. This required a tremendous amount of negotiating as expenses had to be identified specifically and in minute detail. By September, the process was completed, and, after more than a year, the project finally had funds to support it.

Shortly after John's arrival, the project was transferred from the maintenance section of SHD to the construction section. The Sorongan project manager changed and the parameters of the project also began to change.

SHD would not allow realignment of the road. To change the alignment would have meant getting property rights, which was an expensive, time-consuming process and inconsistent with a project that SHD saw as road improvement rather than road construction. This meant that half the design team had no work to do. Their roles had to be quickly changed. For example, the chief design engineer became costing, programming, and budgeting engineer.

The new SHD project manager was inexperienced in his post and concerned about saving money and staying within budget. Because of this, he was loath to hire more workers to run the machinery because the rainy season was coming and construction would slow down. The workers would have to be paid, but little work would be done. By October, with the rainy season in full swing, it was evident that the money allocated to the project was not going to be spent, and the project manager frantically began trying to increase activity. If this year's budget was not spent, it would be very difficult to get adequate funds for the next year. However, it was difficult to spend money in the last months because no preparatory work had been done. It took time to let tenders and hire trained staff.

The new SHD project manager was Hakonese, as was his predecessor. Neither understood the local Tolanese situation. Getting access to gravel and sand sites necessitated dealing with the local population, and this was not handled well, with the result that it took a long time to acquire land rights. The supervisors were also mainly Hakonese and could exercise little control over the workforce. Discipline was lax. Operators wouldn't begin doing any constructive work until 9:30 a.m. They would quit at 11:30 a.m. for a two-hour lunch and then finish for the day at 5:00 p.m. Drivers hauled material for private use during working hours. Fuel disappeared at an alarming rate. One morning when a water truck was inspected before being put into service, the Hazelton adviser discovered the water tank was full of fuel. No explanation as to how

the fuel got there was forthcoming, and it soon vanished again.

Bridges were a problem. It had been almost two and one-half years since the original plans had been submitted, and SHD was now demanding changes. Substructures were not yet in place and the tenders had just been let. When they were finally received by midyear, SHD decided that Canadian steel was too expensive and they could do better elsewhere. The tendering process would have to be repeated, and SHD had not yet let the new tenders.

Although there was no real construction going on, training had begun. A training manager was on site, and the plan was to train the mechanics and equipment operators first. The entire program would consist of four phases. The first phase would involve 30 people for basic operator training. The second would take the best people from the first phase and train them further as mechanics. In the third phase, the best mechanics would train others. The fourth phase would upgrade skills previously learned. SHD cancelled the second phase of training because they considered it to be too costly and a waste of time. They wanted people to be physically working, not spending time in the classroom. Hazelton felt that both types of training were needed, and the cancellation raised difficulties with the financing agency, who considered the training needs paramount.

SHD, as a government agency, was not competitive with private companies in wages. It was not only losing its best engineering people to better-paying jobs elsewhere, it could not attract qualified people at the lower levels. Its people, therefore, were inexperienced and had to be taught the basics of operating mechanical equipment. Ironically, equipment on the project was some of the most sophisticated available.

SHD was directing the construction, but there didn't seem to be any plan of attack. The SHD manager was rarely on site, and the crews suffered badly from a lack of direction. Time, materials, and people were being wasted because of this. Bits and pieces of work were being started at different points with no consideration given to identifying the critical areas.

In June, there was a push to get construction underway. There was a need to give the design people something to do and a desire to get the operators and mechanics moving, as well as the equipment, which had been sitting idle for several months. Finally, there was the natural desire to show the client some concrete results. Hazelton was losing the respect of the people around them. Most people were not aware that Hazelton was acting merely in an advisory capacity. The feeling was that they should be directing the operations. Since Hazelton was not taking charge, the company's competence was being questioned.

The rainy season was due to begin in September and would last until the end of December. This was always a period of slow progress because construction was impossible when it rained. Work had to be stopped every time it rained and frequently work that had been done before the rain had to be redone.

Besides the problem of no progress on construction, some of the expatriate staff were not doing the job they had been sent out to do. Because there was little design work, the design engineer was transformed into a costing and budgeting administrator. No bridges were being built, so the bridge engineer was idle. No training was being done, so the training manager was declared redundant and sent home.

It was difficult for Hazelton to fulfil even its advisory role because SHD personnel were not telling them what they were doing next. A communication gap was rapidly opening between SHD and Hazelton. Communication between SHD in Tola and SHD in Kildona was poor, also. It appeared that the Kildona headquarters was allowing the Tola one to sink or swim on its own. Little direction was forthcoming. Compounding the problems, it didn't seem as if SHD Kildona was allocating its best people to the project.

The one bright spot of the year was that the project was now under the construction section of SHD rather than the maintenance section, and, they understood the situation from a construction point of view. The feeling was that things would improve because now the people in headquarters at least understood what the field team was up against and what it was trying to accomplish.

The Third Year

At the beginning of the year, there was little to be seen for the previous year's work.

The Hazelton staff and their Sorongan counterparts worked out of a small two-storey building in the SHD office compound in Maralinga. The Sorongans occupied the top floor and Hazelton, the bottom. A field camp trailer site had been set up in Corong, the halfway point between Maralinga and Ladawan. The plan was to move construction out from this area in both directions.

John, his mechanic supervisor, and the bridge engineer made the five-hour trip out to the site at the beginning of each week, returning to Maralinga and their families at the end of the week. The second mechanic and his wife lived on-site, whereas the erstwhile design engineer, now in charge of budgeting and administration, stayed primarily in the Maralinga office.

SHD was beginning to rethink its position on using force account labor. There were signs that in the next fiscal year it might hire a contractor to do the actual work because the force account was obviously not working satisfactorily. SHD also underwent another change in project manager. The third person to fill that position was due on-site in April, but arrived the end of May. The new manager began making plans to move the Sorongan base of operations to Corong.

The Hazelton expatriates, for family reasons, would remain based in Maralinga.

The project now also underwent its third status change. It was being given back to the maintenance section of SHD and the budget process would have to be started again. Hazelton, in its advisory role, tried to impress on the SHD staff the advantages of planning ahead and working out the details of the next year's work so that there would be funds in the budget to support it.

Construction had at last started, even though in a desultory fashion. However, Ramadan, the month of fasting for Moslems, was looming on the horizon and this would slow progress. This meant no eating, no drinking, and no smoking for Moslems between sun-up and sundown, which had obvious consequences for a worker's energy level. Productivity dropped during this period. This had not been a major problem the previous year because not much work was being done. Following Ramadan, there would be only two months to work at normal speed before construction would have to slow again for the rainy season.

John's briefing of Dan having been completed, they continued the site check. John wanted Dan to inspect the existing bridges as they arrived at them.

🛡IVEY | Publishing

AN INTERNATIONAL PROJECT MANAGER'S DAY (A)

Lorna Wright wrote this case under the supervision of Professor Henry W. Lane solely to provide material for class discussion. The authors do not intend to illustrate either effective or ineffective handling of a managerial situation. The authors may have disguised certain names and other identifying information to protect confidentiality.

This publication may not be transmitted, photocopied, digitized or otherwise reproduced in any form or by any means without the permission of the copyright holder. Reproduction of this material is not covered under authorization by any reproduction rights organization. To order copies or request permission to reproduce materials, contact Ivey Publishing, Ivey Business School, Western University, London, Ontario, Canada, N6G 0N1; (t) 519.661.3208; (e) cases@ivey.ca; www.iveycases.com.

Copyright © 1986, Richard Ivey School of Business Foundation

Version: 2015-08-13

Situation

The Maralinga-Ladawan Highway Project consisted of 14 expatriate families and the Sorongan counterpart personnel. Half of the expatriates were engineers from Hazelton. The other expatriates were mechanics, engineers and other technical personnel from Beauval and TBL, the other two firms in the consortium. All expatriate personnel were under Hazelton's authority. This is the fifth largest project Hazelton has ever undertaken, with a fee of $3.26 million.

You arrived in Maralinga late on April 25 with your spouse. There was no chance for a briefing before you left. Head office had said John Anderson, the outgoing project manager, would fill you in on all you needed to know.[1] They had also arranged for you to meet people connected with the project in Kildona.

On April 26, you visited the project office briefly and met the accountant/administrative assistant, Tawi, the secretary, Julip, and the office messenger/driver, Satun. You then left immediately on a three-day site check

[1] See Hazelton International Limited, 9A84C040

of the 245-kilometer highway with John. Meanwhile, your spouse has started settling in and investigating job prospects in Maralinga.

On your trip you stopped at the field office in Corong. Chris Williams, second mechanic and his wife, Beth, were living there. Chris was out at the timber company site to get help in recovering a grader that had toppled over the side of a ravine the night before, so you weren't able to see him. However, you met his Sorongan counterpart and he advised you that everything was going well, although they could use more manpower.

You noted that Corong did not have any telephone lines. The only communication link, a 2G cellular phone tower, had been unserviceable for the past few weeks. If you needed to contact Chris, it would involve a five-hour jeep ride to Corong to deliver the message.

You were able to see the haphazard way the work on the road was proceeding and witnessed the difficulty in finding appropriate gravel sites. Inspecting some of the bridges you had crossed made you shiver, too. Doing something about those would have to be a priority, before there was a fatality.

You returned to Maralinga on April 29 and met some of the staff and their families. Their comments made it clear that living conditions were less than ideal, the banking system made it difficult to get money transferred and converted into local currency (their salaries, paid in dollars, were deposited to their accounts at home), and the only school it was possible to send their children to was not appropriate for children who would have to return to the North American educational system.

That evening John left for another project on another continent. It is now Wednesday morning, April 30. This morning, while preparing breakfast with your spouse, the propane gas for your stove ran out. You have tried, unsuccessfully, on your way to work to get the gas cylinder filled, and have only now arrived at the office. It is 10 a.m. You had planned to have lunch with your spouse at noon and you are leaving for the airport at 2 p.m. for a week in Kildona to visit the Beauval office, the Sorongan Highway Department (SHD) people, and the International Aid Agency (IAA) representative for discussions concerning the history and future of this project (it takes about one-half hour to drive to the airport). This trip was planned as part of your orientation to the job. Since the IAA representative and the senior man in the Beauval office were both leaving for other postings at the end of the month, this may be the only opportunity you will have to spend time with them.

On your arrival at the office, Julip tells you that Jim, one of the surveyors, and his wife, Joyce, are arriving at 10:30 a.m. to discuss Joyce's medical problems with you. This is the first opportunity you have had to get into your office and do some work. You have about 30 minutes to go through the contents of your in-basket and take whatever action you feel is appropriate.

Instructions

For the purpose of this exercise, you are to assume the position of Dan Simpson, the new project manager for the Maralinga-Ladawan Highway Project.

Please write out the action you choose on the Action Forms provided. Your action may include writing emails and text messages or making phone calls. You may want to have meetings with certain individuals or receive reports from the office staff.

For example, if you decide to make a phone call, write out the purpose and content of the call on the Action Form. If you decide to have a meeting with one of the office staff or another individual, make a note of the basic agenda of things to be discussed and the date and time of the meeting. You also need to think about establishing priorities for the various issues.

To help you think of the time dimension, a calendar follows (see Exhibit 1). Also, Maralinga is 12 hours ahead of Eastern Standard Time.

Exhibit 1: Dan Simpson's Calendar

dansimpson@hazeltoninterna... Calendar Tasks ×

Synchronize Event Task Tasks Edit Delete

April 2014 ◀ ○ ▶
Su	Mo	Tu	We	Th	Fr	Sa
30	31	1	2	3	4	5
6	7	8	9	10	11	12
13	14	15	16	17	18	19
20	21	22	23	24	25	26
27	28	29	30	1	2	3
4	5	6	7	8	9	10

◢ Calendar
☑ Home
☑ Hazelton

Events in the Next 7 Days ⌄ contain

Title	Start	End	Category
Visit to Kildona	Wednesday, April 30, 2014 All Day	Wednesday, May 7, 2014 All Day	
Flight departs to Kildona	Wednesday, April 30, 2014 2:00 PM	Wednesday, April 30, 2014 3:00 PM	

◀ Today ▶ April 13 – May 10, 2014   CWs: 16-19   Day | Week | **Multiweek** | Month

Sunday	Monday	Tuesday	Wednesday	Thursday	Friday	Saturday
13 Apr	14	15	16	17	18	19
20	21	22	23	24	25	26
					7:00 PM Arrival in Maralinga	Site check with John
27	28	29	30 Apr **Wednesday**	1 May	2	3
Site check with John	Return	Visit to Kildona / 2:00 PM Flight departs to Kildona	Visit to Kildona	Visit to Kildona	Visit to Kildona	Visit to Kildona
4	5	6	7	8	9	10 May
Visit to Kildona	Visit to Kildona	Visit to Kildona	Visit to Kildona	Return to Maralinga		

🗓 Today Pane ∧

Exhibit 2

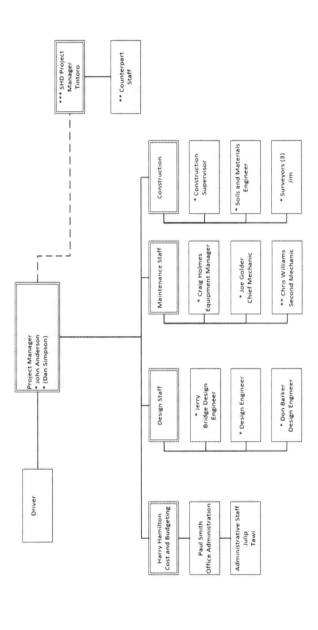

Notes:

*   These people travel to Corong and other locations frequently.

**   Stationed in Corong.

***   Located on the floor above Dan Simpson in the same building.

The two expatriates responsible for training have been sent home. The remaining six expatriates called for under contract have not arrived yet in Soronga and the two construction supervisors recently requested by SHD would be in addition to these six people.

Transportation Availability: (1) PROJECT OWNED - a) 1 Land Rover for administrative use by HQ Staff, b) 1 car shared by all the families, c) most trucks are in Corong, however there usually are some around Maralinga (2) PUBLIC - a) peddle-cabs are available for short distances (like getting to work), b) local "taxis" are mini-van type vehicles which are usually very overcrowded and which expatriates usually avoid, c) there are a few flights to Kildona each week.

David Wesley wrote this case under the supervision of Professors Henry W. Lane and Mikael Sondergaard solely to provide material for class discussion. The authors do not intend to illustrate either effective or ineffective handling of a managerial situation. The authors may have disguised certain names and other identifying information to protect confidentiality.

Ivey Management Services is the exclusive representative of the copyright holder and prohibits any form of reproduction, storage or transmittal without its written permission. Reproduction of this material is not covered under authorization by any reproduction rights organization. To order copies or request permission to reproduce materials, contact Ivey Publishing, Ivey Management Services, c/o Richard Ivey School of Business, The University of Western Ontario, London, Ontario, Canada, N6A 3K7; phone (519) 661-3208; fax (519) 661-3882; e-mail cases@ivey.uwo.ca.

Copyright © 2008, Northeastern University, College of Business Administration   Version: (A) 2010-02-26

In early February 2006, Astrid Nielsen, group communications director of Arla Foods, faced the greatest crisis of her career. Tens of thousands of Muslims in cities around the world had taken to the streets to protest the publication of caricatures of Muhammad by a Danish newspaper. The caricatures, which most Muslims viewed as blasphemous and offensive, prompted some to attack Danish embassies and businesses. In several countries, protests turned deadly.

Saudi Arabia was able to avoid much of the violence seen elsewhere. Instead, consumers protested by boycotting Danish products. For Arla Foods, which owned a large dairy in Saudi Arabia, the result was nothing short of disastrous. As other countries began to join the boycott, Nielson wondered what, if anything, her company could do to mitigate the total loss of Arla's Middle Eastern business.

Background

Arla Foods, a co-operative owned by 10,000 milk producers in Denmark and Sweden, was formed in 2000 through the merger of MD Foods of Denmark and Arla of Sweden. Arla was Europe's second largest dairy company, with 58 processing plants in Scandinavia and Britain, and annual revenues of nearly US$8 billion. It enjoyed a near monopoly on domestic dairy products, with market shares of between 80 and 90 per cent in most categories. The United Kingdom was the company's largest market, accounting for 33 per cent of total sales, followed by Sweden and Denmark at 22 per cent and 19 per cent, respectively. The rest of Europe accounted for another 13 per cent.

Outside Europe, the Middle East was Arla's most important market (see Table 1). The company exported approximately 55,000 tons of dairy products from Denmark and Sweden to Saudi Arabia, and produced around 30,000 tons through its Danya Foods subsidiary in Riyadh. Local production was based mainly on non-perishable goods and included processed cheese, milk, and fruit drinks. In Saudi Arabia, which accounted for 70 per cent of total Middle East sales, the company's Lurpak, Puck, and Three Cows brands were market leaders in butter, cream, dairy spread, and feta categories. Other important Middle East markets included Lebanon, Kuwait, Qatar, and the United Arab Emirates.

Table 1 Arla Foods: Middle East Key Facts

Annual Revenues	$550 million
Net Income	$80 million
Danish Expatriate Workers	20
Non-Danish Workers[1]	1200
Average Annual Growth	10–12%

Other overseas markets included Argentina and Brazil, where Arla produced cheese and whey products. Arla also exported significant quantities of Danish cheese to Japan, and milk powder to less developed countries in Asia and Latin America. In North America, Arla cheeses were produced under a licensing agreement.

The Muhammad Cartoons Crisis

Terrorism and Self-Censorship

In 2004, controversial Dutch filmmaker Theo van Gogh produced a short film on Islam titled "Submission."[2] The 10-minute documentary, written by Dutch Member of Parliament Hirsi Ali, featured the stories of four abused Arab women. It intentionally provoked some Muslims by showing a woman dressed in a semi-transparent burqa, under which verses from the Qur'an were projected on her skin.

After the film was shown on Dutch public television on August 29, 2004, van Gogh and Ali began to receive death threats. Then, on November 2, 2004, Van Gogh was murdered while riding his bicycle in downtown Amsterdam.[3] The assailant attached a note to his body calling for Jihad against "infidel" America and Europe and threatening a similar fate for Ali.

Van Gogh's murder created broad awareness of his film, which was subsequently rebroadcast on Italian and Danish public television and widely distributed on the Internet. In Denmark, tension was already high following another well-publicized incident in which a lecturer at the University of Copenhagen was assaulted by five Muslim youths for reading the Qur'an to non-Muslims.[4] The killing of Van Gogh only served to heighten the cultural distance between Muslim immigrants and native-born Danes. Although most Europeans decried the violence of radical Islamists, many publishers, authors, and artists were reluctant to participate in projects that could offend Muslims and invite the wrath of terrorists.

Fear and Self-Censorship

In the summer of 2005, Danish author Kåre Bluitgen decided to write a children's book on the life of the Prophet Muhammad. He had hoped that such a book would help Danish children learn the story of Islam and thereby bridge the growing gap between Danes and Muslim immigrants. Yet the illustrators who collaborated with Bluitgen on other books feared reprisals from extremists and, therefore, refused to participate.[5] They understood, perhaps better than Bluitgen,

---

[1] Most of Arla's non-Danish staff was comprised of Muslim migrant workers from less developed countries. Many entered Saudi Arabia as Hajj pilgrims and remained in the country at the end of their pilgrimage.
[2] Submission is the English translation of the word Islam.
[3] Gunman kills Dutch film director, *BBC News*, November 2, 2004.

[4] Overfaldet efter Koran-læsning, *TV 2 (Denmark)*, October 9, 2004.
[5] Allah und der Humor, *Die Zeit*, January 2, 2006.

that graphical depictions of Muhammad were considered blasphemous by many Muslims.[6]

Bluitgen eventually found an artist willing to illustrate his book anonymously. However, when the culture editor of the Danish newspaper Jyllands-Posten heard Bluitgen's story, he was incensed. "This was the culmination of a series of disturbing instances of self-censorship," Flemming Rose later wrote.

> Three people turned down the job for fear of consequences. The person who finally accepted insisted on anonymity, which in my book is a form of self-censorship. European translators of a critical book about Islam also did not want their names to appear on the book cover beside the name of the author, a Somalia-born Dutch politician who has herself been in hiding.[7]

Danish Cartoons: Muhammad As You See Him

To counter what he saw as a move against free speech, Rose invited 40 artists to submit drawings of "Muhammad, as you see him." Twelve artists responded, including three members of the Jyllands-Posten staff. When the cartoons first appeared on September 30, 2005, Rose wrote in the accompanying article,

The modern, secular society is rejected by some Muslims. They demand a special position, insisting on special consideration of their own religious feelings. It is incompatible with contemporary democracy and freedom of speech, where you must be ready to put up with insults, mockery and ridicule ... We are on our way to a slippery slope where no-one can tell how the self-censorship will end. That is why Jyllands-Posten has invited members of the Danish editorial cartoonists union to draw Muhammad as they see him.[8]

Muslim Reaction

Two weeks after the publication of the 12 cartoons, Danish imams organized a protest in downtown Copenhagen. More than 3,000 Danish Muslim immigrants gathered to show their disapproval of the cartoons. The most offensive cartoon, in their opinion, featured Muhammad wearing a turban filled with explosives. On the turban was written the Shahādah (Islamic creed),[9] while a lit fuse emerged from the back of his head.

Another image featured a schoolboy named Muhammad scribbling a message in Farsi[10] on a blackboard. "The editorial team of Jyllands-Posten is a bunch of reactionary provocateurs," it states. Ironically, artist Lars Refn was targeted by both sides in the ensuing quarrel. He was the first artist to receive death threats, while at the same time secular free speech advocates accused him of cowardice for not drawing the prophet.

---

[6] Not all Muslims agree on the interpretation of Muslim scholars who have issued fatwas against images of the prophet Muhammad. Some argue that Islam has a centuries-old tradition of paintings of Muhammad and other religious figures. The more famous of these continue to be displayed in palaces and museums in various Muslim countries, including Iran. Source: Bonfire of the Pieties: Islam prohibits neither images of Muhammad nor jokes about religion, *The Wall Street Journal*, February 8, 2006.

[7] The Dutch politician refers to Hirsi Ali, who collaborated with Theo Van Gogh on the film Submission. Why I Published Those Cartoons, *Jyllands-Posten*, February 19, 2006.

[8] Translated from Muhammeds ansigt, *Jyllands-Posten*, September 29, 2005.

[9] The Shahādah is the declaration of belief in the oneness of God and in Muhammad as his messenger. Recitation of the Shahādah is considered one of the Five Pillars of Islam by Sunni Muslims. In English the Shahādah reads: "There is no god but God and Muhammad is his messenger."

[10] Farsi is a Persian language spoken in Iran, Afghanistan, and several other Middle Eastern countries.

In apparent defense of Refn's decision to not draw the prophet, Rose explained in an editorial,

> I wrote to members of the association of Danish cartoonists asking them 'to draw Muhammad as you see him.' We certainly did not ask them to make fun of the prophet.[11]

A few days later, eleven ambassadors from Islamic countries sought a meeting with Danish Prime Minister Anders Rasmussen to demand government action against the cartoons. The prime minister refused, noting that such a meeting would violate the principles of Danish democracy. "As prime minister I have no tool whatsoever to take actions against the media, and I don't want that kind of tool," he replied.[12]

Cartoons Circulated Abroad

Meanwhile, Danish imam Abu Laban decided to take matters into his own hands. He sent a Muslim delegation on a tour of Egypt, Lebanon, and Syria, where dignitaries, religious leaders, and journalists were shown the cartoons. The greatest stir, however, was not caused by the Danish cartoons, but by three additional images that were far more graphic and offensive than those published by the newspaper.[13] While the origin of the three additional images was unknown, within days they were circulated on Islamic websites and chat rooms, causing outrage among Muslims who thought they had been published in Danish newspapers.[14]

In December, the cartoons were circulated among heads of state at a Summit of the Organization of the Islamic Conference (OIC) in Saudi Arabia. The OIC later issued a statement calling on the prime minister of Denmark to apologize. When he refused, the OIC's secretary general for Islamic education and culture urged the organization's 51 member states to boycott Danish products until they received an apology.[15] Since the entire Middle East accounted for less than one per cent of Denmark's exports, Danes showed little concern over the threat of a boycott. Moreover, a poll conducted in late January by the Epinion Research Institute found that 79 per cent of Danes supported the prime minister's decision to not apologize for the cartoons.[16]

Outside of Denmark, the OIC found wider support. United Nations human-rights commissioner Louise Arbour proclaimed her "alarm" at the "unacceptable disregard for the beliefs of others." Both the Council of Europe and the Arab League condemned the cartoons.[17]

European Media Reprint Cartoons

When the OIC called on Muslim countries to boycott Danish products (see "Arla and the OIC Boycott" below), many Europeans saw it as an attack on free speech. In protest, newspapers and magazines across Europe began reprinting the cartoons. Between the beginning of January and early February, the original cartoons appeared in more than 50 European newspapers and magazines. Prominent periodicals, such as France's Le Monde and Germany's Die Welt, displayed some of the images on their front pages.

In explaining his reason for reprinting the cartoons, the editor of Le Monde stated,

[11] Why I Published Those Cartoons, *Jyllands-Posten*, February 19, 2006.
[12] The Danish Cartoon Crisis: The Import and Impact of Public Diplomacy, USC Center on Public Diplomacy, April 5, 2006.
[13] Anatomy of a Global Crisis, *The Sunday Herald (Scotland)*, February 12, 2006.
[14] Child's tale led to clash of cultures, *The Guardian Unlimited*, February 4, 2006.

[15] Muslim organization calls for boycott of Denmark, *The Copenhagen Post*, December 28, 2006.
[16] OIC Demands Unqualified Danish Apology, *Arab News*, January 29, 2006.
[17] Prophetic insults, *The Economist*, January 5, 2006.

"A Muslim may well be shocked by a picture of Mohammed, especially an ill-intentioned one. But a democracy cannot start policing people's opinions, except by trampling the rights of man underfoot."[18] Likewise, The Economist, which did not reprint the cartoons, stated that European newspapers had a "responsibility" to show "solidarity" with Jyllands-Posten.

> In the Netherlands two years ago a film maker was murdered for daring to criticize Islam. Danish journalists have received death threats. In a climate in which political correctness has morphed into fear of physical attack, showing solidarity may well be the responsible thing for a free press to do. And the decision, of course, must lie with the press, not governments.[19]

For many Muslims, the reprinting of the cartoons was seen as further provocation. Some protested peacefully, while others reacted with violence. In some countries, buildings were set ablaze and shops selling European goods were vandalized. In Lebanon and Syria, the Danish and Norwegian embassies were firebombed. Elsewhere, clashes with police and security forces in Afghanistan, Pakistan, and other countries left as many as 300 people dead (see Exhibit 1). In northern Nigeria, Muslims went on a rampage, burning churches, shops, and cars belonging to the Christian minority. The violence left scores of dead and as many as 10,000 homeless.[20]

Arla and The OIC Boycott

At first, Arla viewed the cartoon crisis more as a security concern than an economic one. "It will be a serious blow to us if the situation becomes so grave that we are forced to withdraw our Danish workers," explained Arla Executive Director Finn Hansen.

Exhibit 1 Selected News Headlines

Prophetic insults; Denmark and Islam, The Economist, January 7, 2006

Free speech clashes with religious sensitivity: For much of last year, various squabbles have simmered over several prominent Danes' rude comments about Islam. Now a schoolboy prank by a newspaper has landed the prime minister, Anders Fogh Rasmussen, in the biggest diplomatic dispute of his tenure in office.

Denmark Is Unlikely Front in Islam-West Culture War, The New York Times, January 8, 2006

Editorial cartoons published in a Danish newspaper have made Denmark a flashpoint in the culture wars between Islam and the West in a post-9/11 world.

After Danish Mohammed cartoon scandal, Norway follows suit, Agence France Presse, January 10, 2006

A Norwegian Christian magazine on Tuesday published a set of controversial caricatures of the prophet Mohammed following months of uproar in the Muslim world over a Danish paper's decision to print the same cartoons.

Drive to Boycott Danish, Norwegian Goods Takes Off, Gulf News, January 23, 2006

Riyadh: A vigorous campaign has been kicked off in Saudi Arabia calling for boycott of Danish and Norwegian products in response to repeated publishing of offensive cartoons of the Prophet Mohammad by some newspapers and magazines in those countries.

---

[18] France's Le Monde Publishes Front-Page Cartoon Of Mohammed, *Agence France-Presse (AFP)*, February 2, 2006.

[19] Cartoon wars, *The Economist*, February 9, 2006.

[20] Although the latest hostility was sparked by the cartoon crisis, ethnic violence has been part of an ongoing conflict that has claimed 10,000 lives in Nigeria since 1999.Source: Nigerian religious riots continue, *BBC News*, February 24, 2006.

Exhibit 1 (continued)

Threats by Militants Alarm Scandinavians; Denmark and Norway feel the backlash from cartoons, Los Angeles Times, January 31, 2006

Denmark warned its citizens Monday to avoid Saudi Arabia, and gunmen in the Gaza Strip said any Scandinavians there risked attack over newspaper cartoons of the prophet Muhammad.

Caricature of Muhammad Leads to Boycott of Danish Goods, The New York Times, January 31, 2006

A controversy over the publication of caricatures of the Muslim prophet by a Danish newspaper boiled over into a boycott.

Cartoons of Prophet Met With Outrage; Depictions of Muhammad in Scandinavian Papers Provoke Anger, Protest Across Muslim World, The Washington Post, January 31, 2006

Cartoons in Danish and Norwegian newspapers… have triggered outrage among Muslims across the Middle East, sparking protests, economic boycotts and warnings of possible retaliation against the people, companies and countries involved.

Danish Paper's Apology Fails To Calm Protests; Cartoons Trigger Muslim Outrage, The Boston Globe, February 1, 2006

An apology by Denmark's largest newspaper… failed yesterday to calm a controversy that has ignited fiery protests across the Islamic world and provoked death threats against Scandinavians by Muslim radical groups. Muslim political and religious leaders and jihadists added their voices to the fury already thundering from mosques and blaring from television and radio stations from Morocco to Pakistan.

Bomb threat to repentant Danish paper, The Guardian, February 1, 2006

The offices of Denmark's bestselling broadsheet newspaper were evacuated last night following a bomb threat – a day after the editor-in-chief apologized for publishing cartoons of the prophet Muhammad that offended Muslims.

Anger as papers reprint cartoons of Muhammad: French, German and Spanish titles risk wrath: France Soir executive 'sacked' for defiant gesture, The Guardian, February 2, 2006

Newspapers in France, Germany, Spain and Italy yesterday reprinted caricatures of the prophet Muhammad, escalating a row over freedom of expression which has caused protest across the Middle East. France Soir and Germany's Die Welt published cartoons which first appeared in a Danish newspaper, although the French paper later apologized and apparently sacked its managing editor.

Islamic Anger Widens At Mohammed Cartoons, The Boston Globe, February 3, 2006

An extraordinary row over newspaper cartoons depicting the Prophet Mohammed intensified yesterday, with street demonstrations from North Africa to Pakistan, threats of violence against Europeans in the Middle East, and diplomatic protests by Muslim nations.

BBC shows the Islam cartoons, Daily Mail, February 3, 2006

The BBC and Channel 4 risked a Muslim backlash yesterday by showing 'blasphemous' cartoons of the prophet Mohammed that have caused outrage in the Islamic world.

Cartoons spark Islamic rage *Europe's leaders step in as controversy escalates *More newspapers publish offending images *Mideast consumer boycott hits Danish products, Financial Times, February 3, 2006

European leaders tried to contain the controversy over newspaper cartoons of the Prophet Mohammed, as the international dispute escalated into a consumer boycott and risked the gravest cultural clash with the Muslim world since the Salman Rushdie affair.

Gaza gunmen on hunt for Europeans: Aid workers, journalists, diplomats flee in fear for their lives; protests spread to Pakistan, Iraq, Ottawa Citizen, February 3, 2006

Militants threatened yesterday to kidnap or murder western citizens, in retaliation for the publication of caricatures of the Prophet Muhammad.

Exhibit 1 (continued)

Broadcasters show prophet cartoons despite Muslim rage, The Herald, February 3, 2006

British broadcasters last night defied Muslim anger when they showed cartoons which have caused a storm of protest in the Islamic world.

Danes call envoys home over prophet cartoons, The Irish Times, February 3, 2006

Denmark has summoned its ambassadors back from abroad to Copenhagen for talks today about the controversial newspaper cartoons of the Prophet Muhammad that have triggered protests in the Arab world and threats by militant Muslims.

Embassies burn in cartoon protest, BBC News, February 4, 2006

Syrians have set fire to the Norwegian and Danish embassies in Damascus in protest at the publication of newspaper cartoons of the Prophet Muhammad. Protesters scaled the Danish site amid chants of "God is great," before moving on to attack the Norwegian mission.

Danish embassy in Beirut torched, BBC News, February 5, 2006

Lebanese demonstrators have set the Danish embassy in Beirut on fire in protest at the publication of cartoons depicting the Prophet Muhammad.

Protests Over Cartoons of Muhammad Turn Deadly, The New York Times, February 6, 2006

Demonstrations against the publication of cartoons of the Prophet Muhammad by newspapers in Europe spread across Asia and the Middle East today, turning violent in Afghanistan, where at least four protesters were killed and over a dozen police officers and protesters injured.

Nigerian religious riots continue, BBC News, February 24, 2006

Violence is continuing across Nigeria where religious riots have claimed more than 100 lives this week. Some 10,000 people are still sheltering in barracks in the south-east town of Onitsha after violence there killed 80.

Our tremendous success in Saudi Arabia is thanks in large part to the fact that over the past 20 years, we've kept a number of our most talented managers constantly stationed in the country. It will hurt our credibility to pull out our Danish workers, and in the long term, it will impact sales. But I don't think things will get that bad. The Irish and Dutch dairies we compete with in Saudi Arabia are keeping their workers down there for now as well. Consumers in Saudi Arabia will continue to buy food, regardless of the terror threat. So I don't think our customer base will disappear.[21]

However, within a few weeks it became clear than Arla had underestimated the threat to its business. In Saudi Arabia, its products were featured in news stories about the boycott campaign and religious leaders across the country called on worshipers to avoid Danish goods. By the end of January 2006, Danish products were removed from store shelves, replaced with signs stating "Danish products were here." Egypt, Kuwait, Qatar, Bahrain, and the United Arab Emirates soon joined the boycott (see Exhibit 2 for a timeline of key events).

The boycott also aroused the anger of many local Muslims, some of whom threatened and harassed Arla employees as they went to and from work. In two separate incidents, workers were physically assaulted as they removed banned Arla products from store shelves. As a result, Arla provided employees with additional security escorts.

In early February, Iran became the first country to officially sever all economic ties with Denmark.[22] It made a further symbolic

---

[21] Terror threaten dairy exports, *The Copenhagen Post*, January 7, 2006.

[22] EU warns Iran over boycott of Danish goods, *China Daily*, February 8, 2006.

Exhibit 2 Timeline of Key Events

November 2, 2004	Film director Theo van Gogh is murdered in Amsterdam.
September 30, 2005	Jyllands-Posten publishes 12 cartoons portraying Muhammad.
January 20, 2006	The Saudi grand mufti calls for a boycott of Danish products.
January 24, 2006	In Saudi Arabia and Kuwait Arla's products begin to be removed from 50 grocery store shelves.
January 26, 2006	Arla products were removed from 300 stores.
January 28, 2006	Arla products were removed from 500 stores.
January 31, 2006	Arla products were removed from 50,000 stores, representing 95 per cent of the market.
February 1, 2006	Cartoons reprinted in several newspapers across Europe.
February 3, 2006	Danish and Norwegian embassies in Damascus are set on fire.
February 4, 2006	Danish embassy in Beirut is set on fire.
February 6, 2006	Iran officially bans Danish products.

gesture by renaming domestically produced Danish pastries as "Roses of the Prophet Muhammad."[23] "The Commerce Ministry will not allow Danish brands or products which have been registered in Denmark to clear customs," announced Iranian Commerce Minister Massoud Mir-Kazemi.

Iranian importers, including state-affiliated organs and companies, have three months to designate substitute products for Danish goods and then we will enforce the law. All on-going negotiations or contracts with Denmark which are pending will also be suspended, and all signed contracts will be reviewed. The exchange of delegations between the two countries will be suspended until further notice.[24]

The rapid deterioration in relations between Denmark and the Middle East stunned Arla Foods executives. Although they had been monitoring the situation since the cartoons were first published,

the boycott "was hard to foresee," Nielsen explained.

Some of our customers are extremely influential and powerful people. One of the retailers owns a large chain of grocery stores and he is extremely religious. Everyone else looks to see how he will react ...

We were in constant contact with our customers, and they never suggested that they were going to boycott our products. But they had to react when the religious community told them to. Even after the boycott was announced, retailers said to us, "We want to do business with you, but we can't."

The immediate impact of the boycott was extensive. "Our business has been completely undermined," Hansen lamented. "Our products have been taken off the shelves in 50,000 stores. Without a quick solution, we will lose our business in the Middle East."[25] Meanwhile, Arla was losing sales worth $1.5

[23] Iran targets Danish pastries, *Aljazeera.net*, February 17, 2006.

[24] Iran bans import of Danish products, *Islamic Republic News Agency (Iran)*, February 6, 2006.

[25] Muslim protest spreads to Danish butter, *The Sunday Times*, February 3, 2006.

million per day, or about eight per cent of the company's worldwide revenues.[26]

Other companies preemptively distanced themselves from the cartoons. Switzerland-based Nestlé bought front-page advertisements in Arab newspapers to explain that its powdered milk was "neither produced in nor imported from Denmark." French supermarket giant Carrefour went further, removing Danish products from store shelves with a notice declaring "solidarity with the Islamic community." Other signs read "Carrefour doesn't carry Danish products."[27]

European Criticism: "The Right to Offend"

In Europe, some viewed attempts by European companies to show "solidarity" with Muslim protesters as cowardice. At a Berlin rally, Hirsi Ali, who rarely made public appearances in the face of the numerous threats against her life, expressed outrage. "I am here to defend the right to offend," she proclaimed.

> Shame on those European companies in the Middle East that advertised "we are not Danish" or "we don't sell Danish products". This is cowardice. Nestlé chocolates will never taste the same after this, will they? The EU member states should compensate Danish companies for the damage they have suffered from boycotts. Liberty does not come cheap. A few million Euros are worth paying for the defense of free speech.[28]

European Union President José Manuel Barroso also felt it his duty to uphold the principles of free speech. "I have spoken with the Prime Minister of Denmark and expressed [our] solidarity," he noted.

I want to send my solidarity to the people of Denmark as well; a people who rightly enjoy the reputation as being amongst the most open and tolerant, not just in Europe, but in the world. Our European society is based on respect for the individual person's life and freedom, equality of rights between men and women, freedom of speech and a clear distinction between politics and religion. Our point of departure is that as human beings we are free, independent, equal and responsible. We must safeguard these principles. Freedom of speech is part of Europe's values and traditions. Let me be clear. Freedom of speech is not negotiable.[29]

The Crisis and Communications Group

As the seriousness of the boycott progressed, Arla CEO Peter Tuborgh decided to convene an emergency meeting with senior executives, dubbed "The Crisis and Communications Group." Earlier in his career, Tuborgh had worked in Saudi Arabia for four years as an operations manager. He understood the seriousness of the boycott, but he also felt that the company should not stray in any way from its global mission statement (see Exhibit 3). Any action taken by Arla would need to be consistent with the company's overall vision and reflect its values.

Jens Refslund, director of Arla's production division, suggested that the company needed to act quickly to cut production to reduce costs. He explained,

> Once sales in the Middle East have come to a standstill, it will inevitably have consequences for production. A decision about what we do next must be taken within the next few days.[30]

[26] Danish Companies Endure Snub by Muslim Consumers, *The New York Times*, February 27, 2006.

[27] Carrefour JV with MAF in Egypt halts sale of Danish products, *AFX News Limited*, February 3, 2006.

[28] From a speech titled "The Right to Offend" given in Berlin on February 9, 2006.

[29] EU President Barroso's Statement On The Issue Of The Cartoons Of Prophet Muhammad, *Press and Public Diplomacy Delegation of the European Commission*, February 15, 2006.

[30] Arla dairy sales crippled by Middle East boycott, *Dairy Reporter*, January 31, 2006.

Exhibit 3 Arla Mission Statement

Our Mission is:	Our Vision is:

"To offer modern consumers milk-based food products that create inspiration, confidence and well-being"

Arla Foods' primary objective is to meet consumers' wishes and requirements. Its mission underlines the company's focus on the consumer.

"Modern consumers" covers consumers of all ages who look for inspiration, variety and innovation.

"Milk-based products" means that the products must contain milk or milk components.

Arla Foods is committed to providing consumers with inspiration by offering a multitude of ways of utilizing its products.

Arla Foods creates confidence and well-being by providing tasty and healthy products that not only meet statutory quality requirements, but also satisfy consumers' demands for "soft" values. Consumers can be assured that Arla Foods consistently demonstrates its concern for the proper exploitation of resources, the environment, animal welfare, ethics, etc. throughout the entire production process.

"To be the leading Dairy Company in Europe through considerable value creation and active market leadership"

Through its vision, Arla Foods wishes to demonstrate that its activities are designed to create value for both the company and its owners.

By using the term "value creation" instead of "results," we wish to emphasize that our objectives are based on the long-term rather than short-term financial gains.

To become the world leader in value-creation within the dairy sector, Arla Foods must be:
* Northern Europe's preferred dairy group among consumers, customers and milk producers
* Northern Europe's market leader within all types of dairy products with a broad range, strong brands and a high degree of consumer confidence
* Represented in Southern Europe with a selected range of cheese and butter
* Represented in a number of markets outside Europe through a range adapted to individual markets

---

Refslund estimated that the company would need to layoff as much as one third of the staff at a havarti cheese plant in Denmark, or approximately 50 employees. To avoid delays, negotiations with the dairy workers' union needed to begin immediately. Moreover, numerous Scandinavian dairy farmers faced a loss of some of their income if the Middle East market remained closed to Danish dairy products.

Nielsen expressed concern about the company's ability to recover from the crisis.

One billion customers have rejected our products because it has suddenly become a synonym for the insult to the Prophet Mohammed. What can we do?

We can't edit newspapers, we can't comment on government actions, we can't get involved in politics and we certainly can't address religion.

Nevertheless, Finn Hansen, who had responsibility for the Middle East, remained hopeful. He believed that in order for Arla to recover, it had to communicate with the individual consumer.

Arla has been producing dairy products in Saudi Arabia for so long that we believe the authorities consider us a local dairy. It is not enough to persuade the supermarket chains to put our products back on the shelves. We should take our message directly to the consumer.

PART II
Leading People across Contexts

4

Interpersonal Skills for International Management: Map–Bridge–Integrate for Effectiveness at the Point of Action

> Organizational behavior is about effectiveness at the point of action.
>
> Dr. David Fearon

"Effectiveness at the point of action." We heard this phrase from Dr. Fearon, recounting a moment when Dr. Peter Vaill, his Organizational Behavior professor, expressed the idea that profoundly influenced his academic career. This statement immediately resonated with us, and defines our orientation and our objective in writing this book. We want to help current and future managers become mindful global leaders who are effective at the point of action, which includes the purpose, place, and moment of action. The point of action in international management usually happens when people from widely different backgrounds interact with each other. So far in the book, we've been looking at the context of international management and the context of different cultural backgrounds. We've emphasized the importance of mindful approaches to the context. All of this provides the framing for effective international management behavior. In this chapter, we turn to the basics of interaction among people.[1]

Effectiveness at the Point of Action: Conversations That Create Value

Bettina (German) and Seif (Emirati from Dubai) were both senior partners in a global strategic consulting firm. Both were typical of their cultures, and both were experienced and mindful global leaders. Seif had been with the firm since

---

[1] The research and many of the examples shared in this chapter are based on work we conducted and published with our colleague J. DiStefano. We gratefully acknowledge his insights particularly in this chapter.

graduating from his MBA program, and was well-respected throughout the firm. Bettina had recently joined the firm through the acquisition of a boutique firm in which she was a senior partner. The two were assigned to lead a project with a global consumer goods company. The firm generally had a good relationship with the client company, but the client had been unsatisfied with the most recent project. This project would give the consulting firm a chance to repair the relationship with the client. Here is a sample of the conversations during Bettina and Seif's first meeting:

Beginning the meeting (Task vs. Relationship)	*Bettina*: Hi Seif. I'm looking forward to working with you. I know you've worked in a lot of parts of the firm, I'm sure you've got stories to tell!
	Seif: Hi Bettina. Thanks, I'm looking forward to working with you too. I know you bring a lot of industry experience, I'm sure you've got stories too. [They share background information and experiences for about 5 minutes]
	Seif: Well, let's talk about that more over lunch. Should we take a look at this project?
	Bettina: Sounds good.
Sharing knowledge about the client (Status vs. Egalitarian; Direct vs. Indirect)	*Seif*: As two senior partners, we'll both feel responsible for an excellent outcome for the client. You may know we are a bit vulnerable now, with a fragile relationship with the client. Your industry knowledge will complement my knowledge of the firm and the client.
	Bettina: Yes I've heard we have a bit of repair work to do. I'm sure with our combined expertise and our networks of resources we'll deliver great value. Who else from the firm should be on our project team?
Agreeing on next steps (Risk vs. Certainty; Interdependent vs. Independent)	*Bettina*: Normally I like to get started quickly – get some parallel work streams going and test some early ideas with the client before refining. What's your norm for early stages?
	Seif: I can see the benefit of efficiency in that process. I normally prefer to have some solid analysis before going to the client though. I'm also concerned about having to backtrack if the parallel streams go in different directions – I prefer to keep continuous dialogue so they can build on each other.
	Bettina: Yes, that makes sense too. How about ... [Discussion about process]
	Seif: So to summarize, we'll start parallel work streams, and have calls two times per week for sharing and coordination. After three weeks, we'll set up a prototyping blitz with the client, to get their input on the analysis so far and set up the next phase.

Seif and Bettina led a project that kept to all milestones and delivered on time. It was not simple to work together with their different preferences and norms, but both knew the value was worth the effort. The project deliverables exceeded the client's high expectations. Seif and Bettina ensured that everyone on the project learned a lot from the experience, and the firm was therefore better positioned to work on projects like this in the future.

Seif and Bettina were mindful global leaders in their interaction. They demonstrated global mindsets by showing awareness of each other's perspectives, even anticipating them. Rather than blindly stick to rules and routines from the past, they adapted ones appropriate for the current situation. Through mindful management at the point of action, Seif and Bettina created synergy in this cross-cultural interaction. This chapter will explore the Map–Bridge–Integrate framework, a tool for engaging in effective cross-cultural interaction. We'll examine exactly how Seif, Bettina, and many other leaders create professional value and personal growth from working across cultures.

Map–Bridge–Integrate for Mindful Cross-Cultural Interactions

Our research shows that performance in diverse interactions, especially multicultural ones, derives from a basic set of interactions we call Map–Bridge–Integrate, or MBI (DiStefano and Maznevski, 2000; Maznevski, 1994a, 1994b). Mapping is about understanding cultural and other differences between each other, and providing context for the similarities. Bridging is communicating effectively, taking those differences and similarities into account. Integrating is bringing the different perspectives together and building on them. When these three skills are executed well, interactions between individuals result in high performance. The basic model is shown in Figure 4.1. Integrating leads directly to effectiveness, but our research found that Bridging is the most important process. If Bridging is done well, Integrating almost follows naturally; if Bridging is not done well, there is likely to be no Integrating. Moreover, Bridging cannot be done without good Mapping, no matter how skilled or well-intentioned are the people involved. Below, we discuss and illustrate each of these skills.

Much of the research on cross-cultural interaction is conducted by studying teams – groups of at least two or three people working together toward a joint outcome. In this chapter we'll often refer to teams as the context for effective

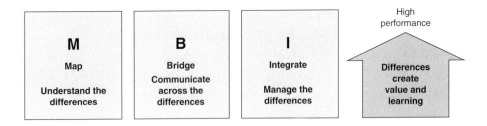

Figure 4.1 MBI in brief

interaction, but we'll focus on the interaction itself. See Chapter 5 for teams as organizing units for work.

Mapping to Understand and Describe Differences

In Chapter 3, we introduced the metaphor of mapping culture. Mapping is systematically and objectively describing characteristics of people and identifying similarities and differences that can be used to help each other perform. The most useful Mapping uses data and summaries of facts, organized with frameworks that help compare the data and facts across groups and individuals. The GlobeSmart dimensions map culture (see pp. 62–73 in Chapter 3), but it is possible – and often desirable – to map other characteristics such as personality, profession, or gender.

Most people are afraid of Mapping because they worry it will lead to stereotyping. They resist being put into a box as an unthinking representative of a group, and do not want to categorize others that way. This is a healthy fear and resistance, and we encourage it. And like any tool, Mapping can be misused. However, Mapping is such a powerful tool that it is worth using. Maps are objective descriptions of characteristics that are relevant to an interaction. They help people respect each other's values and perspectives, and give people suggestions about how to use each other's ideas better. Maps are revised whenever new data are available, and are constantly tested as hypotheses rather than taken for granted as truths. Maps should be seen as windows to the complex territory of human beings, ways of entering the different perspectives and really seeing the person inside.

Stereotyping, on the other hand, is not mindful. Stereotypes are subjective descriptions of groups of people that are normally used to judge those people, often in a negative way. Stereotypes are assumed to be true and are neither tested nor changed with new information. They usually lead people to close doors – making assumptions about how people will behave – rather than open windows. The differences between Mapping and stereotyping are subtle, but important (Adler, 2008; Bird and Osland, 2000). Mapping leads to healthy dynamics among individuals, with people casting aside the maps as they develop more insight into the territory.

Research shows that without explicit intervention, teams tend to spend most of their time discussing information that all team members share, and only a small portion of the time discussing information that only one or a few team members have (Stasser, 1999). This dynamic is not conducive to high performance, especially if the task is complex and multidimensional. Explicit Mapping is an excellent way to avoid this dynamic. If team members are aware of the different perspectives – the different points on the map – and of the potential contributions, they are more likely to bring them into team discussions and to create better solutions. Among individuals, such as between a leader and a subordinate or between a customer and a supplier, Mapping helps prevent conflict and aids in seeing opportunities. The more the people involved understand the nature of each other's different perspectives, the more they can use those differences to achieve high performance.

In the opening conversation, Seif and Bettina were both adept at Mapping. Their two cultures' GlobeSmart profiles are shown in Figure 4.2.

If you look back at the conversation, you'll see that Bettina started by building relationships with Seif, in respect of his cultural preferences. Seif reciprocated by postponing the relationship discussion until lunch, moving to task more quickly than he would have done in his own culture. Seif clarified their status as equals – demonstrating his own sensitivity to status markers while acknowledging their equal status – and he spoke of the client relationship indirectly. Bettina spoke about the client relationship directly, and focused on expertise and networks, a more egalitarian approach. When they asked each other about preferences for work, Bettina expressed preferences for Independent (work in parallel)

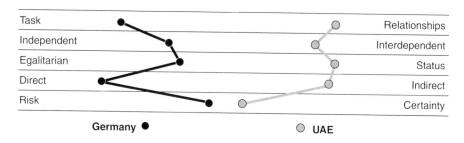

Figure 4.2 Cultural maps for Germany and UAE, based on GlobeSmart

and Risk (go to the client early to test ideas) norms, while Seif expressed preferences for Interdependent (work in close collaboration) and Certainty (get it right before going to the client) norms. Seif and Bettina, as mindful global leaders, were aware in advance of the potential for these differences. They asked each other questions and listened to each other's responses carefully to make sense within the context. This Mapping set them up for excellent Bridging in the conversation and the project.

Cultural differences are not the only ones that influence cross-cultural interaction. People differ, of course, with respect to personality, educational background, experience, gender, and many other dimensions. It's especially important to make cultural maps explicit because they are usually hidden beneath the surface and affect interactions in unintended ways. In addition to mapping culture, it's important to map some of these other dimensions as well. One helpful tool for quickly mapping some key personality and communication style preferences is the Trialogue tool (Ekelund, n.d.). Trialogue uses a short survey and a specific process to get people to explore the different team roles they prefer to contribute and the implications for the team. The combination of the Mapping survey and discussion process creates a positive environment for conversations about differences and similarities, opening people up to Mapping and the entire MBI process.

Mapping is summarized in Figure 4.3.

Mapping in Action: A New Team

How important is it to sit down and create detailed maps, with survey data about individuals involved, or can you just know the general patterns and

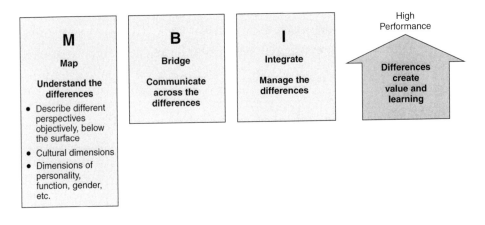

Figure 4.3 Mapping in MBI

map from there? There is a trade-off between investment and results. Explicit Mapping takes time, but it pays off in more ideas coming into the group, more comprehensive examination and analysis of the ideas, and more possibility of building on ideas in innovative ways. The more important the task and/or the more diverse the people involved, the more critical Mapping is.

In our experience, it is best for a group to go into detailed Mapping on at least two dimensions that are important to the group's work, such as culture and personality or gender, then use those discussions to access Mapping on any other relevant dimensions. The use of an outside facilitator to help with Mapping is not necessary, but some managers prefer it, for example if the leader would prefer to be a neutral participant rather than lead the process. Some maps, such as many personality surveys, must be administered and facilitated by a certified professional, so if you want to use these maps an outside facilitator may be necessary.

Reinhard was appointed to lead the global marketing group for a new, highly innovative medical product. The product was based on a combination of robotic, bionic, wireless, and biologic technologies, and had the potential to revolutionize the treatment of debilitating diseases. It could be the next big thing for the company, and everyone involved was excited about its impact. Reinhard knew he needed a diverse team of professionals to tap into different ideas and different aspects of the task and the market, so he deliberately recruited his ten direct reports to reflect a range of organizational veterans and newcomers, medical professionals, engineers and social scientists, young and experienced people, and people from multiple country cultures and with different personality types.

Shortly after the team launched, Reinhard brought the team together for a Mapping exercise. Given the importance of the product launch, the sensitivity of the product, and the diversity of the team, he decided to work with an outside facilitator although he remained very active in the Mapping process and often took the lead. He first used Trialogue, described above, to look at preferences for interaction styles and roles, to help them become comfortable with Mapping and to create a positive environment for exploring differences (Ekelund, n.d.).

Then Reinhard had the team map their personalities and cultures, the former using the Myers-Briggs Type Indicator (MBTI), the latter using GlobeSmart (Briggs et al., 1998). For each of these maps, the team discussed patterns associated with different dimensions, such as the examples we described for culture in Chapter 3, and identified each individual's position on the map. Who prefers extraversion and who prefers introversion as a personality dimension? Who prefers Task and who prefers Relationships as a cultural dimension? In this

Mapping discussion, people identified specific potential contributions of individual team members. For example, the Task-oriented members will help us remember to take charge of the market, and identify what we can control; the Relationship-oriented members will help us remember to keep in mind all the stakeholders, and how we can work with them to co-create solutions.

After these discussions, the team created a large grid on the wall, with team members' names down the left as rows, and dimensions of diversity across the top as columns. The grid with some of the team members' names is shown in Figure 4.4. By the end of the process, team members were even more excited about working together, learning from each other, and using the different perspectives and some newly-discovered commonalities to create a great product launch.

The team succeeded beyond the company's expectations in terms of creating new markets and value for both customers and the company. This initial Mapping set them up well, and as a team they took their interaction seriously,

	Cultural Emphasis	Trialogue	Personality (MBTI)	Gender	County Location	Organizational function (education)	Hobbies
Reinhard	Task Egalitarian Certainty	Blue (red,green)	ENTJ	M	Switzer-land	Director (Sciences)	Family, sports, outdoors
Rachna	Relationships Interdependent Status	Red (blue)	ESTP	F	Belgium	Purchasing and logistics (Engineering)	Family, arts
Alejandro	Relationships Interdependent Indirect	Red (green)	INFP	M	South Korea	Business development (engineering)	Music, sports
Takashi	Task Status Risk	Blue	ESTP	M	Japan	Marketing & advertising (business)	Movies, sports
John	Interdependent Egalitarian Risk	Green	ENTP	M	USA	Technology, sales (Business)	Technology, travel
Marije	Egaitarian Indirect Certainty	Green (red)	ENFJ	F	Switzer-land	Post sales technical management (medicine)	Outdoors, travel
Claire	Interdepenent Direct Certainty	Blue (green)	ISTJ	F	Dubai	Finance (Economics)	Theater, classical music

Figure 4.4 MBI: example of a team's map

engaging in reflection and development frequently. Three years later the five most senior members of the team (including Reinhard) had been promoted to lead other big opportunities across the globe, and one of the more junior members of the team was successfully leading the team to innovate and perform even more. Reinhard is clear that good Mapping started the team in the right direction, and continues to use the process with all his new teams.

Bridging Differences through Communication

Mapping to understand the lens through which others see the world is an enormous aid to intercultural effectiveness. But this understanding provides little benefit as long as it remains latent. It must be put into use to help the flow of ideas among people in a conversation, a team, or an organization. The goal of these interpersonal flows is effective communication, or the transfer of meaning from one person to another as it was intended by the first person. Most managers recognize that effective communication within one's own culture is difficult enough. Interactions with people from different cultures are even more difficult. The challenge is to interpret correctly what a person from a different culture means by his or her words and actions. Even if interaction is aided by slowing speech, speaking more distinctly, listening more carefully, or asking more questions, there still remains the problem of interpreting the message. When your Japanese direct report says "yes," what does she mean? That she agrees, that she will undertake the action, that she accepts the importance of your input? It can make a big difference in implementing strategy!

Resolving miscommunication depends, in large part, on a manager's willingness to explain the problem rather than to blame the other person. And the quality of the explanation depends, in large part, on the manager's ability to map the other person's culture or background with respect to his or her own.

Although language is an important part of communication, communication is not simply a matter of understanding and speaking a language. Communication is broader than language alone. Someone who is able to speak five different languages still may not be able to understand the issues from the viewpoint of those from another culture. Or, put more eloquently by an Eastern European manager to the Australians in an English-speaking group, "I can speak to you in your language, but I can't always tell you what I am thinking in my own language."

There are three skills important to effective communication in a cross-cultural setting: **engaging, decentering,** and **recentering**. These three skills help improve all communication anywhere. In interactions within a single culture, people generally operate under the same set of background assumptions, so the steps can be conducted implicitly, often without people even being aware they are taking them. The more culturally diverse the setting, the more difficult it is to accomplish these steps, and the more explicit they should be. But they also result in bigger payoffs.

This Bridging component of the MBI model is summarized in Figure 4.5.

Engage to be Open, Optimistic, and Active

Engaging is about setting the ground for communication. The most important place to set the ground is in one's own mind. Motivation is having the will to communicate across a cultural boundary both to be understood and to understand others. We are usually very good at the former, but not as good at the latter. Motivation often comes with confidence from experience of effective communication, creating a virtuous cycle. People encountering important cross-cultural interactions for the first time are often worried about misunderstanding. However, with practice and even small success, confidence increases rapidly and combines with motivation for positive engagement.

Engagement and motivation may sound simple, but actually acting this way is difficult in the rush and pressure of making decisions and getting things done. We have a tendency to assume that others are like us, and to forget the importance of deliberately seeing things differently. There are some simple things we can do to help ourselves, aside from just trying to remember to be motivated. For example,

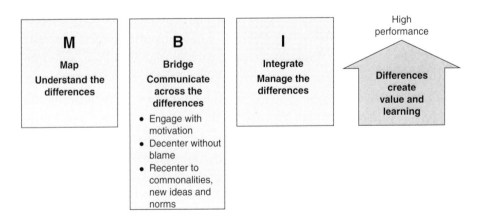

Figure 4.5 Bridging in MBI

learning even some of the others' language signals motivation and optimism, and opens doors into how the others think and what they value. Learning the language creates a positive, reinforcing cycle in cross-cultural communication, even if you do not approach fluency. Reading and studying other countries' cultures, meeting people from the culture and asking them to help you immerse yourself in the culture, watching their movies, are other ways of increasing your confidence in your cross-cultural communication ability. Mastering a cultural framework or "map" gives you the motivation and confidence to ask questions that will be especially helpful in preparing yourself for future understanding.

Both Seif and Bettina, in our opening example, engaged with motivation. In the very first part of the interaction, each prioritized the other's norms. This shows their positive attitude toward the value that can come from cross-cultural collaboration, as well as their experience (they had some ideas of the maps).

Decenter to Transfer Meaning

Decentering is actively pushing yourself away from your own "center." It involves moving into the minds of other people to send messages in a way they will understand, and to listen in a way that allows you to understand the others from their own point of view. The fundamental idea of decentering is **empathy**: feeling and understanding as another person does. But decentering requires going beyond just having empathy, to using one's empathy in hearing and speaking. A child sees two cookies on the table and is about to take both. The mother says, "Now, if you take both cookies, how will your sister feel?" The child knows her sister will feel terrible (strong empathy), but goes ahead and takes both cookies anyway (not decentering). This interaction happens all the time in cross-cultural situations. The Canadian manager says, "I know that being Chinese it's hard for you to disagree openly with your boss, but I want you to know it's okay to do that with me. I don't mind when you disagree with me, in fact I expect you to." Or the Brazilian manager, "I know that in your [Scandinavian] culture it's not good to be open about feelings, but I am Brazilian and in my culture it's fine. So when I express my anger, don't worry, it's okay." We all know people who understand exactly how we feel, but nevertheless go ahead and say or do something awkward or hurtful anyway. This is practicing empathy without decentering.

There are two main elements to decentering. The first is perspective taking, which is the skill of being able to see things from the other person's point of view to the extent that you can speak and listen that way. The second is explaining without blame. When problems in communication do occur, and they inevitably will, it is critical that no one blames the other in a personal way, but that all parties seek an explanation in the situation: the differences in initial starting assumptions.

People who withhold blame and search for situation-based explanations of miscommunication interact more effectively. In our research this emerged as the single best predictor of effective cross-cultural interaction. (DiStefano and Maznevski, 2000)

Consider the sequence of events initiated when blame is suspended; this simple act leads an interaction into a positive cycle of decentering, exploring alternatives to build a shared reality, developing trust and common rules, and engaging with motivation to use different perspectives productively. This process not only resolves the present miscommunication, but also prevents some further ones and provides ideas for creative synergy.

Good decentering is largely dependent on good Mapping. The map warns you that surprises and problems may have different explanations, and also provides you with some alternatives to explore. The Describe–Interpret–Evaluate framework identified in Chapter 3 is also very helpful here (see p. 56). When differences are encountered, the people involved should try to come to a point where they can agree on a description: What are the tangible, concrete facts we are talking about? Next they should explore their different interpretations: What do those facts mean to each person, and why? This is where the map provides a common language for sharing the analysis of interpretations. Finally, they should try to understand the different evaluations of the facts: Why do some people see something as an opportunity and others as a threat? In cross-cultural situations, the greater the tendency to judge events, the greater the probability of making errors. Resisting the interpretive and evaluative modes while maintaining a descriptive posture for as long as possible is the best protection against cultural gaffes.

In our opening conversation, Seif and Bettina practiced effective decentering. Not only did they begin by acting according to each other's norms (see the earlier discussion of engagement in this chapter), they were careful to ask each other about norms and preferences, and to discuss these openly. This decentering set them up well for recentering around project norms and ideas.

Decentering in Action: Scandinavian Managers Abroad

During our culture research studies, we developed a dialogue called "the Dark Side of Scandinavian Management." Scandinavian (the collective name that encompasses Norway, Sweden and Denmark, sometimes Iceland, but not Finland, which is Nordic but not Scandinavian) management has often been described as unique, and several groups of Scandinavian managers asked us to help them understand the challenges they were facing when they worked with people from other cultures. Based on our own research and work done by Smith and colleagues, we developed a data-based picture of the Scandinavian management style (Mapping) (Smith et al., 2003; Smith, Peterson, and Schwartz, 2002). Although all organizations and all leaders are different, and the Scandinavian country cultures differ from each other, Scandinavian managers and those from other cultures who work with Scandinavians agreed that the picture was generally accurate. We mapped Scandinavian management style as:

- **Strongly interdependent** – especially with respect to co-workers and society in general; the group is important, it is critical to get everyone aligned and on board, opinions of co-workers and subordinates are very important.
- **Strongly egalitarian** – power and influence come not from your position but from your ideas and values and contributions to the group; considering your co-workers' and subordinates' ideas is often more important than considering your boss's ideas.
- **Action-oriented and pragmatic** – take control of situations, influence them, get things done, task focus, change actions as necessary to achieve the goals.

Based on this Mapping exercise, we created a typical conversation between a Scandinavian manager and his or her non-Scandinavian subordinates, outside Scandinavia. This hypothetical conversation brought tears of laughter to Scandinavian executives who recognized themselves in the middle of it:

1. Scandinavian manager ...

Asks subordinates and co-workers for their opinions, tries to negotiate alignment.

2. The "others" ...

Don't understand why the Scandinavian boss can't just decide. May want to make decision quickly so planning phase can begin.

3. Scandinavian manager ...

Responds to the requests and anxiety for decisions by asking more questions to get ideas and create alignment.

4. The "others" ...

Become even more frustrated with the lack of decision-making, we'll never get to planning.

(cont.)

5. Scandinavian manager ...

Becomes paralyzed by not wanting to act in an authoritarian way. Not sure what to do.

6. The "others" ...

Are frustrated with lack of speed, lose respect for the business capability of the Scandinavians.

7. Scandinavian manager...

Finally, in frustration, makes and announces a decision.

8. The "others"...

Relieved, voice agreement with the boss.

9. Scandinavian manager ...

Assumes agreement = alignment and signals readiness for action, shifts attention to other matters.

10. The "others" ...

Either wait for further directions for action, or act in unaligned ways (depending on culture and situation).

11. Scandinavian manager ...

Becomes frustrated by lack of action or unaligned action, waits for it to improve.

12. The "others" ...

Continue to wait or to act in many different directions.

13. Scandinavian manager ...

Becomes frustrated with unenlightened subsidiaries.

14. The "others" ...

Under-perform according to standards or expectations.

15. Scandinavian manager ...

"Knows" (assumes) that everyone will contribute to their potential for the group, and will self-correct performance. Does nothing.

(cont.)

	16. The "others" ... "Know" (assume) everything is fine because the boss has not said anything. Nothing changes.
17. Scandinavian manager ... Waits patiently for performance to self-correct; perhaps manages the environment to make it easier for people to self-correct.	
	18. The "others" ... Start to recognize performance problem but see that boss doesn't "care" about it. Nothing changes.
19. Scandinavian manager ... Becomes frustrated with unenlightened, unempowered subsidiaries.	
	20. The "others" ... Become convinced that Scandinavians avoid conflict and are weak managers.

This conversation shows what happens when decentering is not practiced by anyone involved. Notice the evolution to blaming that comes from not understanding each other's starting point: Scandinavian managers assuming the others are unenlightened, the "others" assuming Scandinavian managers are weak. Scandinavian managers who are effective in other cultures adapt this process through decentering in several ways. They report they believe that in most situations getting ideas from subordinates and developing alignment is the best way to make decisions and implement change. However, when they first go to a new culture where hierarchy is stronger, they are more likely to use their position as boss to manage explicitly a process of getting ideas from others. They "command" people to take part and contribute their own ideas directly, and they use the hierarchy to dictate each part of the process. Effective Scandinavian managers abroad are also more likely to incorporate specific planning into the early discussions, recognizing others' need to make firm plans.

Recenter to Align and Agree

The final step to effective communication is **recentering**, or establishing a **common reality** and agreeing on common rules. Like the other elements, this is easier said than done. For example, the implicit definition and purpose of "a meeting" varies from one culture to the next, with some cultures using meetings to discuss perspectives and come to a joint decision, and other cultures using meetings to publicly formalize decisions that were discussed informally among smaller subgroups of a team. A multicultural team that has not addressed even this basic definition is bound to find at least some members very frustrated with the first meeting. Good mapping helps to find a common definition and give the team a point of leverage.

Members of a multi-site global research and development (R&D) team differed enormously on every cultural dimension except one: virtually all preferred Certainty strongly over Risk. They were able to use their common ground of the preference to plan carefully to discuss their differences and work together. A team managing a strategic alliance in a manufacturing technology firm consisted of members from all over Europe, North America, and Asia. Like the team of R&D scientists, they had strong differences on many cultural dimensions. Coincidentally, though, all were engineers for at least some part of their career, and they shared the same focus on Task first, with a balance of Certainty and Risk. Their common reality was based on what had to be done (changed and controlled), and they used this point to launch discussions about how to divide the work and what task processes to use.

Common norms for interacting must be established. Interestingly, it is less important to agree on a single set of norms for everyone, and more important to agree on a range of acceptable norms, with acceptance for some degrees of freedom for individual team members. As we showed in the opening of this chapter, it is futile to expect someone to behave in a way that is uncomfortable to them, yet still expect them to participate to their full potential. Asking someone who prefers a thinking orientation to jump in and "do" because that is the dominant mode and "you'll just have to adapt," is like asking that person not to bother contributing his best ideas to the group.

The most effective groups find ways of allowing different members to work with the group differently. Finding these norms is a creative process. It takes time and relies on strong relationships and trust within the group. But, like good preparing and decentering, the effort is well worth it. When the processes are not explored or discussed to find common ground, serious misunderstandings can occur, even when the cultures are not dramatically different.

In our opening conversation, Seif and Bettina recentered around the objective for the project (to include mending the relationship) and norms (some work in parallel, with frequent coordination and sharing meetings). This recentering allowed everyone to draw on their strengths, and identify clear, high expectations for the deliverables.

Recentering in Action: A Multicultural Team

We captured a classic example of cross-cultural communication when we videoed a group of executives discussing the possibility of their company acquiring another firm. The group consisted of five senior managers from the USA (two members), UK, Japan, and Uruguay. We video-recorded them at their request to help them develop their Bridging skills. After studying various aspects of the potential deal, they had come together to make a recommendation.

The discussion was dominated by the American and the British managers, who were concerned about the lack of compatible strategies and financial problems in the negotiations. In the first hour, two key incidents happened which showed the need for recentering. First, the Uruguayan manager tried three times to introduce the issue of who would constitute the top executive team should the deal be struck. Would the buying company or the acquired organization supply the key executives for the merged entity? Each time he tried to raise the issue, the four others brushed his comments aside, and he eventually became frustrated. Second, after forty minutes of discussion, the British manager stood up and went to the flip chart and wrote: "Do Nothing!" He added, "I don't usually entertain this option, but I really think in this situation it is our best choice. The deal is far from being ready to make." There was a moment of silence, then the Japanese manager quietly said, "Wait." The others thought that he was asking for a chance to discuss the "Do Nothing" option, but he said nothing more. The British manager crossed out "Do Nothing" and wrote next to it, "Wait," then he proceeded with his next point.

After one hour of discussion, the group stopped and looked at their video before continuing. They analyzed the two incidents above. Regarding the Uruguayan's concerns, the group learned that, for him, relationships were fundamental and were related to the financial and strategic analysis of the deal. If certain members of the acquired organization were maintained, the price could be lower and returns could be more certain than if those individuals were not part of the deal. The Anglo-American managers were more focused on quantitative and product-market issues and missed the potential link. Through this discussion, the group recentered around a new common objective: to identify combinations of factors that could create a positive investment outcome, then to analyze the extent to which it was possible to create those combinations of factors. This was a more complex goal, but one that the group members all agreed to and that eventually led to better value creation for the company.

The group then explored the British "Do Nothing" versus the Japanese suggestion to "Wait." The British executive literally meant "Don't do anything more; proceed to look for other deals unless the other party indicates a change in the conditions." In contrast, the Japanese executive's "Wait" was filled with subtle actions including continuing to get to know the other parties, extending attempts to get more information about their business, and so on. Both wanted action, but in the British manager's mind, "waiting" was a passive mode and to be avoided. It was better to do nothing on this deal, and move on with other things. In the Japanese manager's mind, "waiting" was a very active mode and would help create the conditions for a good deal. The group members realized that the two actions could be complementary and recentered around a more comprehensive strategy of concerted dialogue and extended research, including into alternative deals.

Finally, the group discussed some of the norms they saw, such as the dominance of three of the members. They realized that the Uruguayan had posed his ideas in the form of questions ("Don't you think we should explore from which company the top officers will be drawn?"), an indirect mode of communication. The Anglo-Americans were much more direct in their phrasing ("That's irrelevant until we get the financials and strategy agreed to!"). The team learned to recenter on norms by picking up the Uruguayan's cues about his opinions and learned to listen and take him seriously, even when he phrased his ideas as questions. It was also quite evident from the video that the Japanese manager rarely spoke unless someone asked him a question directly. All the others knew that this was a characteristic of Japanese culture, but they had not developed a set of norms that would constructively encourage the Japanese member's participation. They recentered with an agreement that in the future, at the beginning of every new stage of the discussion, they would go around the table and have each person make a two-minute statement. They would assign a facilitator (a rotating role) to ensure this happened with discipline, and that facilitator also had the responsibility of ensuring balanced contributions afterwards.

By recentering around a common view of the task and situation, and around specific norms that facilitated participation, the team members enhanced their Bridging and were able to provide much more valuable advice to the company.

Integrating to Manage and Build on the Differences

The final component of the MBI model is **integrating** the differences. Communicating effectively (Bridging) means the people in the interaction understand each other. But they still may not be able to agree or collaborate. For example, Seif and Bettina understood each other's different preferences for working on the project (Independent versus Interdependent; Risk versus Certainty), but it was not obvious how to develop a work method that would integrate the best of both.

Integrating is where cultural synergy actually gets created. In Chapter 3 we repeated the notion many times that no one culture is inherently better than others. Every culture was developed by a group of people to help them be efficient, and to identify each other as a group that helps each other. In a highly complex environment, such as the one we face now, no one culture can ever provide all the answers. Integrating is the process of drawing on the strengths of each culture for the situation at hand, and combining them for synergy. With effective Bridging, the people interacting have a good understanding of what each other brings to the situation. In fact, as we said earlier in this chapter, great Bridging almost automatically leads to effective Integrating, because great Bridging conversations set up all the elements for Integrating. Here we identify the three main behaviors for ensuring that great Integrating happens as well: empowering participation, resolving conflicts, and building on ideas.

Integrating is summarized in Figure 4.6.

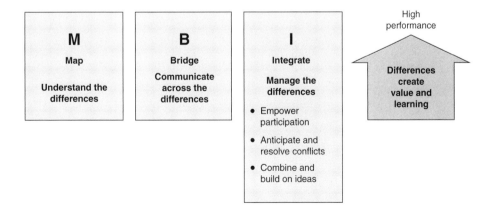

Figure 4.6 Integrating in MBI

Empowering Participation

To realize the benefits of different perspectives and ideas, it is necessary to express and listen to the ideas in the first place. Different cultures have different ways of offering information and input, and the norms of one culture often suppress participation from people of other cultures. People from cultures with a strong Status orientation, for example, are not likely to state their ideas directly in a group in which their direct superior or a higher-status person is also a member. In contrast, people from Egalitarian cultures are more likely to assert their ideas and assume that if someone has an idea, they will say it (and conversely if they've said nothing, they have no ideas). The first Integrating challenge in a multicultural interaction, then, is to ensure that all the ideas are contributed and heard.

It is especially helpful to notice whether there are systematic differences in participation rates in dialogue. Does one person speak more than others? Do people from one culture speak more than people from others? As long-time professors in multicultural settings, we know there is a strong tendency for people from Anglo cultures to dominate class and small group discussions in terms of amount of time spoken, even when they are a small minority culturally and even when the class is not taught in English. Anglo norms generally combine a first priority for Task rather than relationships, with preferences for Independent, Egalitarian, and Direct norms and Risk-taking in action. This combination of preferences is associated with a definition of meetings as a place "to discuss openly and decide," and the combinations reinforce each other to encourage and reward people speaking up freely to offer ideas, (inadvertently) suppressing contributions from others.

There are ways of engaging all group members and facilitating their participation. In the example given earlier, the Japanese manager hardly spoke in the first half hour; his "Wait" was his lone contribution during the first forty-five minutes. After the break to analyze the video and recenter, one of the Americans in the group noticed his silence and invited participation by saying, "If I recall, Sugano-san, a couple of years ago you had some experience in a merger similar to the one we are discussing. What do you think about this situation?" (Notice that the invitation drew on the Japanese manager's experience, respecting this Status-orientation cue.) What followed was a highly relevant discourse, fluidly expressed, which had a big impact on the shape of the group's recommendation. When his involvement was sought in a way that acknowledged his own cultural norms, this otherwise infrequent participant made an important contribution.

The most important way of **empowering participation** is to vary the modes of engaging; to broaden the definition of "meeting" to include a series of connected interactions. For example, people from some cultures – such as those preferring Status-oriented norms – may prefer to provide written input than to appear to be dominating or advancing their own interest by speaking in the group. Circulating written agendas well in advance of a meeting can help members prepare themselves this way and to provide written responses before the meeting. In some cultures – such as those preferring Indirect norms – it's more appropriate to provide ideas outside the context of formal group meetings. A series of private, face-to-face meetings can be sequenced to gather ideas and input for broader discussion, without attributing them to individuals.

Most people find creative ways to get everyone's input, once they accept the possibility of having different norms for different people. In a situation with extensive multicultural interaction, such as a team or a negotiation, it is helpful to identify someone to play the role of facilitator to ensure that participation is genuinely empowered. This can even be a rotating role, to develop further Mapping and Bridging capabilities.

Anticipating and Resolving Disagreements

As more ideas from various viewpoints are expressed, there is an increasing likelihood that there will be disagreements. The way these conflicts are handled then becomes the next cross-cultural challenge. Even the way conflict is expressed, quite apart from how it gets resolved, varies in different cultural traditions. In Indirect cultures, it is inappropriate to express conflict openly. For a manager from a Direct culture, where open expression of disagreement is valued, the first problem becomes detecting the existence of the conflict. Moreover, in Indirect cultures, a disagreement may be expressed very subtly or indirectly through a third party. In Direct cultures, conflict is more likely to be stated bluntly, in words of little ambiguity. When these norms are not understood, frustration or anger is likely to be the result. If I am accustomed to norms of expressing conflict more directly, I may be frustrated by behavior that I read as sending "mixed signals," or I may conclude the other person is confused or cannot make up his or her mind. If I expect indirect expression of conflict, I might feel insulted by what I experience as impolite or crass comments from the other person who feels she or he is "just putting the issue on the table."

The best way to deal with these issues is to use the Mapping and Bridging components of the model noted in the previous sections. Mapping provides a way to anticipate when the conflict may occur; the Bridging techniques (engage, decenter, recenter) give tools for reaching a common understanding and a common set of rules or norms for resolving the conflicts and avoiding them in the future. Remember that the single best predictor for effective cross-cultural interaction is refraining from judgment or blame; but, instead, looking for explanations for different views. Effective communication is more than half of effective conflict resolution.

Building on Ideas

Even if the Mapping framework is well understood, the communication skills are well developed, and participation and conflict issues are managed effectively, there is still a key component to realizing the potential in cross-cultural encounters, namely, moving forward and building on the ideas. There are cultural barriers in this phase of activity, too. Some cultural preferences would lead a person to push their ideas (Independent), while another orientation (Status) is more likely to lead to deference to authority. If you are in a group with several cultures, there might be an agreement (common rules of interaction) to surface ideas without attributing them to individuals or using an individual's ideas as a starting point for discussion. The main idea is to encourage the exploration of ideas with the conscious attempt to invent new ideas, to build on the ideas initially surfaced. A real stimulus to innovation is to try to do more than combine ideas and to avoid compromises. Finally, striving to find solutions to issues or problems that are acceptable to all (another rule for interaction or norm for behavior) is another way to increase the probability of getting synergy from the diversity in the group. Trying to invent new ideas from those available and reaching for solutions to which everyone can agree are ideals that are difficult to accomplish. But even setting them as objectives will help a multicultural team achieve its potential for high performance.

The award-winning design firm IDEO has developed and refined processes that take diverse ideas and inputs, and build on them to create highly value-creating solutions (Kelley and Littman, 2002, 2016). Their rules and techniques for brainstorming and prototyping are especially helpful with diverse teams. The firm's founder, Tom Kelley, says this about "brainstormers":

Hot brainstormers may generate a hundred or more ideas, ten of which may be solid leads ... People talk after brainstormers, sharing wild or practical ideas. A greater brainstormer gives you a fantastic feeling of possibility, and an hour later you walk out of the room a little richer for the experience. I think that sense of spontaneous team

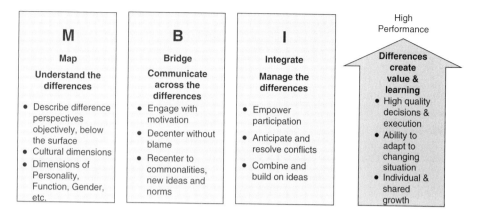

Figure 4.7 MBI full model

combustion is why we've been able to find so many unusual solutions to seemingly intractable problems. (Kelley and Littman, 2002)

We will discuss more about design thinking in Chapter 9; here, we want to highlight these techniques in their Integrating role.

The complete MBI model is repeated here for convenience, in Figure 4.7.

Troubleshooting Your Cross-Cultural Interaction: Destroying and Equalizing

Although there are many ways in which cross-cultural interaction can go wrong, they tend to fall into two basic patterns: destroying and equalizing. The two patterns have different starting points and dynamics, but both can end in sub-optimal performance and require repairs to be made. In this section we'll diagnose them both, compare them with the positive dynamic of creating value described in the MBI model, and identify how to avoid them or turn them around.

Destroying Value

Here is how the conversation between Seif and Bettina might have looked, if they had started on a **Destroying** path. Notice that neither is intending to be destructive, both are trying to move things forward in what they think is the most appropriate way. But neither is mindful about Mapping, Bridging, or Integrating in this cross-cultural encounter.

Beginning the meeting (Task vs. Relationship)	*Bettina*: Hi Seif. I know we don't have much time for this meeting, so let's start with the client's current value proposition and industry positioning.
	Seif: We'll be working together a lot, let's find out more about each other's experiences first. Why don't you tell me about your time in Japan last year?
Sharing knowledge about the client (Status vs. Egalitarian; Direct vs. Indirect)	*Seif*: I'm sure you saw from the firm's directory that I've been a partner for many years. In my experience, we may want to look deeper at the client's customer interface.
	Bettina: Look, the firm's relationship with the client is not great. We almost missed delivery on the last project. We have to start on the supply chain. My industry experience says that's where the quick wins are.
Agreeing on next steps (Certainty vs. Risk; Interdependent vs. Independent)	*Bettina*: Okay, I'll work on the supply chain analysis with my team. You look at the customer interface with yours. We'll have a weekly call to update each other, and our recommendations ready in three weeks.
	Seif: Hold on, hold on! First, supply chain and customer interface are related, we can't work on them separately. Second, we need much more planning before dividing the work, and the recommendations will likely take longer to develop. We have to be sure!

This exchange is likely to spiral into conflict and missed deadlines, with a deliverable below the client and/or the firm's expectations. Both Seif and Bettina may blame the problems on the other person, and both could end the project without learning as much as they could have.

The Destroyer dynamic is common because of the efficiency of within-culture interactions. We are so used to our culture's assumptions about how things are done, we all tend to jump straight to those patterns rather than question them. When two people "mindlessly" pursue two very different paths in parallel, each of which is efficient in itself but incompatible with the other, the result is conflict and inefficiency. Moreover, the Destroyer dynamic is toxic because of the nature of identity associated with culture. When someone doesn't seem to respect our norms and values, the ones we know deeply and take for granted, we experience this as identity threat. Implicitly, below the surface, we feel we're being told that the way we do things is wrong and devalued; that we should suppress a part of who we are. This tends to make us feel defensive and closed, and therefore less likely to be open to seeing things the other person's way.

If performance milestones are being missed or deliverable quality is below expectations, you're probably well into the Destroyer dynamic and it may be extremely hard to turn it around. The best way to recognize the Destroyer dynamic early is to pay attention to (be mindful of) your own and others' emotional reactions and surprises. If you find yourself negatively surprised with the way someone has responded about how to work together or progress on task, pause and ask yourself if you may have different ways of working that you haven't articulated yet. Even more important, but also more difficult, is to notice (be mindful of) negative surprises that your behavior creates for others. What assumption did you just challenge for the other person? In these situations, ask the kind of question Seif and Bettina asked at the beginning of this chapter: "How would you normally ...?" or "In your experience, what would you ...?" or "What did you learn from projects like this before?"

In sum, the Destroying pattern spirals downward for two reasons. It engenders conflict and interrupts efficiency and acceptance of ideas and ways of doing things; and it leads to defensive emotions and behaviors, with people less open about understanding others. The best way to avoid or turn it around is to be mindful of negative surprises, both in yourself and in others, and to ask questions that value and explicitly request other perspectives.

Equalizing Value

Most people working in cross-cultural interactions want to avoid conflict, and want the best outcome for all involved. Ironically, because of these intentions, the **Equalizing** pattern is very common. It can lead to expected performance quality in the short term, and people are caught completely by surprise if it turns suddenly into the Destroying dynamic. This is why it's critical to be aware of the pattern and prevent it before the turning point.

The Equalizing dynamic focuses on common ground – it sticks to what we share, the overlap of our perspectives, something we can all agree on. These are often professional norms or company policies. They could also be a minimum set of norms from the dominant culture, such as the "common global business culture" (which most people see as very close to Anglo norms) or the headquarters culture. Here is the Seif and Bettina conversation recast in an Equalizing, drawing on the norms of their global consulting firm:

Beginning the meeting (Task vs. Relationship)	*Bettina*: Let's start by framing our analysis. We need input on the value proposition and industry positioning. You've got experience with the client, how would you start on the value proposition analysis?
	Seif: Sure I can outline that. And as we work through the template, we can fill in a lot on positioning with your industry experience.
Sharing knowledge about the client (Status vs. Egalitarian; Direct vs. Indirect)	*Seif*: I know the lead partner in the consumer goods practice. I'll call her to get some analysis for market trends. That might address an issue they've been wanting to solve.
	Bettina: Okay. Meanwhile I'll tap into the expert networks to find people in the firm who know about this segment, then follow up with whoever's got the expertise. We've got to give them a better recommendation than last time.
Agreeing on next steps (Certainty vs. Risk; Interdependent vs. Independent)	*Bettina*: Who will be the lead contact for each of these areas? Normally we work with one person from the client for each target demographic, but in this project I think one person can handle two segments. I'll set up work stream meetings for me with them.
	Seif: There's still some background research we need to do before we're prepared for those meetings. Let's discuss the prep materials we have in more depth, and decide what research we still need. I'm pretty sure we should stick to one contact per demographic segment. Anyway, when we get to that stage, I'd like to have visibility on the work stream meetings too, so we can keep coordinated.

In this Equalizing dialogue, both Seif and Bettina refer to templates, processes, and mechanisms in the firm to get the project work going. The conversation is very efficient, and cultural differences are almost invisible. Typically, for a relatively straightforward or short-term task or interaction, performance will meet expectations. Why is this a problem, then?

The first problem is simply about sub-optimizing performance quality. The Equalizing approach doesn't take advantage of the different resources brought to the interaction, and is unlikely to create extra value for the customer or the firm. It's also unlikely to lead to learning and development – the people involved won't be better prepared to take on more challenging tasks in the future, for example.

But still, it looks less risky and certainly less time- and effort-consuming than Creating, right? So why not Equalize? The deeper problem with Equalizing is that, like Destroying, it suppresses part of who people think they are, part of their sense of identity. This is especially true if the Equalizing norms are based on "global business culture" or the headquarters culture.

Think about a time when you worked on a team where you felt like you couldn't be yourself, when you had to work, for a sustained period of time, in a way that was not comfortable for you. When someone's perspectives and ways of working are suppressed over time, they act through a filter. They're constantly spending energy thinking about how to present their ideas and how to participate, rather than on the act of creating and presenting ideas and reflecting on others' ideas in the first place. Most people in this situation eventually become frustrated and disengaged. They may even initiate serious conflicts or, more likely, simply leave the situation. So what looks like a safe approach – Equalizing – very often turns into a Destroying approach over time.

It is hard to recognize the Equalizer pattern in its early stages, because it can look very positive. People are happy to talk with each other, and things are moving smoothly on the surface. The best way to avoid Equalizing in the first place is to engage in a Mapping exercise – a conversation that explicitly engages both similarities and differences in a systematic way. This creates a positive norm about bringing uniqueness to the interaction. Further down the line, be mindful of comments like "It's what we have in common that matters, we don't need to worry about differences," and "We have lots of cultures involved but we never even notice cultural differences, they certainly don't get in the way." When you notice these comments, it may be time to revisit Mapping. You may have observed that the Creating conversation that started this chapter off was longer than either the Destroying or Equalizing conversation. Avoiding Equalizing takes time and effort – if you invest this at the beginning, it will pay off with greater effectiveness later.

In sum, the Equalizing pattern is a problem for two reasons. It sub-optimizes performance by ignoring the great resource of different perspectives for innovation; and over time it almost inevitably transitions into a Destroying pattern because at least some people in the interaction must suppress an important part of their sense of identity. The best way to avoid it is to engage in Mapping at the beginning, and be mindful of a focus on commonality without valuing difference.

A Note on Email and Virtual Interaction

So much of cross-cultural communication happens over email, phone, or other technology, that it's important we address the implications. As we've seen through Chapters 2 and 3, mindful global leadership requires taking account of the context of the interaction. In this chapter, we again emphasized the importance of understanding the other, in order to decenter and recenter in Bridging. We cautioned that we tend to take for granted that others' contexts and deep-level assumptions are the same as ours, so for effective interaction we need to explicitly overcome that tendency and learn more about others in a non-judgmental way.

The main challenge with interacting through technology is that the context of a message is either completely stripped away (e.g., with email) or it is greatly diminished (e.g., with video). We therefore have an even greater tendency to ignore context and deeper understanding behind the message. We send emails, forgetting that the sender may not read the email with the same background assumptions, and therefore may interpret it differently than intended. We don't see the context in which the sender receives the email, so we don't know the initial reaction (confusion, frustration ...). We present information in video-conferences with as little "background distraction" as possible, forgetting that the "background distraction" would actually provide contextual information for the other person, to help them better understand the meaning of our messages. Every global leader we know – even the highly skilled ones – has had the experience of an unfortunate misinterpretation of an email they've sent in a hurry.

At the same time, technological communications, well used, can help cross-cultural communications enormously. For example, because emails are written, senders can revise them several times to make sure they have the right meaning, even check with others before sending "for real." Receivers can read them several times over to make sure they have the right interpretation. We've seen several innovative best practices that combine different technologies for very high quality cross-cultural communication.

For example, a great sequence is email/voice or video call/email. The first email sets up the context of the conversation:

Let's have a conversation about the concrete and cement accounts. I'd like to share with you some analysis from the R&D team about technical applications for a new compound, and get your ideas about potential customers. The initial analysis is attached. Is tomorrow (Wednesday 17) at 14:30 your time (8:30 my time) good for a video call, using our desk systems?

Notice that the email doesn't make any conclusions or recommendations. It does set a clear agenda, with clear roles. It also shares information for future discussion, and provides a good context for that information. It sets up a time for a phone call that gives the receiver enough time to read and reflect on the question and analysis, and it specifies date and time zones explicitly,

using unambiguous formats (decentering). During the video call, both parties can take advantage of the synchronous communication and the ability
to see facial expressions, share screens, draw pictures, and so on for a rich
discussion.

After the video call, an email follows quickly:

*Thanks for the call today. Here is what I heard from you about potential customers ...
[summary of discussion]. I also heard you say that the new compound should ideally be
adjusted more for hot weather and typhoon applications. I believe we agreed that next
steps for me are ... and for you are .... Would you please let me know what I might have
missed in my summary? Or any other ideas you've had since?*

Again, note the clear decentering and recentering in the email. This email/call/
email sequence is ideal for combining the cross-cultural needs for contextual
understanding and careful reflection, with the richness of interactive dialogue.
By varying the modes of participation, it allows for different cultural preferences to play their strengths at different times.

Another creative best practice we've seen uses easily available translation
software, such as Google Translate. We know that the translations are not flu-
ent, but they are very useful in a "reverse translation" technique. Let's imagine
an interaction between a Japanese and a French manager, neither of whom
speaks the other's language. The French manager writes an email in French,
puts it into Google Translate to translate into Japanese. Then the French manager opens up another window of Google Translate, takes the Japanese translation and translates it into French. Likely, the two French versions are different
in some important ways. The French manager therefore goes back and clari-
fies the original French text, perhaps adding more sentences and context, then
repeats the reverse translation process until the two French versions are similar.
At that point, the French manager sends the Japanese translation. The Japanese
manager would apply the same technique in responding. One interesting impli-
cation of this technique is that both managers, over time, are likely to become
more precise and mindful in their native language so that the translate/retrans-
late cycle becomes shorter and communication more effective.

In sum, communication technologies enable cross-boundary communication, and smart combination of the technologies can enhance interaction effectiveness. This requires very mindful leadership, consciously taking into account
context and explicitly Bridging. The lack of context in communication over
technology often leads to people forgetting the importance of context, and poor
interaction.

Who Should Adapt?

The MBI process assumes that at least some people involved in an interaction are adapting to the others. But who should adapt? This is a difficult question.

A number of factors influence the answer. As a general rule, the burden for adaptation usually rests with the party who is seen as the foreigner. The sheer force of numbers probably influences this. But this rule of the majority also misses significant opportunities for learning and inventing, as we saw in the example of the culturally mixed team of managers discussing the acquisition.

Power of resources is another strong factor. An American joint venture in Dhaka may choose to emphasize American cultural values and management practice in spite of the location and overwhelming majority of Bangladeshi population, simply as a recognition of the need to acquire information. The buyer almost always expects the seller to adapt, unless the seller has something extremely rare for which there are many willing buyers.

Individual preference may also enter the equation. An expatriate dealing with Chinese in Hong Kong may attempt to adapt to Chinese traditions, even though there is no expectation from the Hong Kong staff to do so. The motives for adaptation in this situation may range from showing courtesy to a desire to learn and to increase one's own repertoire of behavior. Furthermore, no matter where a company is operating, an attempt to adapt to others' customs will be appreciated and will have a positive influence on relations.

We usually give a different but quick and easy answer to the question of who should adapt: whoever cares about performance. There are a lot of contingencies that influence who *tends to* adapt and who is *expected to* adapt. But as our description of the MBI process should emphasize, the more everyone adapts mindfully, the more potential there is for performance to improve. If one party adapts, it is better than if no one adapts. However, if everyone adapts, performance can be even higher. Discussing "who should adapt" often becomes a negotiation of power. Discussing "how we can perform together" becomes a dialogue of empowerment.

Continuous Learning for Development and Effectiveness

Managers often feel discouraged when they realize the complexity and depth of skills needed for interacting effectively across cultures. However, there is good news. A little bit of skill goes a long way. Doing a bit of Mapping will help you ask a couple of questions differently in Bridging. You'll get rich answers, which will lead you to avoid or manage a conflict differently, and you'll see yourself on the way to higher performance. This gives you and others more motivation to engage, you ask more Mapping questions, engage in more Bridging, and people will volunteer some ideas you hadn't heard before. Performance looks even better. And so on.

Being able to learn continuously comes from mindfulness: paying attention to your actions, selecting your behaviors carefully, concentrating on the results, managing the impact, and learning to prepare yourself for the next set of actions. Much more important than avoiding mistakes completely (because it is impossible) is learning. Ask questions about what you should have done. Ask them in a way that's appropriate to the culture. Provide "what if" scenarios and ask for people's reactions. Experiment when it feels safe. Then learn the new information and incorporate it into your maps for next time. Experienced managers love sharing stories about these incidents with each other. Both authors and all our colleagues have experienced many of them, even recently!

Susan, a businesswoman, was excited about her first trip to Saudi Arabia. After a few days of different types of meetings (always accompanied by a male guide and a male host), she met with a senior woman entrepreneur and her team. During the meeting the entrepreneur invited Susan to remove her hijab (headscarf), even though there were men present. Normally Susan would have declined immediately and left the hijab on, but there were several aspects of the situation that made it ambiguous, and she was not sure what to do. She made a decision, which seemed to be appropriate, since the Saudi woman continued the meeting as before with genuine warmth. But the most important part of the learning came afterwards. Susan asked a mixed group of Saudi men and women she knew well, what she should have done (without telling them what she had done). The spirited discussion lasted for an hour, and there was no consensus. All agreed that either action would have been fine, but they disagreed about what messages would be sent by leaving the hijab on or taking it off, with arguments for both being "better" or "less offensive." The group offered many examples of factors that should be taken into account – Did she see you as an expert or as a peer? How covered was her own hair? What does she do with her relatives and outside her business context (some of them knew the woman)? What kind of statement would she have wanted you to make? Who were the men in the room? Did you get the sense she was offering this to you as a gift? And so on. They also agreed that they were fairly liberal as a group, there would be many people in the country who would disagree with them that either option was fine, and that there might be different answers if only men or only women were asked, rather than a mixed group. This led to a discussion about dynamics in different parts of the country. Susan knew when she made her decision about the hijab that either leaving it on or taking it off could be a mistake, and she counted on her cultural competences to manage whichever impact evolved. But the learning from the situation was invaluable and became input for the next set of interactions.

If you create a negative impact you didn't intend, make sure you manage that impact. That means first of all, you must be watching for these impacts with mindfulness. Become sensitive to the cues that you have inadvertently created offense, such as the other person switching the type of pronoun to a more formal one, or using more structured language and actions. If you see the signs, first apologize sincerely. A genuine and respectful apology goes a long way to creating the conditions for turning it into a learning situation. Then, being mindful, learn for next time. If you are sincere in your attempts to learn and improve, you almost always get at least one more chance and people willing to help you learn.

In the remaining chapters of the book, we look at many different contexts for international management. Sometimes we draw on the MBI model explicitly; often we incorporate other lenses to focus on other aspects of the situation. But MBI is always assumed to be a foundation underneath the other processes, to be drawn upon in all situations.

Reflection Questions

The reflection questions for this chapter involve three sets of observations and actions to become more mindful about Mapping, Bridging, and Integrating in your own interactions.

1. Mapping. Think of someone you need to work with, who's quite different from you. Map the ways in which you're different – culture, gender, personality, work preferences, educational or experiential background. Go beyond the surface characteristics and try to understand how those differences could add value to your work together. After you've developed some ideas, have a conversation with the person to get their own perspective.

2. Bridging. Observe a wide variety of interactions, paying attention to how often people jump to judgment and even blame without considering that there may simply be different perspectives. Try listening to conversations, watching documentaries and movies, or reading commentary and opinion articles. Then pay attention to your own communication. How often do you move into judgment mode without considering all the perspectives? It's

impossible to eliminate this leap – it's part of what we do as human beings. But it's important to become aware of it.

3. Integrating. This reflection will focus on empowering participation. Think about a meeting that you go to on a regular basis that involves at least three people. It could be a weekly sales meeting, a production review meeting, a planning and reporting meeting, a club meeting, or anything else. What are the norms for participation? For example, who speaks when, and how do you know whose turn it is? Does everyone feel comfortable with these norms? Are there people who might say more, or provide more innovation, if the norms were different? If you can, encourage different modes of participation during the meeting. For example, try having everyone write individual responses before anyone shares, or having small subgroups discuss ideas before sharing with everyone. Explicitly reinforce ideas that are different from the others. What effect does this have on the meeting? On people engaging? On you?

Further Resources

The GlobeSmart resources, identified in Chapter 3 (www.globesmart.com) provide comprehensive information, including videos and advice, for Mapping and Bridging across different country cultures.

Diversity Icebreaker, also known as Trialogue, is an excellent tool for setting up Mapping, Bridging, and Integrating with any size group. The easy-to-use assessment provides a simple Mapping framework for communication and interaction preferences, which can be related to personality and cultural dimensions. The online resources provide guidance and tools for facilitating a process that makes Mapping, Bridging, and Integrating explicit and constructive. See www.diversityicebreaker.com or www.trialogue.com for further information.

Bibliography

Adler, N. J. (2008). *International Dimensions of Organizational Behaviour*, 5th edn. Thomson South-Western.

Bird, A., & Osland, J. (2000). Beyond Sophisticated Stereotyping: Cultural Sense-Making in Context. *Academy of Management Executive*, 14, 65–79.

Briggs, M., McCaulley, M. H., Quenk, N. L., & Hammar, A. L. (1998). *MBTU Manual: A Guide to the Development and Use of the Myers-Briggs Type Indicator*. Consulting Psychology Press.

DiStefano, J., & Maznevski, M. (2000). Creating Value with Diverse Teams in Global Management. *Organizational Dynamics*, 29, 45–63.

Ekelund, B. Z. (n.d.). *Trialogue – The Diversity Icebreaker*. Retrieved October 2017 from: www.diversityicebreaker.com or www.trialogue.com

Kelley, T., & Littman, J. (2002). *The Art of Innovation: Lessons in Creativity from IDEO, America's Leading Design Firm.* HarperCollins.

Kelley, T., & Littman, J. (2016). *The Art of Innovation: Lessons in Creativity from IDEO, America's Leading Design Firm.* Profile Books.

Maznevski, M. (1994a). Synergy and Performance in Multicultural Teams. Dissertation, Western University, Canada.

Maznevski, M. (1994b). Understanding our Differences: Performance in Decision-Making Groups with Diverse Members. *Human Relations*, 47, 531–552.

Smith, P. B., Andersen, J. A., Ekelund, B., Graversen, G., & Ropo, A. (2003). In Search of Nordic Management Styles. *Scandinavian Journal of Management*, 19, 491–507.

Smith, P. B., Peterson, M. F., & Schwartz, S. H. (2002). Cultural Values, Sources of Guidance, and their Relevance to Managerial Behavior: A 47-Nation Study. *Journal of Cross-Cultural Psychology*, 33, 188–208.

Stasser, G. (1999). The Uncertain Role of Unshared Information in Collective Choice. In D. M. Levine & L. L. Thompson (eds.), *Shared Cognition in Organizations: The Management of Knowledge.* Lawrence Erlbaum Associates.

5   Leading Global Teams

Alone we can do so little, together we can do so much.

Helen Keller

Most work in organizations today is done in some configuration of teams: small groups of people working together to accomplish something. Although researchers know a lot about teams in general, teams in international management are highly complex and we know less about how to be effective in global teams. Certainly, leaders and members of these teams have to excel at the basics of teamwork. In addition, they must be adept at bridging diversity and collaborating virtually. Global teams are often interconnected with other team configurations, so their members should be able to leverage these larger networks effectively.

Let's start by taking a look at a typical global team and its new leader.

Shawna moved from her native Ireland to continental Europe to lead an innovation team for a consumer goods firm. The team's mandate was to help the company spread innovations more systematically throughout the international network of subsidiaries. Shawna quickly saw that although individual projects were done well, team members missed opportunities to build innovation systems and knowledge-sharing. The team worked as a group of individuals assigned in different configurations to projects. To build integration, the team needed to work together in an interdependent way.

Shawna faced significant challenges. The team of twenty-five was highly diverse in terms of nationality, function, and types of experience – this was important for innovation but made it difficult to integrate. Moreover, assignment to the team was considered a three-year development experience for high potentials, so about one third of the team turned over each year. Team members worked in subgroups on projects, and the subgroups did not have much opportunity to interact.

Shawna started by interviewing all the team members and some important external stakeholders individually. Based on this initial input, she structured roles more clearly within the team, including the leadership role. She implemented a comprehensive set of performance expectations and an assessment system combining team priorities and stakeholder input. She began to bring the team together more often to develop common ways of working and joint priorities. She shifted the agenda of the semi-annual week-long workshops. In the past they had focused on reporting and administrative issues as well as general team-building. Instead, Shawna had the entire team create joint knowledge books around key competency areas, which they could all then deploy. To identify the priorities and key competency areas, team members worked together in these meetings to assess all current and potential projects against the company strategy. Once the projects and basic competences were assessed, team members finished the competency books when working apart from each other, and shared them virtually. The workshops also included significant team-building activities to increase trust and communication among team members when they weren't together.

Next Shawna started to work on larger system challenges and opportunities. She put in place a clear recruitment and succession plan so the team could become more stable in terms of skills and capabilities. This also facilitated knowledge transfer in the team, and increased the company's retention of these individuals after their "tour" with the team. The team implemented a structured orientation program, which included helping newcomers to the team develop their networks and relationships in the team and among key stakeholder groups. They developed an alumni group to leverage the relationships of people who had "graduated" from the team and help make innovation more systematic throughout the firm.

Shawna addressed all the aspects important to complex teams in international organizations. She reviewed the basic dynamics of the structure, task, and social processes, and built more complex dynamics including trust and boundary-spanning in addition to the team's already well-developed innovation processes. She set up the team to manage its dispersion well, and leveraged the team's networks. The team began to achieve its higher mandate of spreading innovation more systematically.

Teams Are the Basic Unit of Work and Collaboration

Formally, a team is a group of people who work together to achieve a particular outcome (Eagly and Gibson, 2002). There are different kinds of teams, each with different tasks, structures, and other characteristics. For example, a resources company identified five categories:

- **Project teams**: Teams with defined duration, clear deliverables, core membership and networking with experts and other stakeholders outside; e.g., exploration team for a new potential drilling site.
- **Management teams**: Teams with indefinite duration, clear membership representing different departments; high-level deliverables, coordination, and communication are key to the mandate; e.g., global lubricants management team.
- **Production/work teams**: Teams with indefinite duration, clear membership, specific and clear deliverables; team does regular and ongoing work together; e.g., production team operating a refinery.
- **Service teams**: Teams with indefinite duration, clear membership; deliverable depends on serving other people's and teams' deliverables; team members provide regular and ongoing support to others; e.g., IT or HR support for a global business unit.
- **Action teams**: Teams with defined duration, clear deliverables, created as needed from a network of potential members; team members work together in a fast and fluid way; e.g., emergency response team for a refinery fire.

Teams have become more complex in today's international economy, and there is no simple "how to" guide that fits all teams. With the wide variety of tasks that groups of people work on jointly, managers must develop a sophisticated view of contingencies (Maznevski and Athanassiou, 2006; Maznevski and Chui, 2013).

Getting the Team Basics Right

When members of a global team first get together, they often notice the complexity: people from different cultures, working across countries and time zones. Too often they forget to establish the basics of being a good, solid team. Researchers have been looking at teams in organizations for decades, and we have a strong understanding of the basics of teamwork. Here we'll start with the results, then work back to look at how teams achieve those results with specific levers and builders. The basic model is shown in Figure 5.1.

Team Results: What Should We *Get* from the Team?

High-performing teams perform well not just on the current task, but they also set themselves up for long-term success. In Formula 1 car racing, one of the keys to a fast race is the speed of tire changes during a pit stop. A pit stop team can have up to twenty members who coordinate their movements and equipment to remove and replace four tires. The record-setting pit stop in Formula 1 was in 2016, where the Williams team replaced Massa's tires and got him away in 1.89 seconds. Teams that have the fastest pit stops tend to perform well on this task over time, constantly decreasing their average speed. They are also the crews that perform well on other aspects of car tuning and maintenance, with better overall performance in racing.

High-performing teams excel on three dimensions. First is of course the task deliverable. They deliver high quality, according to the criteria set by the manager, customer, or other stakeholders. They also deliver in a timely, efficient way, again according to criteria set by the stakeholders. Second, they make the team better over time. They work together in a way that is sustainable. The team members don't have to like each other, although this may make sustainability easier. High-performing team members do respect each other and appreciate each other's contributions. They also improve their ability to work together as a team over time, so the team can complete more challenging tasks with better quality. Third, high-performing teams make their individual members better over time, too. They help members improve and develop new skills, so they can contribute more to the team and to the organization. They also work together in a way that motivates and intrinsically rewards team members, so they are inspired to engage with the team and the organization as a whole.

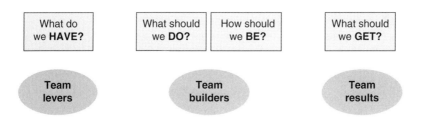

Figure 5.1 Basics of team performance: overview

The task deliverable may be the performance the team or the organization cares about most, and the one that managers and team leaders focus on. However, the other two aspects of performance – team enhancement and individual enhancement – are at least as important to monitor and develop. Quality of the task deliverable may be difficult to measure during the team process, but team enhancement and individual enhancement are often good indicators of the eventual task deliverable quality, so they can provide early diagnostics of poor quality. Moreover, team enhancement and individual enhancement are performance criteria that are associated with high-performing teams over time. In Shawna's example at the beginning of the chapter, we see that Shawna monitored all aspects of team performance, and put particular focus in her leadership on team and individual enhancement, using those as vehicles for helping the teams develop ways to excel on deliverables.

Team Levers: What Do We Need to *Have* as a Starting Point in the Team?

Teams have a variety of levers they can pull at the beginning of a team's life to structure the team well and prepare it for strong dynamics and performance. They can be categorized as levers about what, who, and where.

What Will the Team Accomplish?

The starting point is the "*what*" of the team: the definition of the task and timelines, with a clear understanding of the level of complexity (Is this a structured task with clearly identified inputs and outputs, or is it more ambiguous with potential for change mid-task?). Team members must know clearly what their task and objectives are, even if there is ambiguity, in order to achieve them reliably. For example, the Savory Flavors R&D team at a fragrance and flavors company has the mandate of developing new flavors for salty (rather than sweet) foods, such as soups and sauces. The account sales team at an Internet bank has the objective of selling new accounts. This sounds obvious, but many teams do not understand their objectives well or do not agree on them. Sometimes this is due to lack of clear communication from the leader, who may present a set of objectives that are clear to him- or herself but are difficult or ambiguous from the point of view of the team. More often, team members have different interpretations of the task and objectives. For example, a specialty chemicals company launched a new industrial product, with a multi-functional team guiding the launch. Their mandate from the CEO was to launch the product successfully. The vice president of marketing on the team defined this as high market share, while the financial director defined it as high profitability. These two objectives could be conflicting, and this team did not identify their different ideas until well into execution phase, when they had already created unaligned actions. The simple lesson here is: make sure the team has a clear mandate, and be mindful about the level and type of complexity. In complex teams such as those in international settings, you will have to revisit the goals and objectives many times.

Who's on the Team?

Next is the "*who*": Who do we need on the team, and in what roles? Teams need the right combination of skills among members. The right combination depends on the task, and includes technical skills, functional and geographical knowledge, skills important for managing the team processes, and people who can access external resources of all types. It is helpful to have diversity in personal characteristics among team members to boost innovation and increase the quality of decision-making. Teams are often composed based on convenience – who is available – rather than careful assignment, and sometimes the necessary skill combination is not available. As a result, teams frequently have significant skill or knowledge gaps which should be addressed by adding members or developing the necessary knowledge or skills.

Roles are sets of specific responsibilities within a group. Teams function best when different members take responsibility for different aspects. Should roles be explicitly assigned, or should they emerge? We have heard managers of teams argue strongly for both: "Our team worked well because we assigned and followed clear roles," and "Our team worked well because we let each person's role in the team emerge in a fluid way, shifting as necessary." Teams can perform well in either case. It is safer to assign roles, especially in a team of people who have not worked together before, or in complex situations like international teams. The best teams normally use some combination of assigning roles and adjusting them as necessary.

Where Does the Team Work?

This is the most neglected lever, but it is also important. To function well, a team needs a supportive environment and access to a network of stakeholders for team resources. The supportive team environment could include a physical environment, such as a team room with white boards to track work and interactive spaces for discussion. It should also include virtual space, such as shared network drives and collaboration platforms. Perhaps even more important, though, is the organizational culture around teaming. Often, team members will work part-time on this project and part-time on other work. Managers must be supportive of this work arrangement, giving team members enough time and resources to focus on the team. If the organizational climate is supportive to teams, then the physical and virtual environments are more likely to be appropriate.

Team Levers: Set Up Well at the Beginning, Then Adjust as Needed

We call these structural elements the team levers because they are usually structured by managers outside the team rather than by team members themselves. They are the starting conditions, and as such, they have a great influence on the team's trajectory. Of course, as the team works together, it may become apparent that some of the levers need to be adjusted. For example, the team may find that the task definition needs to be refined, based on new analyses about market segments or suppliers. Or they may find they need specific expertise that is not on the team, and they need the expertise integrated as a team member rather than accessed through a network. A manager who is creating a team to accomplish something should continue to pay attention to these levers. Similarly, team members should be aware of the possibility to adjust the levers after they start working together, and should maintain strong dialogue with their external stakeholders regarding these structural conditions.

Team Builders: What Should We as a Team *Do* in Our Work Together, and How Should We *Be* Interacting?

Most research on teams focuses on the social processes and conditions inside the team itself, and indeed this is where team members have the most influence on their own team performance. This section will refer frequently to Chapter 4 on interpersonal effectiveness with Map–Bridge–Integrate, because interpersonal interaction is the foundation for effective team builders.

What Should We *Do*? Task and Social Processes for Teams

Team processes are the actions that teams engage in, the behaviors they do, in order to perform well as a team. It's helpful to identify two important categories of actions: task and social.

Task Processes: Working Directly on the Deliverable

This is often thought of as "doing the work." The three main types of task processes are planning and tracking, analyzing and deciding, and executing.

Planning and tracking are often referred to as project management and are the subject of many books, articles, guides, and software packages. Simply put, teams are more likely to achieve results if they plan clear processes with activities, milestones, and deliverables, if work and sub-tasks are allocated clearly to members, and if the team tracks progress compared to plan, adapting the plan when necessary. Planning and tracking are enhanced if communication and conflict management – two social processes – are effective. Without good communication and conflict management, plans are unlikely to be complete or comprehensive, and tracking is likely to be inaccurate.

Analyzing and deciding are integral as most teams have to make a variety of recommendations and decisions, all of which require gathering and analyzing data. They may be deciding on production parameters, product attributes, candidates to hire or promote, or any other organizational issue. Again, analyzing and decision-making are the subject of many books from project management to strategy. In a team, the key is to use the benefit of multiple team members to increase the scope of alternatives considered, to enrich the analysis, and to debate and explore implications of different decisions. As we will examine in a later section, this can be particularly challenging in diverse teams, which are typical of global teams.

Executing is about individual team members accomplishing their own parts of the task – whether it is data gathering, analysis, report-writing, or other things – and the group as a whole combining the individual outputs to create a joint deliverable. This requires individual discipline – team members need to finish their own parts on time and come prepared to meetings – as well as group commitment, with team members helping each other out as unexpected challenges arise. For some team tasks, executing also involves actually implementing. For example, an equipment purchasing team formed after two companies merged was charged with identifying the best few suppliers from among the two companies' previous relationships. Then the team negotiated new contracts with these suppliers and worked with the suppliers and individual purchasing departments to adjust volumes and delivery conditions until new routines had been established.

Social Processes: General Interactions that Enable the Team's Work

Social processes are those that facilitate interaction, commitment, and motivation within the group. They are the interactions that enable high quality task processes. For teams, the most important social processes are effective communication, anticipating and resolving conflicts, and innovating by building on ideas. Chapter 4 covered these social processes extensively, so we refer the reader there.

Although we've presented task and social processes separately here, it's important to remember that they work together. Moreover, they do not necessarily begin in this order. Recall that cultures differ in their preference for prioritizing tasks or relationships. They also differ, therefore, in terms of where they prefer to begin teamwork – with the task or the social processes. What's important is for a team to monitor both sets of processes. Whenever one type seems to be stalled or in conflict, it often helps to go to the other to look for resolution and progress.

How Should We *Be*? The Importance of Internal Team Conditions

Teams need to create a set of norms and a way of "being" that promotes healthy task and social processes, especially to achieve sustainable, adaptive performance. It helps to think of these ways of being as sets of beliefs that team members have about the team as a whole, like a team culture. Certain sets of beliefs allow the team to interact in a way that facilitates processes like planning, analysis, deciding, executing, communicating, resolving conflict, and innovating. The ways of being that most affect performance are psychological safety, cohesion, and trustworthiness.

Psychological safety is a belief that team members look after each other's identity, or sense of self, and that people are valued for being in the team. When there is strong psychological safety, team members contribute ideas without fear of ridicule or pressure for conformity. The team is more likely to communicate effectively, resolve conflicts constructively, and innovate well. Behaviors that reinforce psychological safety are open and active listening, showing empathy and compassion, and encouraging each other to bring unique perspectives to the team.

Cohesion is a strong sense of identity as a team. It means that team members believe that the performance of the team as a whole is at least as important as their own individual contributions, and they are willing to invest a lot in helping each other to achieve the team's deliverables. Cohesion is particularly important when there is conflict, or when the task or environment change as the team works together, and roles need to be fluid and changing. With strong cohesion, individual team members are willing to put aside their individual concerns and shift for the sake of the team.

Trustworthiness is the belief that team members will act in ways that are reliable, and that they will look out for each other in situations of ambiguity, risk, or vulnerability. We often talk about two kinds of trust: cognitive and affective, or head trust and heart trust.

Head trust is the belief that someone will do what they say they are going to do. Head trust comes from experience with the other person's expertise, capabilities, resources, and conscientiousness. Heart trust is the belief that someone will look after your interests as much as they can, even when you're not there. Heart trust comes from experience with the other person's values, and with the other person looking after you when you're in a state of vulnerability or taking a risk. Head trust is necessary for any kind of teamwork. Without head trust, team members feel the need to monitor each other's work constantly, to re-check and re-do. This leads to redundancies and inefficiencies, and poor performance. Heart trust is necessary for the team to engage in tasks that stretch the team's capabilities, tasks that are ambiguous or complex, and tasks that require adaptation along the way. All of these latter situations require that people in the team act on behalf of the team, without everyone present or clear about the direction.

All of these team conditions, or team ways of being, have to develop with experience. Team members may begin with initial "trial" levels of psychological safety, cohesion, and trust, but their experiences together will determine whether the conditions increase or decrease. Full safety, cohesion, and trust can only be built with deep and challenging experiences over time.

Team Builders Are Reciprocal, Not Sequential

We've presented the team builders as linear, with task and social processes, and team conditions. In fact, they are and must be completely reciprocal, affecting each other constantly. Effective communication and conflict resolution lead to strong team conditions. With strong team conditions, the team has better planning, analysis, execution, and innovation. Good task progress provides a context for extensive communication, and together these build more cohesion.

With strong processes and conditions, when the team hits a challenging part of the task, for example a failure with a customer, team members pull together to solve the problem. This experience in turn provides a context for developing better processes, and creates deeper psychological safety, cohesion, and trust. The reinforcement can easily become a negative cycle, rather than a positive one, with poor processes leading to poor team conditions and the poor conditions, in turn, making it more difficult for team members to engage in good team processes. Good team leaders, team members, and those who support teams from the outside all pay attention to both the processes and the conditions, working to create momentum on positive cycle.

Team Basics in Action: Shawna's Innovation Team

The full model of team basics is shown in Figure 5.2. Let's look back at Shawna's team to see how the team basics worked together to empower a high-performing team.

Team Results

Shawna was clear on what she wanted to get out of the team. She clearly articulated the three types of performance objectives: the task deliverables (innovation for internal clients), team enhancement (improved knowledge management and team capabilities), and individual enhancement (preparing team members

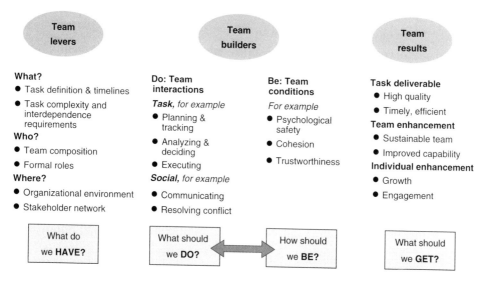

Figure 5.2 Team basics: full model

for succession roles in the organization as a whole). She explicitly used all three types of performance to identify the team levers, and to enable team builders.

Team Levers

Shawna developed processes and worked more closely with clients to identify key deliverables and timelines. She acknowledged the complexity of innovation, and its requirement for a lot of interdependence among team members and with the client, and she set up processes for project teams to work together intensively. She became more systematic about recruiting people into the team and orienting newcomers, and she worked with the teams to develop clear role profiles that were appropriate for organizing the work. She, herself, spent a lot of effort advocating for the team's resources and developing the right stakeholder network.

Team Builders

Shawna guided the team to develop strong task and social processes. She role modeled and facilitated to start with, then reinforced the team members as they developed the norms on their own. She carefully planned large team meetings and experiences to provide opportunities for building good team conditions over time, then to rotate new team members into the strong team culture as it evolved.

Shawna went beyond the basics to take advantage of the global team composition and to manage its global dispersion, as we'll explore in the next section. However, Shawna knew about the importance of getting these basics right. She invested more energy into this than most managers do, but the results paid off. Further, once the team was performing exceptionally well, Shawna herself could turn her attention to raising the team's and the company's ambitions for developing even more value for customers.

Culturally Diverse Teams: Creating, Equalizing, or Destroying Value

Global teams tend to be much more diverse in their composition (an important team lever) than domestic teams are. Of course, team members usually come from different country cultures. Moreover, global teams tend to be initiated for complex, globally-relevant tasks (another important team lever). Once the team leader has included all the different skill sets needed for the task, global teams tend also to be multi-functional, and their members tend to come from very different parts of the organization or even different organizations (such as a customer, supplier, or expert organization).

Most people assume that highly diverse teams perform better than less diverse teams. They certainly have the potential for higher performance. They have access to more resources, from information to stakeholders, and they can therefore "cover" more of the information and analysis needs for the task. In addition, people from different cultures and backgrounds tend to ask different questions and confront assumptions differently, so highly diverse teams have more potential for innovation and more integrative ways to resolve conflicts than less diverse teams.

Unfortunately, as we foreshadowed in Chapter 4, diverse teams find it very difficult to use their resources well and turn them into performance. In a recent meta-analysis, we found that the basic relationship between cultural diversity and performance is zero; that is, there was no correlation at all between cultural diversity and performance. What we found instead is that multicultural teams, and highly diverse teams in general, tend to perform either better *or* worse than teams with low diversity, with the two patterns averaging each other out. The pattern of team results is summarized in Figure 5.3 (Adler, 1986; Maznevski, 1994; Maznevski and DiStefano, 2000; Stahl et al., 2010).

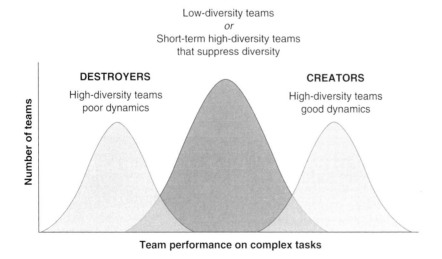

Figure 5.3 Relationship between team diversity and team performance

Just as for interpersonal interactions, people are often worried about differences getting in the way of team performance. So most diverse teams suppress diversity by equalizing everyone to the lowest common denominator. They do this with good intentions – they believe it is the best way to have smooth task and social processes, and to build strong team conditions. In teams, this suppression is problematic for two reasons. The obvious shortfall is that it does not realize the potential of the team. It leaves unused resources on the table, and sub-optimizes decision quality and implementation. "Okay," some managers respond, "it's not worth the effort or the risk of conflict. For us, it is a good rational decision not to invest in the diversity." Maybe, in the short term.

Just as for interpersonal interactions, the equalizer approach of suppressing diversity inevitably demotivates team members whose beliefs, values, or norms are different from the dominant ones of the group. Not only do they stop contributing their knowledge, they also stop engaging with energy in the team. They may even initiate serious conflicts or, more likely, simply leave the team. This is why Figure 5.3 shows the equalizer performance as working for highly diverse teams in the short term. In the long term, diverse teams that try to equalize end up destroying.

Managing Fault Lines: Why Different Sources of Diversity Align

Global teams face yet another challenge that is less relevant for single-culture teams: managing fault lines. Fault lines are rifts in teams created by alignment of different types of diversity (Lau and Murnighan, 1998; Maloney and Zellmer-Bruhn, 2006). For example, a global team may consist of two production engineers, two marketers, and two R&D scientists, from the USA, Japan, and Germany. If the engineers are from the USA, the marketers from Japan, and the scientists from Germany, then the functional and cultural divisions are aligned and it is more difficult for team members to recenter and bridge across differences. On the other hand, if each of the functions is represented by people from different countries, the subgroups will be less evident and the group will find it easier to balance divergent and convergent processes.

On a team that was developing a new global pricing strategy for the company's service offerings, all the finance expertise on the team came from the headquarters country. The other members of the team assumed that whatever the finance people suggested represented the headquarters' point of view, so the others on the team were unwilling to question the finance members. The company eventually took one of the headquarters people out and brought in a finance director from a moderate-sized subsidiary on a different continent, and this changed the dynamics significantly in a positive way.

Diverse Teams Do Perform Well

The good news is that highly diverse teams *can* and *do* perform extremely well. As in Shawna's example above and Reinhard's team and others profiled in Chapter 4, the highest performance on complex tasks in organizations is typically achieved by teams that engage their diversity well. To do this, they apply the Map–Bridge–Integrate principles with discipline to achieve the team builders outlined above. There is no magic wand or silver bullet, but there is a lot of effort toward mindful global leadership.

Virtual Teams: Managing the Impact of Geographic Dispersion

Not only are global teams highly diverse, their processes are also hindered by the fact that they often conduct most of their interaction while the members are physically in different locations. Virtual team members are distributed widely, often around the globe. Some of the consequences are obvious. You may be familiar with the Tokyo–Berlin–Rio conference call scheduling dilemma! A more subtle challenge is with different infrastructures: communicating seamlessly over different network types is often impossible.

These teams are often called **virtual teams** because much of their interaction happens in the virtual space of digital information and communications technologies. Today's technologies facilitate communication and collaboration much more easily than those of even five or ten years ago, and they are becoming more powerful and more intuitive at a fast pace. Still, as human beings we have hundreds or thousands of years of experience in face-to-face teams and only a decade or two in virtual teams, so interacting virtually still presents a learning curve for us together.

If we go back to the basics model, we see that virtual teams are still teams first. They ought to achieve all three types of team results. With respect to team levers, they likely have diverse composition and a rather complex task. The real challenge is that all the team builders need to rely on technology. Research and practice suggest four important sets of recommendations for virtual teams, to be adapted according to the needs of the specific team.

Organize and Discipline: A Lifeline for Virtual Teams

Face-to-face teams can get away with being unorganized and undisciplined. When members see each other, they catch up on the task, and they muddle through an agenda even without preparation or clear process. For virtual teams, lack of organization and discipline is deadly. High-performing virtual teams set up their norms for organizing and disciplining early in the team's life, and follow them with commitment. They clearly identify norms for both task and social processes. Some norms may seem trivial, such as an agreement to respond to every team email within one work day, even if the response is "I see it but I can't get to it right now." Although this may seem minor, it is the kind of norm that builds trust and also keeps the task and communication going. Other norms may be more comprehensive, such as committing to conducting an action review on a regular basis, or always starting a new task phase with individual insight contributions from each member. High-performing virtual teams also understand that the definitions, milestones, norms, and roles will change as the team and the task evolve. They articulate these clearly at the beginning of their work together, and revisit them regularly to adapt as necessary.

Get to Know Each Other: People and Context

As we discussed in Chapter 4, virtual technology takes most or all of the context out of communication (see p. 136). This context, though, is critical for cross-cultural effectiveness. And the lack of context makes it very difficult for people to build relationships, which are also critical for cross-cultural effectiveness. Throughout this book we emphasize that mindful global leaders are particularly sensitive to context, relationships, and process. This needs especially to be the case in virtual teams.

It's important that virtual team members take extra time at the beginning of their teamwork to get to know each other, and each other's contexts. For example, we've worked with many teams whose members have a specific folder or thread on their team communication site for team-building. They may begin by posting an easy phone video of themselves in their workplace, introducing their colleagues and work spaces. Some people are comfortable sharing personal information, such as family or hobbies, and of course some cultures encourage this. Other individuals are less comfortable and some cultures discourage it. Team members should share personal information at the beginning if they're comfortable, but not require it from everyone.

Each virtual interaction should try to take at least a few moments for contextual social information, and it's important to schedule this into the time expectations. It would usually happen naturally in face-to-face encounters, but it must be carefully structured into virtual meetings so it's not forgotten. People in all cultures are comfortable with sharing some kind of contextual information, whether it's weather, sports scores, current events, music and theater, or other topics. A team should start with what's comfortable for people, and only move into more personal or sensitive topics (e.g., political conflicts) as trust builds. Every virtual interaction should also share their context with respect to the business itself. For example, what are the local customers like? What are the challenges and opportunities the different business units are facing, whether or not they are directly linked to the task of the team?

The Right Technology: Match Richness with Message, from the Receiver's Point of View

Virtual teams are faced with a wide array of technologies and applications. However, there is no correlation between specific technologies and performance. Some good teams use mainly email and telephone calls; others use high-tech voice and video over Internet and shared live websites with extensive use of chat. High-performing teams use a menu of technologies and select the right one for the team process at a given time.

The one important heuristic is this: the more complex the message you're communicating, the more you should use rich media. Rich media are those that allow for multiple modes of communication at the same time. High-end video conferencing, for example, is more rich than text messaging. Face-to-face is the most rich communication. Remember though that communication is about a receiver understanding the message as you intended it. Complexity, therefore, should be defined from the receiver's point of view, not the sender's. Even if something seems straightforward to you, if there is a chance that the receiver will not see it the same way, a more rich technology is in order. In other words, it is often better to pick up the phone or send a quick video of the context, rather than send an email that could be misinterpreted.

The other corollary of this rule of thumb is that rich technologies should not be used for straightforward messages. Rich technologies are expensive, in terms of coordination time even if not financial investment. It is much more efficient to use a non-rich media, such as shared document space or email, to share a routine sales report, and to save the rich media time for more complex messages such as problem-solving.

Create a Heartbeat

When should we get together in person? Leaders often assume that high-performing teams get together whenever things become complex, for example, a situation of intense conflict or when it's important to make a big step on a task. Our research and experience, however, suggest otherwise. Quite simply, high-performing virtual teams get together on a regular schedule, creating a **heartbeat** for the team (Maznevski and Chudoba, 2000).

Teams should set a schedule of regular face-to-face meetings, perhaps once a quarter or twice a year. These meetings can be planned in advance to coincide with events such as professional association meetings or larger management meetings. Heartbeat meetings should focus on progressing the team builders: task and social processes, and team conditions of psychological safety, cohesion, and trust. A two-day agenda of presentations sharing PowerPoint results from the last quarter will do nothing to help the team. But a two-day agenda of customer visits, site visits, and discussion of difficult cases to share knowledge and advice will pump the equivalent of high quality oxygen into the team's circulatory system.

The heartbeat rhythm does not need to coincide with major decision points or milestones. A high-performing team can handle intense conflict and heavy deliverables in virtual mode if it has developed strong norms for the team "Do's" and strong conditions for the team "Be's." Rhythm is critical. Like a human heartbeat, a team's heartbeat should be adjusted depending on the situation. If the team is less fit – for example, if there are new members or if trust has been damaged through a difficult situation – then the heart should beat faster than if the team is highly fit. If the team's task is more difficult – includes more ambiguity, more strategic importance, or the environment changes unexpectedly – then the heart should beat faster than if the team's task is simpler or more predictable.

Ideally, heartbeat meetings are in person, supplemented with interim virtual heartbeats. We also have seen successful teams that cannot meet face-to-face, who develop strong heartbeats using virtual technologies. These teams consciously keep the task and social processes moving, and find ways to build strong team conditions creatively. For example, members use simple multimedia technologies – digital cameras and webcams – to share what is going on in

their separate worlds, and they explicitly develop social relationships by sharing family and personal information as they increase their trust.

Virtual Teams Are Complex, But Can Create Great Value

We are often asked "What's the secret?" as if there is some simple key that
will unlock virtual team performance. Unfortunately, there is no such key.
Collaborating across dispersion and diversity brings challenges. But it also
brings opportunities that are worth the investment. Beyond their task mandate,
virtual teams expand our possibilities. In today's organizations, well-managed
virtual teams create development experiences with exposure to other cultures
and situations. When virtual teams try to replicate their face-to-face teams,
they are usually disappointed. But when they develop new skills to address the
challenges discussed here, they achieve high performance and create competences that the organization as a whole can benefit from.

Beyond Teams: Connecting Networks for Social Capital

How big can a global team be? A global brand manager for a large consumer
electronics group said, "My team has 100 people; that is probably too much,
but that's the real group of people who need to work together on this." A global
supply chain manager for an industrial parts manufacturing group said, "I have
purchasing teams, production teams, logistics teams, and integration teams,
and they all need to work together at different times. Which sets of teams should
I apply these principles to, and how, when they are always shifting?"

   The idea of "team" tends to limit us to thinking about a group of people that
is relatively stable over time, doing a single task. However, most collaborations
in international organizations are not really that stable or one-dimensional. It
is helpful to think in terms of social networks and the social capital they carry.

Networks Are Maps of Social Connections

A network is a set of relationships among people. We visualize networks by
drawing them as a set of points representing people (or organizations, or teams,
or other social entities), with lines linking them to represent relationships.
Figure 5.4 shows the network of a ten-person account team for a marketing and

advertising firm. In the center are the ten core members, from the USA, Europe, and Asia. Team member 1 is the managing director, 2 is the assistant director, and the others are relatively equal in the team hierarchy. The arrows show information relationships among the core members of the team: Who goes to whom for advice about the client and the task? The second layer adds relationships between team members and others in the firm: Who do the core team members go to, outside the team but within the firm, for advice about the client and the task? The third layer adds relationships between the team members and people in the client firm: Who do the core team members go to at the client firm for advice about the client and the task?

This network view shows many things that a simple team perspective cannot. For example, the managing director of the account does not interact with many of the account team members, and it may seem he is a negligent team

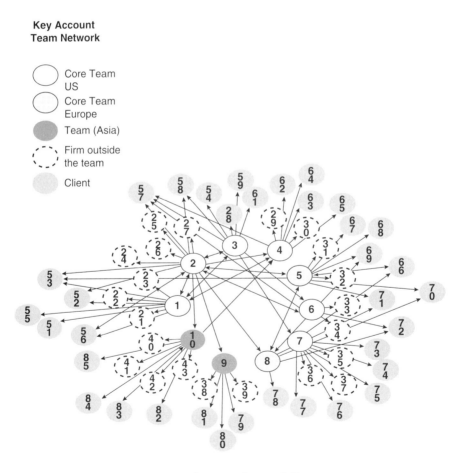

Figure 5.4 An account team's networks: team, firm, and client

leader. However, as we see by the network, he does interact frequently with the most senior people at the client, and this helps the success of the team. Another important insight is related to team members 9 and 10 in Asia, the newest location for this account. The assistant director goes to them whenever she needs information from them. But members 9 and 10 are otherwise not integrated into the core team. The two Asian representatives went only to people in their own office and in the client's local offices to work on the account. Their contacts at the client don't overlap with anyone else's, so if they were to leave the team, the team would lose these client contacts. Learning and synergy opportunities are also being missed. After seeing this map, the assistant director started incorporating the two Asian members into more team meetings.

Social Capital: The Assets in Relationships

Relationships are important for many aspects of business performance. To assess these relationships, it is useful to draw on the notion of social capital: the assets in networks of relationships that can be valuable to achieve objectives (Adler and Kwon, 2002; Cross and Parker, 2004; Lin, 1999). Like other assets, building social capital requires investing, and the payoff may be immediate or long-term. Using social capital can increase it, and not using it can decrease it. Unlike other assets, though, social capital exists entirely in a relationship between parties. One person cannot own social capital by him- or herself.

Social networks, like the structure shown in Figure 5.4, are holders and carriers of social capital. Social capital flows along the connections to and through people to other parts of the network, to get things done. Social capital moves four types of resources through networks (Lin, 1999):

- Information flows
- Influence for decision-making
- Reputation and credibility
- Identity

Relationships that increase information flow, provide influence, clarify credentials, and reinforce identity enable the actor to access and use social capital to enhance their performance.

In the marketing account team described above, all four aspects of social capital – information, influence, credibility, and identity – were facilitated by social networks. Team members used their relationships to influence people whose cooperation they needed, and to facilitate information flow. Relationships with the client were important for obtaining the information and detecting its valid-ity. Relationships among team members were important for sharing information and creating a comprehensive picture of the client firm's needs. Team members with strong influence encouraged other team members to increase their com-mitment to the client and the team, providing better solutions for the client. Relationships with the client were also used to influence the client's propen-sity to accept the firm's advice. Team members' relationships with their profes-sional associations influenced their credibility, and the senior leader in this team derived enormous credibility from the quality of his relationships with other senior leaders in the firm and senior managers at client firms. Finally, the mar-keting and advertising experts' identity as professionals was enhanced when the team produced a market plan and brand idea that won awards in the industry.

Network Structure: Not All Networks Are Created Equal

To understand which organization structures are best, we look at the character-istics of strength and density.

Connections between people, or ties, can be weaker or stronger (Granovetter, 1985). Weak ties are those among people who have met briefly, perhaps exchanged business cards, and connect with each other infrequently; or, they may have connected more frequently but without a close relationship. Weak ties are good for accessing information, such as learning about new products or customers, or for looking for job candidates or jobs. They are relatively easy to maintain. Strong ties are those among people who have known each other longer, and who have a personal relationship and maybe even deep trust in each other. Strong ties are good for getting in-depth information, scarce resources, and commitment to new ventures. Strong ties are relatively difficult to maintain.

Internet social networking sites such as Facebook, LinkedIn, Twitter, and Instagram show connections among people. They have developed innovative ways to indicate and leverage strength of ties. Facebook is aimed at linking together social networks of friends. For example, LinkedIn, which creates net-works of professionals, emphasizes that you should only accept as connections people you know and trust, since others who can see your network will be able to see and possibly leverage those connections. LinkedIn provides mechanisms for recommendations and endorsements, which is another way to indicate strong ties. As social media applications come and go, different ways of build-ing and using social capital over technology emerge and shift.

Density is a measure of how interconnected people are with each other. The more everyone is connected to everyone else, the higher the density. In high-density networks, information is passed quickly. There tends to be redundancy in information, as everyone is talking to the same sources. In low-density networks, information is passed less efficiently and may miss network members. However, low density networks tend to access a broader set of resources and information, with less overlap.

Strength and density combine to create many different types of networks. Two important patterns are fishing nets and safety nets. Fishing nets are lower-density structures with many relatively weak ties, often formally referred to as networks with structural holes (Burt, 1992). Like "real" fishing nets, they can be cast in the right place to cover an area and catch things in that expanse. Fishing "social" nets catch ideas, job candidates, customers, suppliers, and other opportunities. They can work when the network owner is not actively involved, but they must be checked from time to time in order to bring in the catch. These nets must be maintained at regular intervals, checking that the connections are still in place and replacing those that have ripped. A real fishing net that is too dense brings in too many fish that are too small; not dense enough and it doesn't catch anything. Likewise, a fishing social network that is too dense brings in too much of the same kind of information. One that is not dense enough brings in too little information or resources.

Figure 5.5 shows a global engineering company's fishing net. This company has quite good fishing nets, with connections broadly distributed across all geographies and specialties. But this diagram highlighted two members from Latin America, "She" and "Bab," who were not connected to the rest of the company. Their operations had developed expertise in mining that would have been very valuable to the rest of the company, but it was not being "caught" by anyone else. After they saw this diagram, managers in the company worked to repair these holes and transfer more information. Global teams should assess their fishing net to ensure it is catching and holding the right resources, and build fishing nets where necessary.

Safety nets are higher-density structures with relatively strong and flexible ties. Like "real" safety nets, they catch people when they fall, and bounce them back up again. They are rarely used, but must be carefully maintained in case they are needed. Human safety nets usually include family members and a few close colleagues. Some people think it is best to never use a safety net, but we disagree. In fact, when one is training in trapeze and tightrope, the first instructions are always about how to use the safety net. If you talk to any circus

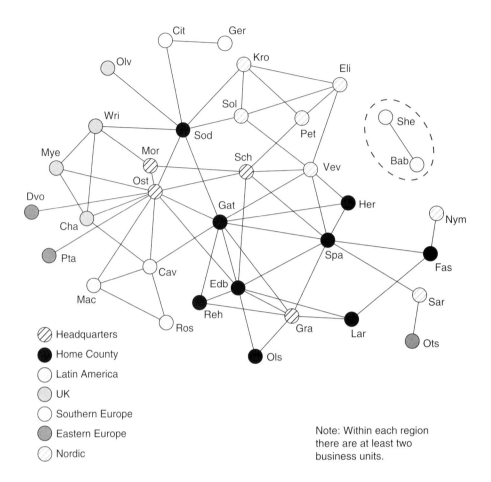

Figure 5.5 An international engineering company's cross-business unit, cross-geography fishing net

performer, they will tell you, "If you're not using your safety net during train-ing, you are not learning enough."

Figure 5.6 shows one manager's business network, clearly structured as a safety net. This manager is an investment banker in a highly volatile country, and knows that structuring his business network in this way is critical to achiev-ing success in the business (Maznevski and Shaner, 2011). One of the peripheral members of the network is his golf instructor, whom he is introducing to every-one else in his network to facilitate interaction during a leisure activity.

Just as all individuals should consider building both fishing and safety nets, all teams should incorporate relationships of fishing and safety nets. The core team itself may be a safety net. One top management team of a global com-pany we worked with realized that members' divisional roles left them feeling isolated and frustrated, with nowhere to turn for advice. They began to create

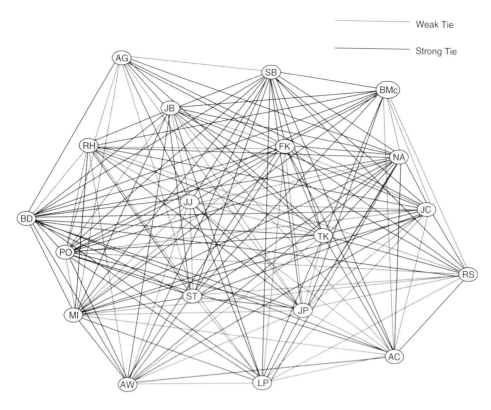

Figure 5.6 An investment banker's safety net for business execution in a volatile market

relationships among themselves to become the safety net for each other, and explicitly used the safety net to help the company take some bold but important steps in a coordinated way. Although the company is in an industry that has been hit hard by the current global turmoil, they were much better positioned than their competitors and weathered the storms very well.

There are many other ways of looking at social networks and social capital that are very useful, and we encourage such teams to consult the many good references on this topic.

Complex, Large, Distributed Global Teams: Ambitious Configurations to Achieve Ambitious Goals

The most determined global organizations combine a global team, a virtual team, and social network configurations and processes to achieve ambitious goals. In our experience, global not-for-profit organizations are at the leading edge of experimenting with networked team structures. Their mandates are highly complex and multifaceted, and they need to develop and implement solutions in close interdependence with highly complex environments. For example, they may be enforcing peace, delivering humanitarian aid in conflict zones, or preventing or reducing climate change.

One example is the World Wide Fund for Nature, more commonly known as WWF and by its panda logo. WWF's global structure is like a federation of country organizations with a combination of fundraising and conservation project responsibilities. This structure has been very effective for raising awareness and funding in different countries, and sponsoring conservation projects in over 100 countries around the world. Throughout its history, some projects and initiatives crossed country and regional borders; these were hard to implement with the federation-like structure, but until recently the benefits of the decentralized structure and the challenges of changing outweighed the need for more formal coordination.

However, with the current state of the physical environment, WWF saw a need to change how they work. Conservation needs are clearly global and not national. WWF recently took the bold step of adding a new formal vehicle for coordinating to prioritize nine global practices: forests, oceans, wildlife, food, climate and energy, freshwater, finance, markets, and governance. This new overlay on the federated structure is a networked, global team-based structure.

Each practice is headed by a Practice Leader, who has a small management team. Each country office has one (or more, if appropriate) member of the Practice, called a Focal Point. A small team of key Focal Points works with the Practice Leader to lead the direction of the Practice. Practice Leadership teams meet twice per year physically, at the same time as other meetings. At all other times they meet and work virtually. Almost all the work done by Focal Points in the practice is done virtually. All of the Practices partner with organizations outside WWF as well as members internally, and Focal Points are encouraged to develop those networked connections. The Practice Leaders, themselves, work together as a team of nine to identify synergies and reduce redundancies. Together they are accountable for delivering on the strategy of WWF globally (WWF, n.d.; WWF, 2016).

WWF's new Practice Leaders are applying everything from this chapter, in many different ways. They identified performance goals that cover all three types of Team Results (*Get*) for themselves as a team and for the Practices they lead. They began with a planning period during which they carefully considered all of the Team Levers (*Have*): they defined tasks and goals (*What*), identified the characteristics of people and the roles they needed on their leadership teams (*Who*), and worked closely with the WWF global organization to identify what kind of support they needed to facilitate the teams. In late 2017, they were beginning to launch Team-Building, and were paying close attention to task and social processes (*Do*) as well as how to ensure the best team conditions (*Be*). Since most of their work is virtual, they were mindfully developing organization and discipline. They experimented with building a portfolio of technologies to work with, including very innovative use of web-based video programs for multi-day conferences incorporating break-out work sessions. They carefully structured an annual rhythm of face-to-face and virtual meetings into the calendar, two to three years in advance for the major meetings. And they are very strategic in structuring both teams and networks for different aspects of the tasks.

WWF knows that the team- and network-based structure they're implementing is challenging, and Director General Marco Lambertini led a two-year highly inclusive planning process to help prepare the organization for implementation. WWF staff strongly believe this level of interdependence is the only way to "help WWF unleash our full potential to support the urgent transition needed toward an ecologically sustainable future, vital for natural and human well-being." While it is too early to compare the results with the previous structure, it is clear that WWF staff members in country offices around the world are engaged and contributing actively to the process. As we saw when looking at team results, this level of engagement is a good predictor of motivation to engage in positive team builders.

Managers facing complex international coordination – at WWF and other organizations – appreciate the combination of the team and network perspective since it helps them find and manage patterns in the complexity of their task. They know the task is difficult and that simple solutions and principles will only go part of the way. Even if the perspectives here are not simple to apply, they are systematic, and they provide ways of working toward performance and assessing progress.

Teams in International Management Start with the Basics and Add Sophistication

As work in international firms becomes more interdependent, the need for coordination increases. The most common way to coordinate is with teams. Most managers are part of multiple teams of different configurations, with at least some of those teams having members distributed across space. It's important to set the team up well from the start, pulling the right levers. To turn those inputs into performance, managers must lead and facilitate team builders, adapting as the team works together. The team levers and builders are part of leaders' traditional knowledge; however, managers of global teams must be able to lead them very well and in new contexts. The newer skills that are important in global organizations are managing virtual teams, and managing with networks in mind. Today's Internet-raised generations will likely lead with yet an additional set of team skills. Teams will never disappear, and good global leaders will keep evolving with them.

Reflection Questions

These reflection questions suggest that you think back to different team experiences you've had to analyze the different elements and their impact on the deliverable, team enhancement and individual member enhancement.

1. Identify several teams you've worked on that had very different tasks. Which required more or less interdependence among members? How did that relate to the intensity of interaction required? When more interdependence was needed, did the team have the ability to deliver it? Why or why not?
2. Have you experienced some teams with positive ways of being (cohesion, psychological safety, trust), and others with negative ones? What led to the team having those states? What impact did they have?
3. What is your experience with highly diverse teams? When did the diversity lead to high performance, and when were the results disappointing? How can you link the ideas from this chapter and from Chapter 4 (Map–Bridge–Integrate) to explain the performance?
4. Most people have worked on a team that does much of its work virtually, even if the team members are located in the same geography. How well have your virtual teams managed organization and discipline, getting to know people and context, and using a good portfolio of technologies? Have you developed strong rhythms? What other best practices have you observed?

After reflecting, try facilitating some new practices in your current teams, whether you are leading or a member. As you observe what happens and adjust your behavior, you'll be practicing a process orientation, an important part of mindfulness and a global mindset.

Further Resources

For more on multicultural and virtual teams, Lena Zander's recent articles summarize the current state of knowledge well:

Zander, L., Mockaitis, A. I., & Butler, C. L. (2012). Leading Global Teams. *Journal of World Business*, 47, 592–603.
Zander, L., Zettinig, P., & Mäkelä, K. (2013). Leading Global Virtual Teams to Success. *Organizational Dynamics*, 42, 228–237.

Tsedal Neeley and colleagues' work on virtual teams in general, and language in multilingual organizations, is also helpful. See for example:

Neeley, T. B. (2015). Global Teams That Work. *Harvard Business Review*, 93, 74–81.
Neeley, T. B., Hinds, P. J., and Cramton, C. D. (2012). The (Un)hidden Turmoil of Language in Global Organizations. *Organizational Dynamics*, 41, 236–244.

For more on social networks and their role in organizations, Rob Cross's work is helpful. Two practical articles are:

Cross, R., Ehrlich, K., Dawson, R., & Helferich, J. (2008). Managing Collaboration: Improving Team Effectiveness through a Network Perspective. *California Management Review*, 50, 74–98.
Cross, R., Nohria, N., & Parker, A. (2002). Six Myths about Informal Networks and How to Overcome Them. *MIT Sloan Management Review*, 43(3): 67–75.

Bibliography

Adler, N. J. (1986). *International Dimensions of Organizational Behaviour*. Kent Publishing.
Adler, P. S., & Kwon, S.-W. (2002). Social Capital: Prospects for a New Concept. *Academy of Management Review*, 22, 28–51.
Burt, R. S. (1992). *Structural Holes: The Social Structure of Competition*. Harvard University Press.
Cross, R., & Parker, A. (2004). *The Hidden Power of Social Networks*. Harvard Business School Publishing.
Eagly, P. C., & Gibson, C. B. (2002). *Multinational Work Teams: A New Perspective*. Lawrence Erlbaum Associates.

Granovetter, M. (1985). Economic Action and Social Structure: The Problem of Embeddedness. *American Journal of Sociology*, 91, 481–510.
Lau, D. C., & Murnighan, J. K. (1998). Demographic Diversity and Faultlines: The Compositional Dynamics of Organizational Groups. *Academy of Management Review*, 23, 325–340.
Lin, N. (1999). Building a Network Theory of Social Capital. *Connections*, 22, 28–51.
Maloney, M. M., & Zellmer-Bruhn, M. (2006). Building Bridges, Windows and Cultures: Mediating Mechanisms between Heterogeneity and Performance in Global Teams. *Management International Review*, 46, 697–720.

Maznevski, M. (1994). Synergy and Performance in Multicultural Teams. Dissertation, Western University, Canada.

Maznevski, M. L., & Athanassiou, N. A. (2006). A New Direction for Global Teams Research: Introduction to the Focused Issue. *Management International Review*, 46, 631–646.

Maznevski, M. L., & Chudoba, K. M. (2000). Bridging Space over time: Global Virtual Team Dynamics and Effectiveness. *Organization Science*, 11, 473–492.

Maznevski, M. L., & Chui, C. (2013). Leading Global Teams. In M. E. Mendenhall, J. S. Osland, A. Bird, G. R. Oddou, M. L. Maznevski, M. J. Stevens, & G. K. Stahl (eds.), *Global Leadership*, 3rd edn. Routledge.

Maznevski, M., & DiStefano, J. (2000). Creating Value with Diverse Teams in Global Management. *Organizational Dynamics*, 29, 45–63.

Maznevski, M., & Shaner, J. (2011). The Relationship between Networks, Institutional Development, and Performance in Foreign Investments. *Strategic Management Journal*, 32, 556–568.

Stahl, G. K., Maznevski, M. L., Voigt, A., & Jonsen, K. (2010). Unraveling the Effects of Cultural Diversity in Teams: A Meta-Analysis of Research on Multicultural Work Groups. *Journal of International Business Studies*, 41, 690–709.

WWF (n.d.). *Our Global Goals*. Retrieved 2018, from WWF Global: www.panda .org/what_we_do/how_we_work/our_ global_goals/index.cfm

WWF (2016). *WWF Launches New Strategy with the Appointment of Eight Global Practice Leaders*, August 30. Retrieved 2018 from WWF Global: www.panda .org/?276775/WWF-launches-new-strategy-with-the-appointment-of-five-global-Practice-Leaders

6 Talent Management: Selection, Preparation, and Mobility of Global Leaders

> Travel is fatal to prejudice, bigotry, and narrow-mindedness.
>
> Mark Twain

Global Talent Management

A McKinsey & Company study, "The War for Talent," published in 1998 (Chambers et al., 1998), identified "the war for senior executive talent [as] a defining characteristic of the competitive landscape for decades to come," and probably ushered the term "talent management" into the management lexicon. Almost twenty years after that original McKinsey report, the Boston Consulting Group said:

Most efforts at developing leaders and talent fail, yet the need for exceptional leadership at all levels has never been clearer ... driving the need to focus on recruiting and retaining leaders and talent amid a growing global talent shortage. (BCG, n.d.)

Brookfield Global Relocation Services in its 2016 "Global Mobility Trends Survey" stated:

Companies continue to find an ever-increasing gulf between the demands of their businesses and the supply of candidates with the required education, skills and future potential necessary to fully execute on both the opportunities, and the challenges identified by the senior management teams. (Brookfield, 2016)

Academics and practitioners tend to agree that the talent management function of corporations has not kept up with the sophistication of their functional counterparts such as finance, marketing, or supply chain. "Waging a war" on talent or "managing the talent pipeline" are easier to talk about and create slogans for than the more difficult job of actually doing it. Stahl et al. state that building and sustaining a talent pipeline is one of the biggest challenges facing companies everywhere (Stahl et al., 2012).

It is no longer sufficient just to find talent. Companies must combine that with development and mobility strategies to ensure managers have the requisite skills and are moved to where they are most needed. Caligiuri and Bonache (2016) advise:

Ensuring that professionals with the right set of cross-cultural competencies and technical skills are in the right assignments at the right time will require both the talent management and global mobility functions to work more closely together. (Caligiuri and Bonache, 2016)

Mindful Global Leaders Are the Key to Managing Complexity

Before examining the process of global talent management, we briefly revisit the discussion about the complexity of the global environment in which global leaders must function. In Chapter 1 we identified several characteristics that work to increase complexity: variety, interdependence, and ambiguity (see p. 13). Each of these characteristics is difficult to manage, but their interconnectedness magnifies that challenge.

Globally, executives are dealing with a wider variety of organizations, governments, and employees. Globalization is not just about "more"; it's about "more and different." There are more competitors and partners, with diverse types of organizations and networks, serving customers with different needs in different markets. Companies have more operations in more locations to manage and, of course, have more governments to contend with.

Companies exist in a world of complex social, political, and economic interdependencies. Interdependence is not only a feature of the external environment. It also is something companies create themselves through offshoring, outsourcing, alliances, and network arrangements related to value chains, often to cope with competitive challenges.

If customers, governments, interest groups, and competitors were passive, a corporation could manage the complexity by simply adding managers and computers. That would be an increase in detail complexity. The increase in interdependence and variety leads to more ambiguity. Ambiguity makes clear understanding difficult. As we have said, the whole system is in constant motion, always changing. And the rate of change seems to be accelerating.

Eliminate or Amplify?

There are two common methods for dealing with increased complexity: eliminating input variety, or amplification. Elimination of variety is the reduction of "noisy" information achieved by not being able, or willing, to see and understand the nuances in the environment; or by creating an artificial state of certainty, misleading executives into thinking they are in control. Such ostrich-like behavior does not usually bring success.

Amplification usually means increasing the number of decision-makers. Organizational structures have become more complex, with more managers and more multidimensional matrices. The more complex structures become, the more unwieldy they are. Moreover, they cannot always adapt quickly to new circumstances, since they are designed to fit a particular set of contingencies. Additional complex sets of policies may not work either. In a continually changing, dynamically complex environment, policies have to be changed continually or lose their effectiveness.

W. Ross Ashby, a pioneer in cybernetics said: "Only variety can destroy variety" (Ashby, 1972) which became known as Ashby's Law of Requisite Variety (Ashby, 1973). In human information processing terms, this means that when there is complex, ambiguous information coming from the environment, organizational decision-makers (managers) must have the cognitive complexity to notice these inputs, decode them, process them, and possess a sufficiently varied behavioral repertoire to act on them properly.

Research has shown that for non-routine or highly complex decisions, teams make better decisions on average than do individuals. Yet simple amplification will not necessarily work. If, for example, executives operating out of a corporate headquarters in Norwich, Connecticut cannot generate the requisite variety in their decisions to match the variety existing in a global marketplace, simply increasing the size of the team may not work. If multiple decision-makers are highly homogeneous, with similar outlooks, a similar vested interest in the outcome, and reliance on the same selected sources for their information, they may be deceiving themselves. That is, they may think they are facing less variety than they actually are.

We believe that the appropriate response to complexity is the deliberate development of human requisite variety. Simply, this means that global organizations must find the right people capable of deciphering the informational content in the environment to create the appropriate responses and organizational processes to execute action plans. Weick and Van Orden stated: "Globalization requires people to make sense of turbulence in order to create processes that keep resources moving to locations of competitive advantage" (Weick and Van Orden, 1990). Jack Welch called this the globalization of intellect: "The real challenge is to globalize the mind of the organization ... I think until you globalize intellect, you haven't really globalized the company" (Rohwer, 2000).

As companies globalize, managers face challenges that require a more complex view of the world or they may be prone to deciding on the wrong, simple solutions to their problems. To paraphrase the American journalist H. L. Mencken, "for every complex problem there is a simple solution. And it is always wrong."

There is little doubt that dealing with the complexity of global operations requires having managers with the orientations, competences, and skill sets beyond those required in domestic organizations. Acquiring and retaining people who can function effectively in this new context becomes a critical human resource management undertaking. High-potential individuals must be carefully selected and given the necessary preparation and professional development. Finally, their careers must be managed responsively so that they remain with the organization, using their new skills to achieve strategic objectives.

International Assignments Come in Many Shapes and Sizes

International assignments have increased in importance not only for strategic reasons but also for career success. Academics and practitioners agree that these assignments are generally considered essential for career development. Bolino, Klotz, and Turnley, writing in the *Harvard Business Review*, state:

Many companies expect their aspiring leaders to work abroad. It's how their executives develop the skills to lead across cultures and learn the inner workings of a global business; it's how rising leaders advance into the senior ranks. (Bolino, Klotz, and Turnley, 2017)

Historically used in a management control role, for decades expatriate managers went abroad for long terms, usually two to three years. Very often they were accompanied by a trailing spouse who did not have a career and was not expected to work. It was viewed as an interesting or exciting opportunity and a possible chance to make additional money or save money. Surviving the assignment was often considered to be a measure of success and on return executives usually stayed with the company.

The scenario has changed. Today managers are transferred to and from the parent company to learn about affiliated operations in other countries, to fill skills gaps, to transfer knowledge and technology, to launch projects, to facilitate integration of the global value chain, to transfer corporate culture, and to improve management development.

Although expatriates on long-term assignments (one year or longer) are common and probably still the majority of international assignees, numerous surveys of multinationals also have shown an increasing use of "non-standard international assignments." These assignment types vary in length including frequent flyer, commuter, rotations, virtual, and short-term (up to 12 months) and extended business traveler (30–180 days) assignments. The people in these new arrangements are now referred to as "**flexpatriates**," defined by the *Financial Times* as "an employee who takes up an international assignment centered on frequent international business trips without locating abroad" (*Financial Times*, n.d.). Research has recently begun to investigate the implications of these assignments for individuals and for companies (Pate and Scullion, 2016).

A major reason for the rise in non-standard assignments is the expense associated with relocating expatriates and their families. The Society for Human Resource Management says that the cost of a three-year assignment for an expatriate and their family may exceed US$3 million as of 2017. Expatriates' salaries are usually higher than those of local managers, and they usually receive benefits to make an overseas move attractive. Benefits often include items like housing or a housing allowance, moving expenses, tax equalization, and schooling for children. Many of these benefits are not usually provided to local employees. In addition to lowering costs, having fewer expatriates has reduced conflict between expatriate employees and local employees.

The use of local managers to reduce costs has increased. Localization also has become a viable option with the increase of host country managerial and technical capabilities. In many developing countries, larger pools of better-educated management talent are appearing. In developed countries, where sufficient management talent exists, there are employment and immigration laws with which a firm must comply. Companies also are now using third country nationals (TCNs) more frequently to reduce labor costs and are converting the status of expatriates to local employees, also reducing costs.

Some companies are attempting to understand and measure the cost–benefit trade-off of international assignments in order to gauge their effectiveness and the return on investment (ROI). Some firms use specific assignments or projects which can be assessed as completed or not, while others attempt to measure more formally the successful completion at the expected cost. Companies are increasingly tracking the costs of international assignments and requiring clear statements of the assignment's objectives and pre-approval by business units and possibly HR. Some are doing cost–benefit analyses, but businesses that measure ROI are in the minority. Brookfield's data show that of the 163 global companies in their survey, 61 percent prepare cost estimates for assignments; 51 percent track actual total costs; but only 26 percent require a cost–benefit analysis.

Expatriates now are more likely to have partners with their own careers. Brookfield Global Relocation Services in its 2016 Survey Report found that 49 percent of the spouses/partners were employed before the assignment but only 16 percent continued to be employed during the assignment (Brookfield, 2016). The career impact and loss of income effects for spouses and partners have become important considerations as executives think about accepting an international assignment.

International assignments are important tools for the coordination and integration of organizational resources, which are essential activities for successful strategy implementation in geographically dispersed companies embedded in differing cultural environments. Although electronic communication and data processing system options allow for the creation of sophisticated enterprise information systems to coordinate dispersed operations and the activities of suppliers and customers, the cultural nuances of information that provide the deepest comprehension of market-specific knowledge are not transferable electronically.

Tacit knowledge, which is deep-rooted and usually not codified, explains the most important nuances of operations in a particular cultural context. This knowledge is acquired experientially and must be shared through face-to-face interactions. Firms gain sustainable competitive advantage from executives acquiring experiences and lessons that are held as tacit knowledge and then shared across the organization.

Given the dispersed nature of multinational organizations, knowledge-sharing is particularly difficult. Some solutions to this challenge include the use of short-term assignments as well as cadres of expatriates and **inpatriates** (an employee transferred from a foreign country to a corporation's home country operation or headquarters) to acquire and share tacit knowledge that exists within the organization. Used strategically, short-term assignments, inpatriation, and expatriation can be used to implement projects, fill positions, or, as a management development experience, to provide high-potential employees with a global orientation – or all three. These employees create global relationships inside and outside the company, and share explicit and tacit operating knowledge. The relationships and knowledge then become essential to the value creation process in global operations (Harzing, 2001).

We have dealt with some companies that were increasing the number of inpatriates to headquarters. These inpatriate assignments were usually short-term, two to three months at headquarters for a special project. This had a double advantage of exposing the inpatriate to headquarters processes, concerns, and perspectives, while allowing headquarters personnel to become acquainted with cultural orientations and views of divisions from around the world. At the same time, some of these firms were establishing formal policies that required international experience as a prerequisite for consideration for promotion to senior ranks, thereby "localizing" management and eliminating many of the perks that were formerly needed as incentives for executives to accept international assignments.

Caligiuri and Bonache have documented some of the important changes and trends in global mobility as shown in Table 6.1.

Table 6.1 **Mobility trends**

	Traditional approach (1960s to the late 1980s)	Modern approach (1990s to present)
Changes in the strategic deployment of expatriates		
Reasons for expatriation	• Control of subsidiaries • Fill gaps for skills unavailable in host countries	• Knowledge transfer around MNC • Professional development of global leaders
Typical mobility flow	• One-directional flow from headquarters to subsidiaries • Mostly from large US, European, and Japanese headquarters	• Mobility in all directions (e.g., lateral moves, reverse expatriations) • MNCs from emerging market and developing countries
Dominant perspective	• Headquarters' perspective was dominant	• Multiple perspectives (headquarters, regional, local) are considered
Changes in assignment types		
Duration of assignments	• Relatively long assignments (two- to four-year period)	• More traveling and short-term assignments
Employment modes	• Relational contracts	• Relational and transactional contracts
Initiating the global experience	• The company requests employees to relocate	• The company posts open requisitions for international assignments • The employees request opportunities for international assignments
Changes in the profile of expatriates		
Gender	• Male executives	• More female expatriates
Age and level	• Middle-aged • Senior level managers and executives	• All ages • From all levels in the organization
Other	• Single-income families • Non-working spouse	• Dual career couples • Elderly parents • Non-traditional families

Source: Caligiuri and Bonache (2016).

Selection

In 1973, published research showed that managers were selected for international assignments based on their proven performance in a similar, usually domestic, job (Miller, 1973). The ability to work with foreign employees was at or near the bottom of the list of important qualifications. Unfortunately, forty-five years later the situation has not changed enough. Very often technical expertise and knowledge as well as previous domestic performance are used as important selection criteria. However, they should not be given undue weighting relative to a person's ability to adapt to and function in another culture. It does no good to send the most technically qualified engineers or finance managers to a foreign subsidiary if they cannot function there and have to be brought home prematurely. Caligiuri stated that:

selection for international work starts where other systems stop in that only those individuals who have a demonstrated competence for the tasks and duties of the job are considered. In essence, international assignment selection attempts to take a group of "qualified individuals" and determine who can effectively deal with the challenges inherent in working with individuals, groups, and organizations that may approach work in a very different way. Not everyone with a proven record of professional success in a domestic context for a given job title will have what it takes to be successful in an international context – even doing the same job with the same job title. (Caligiuri, 2012)

Given the importance of selecting and assigning the right candidates to these international jobs, one would think that companies would have very thorough career management processes. Although some undoubtedly do, this does not appear to be the case overall. Brookfield found that only 23 percent of its surveyed companies had a "specific process for career planning from assignment acceptance"; 33 percent didn't have a process for employees to express interest in an international assignment; 73 percent didn't have a candidate pool for potential assignments; and only 22 percent used formal tools to assess the adaptability of a candidate (Brookfield, 2016).

Effectiveness in the International Assignment: *E = f (PAIS)*

A useful framework for thinking about selection in the context of overseas effectiveness was developed by Daniel Kealey in his work with the Canadian International Development Agency (Kealey, 1990). It focused on three factors: adaptation, expertise, and interaction. He states that for a person to be effective, he or she "must adapt – both personally and with his/her family – to the overseas environment; have the expertise to carry out the assignment and be able to interact with the new culture and its people" (Kealey, 1990). Managerial success in an international assignment comes from the ability to live and work effectively in the cultural setting of an assignment. Effectiveness is a function of professional expertise; plus, the ability to adapt to one's host country; plus, intercultural communication skill to interact with the locals.

Possibly one of the most overlooked and neglected factors in selection for an international assignment is **situational readiness** (Franke and Nicholson, 2002). A way to think about this is to ask the question, "Is an international assignment right for a person at this time with everything going on in their life and with their family?" Some examples of relevant selection criteria include having a family that is willing, able, and probably excited to take the assignment; not having aged or sick parents to care for; or having children with special needs that cannot be accommodated in the host country.

Our shorthand notation for a candidate selection rubric is $E = f (PAIS)$ which stands for *Effectiveness is a function of (Professional expertise, Adaptation, Intercultural interaction, and Situational readiness)*.

Effectiveness on the job is the important outcome for an international assignment. Many studies have used outcome variables such as expatriate satisfaction with an assignment as a surrogate for performance. An international assignee who is satisfied with his or her assignment is not necessarily an effective manager. Neither is a manager with previous international experience necessarily effective, although such managers are likely to be more satisfied in their assignment. Previous experience is related to increased satisfaction, ease of adjustment, and less stress, all of which are good. However, global companies need effective managers and an ineffective one can damage relationships in the host country. Poor performance in an international assignment also can result in high professional and personal costs to the individual and his or her family. Therefore, all the variables in $E = f (PAIS)$ are important.

Women as Global Leaders

The international assignment of female executives has become an important consideration as more women have graduated from business schools and are in line for senior management and international careers. It is also a relevant concern both under employment equity guidelines and legislation in some countries such as the USA, the UK, and Canada. The overall percentage of female international assignees has been rising with historical estimates being between 16 percent and 20 percent. For 2016, Brookfield found that the percentage of female expatriates was 25 percent.

Nancy Adler conducted some of the early, pioneering research on female expatriates (Adler, 1987). Her research showed that, contrary to conventional wisdom at the time, women did want careers as international managers. Another lesson learned about women expatriates was that the perception of men in the home country was more of a barrier than the behavior of men in the foreign country. Men in the company's home country tended not to select women for international assignments in order to protect them from imaginary difficulties in foreign countries. However, Adler learned that a foreign woman is not expected to act like a local woman and being foreign was more noticeable than being female.

Caligiuri and Cascio state, "the four variables predicting a Western female expatriate's success [are] her individual characteristics; the support she receives from her organization; her family; [and] the host nationals with whom she works" (Caligiuri and Cascio, 1998). To this list of four variables we would add that she should be at a senior level and have significant decision-making responsibility so that executives in the foreign company will understand that she is a senior executive and the person with whom they must deal.

Our advice is to select and send the best person for the job. If a woman is the best person to be sent on an international assignment, then she should be sent. However, being a woman expatriate in some countries is undoubtedly more difficult than in others and companies have a responsibility to prepare women well for challenging assignments in difficult countries.

Assignment Destinations

It is now generally accepted that managers aiming for the C-suite will need multiple international assignments and not just in developed countries. Given the demographic profile of aging populations in many developed countries, market expansion into emerging markets is a growth requirement for firms – and not just to the **BRIC countries** (Brazil, Russia, India, and China). Companies are now exploring the CIVETS (Colombia, Indonesia, Vietnam, Egypt, Turkey, South Africa) and the Next 11 countries (Indonesia, Vietnam, Egypt, Turkey, Mexico, South Korea, Bangladesh, Iran, Pakistan, Nigeria, Philippines). The International Monetary Fund (IMF) projects that the GDP growth rate for advanced economies for 2020 will be 1.7 percent while the growth rate for emerging markets and developing economies will be 5 percent.

What does this mean for you as an aspiring global executive? First, some of these countries and markets can be considered challenging destinations. Second, it means that you, or someone who will be reporting to you, could be assigned to one of these countries. There are two dimensions on which to categorize countries as challenging destinations: administrative problems for international program managers (government regulations, immigration, work permits, tax issues, locating acceptable housing); and cultural difficulty for the assignee and family in adapting to a new country, including personal risks, and security and health issues.

Brookfield found that the five top challenging locations for administrators were China, Brazil, the USA, India, and Russia. The most challenging for assignees and their families were the same countries with the exception of Saudi Arabia replacing the USA. The challenges assignees face include language, remoteness, schooling for children, lack of jobs for spouses, living standards, and security and health concerns. These challenges undoubtedly will continue for expatriates assigned to the CIVETS or the Next 11.

Today a successful assignment also means a safe assignment. Companies are formalizing programs to ensure the safety and security of their expatriates and families to minimize international assignment turndowns, attrition, early returns, and failures. Since the events of September 11, 2001, we have seen continued economic and political volatility as well as the rise of global terrorism. Kidnapping and piracy also have become all too common phenomena. Executives could be tempted to say: "The world has become a dangerous place and maybe we should concentrate on places like the United States and Western Europe."

We believe that global business is a long-term proposition. Companies cannot succeed by jumping in and out of countries when the going gets tough. Not only is it expensive, but customers and suppliers often remember when they were "deserted."

Nestlé had some of its operations in South America nationalized and later resumed ownership. It then went through a second full cycle of nationalization and renewed ownership. Although the company contested and fought the actions as best it could, the attitude of senior executives was one of patience, knowing that these things happen and that, eventually, the regime would change and the assets would be returned. Nestlé demonstrated real commitment to its global business and a long-term perspective, both of which have contributed to its consistent success.

Many countries that companies are exploring can be considered difficult places in which to do business and for expatriates to live. It is important to have a realistic attitude toward these situations and to learn to live and work in a world of uncertainty and risk. The more you learn about other countries, the better you understand the risks involved. This enables better decisions to be made about entering a certain country and the steps necessary to manage the risks in that country as the following story illustrates.

One of the authors was having dinner with the president of a British bank's Canadian subsidiary and described his time in East Africa to the bank president. The bank president commented about how risky it was to operate in Africa. This comment surprised the author, who understood the difficulties involved, but had thought it possible to manage them. The bank president then listed the countries in South America in which the bank was operating and making money. To the author, some of these seemed like pretty risky places, and he said so. The bank president replied, "Not really; the bank has been there for a long time, and we understand the situation." Therein lies the moral: Familiarity with and understanding of a country provide the necessary perspective for accurately assessing risks, determining acceptable levels of risk, and managing those risks.

Companies need to have strategic and tactical plans for managing risks. Large companies can develop risk specialists to contribute to informed decision-making, and smaller firms can access consultants for specific decisions. All companies are advised to listen to expatriates and locals working in the field when they provide systematic assessments of their environments, usually required periodically by the home office. Individual managers can add to the quality of their own decision-making by reading broadly, by understanding the history of regions in which they operate, and by seeking (and paying attention to) information from international field personnel.

Duty of Care

What is your company's or university's duty of care policy? If you are sick, in an accident, or caught in an attempted coup d'état, such as the one in Turkey in 2016, does your organization have a plan in place to assist you? Whether you are currently a full-time student or in a part-time or executive education program, has this question ever occurred to you? It hadn't occurred to us either until we happened to read an article, "At the Ready, at the Sochi Games" in the *New York Times*. The article, about a company called Global Rescue, said that they evacuated over 200 people from Egypt during the Arab Spring, evacuated clients from Haiti after the 2010 earthquake, and helped a professional snow-boarder travel from New Zealand to the USA after he broke his neck while training (Martin, 2014). We were designing an executive education program for a company in the Middle East at the time and instantly became interested in the topic for personal as well as professional reasons. There are a number of companies that offer travel risk management services, including Global Rescue, International SOS, and iJET. International SOS defines duty of care as:

the moral and legal obligations of employers to their employees, contractors and related family members in maintaining their well-being, security and safety when working, posted on international assignments or working in remote areas of their home country. (International SOS, n.d.)

Although security tends to be at the forefront of one's mind today for many executives, there are numerous less newsworthy, but serious, threats that expatriates and their families may face, including political unrest, air pollution, natural disasters, illness, disease, traffic accidents, and crime. The bottom line is that companies need to develop a strategy and policies for assisting employees well in advance of crises.

Operating globally is different from operating at home, and those differences must be, and can be, understood. The costs of entering the global game can be high. But the experience can be rewarding financially for the corporation, as well as personally and professionally for the manager. A global viewpoint, an understanding of the culture, political and social situations, and a long-term commitment to global operations are essential.

Training and Preparation for an International Assignment

The training that a person undergoes before expatriation should be a function of the degree of cultural exposure that they will experience. Two dimensions of cultural exposure are the degree of integration into a culture and the duration of stay. The integration dimension represents the intensity of the exposure. A person could be sent to a foreign country on a short-term, technical, trouble-shooting matter and experience little significant contact with the local culture. The same person could be in another country only for a brief visit to negotiate a contract, but the cultural interaction could be very intense and might require a great deal of cultural fluency to be successful. An expatriate assigned abroad for a period of years is likely to experience a high degree of interaction with the local culture simply from living there.

The framework shown in Figure 6.1 suggests that developmental methodologies have different transformative potential that can be aligned to the nature of the international assignment. For example, for short stays with a low level of integration an "information-giving approach," such as area and cultural briefings and survival level language training will probably suffice. For longer stays with higher levels of integration, language training, role-plays, critical incidents, case studies, and possibly stress reduction training would be more appropriate. For people who will be living abroad for extended periods of time and/or will experience a high level of integration into the culture, extensive language training, sensitivity training, field experiences, and simulations are recommended training methodologies. Effective preparation would also stress the realities and difficulties of working in another culture and the importance of establishing good working relationships with the local people.

Characteristics of the "degree of experiential rigor" include the complexity of the experience; whether it generates affect (emotion); how intense the experience is; and how relevant it is to a person's career or goals.

The Canadian International Development Agency (CIDA) developed a useful approach for augmenting assignees' training for long-term international postings requiring high levels of cultural integration. After extensive pre-departure

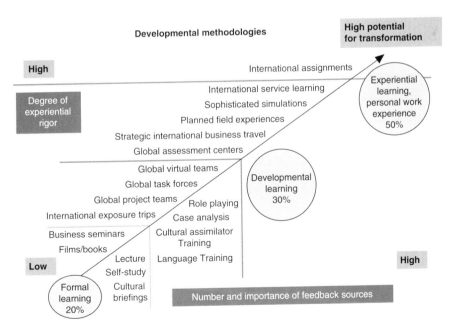

Figure 6.1 Relationship between developmental methodologies and the potential for personal transformation. Adapted from Mendenhall et al. (2017).

training in Canada, expatriates were sent to the field. Shortly after they began in their new posting, more training was provided to them along with their new co-workers, thus facilitating the process of assimilation into their new post. During the expatriates' stay abroad, periodic "refreshers" or debriefing sessions were held. Finally, the expatriates were actively involved in repatriation training both prior to and after their return home. The expatriate's spouse and family were also provided with similar training and resources.

Historically companies provided little, if any, cross-cultural training. But this is an area where some change has taken place. More companies are realizing the value of cross-cultural training and providing it to family members. Brookfield found that 84 percent of its respondents provided cross-cultural training for some or all of its international assignments. However, only 38 percent provided it for all assignments. Thirty-five percent offered it for the assignee and spouse/partner and 55 percent to the entire family. Historically, 44 percent of respondents provided preparation to the entire family and 30 percent to the international assignee and spouse/partner (Brookfield, 2015).

Adaptation and the Reality of Culture Shock

Despite a strong desire to understand and adapt to a new environment, assignees often experience some problems when entering another culture.

A condition associated with a possible failure to adapt – culture shock or, more appropriately, acculturative stress – is rooted in our psychological processes. The normal assumptions used by managers in their home cultures to interpret perceptions and to communicate intentions no longer work in the new cultural environment. Culture shock is not a shock experienced, for example, from exposure to conditions of poverty. Culture shock is the stress and behavioral patterns associated with a loss of control and a loss of sense of mastery in a situation. Culture shock, in normal attempts to socialize or in a business context, can result in confusion and frustration. Managers who are used to being competent in such situations may find that they are unable to operate effectively.

An inability to interpret surroundings and behave competently can lead to anxiety, frustration, and sometimes to more severe depression. Most experts agree that some form of culture shock probably is unavoidable, even by experienced internationalists. People who repeatedly move to new cultures likely dampen the emotional swings they experience and probably shorten the period of adjustment, but they do not escape it entirely. In fact, research on intercultural effectiveness has found that those who eventually become the most effective expatriates tend to report experiencing greater difficulty in their initial adjustment. This is because those who are more sensitive to different patterns of human interaction are likely to be disrupted by changes in these patterns and likely to become adept at new patterns.

There are four typical modes of responding to a new environment (Berry, 1980):

- Going Native (assimilation): "acceptance of the new culture while rejecting one's own culture";
- Being a Participator (integration): "adaptation to the new culture while retaining one's own culture";
- Being a Tourist (separation): "maintenance of one's own culture by avoiding contact with the new culture"; and
- Being an Outcast (marginalization): "the inability to either adapt to the new culture or remain comfortable with one's own culture."

The pattern experienced by people who move into a new culture usually comes in three phases as shown in Figure 6.2: (1) the elation associated with anticipating a new environment and the early period of moving into it; (2) the distress

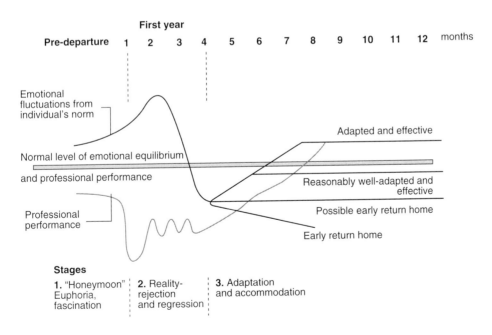

Figure 6.2 Acculturative stress

Adapted from C. Sargent, "Psychological Aspects of Environmental Adjustment" (unpublished paper, n.d.).

of dealing with one's own ineffectiveness and, as the novelty erodes and reality sets in, the realization that one has to live and function in a strange setting; and (3) the adjustment to and effective coping in the new environment.

During the first and second periods, performance is usually below one's normal level. The time of adjustment back to normal or above average performance takes from three to nine months, depending on previous experience, the degree of cultural difference being experienced, and the individual personality.

Frequently observed symptoms of culture shock are similar to most defensive or stress reactions. People reject their new environment as well as the people who live there, often with angry or negative evaluations of "strangeness." Other symptoms include: fatigue; tension; anxiety; excessive concern about hygiene; hostility; an obsession about being cheated; withdrawal into work, family, or the expatriate community; and, in extreme cases, excessive use of drugs or alcohol. The vast majority of people eventually begin to accept their new environment and adjust. Most emerge from the adjustment period performing adequately and some people perform more effectively than before. A smaller percentage either "go native," which is usually not an effective strategy, or experience very severe symptoms of inability to adjust such as panic attacks or even nervous breakdown.

Coping with Culture Shock

Different people have different ways of coping with culture shock. Normal stress management techniques, regular exercise, rest, and balanced diet are helpful. As noted earlier, some use work as a bridge until they adjust. Usually, the work environment does have some similarities to that of one's home culture. But for non-working spouses or partners who are often left to cope with the new environment on their own, the effects can be more severe.

Language training is one effective way of coping and provides an entry into the host culture. Education about the local history, geography, and traditions of the new culture and then exploration of the new environment also help adjustment. Whatever methods are employed, it is wise to remember that everyone experiences culture shock. Diligent preparation can moderate the effect, not eliminate it.

Support systems are especially important during the adjustment period. One obvious source of support is the family. Doing more things together as a family, more often, is a way to cope with the pressures. Another is to realize that it is acceptable to withdraw from the new culture, temporarily, for a respite such as reading newspapers from home or enjoying familiar food from a restaurant chain from home – if not carried too far. It is important to use such temporary interruptions to one's reality as bridges to the new culture, not as permanent anchors to an old environment.

In company situations, it must be understood that the international manager in a new culture goes through these stresses. Local colleagues should not be surprised at less than perfect performance or strange behavior and can provide crucial support for expatriate managers and their families. When one goes overseas, there are two jobs to accomplish. There is the obvious functional or technical job, such as engineering, finance, marketing, or plant management responsibilities. However, too often it is only this job that people identify, focus on, and prepare for. The other, less obvious, job is cultural adaptation. If you cannot adapt successfully, you may be requested to go (or may be sent) home early – often in a matter of months. Such a manager may never get a chance to use his or her technical or functional skills.

You do not have to leave your own country to experience culture shock, as the following demonstrates. A Canadian volunteer on a project in Ghana experienced the symptoms of culture shock, even after participating in an orientation program organized by the sponsoring agency. This same person reported severe symptoms of culture shock on returning to an urban-based MBA program. However, the ultimate culture shock came upon graduating and starting work for a manufacturer located in a small, rural community in one of Canada's Maritime Provinces. In all three experiences, the patterns were the same, and the sharpest disorientation occurred within this person's native country, perhaps because it was least expected. It is important to note that this individual also experienced a "reverse culture shock" on the return home.

Return Shock

"Reverse culture shock," "return shock," or "reentry shock" to one's home culture is an adjustment phenomenon that people need to be prepared for. There can be a significant readjustment to one's home country, especially if a manager has been away for a long period of time.

Osland points out that there can be a high degree of uncertainty surrounding one's career upon repatriation that, combined with a loss of prestige and autonomy of being abroad, may give an executive pause to think about his or her future career with the company (Osland, 1995). Both at work and in one's personal life, a returned international assignee may find that others lack interest in their experience. They have grown personally and changed during their assignment, but people at home only want to hear a 30-second summary of the experience. Their idealized image of how perfect the home country was and how well everything worked there is often shattered upon return. A person who worked for one of the authors in Nairobi, Kenya often commented about how she could not wait to get back to North America where the copy machines worked properly. When she returned she discovered that the copiers often broke down there as well. On a more personal level, returned assignees often find that they miss life abroad. All of these factors probably play a role in the attrition rate of returnees discussed in the next section.

The Return Home

The process of selecting the right people, training them properly, and sending them and their families to their foreign posting is not the end of the story. Reintegrating expatriates into the company after the foreign assignment so that the company can continue to benefit from their experience and expertise is important, and it also has proven to be a problem.

First, companies must contend with failure rates, defined as early return. There are estimates in the academic literature of failure rates of 20–50 percent for American expatriates but these high estimates have been called into question (Harzing, 2002). Respondents to Brookfield's survey in 2015 reported an early return rate of 6 percent. However, that number is still high, especially given the investments firms make in sending employees and their families abroad.

There are many reasons for failure or early return. Various surveys have reported causes such as the inability to demonstrate a global mindset, poor leadership skills, and an aversion to change or a lack of networking skills. Others have found that the key factors of expatriate failure were partner dissatisfaction, family concerns, inability to adapt, poor candidate selection, and the job not meeting the expatriate 's expectations. Usually the number one reason prompting early return is family-related issues such as partner/spouse dissatisfaction. Brookfield's research showed that the top three reasons for assignment failure were family-related issues (33 percent), poor candidate selection (18 percent), and an inability to adapt to the host country (18 percent).

Expatriate attrition also is a problem. Historically, the annual average turnover rate for assignees has been 10 percent, with 21 percent leaving during their tour of duty and 25 percent within the first year after returning. To minimize attrition, companies need to think more coherently about career-pathing for their expatriates and provide them with adequate repatriation support and a wider choice of positions after repatriation, so they can use their newly acquired international experience and skills.

Regardless of the exact numbers on failure rate or attrition, it pays to get the expatriate cycle right – the right people, the right preparation, and the right repatriation. The costs associated with expatriation are large and include moving costs, home leave, housing allowances, cost of living allowances, private international schooling for children, and preparation and language lessons. And these costs do not consider the personal costs to employees and their families from terminating an assignment early. If companies want to retain their internationally experienced managers, they will have to do a better job with their career management processes including the repatriation process. Ways to improve the repatriation process include using the international experience assignees bring home with them, offering job choices upon return, recognition, repatriation career support, family repatriation support, and improving evaluations during an assignment.

An international assignment is an important vehicle for developing global managers; achieving strategic management control; coordinating and integrating the global organization; and learning about international markets and competitors, as well as about foreign social, political, and economic situations. However, the idealized goal of becoming a global, learning organization will only be reached if the right people are selected for foreign assignments, trained properly, repatriated with care, valued for their experience, and then offered assignments that draw on their unique backgrounds.

Ongoing Talent Development: Important for all International Companies

Advances in global talent management have been notable in some companies where they have developed sophisticated talent pipelines with effective selection and development practices (Caligiuri, 2012). But, as we have said, mindful leaders are increasingly important for most companies, even those that don't consider themselves "global." The more that companies approach talent selection, development, and mobility rigorously, the more they will have a strong ongoing cadre of global leaders to help them navigate in the highly complex global environment.

Reflection Questions

This chapter's reflection questions are written in future tense, suggesting you anticipate upcoming international assignments in your career. You can adapt them to reflect on previous assignments, and/or to other people whose careers you are managing.

1. When you apply the equation $E = f(PAIS)$ to your career, which elements are you most likely to be strongest in? Which will you likely need to focus more on developing – Professional expertise, Adaptation, Intercultural interaction, or Situational readiness? What are the implications for how you should engage in your next assignment?

2. Different people find different kinds of conditions challenging – physical environment, social environment, distance from family and close friends, living conditions, and so on. Which are the kinds of conditions you are likely to find most challenging? Which are so extreme for you that you would try to avoid an assignment with those conditions? Which do you think you could manage with support? How can you prepare yourself for that possibility in the future?

3. Experiential development is the most effective way of developing global leadership competences and a global mindset. The experiences must be immersive and stretching, and the learner must engage mindfully, paying attention to context and process. What opportunities for experiential development can you build into your own career, even if your organization does not initiate an international assignment for you? How can you make the experience mindful for yourself? What other resources could you draw on?

Further Resources

Paula Caligiuri's book *Cultural Agility* (2012) is an excellent source on international talent in today's business environment.

To understand and keep up to date on what is happening in the corporate world regarding international assignments of executives, we recommend obtaining a copy of the latest Global Relocation Trends published by Brookfield Relocation Services and available at www.brookfieldgrs.com/insights_ideas/trends.asp.

For a more in-depth discussion of the issue and challenges of calculating ROI of international assignments see the following articles:

McNulty, Y., & De Cieri, H. (2009). Do Global Firms Measure Expatriate Return on Investment? An Empirical Examination of Measures, Barriers and Variables Influencing Global Staffing Practices. *International Journal of Human Resource Management*, 20, 1309–1326.

McNulty, Y., & De Cieri, H. (2011). Global Mobility in the 21st Century: Conceptualizing Expatriate Return on Investment in Global Firms. *Management International Review*, 51, 897–919.

Some suggested readings on the topic of culture shock include:

Grove, C. L., & Torbiörn, I. (1985). A New Conceptualization of Intercultural Adjustment and the Goals of Training. *International Journal of Intercultural Relations*, 9, 205–233.

Oberg, K. (1960). Culture Shock: Adjustment to New Cultural Environments. *Practical Anthropology*, 7, 177–182

Torbiorn, I. (1982). *Living Abroad: Personal Adjustment and Personnel Policy in the Overseas Setting*. John Wiley.

Research on stress and adapting to stressful situations also suggests that there are physiological contributions as well. One reference that links physiology and culture shock is:

Wederspahn, G. (1981). Culture Shock: It's All in Your Head … and Body. *The Bridge*, 6, 10.

An accessible, practitioner article on repatriation can be found at www.relocatemagazine .com/repatriation/repatriation-articles. See also the following articles for further discussions of repatriation:

Bossard, A. B., & Peterson, R. (2005). The Repatriate Experience as Seen by American Expatriates. *Journal of World Business*, 40, 9–27.

MacDonald, S., & Arthur, N. (2005). Connecting Career Management to Repatriation Adjustment. *Career Development Journal*, 10, 145–159.

Bibliography

Adler, N. J. (1987). Pacific Basin Managers: A Gaijn, Not a Woman. *Human Resource Management*, 26, 169–191.

Adler, N. J., & Izraeli, D. (1988). *Women in Management Worldwide*. M. E. Sharpe.

Ashby, R. (1972). *Design for a Brain*. Chapman Hall.

Ashby, R. (1973). *Introduction to Cybernetics*. Chapman Hall.

BCG (n.d.). *Leadership and Talent: Driving Value through Leadership and* talent development. Retrieved February 2017 from BCG People & Organization: www .bcg.com/capabilities/people-organization/leadership-talent.aspx

Beer, S. (1981). *Brain of the Firm: The Managerial Cybernetics of Organization*. John Wiley.

Berry, J. (1980). Acculturation as Varieties of Adaptation. In A. Padilla (ed.), *Acculturation: Theory, Model, and Some New Findings*. Westview Press.

Bolino, M., Klotz, A., & Turnley, W. (2017). Will Refusing an International Assignment Derail Your Career? *Harvard Business Review*, April 18. Available at: https://hbr.org/2017/04/will-refusing-an-international-assignment-derail-your-career

Brookfield (2015). *Mindful Mobility*. Global Mobility Trends Survey. Available at: http://docplayer.net/15337612-2015-global-mobility-trends-survey-report-mindful-mobility.html

Brookfield (2016). *Breakthrough to the Future of Global Talent Mobility.* Global Trends Mobility Survey. Available at: www.globalmobilitytrends.bgrs.com

Caligiuri, P. (2012). *Cultural Agility: Building a Pipeline of Successful Global Professionals.*Jossey-Bass.

Caligiuri, P., & Bonache, J. (2016). Evolving and Enduring Challenges in Global Mobility. *Journal of World Business*, 51, 127–141.

Caligiuri, P., & Cascio, W. (1998). Can We Send Her There? Maximizing the Success of Western Women on Global Assignments. *Journal of World Business*, 33, 394–516.

Chambers, E., Foulon, M., Handield-Jones, H., Hankin, S., & Michaels, E. (1998). The War for Talent. *The McKinsey Quarterly.* August.

Financial Times (n.d.). *Definition of Flexpatriate.* Retrieved from: http://lexicon.ft.com/Term?term=flexpatriate

Franke, J., & Nicholson, N. (2002). Who Shall We Send? Cultural and Other Influences on the Rating of Selection Criteria for Expatriate Assignments. *International Journal of Cross Cultural Management*, 2, 21–36.

Harnden, R., & Leonard, A. (1994). *How Many Grapes Went Into the Wine: Stafford Beer on the Art and Science of Holistic Management.* John Wiley.

Harzing, A.-W. (2001). Of Bears, Bumble-Bees, and Spiders: The Role of Expatriates in Controlling Foreign Subsidiaries. *Journal of World Business*, 36, 366–379.

Harzing, A.-W. (2002). Are Our Referencing Errors Undermining Our Scholarship and Credibility? The Case of Expatriate Failure Rates. *Journal of Organizational Behaviour*, 23, 127–148.

International SOS (n.d.). Retrieved October 2017 from International SOS: www.internationalsos.com/

Kealey, D. (1990). *Cross-Cultural Effectiveness: A Study of Canadian Technical Advisors Overseas.* Canadian International Development Agency.

Lane, H. W., Maznevski, M. L., Mendenhall, M., & McNett, J. M. (2004b). Globalization: Hercules Meets Buddha. In H. W. Lane, M. L. Maznevski, M. Mendenhall, & J. M. McNett (eds.), *The Blackwell Handbook of Global Management: A Guide to Managing Complexity.* Blackwell.

Martin, C. (2014). *At the Ready, at the Sochi Games, New York Times*, February 15. Retrieved October 2017 from: www.nytimes.com/2014/02/16/business/at-the-ready-at-the-sochi-games.html

Matteau, M. (1993). *Towards Meaningful and Effective Intercultural Encounters.* Intercultural Training and Briefing Centre, Canadian International Development Agency.

Mendenhall, M., Dunbar, E., & Oddou, G. (1987). Expatriate Selection, Training, and Career-Pathing: A Review and Critique. *Human Resource Management*, 26, 331–345.

Mendenhall, M., Osland, J., Bird, A., Oddou, G., Stevens, M., Maznevski, M., & Stahl, G. (2017). *Global Leadership: Research, Practice, and Development*, 3rd edn. Routledge.

Miller, E. (1973). The International Selection Decision: A Study of Some Dimensions of Managerial Behaviour in the Selection Decision Process. *Academy of Management Journal*, 16, 239–252.

Osland, J. (1995). *The Adventure of Working Abroad: Hero Tales from the Global Frontier.* Jossey-Bass.

Pate, J., & Scullion, H. (2016). The Flexpatriate Psychological Contract: A

Literature Review and Future Research Agenda. *International Journal of Human Resource Management*. Retrieved October 2017 from: https://doi .org/10.1111/j.1468-2370.2006.00123.x

Rohwer, J. (2000). GE Digs into Asia. *Fortune*, October 2.

Society for Human Resource Management (2017). *Managing International Assignments*, May 1. Retrieved October 2017 from: www.shrm.org/ resourcesandtools/tools-and-samples/ toolkits/pages/cms_010358.aspx

Stahl, G., Bjorkman, I., Farndale, E., Morris, S., Paauwe, J., Stiles, P., Trevor, J., & Wright, P. (2012). Six Principles of Effective Global Talent Management. *MIT Sloan Management Review*, 53, 25–32.

Weick, K., & Van Orden, P. (1990). Organizing on a Global Scale: A Research and Teaching Agenda. *Human Resource Management*, 29, 49–61.

Professor Henry W. Lane prepared this case solely to provide material for class discussion. The author does not intend to illustrate either effective or ineffective handling of a managerial situation. The author may have disguised certain names and other identifying information to protect confidentiality.

Ivey Management Services is the exclusive representative of the copyright holder and prohibits any form of reproduction, storage or transmittal without its written permission. Reproduction of this material is not covered under authorization by any reproduction rights organization. To order copies or request permission to reproduce materials, contact Ivey Publishing, Ivey Management Services, c/o Richard Ivey School of Business, The University of Western Ontario, London, Ontario, Canada, N6A 3K7; phone (519) 661-3208; fax (519) 661-3882; e-mail cases@ivey.uwo.ca.

Copyright © 2005, Northeastern University, College of Business Administration   Version: (A) 2009-09-28

Charles Foster was a U.S. national sales manager for a large multinational technology company headquartered in France. He was concerned about the availability of an important new disk drive that was selling better than anticipated. If he could obtain more of these drives, he was sure that they would sell. Since the product had just been launched with the company's various sales forces and distributors, Foster was worried about losing momentum. The sales force and distributors had literally thousands of products to sell and an availability problem could prove fatal to the product line, as the company's sales efforts were redirected to other products or customers chose to purchase from the competition.

The situation was complicated by the fact that the design and manufacturing of the drive had been assigned to a new Franco-Japanese joint venture (JV) located in France. Not only was the joint venture adapting to a new manufacturing system that had been introduced to produce the drive, it was also adapting to the joint venture's new organizational structure. As it tried to adapt, the joint venture encountered numerous complications, particularly those involving logistics.

Over the previous months, several attempts had been made to resolve the availability issue at lower levels but with no success. Foster decided that the problem had become serious enough to warrant the attention of his supervisor, Richard Howe, vice-president of sales for High Technology Products. Because Foster had a good, informal relationship with Howe, he decided to send him an email explaining the situation.

Howe forwarded Foster's email to Maurice LeBlanc, the head of the Strategic Business Unit (SBU) headquartered in France. In turn, LeBlanc, who previously had been head of new product development for the SBU, forwarded the email to Ahmed Hassan, president of the JV. Hassan, raised in the Middle East, had lived most of his adult life in France (see Exhibit 1).

The Phone Call

A couple of days after sending his email, Foster was in his office completing some sales reports when the phone rang. After he answered the phone, he immediately recognized the accented, emotion-laden voice that spilled out into the room.

This is Ahmed Hassan. Why are you writing such things to my boss in an email? Why are you saying so many negative things about my business? Why didn't you call me?

Foster was stunned. He did not know what Hassan was talking about or what to say. He recalled:

> Ahmed was absolutely livid. And he continued yelling at me for what seemed like an eternity.

Exhibit 1 Email String

1. Email to Richard Howe

To: Richard Howe/Techco@USHQ
Subject: Drives Availability – Further info on XD19

Dick,

I wanted to give you some further info on the XD19 stock situation.

I feel strongly that this is a precursor to what we are going to face when all of our manufacturing goes to the JV. I'm including my thoughts on what is going on and I would like your opinion on what we should do in the organization to get a handle on this before it gets too far out of hand. The issues we are facing seem to be driven by two main factors:

- Marketing is asking for forecasts on product use. Manufacturing does not believe them and makes their own forecasts based on run-rates and then ends up shipping even below that. I think that this is being driven by an inappropriately high emphasis on reducing inventory.
- The manufacturing for the XD19 is done in batches. It is often three to five months between batch runs for a specific drive. With such long lead-times, we are unable to respond to sudden swings in the market or new opportunities.

Our issues right now are magnified by a problem with the firmware[1] on the XD19. This issue is also illustrative of the types of problems that we need to prevent from happening with the JV:

- We have been using Version 07 firmware, but the JV is currently converting all of their stock to Version 08. The Version 08 firmware has a bug that does not provide true three-wire control in a keypad mode, which we consider a major safety issue.[2]
- The JV does not consider this to be a safety issue and has released this firmware for use outside of the U.S. We are going to have to live off of the remaining stock of Version 07 until the release of Version 09 next year.

---

[1] Firmware is a software program that is loaded onto a chip and cannot be modified. "Masked" firmware is etched onto the chip. "Flashable" firmware is not etched on a chip, and new versions can be downloaded onto the chip.

[2] Three-way wire control was "fail-safe" circuitry required in the United States but not required or used in the rest of the world.

Exhibit 1 (continued)

- This problem is magnified by the use of masked firmware instead of flashable. When there is a mistake, as there is in this case, we are stuck with it until the next set of masks is made. (There is a cost savings in using masked units, but I would be willing to bet that we have never realized it since we are always giving customers new drives and new control boards to cover our bugs.)
- The JV does not fully test functionality like we do, resulting in a huge list of bugs with each firmware release once we test it. We then have to live with these bugs until the next release and the next set of bugs. Since these releases are normally masked before we do our testing, the fixes can't be done on the fly.
- We are currently expediting Version 07 units from France to cover the shortfalls, but there are six catalog numbers that will need to be ordered from Japan. It is also likely that we will completely exhaust the remaining supply of Version 07 masks for all of the other sizes before production of the Version 09 firmware begins. With the batch lead times, I expect this to absolutely kill the XD19 launch and it will be a big hit on us for Core Product.

This is SCARY! If an opportunity comes along, forget about it, because we are still filling backlog. I already have OEM salespeople giving up on selling the XD19 because it is not in stock.

It is particularly frustrating being told that we are not meeting top-line objectives when we cannot even ship to the current level of sales.

Charles

2. Email to Maurice LeBlanc

To: Maurice LeBlanc/TechcoInt@HQFrance
Subject: Drives Availability – Further info on XD19

Maurice,

We are having an inventory problem with the XD19 (V07). The issue as I under-stand it is France does not have the inventory and we have to wait on the JV to build its next batch. In the meantime, we are losing orders due to lack of inventory.

I would like to see if you could talk with JV to expedite its manufacturing process as we need drives now. The list below contains the key part numbers that we need with Version 07.

Please see some other concerns identified by our Drives National Sales Manager – Charles Foster – in the attached email.

Thank you for any help you can provide.

Dick

3. Email to Ahmed Hassan

To: Ahmed Hassan/TechcoInt@JVFrance
Subject: Attached emails

Ahmed,

Is this correct what the emails from the U.S. say? Why aren't you following our Standard Protocol SPQ that dictates that we safety test products to the safety standards in the U.S.? I am concerned that the JV is not following our normal engineering review practice.

Maurice

🛡IVEY | Publishing

THE LEO BURNETT COMPANY LTD.: VIRTUAL TEAM MANAGEMENT

Elizabeth O'Neil prepared this case under the supervision of Professor Joerg Dietz and Fernando Olivera solely to provide material for class discussion. The authors do not intend to illustrate either effective or ineffective handling of a managerial situation. The authors may have disguised certain names and other identifying information to protect confidentiality.

This publication may not be transmitted, photocopied, digitized or otherwise reproduced in any form or by any means without the permission of the copyright holder. Reproduction of this material is not covered under authorization by any reproduction rights organization. To order copies or request permission to reproduce materials, contact Ivey Publishing, Ivey Business School, Western University, London, Ontario, Canada, N6G 0N1; (t) 519.661.3208; (e) cases@ivey.ca; www.iveycases.com.

Copyright © 2003, Richard Ivey School of Business Foundation

Version: 2018-06-04

Janet Carmichael, global account director for The Leo Burnett Company Ltd. (LB), United Kingdom, sat in her office wondering how to structure her global advertising team. The team was responsible for the introduction of a skin care product of one of LB's most important clients, Ontann Beauty Care (OBC). The product had launched in the Canadian and Taiwanese test markets earlier that year. Taiwanese sales and awareness levels for the product had been high but were low for the Canadian market. Typically, at this stage in the launch process, Carmichael would decentralize the communications management in each market, but the poor performance in the Canadian market left her with a difficult decision: should she maintain centralized control over the Canadian side of her team? In three days, she would leave for meetings at LB's Toronto, Canada office, where the team would expect her decision.

The Leo Burnett Company Ltd. BackGround

LB, which was founded in Chicago in 1935, was one of North America's premier advertising agencies. It had created numerous well-recognized North American brand icons, including The Marlboro Man, Kellogg's Tony the Tiger, and the Pillsbury Dough Boy.

In 2000, LB merged with two other global agencies to form b|com³ (the actual company name), one of the largest advertising holding companies in the world, but each LB office retained the Leo Burnett company name.

LB had expanded around the globe to include 93 offices in 83 markets. The company employed approximately 9,000 people, and worldwide revenues were approximately US$9 billion.

LB Services and Products

As a full-service agency, LB offered the complete range of marketing and communications services and products (see Exhibits 1 and 2). The company's marketing philosophy was to build "brand belief." The idea driving this philosophy was that true loyalty went beyond mere buying behavior. LB defined "believers" as customers who demonstrated both a believing attitude and loyal purchase behavior. The company strove to convert buyers into believers by building lasting customer affinity for the brand.

Exhibit 1: LB Agency Services

Traditional core agency services included:

Account Management

Account management worked in close partnership with planning, creative, media, production and the client to craft tightly focused advertising strategies, based on a deep understanding of the client's products, goals and competition, as well as insights into contemporary consumer behavior.

Creative Services

In most LB offices, creative was the largest department. Creatives focused its visual art and copywriting talents on turning strategic insights into advertising ideas. This department was a key part of each client's brand team and often interacted with both clients and clients' customers.

Planning

Planners conducted research to gain insights about the consumer and the marketplace. They also provided valuable input to the strategic and creative agency processes in the form of the implications raised by that research,

specifically combining that learning with information about a given product, the social context in which it fit and the psychology of the people who used it.

Media

Starcom was the media division for LB's parent holding company. Its role was to identify the most influential and efficient media vehicles to deliver brand communications to the appropriate audience.

Production

Production staff brought creative ideas to life with the highest quality execution in television, cinema, radio, print, outdoor, direct, point of sale, interactive or any other medium.

In addition to these core services, most offices also offered expertise in more specialized services, including:

- B2B Technology Marketing
- Direct and Database Marketing
- Health-care Marketing
- Interactive Marketing
- Multicultural Marketing
- Public Relations
- Sales Promotion and Event Marketing

One of the most important measures of an agency's success was the quality of the creative product that was developed to connect brands to their end consumers. Each local office strove to produce outstanding creative advertising to break through the clutter of marketing messages that the general public was subjected to daily, and truly reach the consumer in a memorable way. Award shows were held nationally and internationally to recognize this effort, one of the

most prestigious being the annual festival in Cannes, France. With each award, individual employees (usually the art director and copy writer who had worked together to develop the ad) were recognized, as was the local agency office where they worked. These creative accolades were instrumental in helping an office win new client business. Even within the global LB network, awards were given to the local offices that produced the most outstanding creative work.

Exhibit 2: LB Agency Products

Traditional Advertising Products

Television Broadcast Advertising – Usually 30-second (:30s) or 60-second (:60s) TV ads that ran during local or national television programming. This also included sponsoring specific programs, which usually consisted of a five-second announcement before or after the show, i.e., "This program is brought to you by …" accompanied by the visual of the sponsoring company's logo.

Radio Broadcast Advertising – Usually 15-, 20-, or 30-second (:15s, :20s, :30s) radio ads that were placed throughout local or national radio programming. Radio ads could include sponsoring specific programs, which usually consisted of a five-second announcement before or after the show, i.e. "This program brought to you by …"

Print Advertising – Included black and white and color print ads in local, national or trade newspapers, journals and magazines. Magazine ads could be single-page ads or double-page spreads (two pages facing each other.)

Exhibit 2 (continued)

Non-Traditional or "Below the Line" Advertising Products

Direct Marketing – Normally a series of mail-out items (letters, post cards, product samples, etc.) sent to a specifically targeted population(s) called "cells", e.g., companies might send promotional mail-outs to current customers, former customers who have not shopped with the company for a period or time, and new prospective customers – each of these groups would be considered a cell.

Digital or Interactive Marketing – Any marketing efforts that were delivered to the consumer online or by wireless networks (e.g., hand-held wireless devices). This could include Web site design and production, banner advertising and promotions on other Web sites, e-mail marketing, and internal corporate marketing tools such as customer relationship marketing or database building tools.

Collateral – Any piece of print material that was not strictly advertising, for instance brochures, annual reports, posters, flyers and in-store materials.

Promotions – Any marketing effort that included a time-limited offer or incentive to either purchase a product or offer personal data. Promotions could involve advertising, direct marketing, interactive marketing, product packaging and/or outdoor marketing.

LB Internal Team Structures

A multidisciplinary team serviced each brand. Each team had representatives from all core areas of the agency as well as members from the specialized services as appropriate for the brand. In most cases, team members had two sets of reporting lines.

First and formally, they directly reported to the supervisor of their home department (for example, account management). It was this formal supervisor who was responsible for conducting performance evaluations and assigning and managing an employee's workload.

Informally, the team members reported to a project team leader, the senior account services person, who usually was an account director or a vice-president of client services director. It was this team leader's responsibility to manage the project in question, ensure that the client was satisfied with project progress, and build and manage the overall relationship between the client and the agency. Employees on the project team would be responsible to this person for meeting project deadlines and managing their individual client relationships. This team leader would often provide input to a team member's performance evaluation, along with other agency colleagues (see Exhibit 3).

At any given time, an agency employee typically worked on two or three different brand teams, virtually all of them face-to-face teams servicing local clients.

LB Typical Office Environment

Most LB employees were young (in their 20s and 30s) and worked about 60 hours per week. Client needs and project deadlines dictated work priorities, and the volume of work often required late nights at the office. Agency office environments were often open-concept and social. Employees spent many hours each day up and about, discussing projects with colleagues and responding to client requests. The pace was fast and the general spirit was one of camaraderie; it was common for LB employees to socialize together after a late night at the office.

LB Toronto

LB's Toronto office was founded in 1952 to service the Canadian arms of the Chicago-based clients. It was LB's first expansion beyond Chicago. It employed a staff of approximately 200 people and billings were approximately $200 million.

Exhibit 3: Lb Agency Formal and Informal Reporting Lines

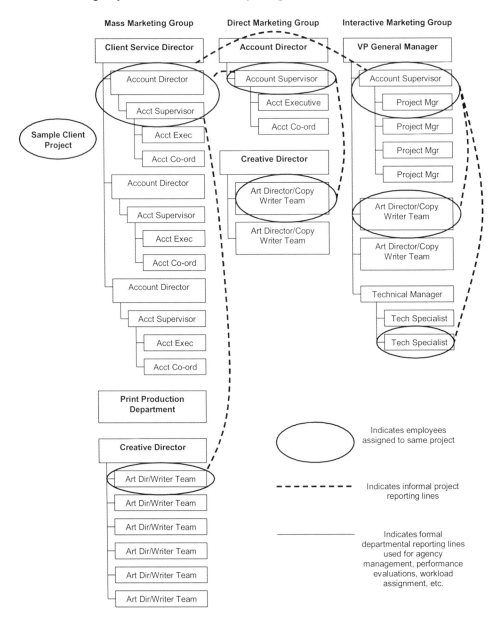

LB United Kingdom

LB acquired its London, United Kingdom, office in the mid-1970s as part of an expansion into Europe. The office had grown to over 350 employees and billings were approximately $400 million. London was also the regional LB headquarters for all European, Middle Eastern and African offices.

LB's Relationship with Ontann Beauty Care

Ontann Beauty Care (OBC)

OBC was a leading global manufacturer of health and beauty care products. OBC made a strategic decision to centralize the global marketing of its brands and products, designating a global team to define the global strategy for a given brand and develop the core communication materials as templates for local markets to follow. Local offices were given the responsibility for adapting the global materials and developing local "below the line" (BTL) materials, which would synergize with the global vision and creative templates. Below the line materials included direct marketing, in-store materials, digital marketing, public relations and promotions (that is, everything except strict advertising). In practice, on established brands with well-defined communication templates and strong local knowledge, some local markets (at least key regional markets) were awarded more opportunity to develop their own communication material. The global team, however, retained veto power to ensure all communications were building a consistent personality and look for the brand.

Each OBC global office had as many teams as it had brands. An OBC brand team usually consisted of the global category director, the brand manager and an assistant brand manager, plus a representative from each of the various departments: marketing technology, consumer, trade/distribution, PR, sales, product development, and production.

Relationship Between LB and OBC

OBC, which, like LB, was founded in Chicago, was one of LB's original clients. As one of the top three LB clients worldwide, OBC did business with most LB offices. OBC, however, awarded its business to advertising agencies brand-by-brand. As a result, other advertising agencies also had business with OBC. Competition among advertising agencies for OBC business was strong, in particular when they had to work together on joint brand promotions.

OBC had been a client of LB's Toronto office since 1958 and of LB's London office since its acquisition in the mid-1970s. Both the Toronto and London offices initially developed advertising and communications materials for various OBC facial care brands and eventually also worked on OBC's skin care brands.

To better service OBC, LB also centralized its decision-making for this client's brands and appointed expanded and strengthened global teams with the power to make global decisions. For its other clients, LB's global teams were significantly smaller, tending to consist simply of one very senior LB manager who shared learning from across the globe with a given client's senior management.

A New OBC Brand: Forever Young

The OBC London office announced a new skin care line called "Forever Young." Product formulas were based on a newly patented process that addressed the needs of aging skin. For OBC, this brand presented an opportunity to address a new market segment: the rapidly growing population of people over the age of 50. The product line was more extensive than other OBC skin care brands. It also represented the company's first foray into premium-priced skin care products. Product cost, on average, was double that of most other OBC brands, falling between drug store products and designer products. OBC intended Forever Young to be its next big global launch and awarded the Forever Young advertising and brand communications business to LB.

Global Advertising and Communications Team for Forever Young

Team Formation

For LB, a successful launch of this new product would significantly increase revenues and the likelihood of acquiring additional global OBC brands. An unsuccessful launch would risk the relationship with OBC that LB had built over so many years. LB management in Chicago decided that LB London would be the global team headquarters. This decision reflected the experience that the London office had in leading global business teams and the proximity to the OBC global team for Forever Young. It was also likely that the United Kingdom would be the test market for the new product.

In LB's London office, Janet Carmichael was assigned as brand team leader for the Forever Young product. Carmichael was the global account director for OBC. The 41-year-old Carmichael, a Canadian, had begun her career at LB Toronto as an account executive, after completing an MBA degree at the University of Toronto. Later, Carmichael moved to Europe, where she continued her career with LB. She became an account supervisor in Italy, an account director in Belgium, and finally a regional and global account director in Germany before taking on a global account director role on OBC brands in the United Kingdom. She was very familiar with OBC's business and had built excellent relationships with the OBC skin care client group.

LB's initial Forever Young brand team had six members who were all employees of the London office: Carmichael as the team leader, an account director, an account executive (she formally supervised these two employees), the agency's creative director, and two "creatives" (an art director and a copy writer). Carmichael outlined a project timetable (see Exhibit 4).The LB team worked with the OBC team on consumer research, market exploration, brand creative concepts (creative), packaging samples and global copy testing throughout North America and Europe. Carmichael viewed marketing a new product to a new consumer segment in a crowded category as challenging; however, after several months of testing, LB's Forever Young brand team developed a unique creative concept that was well received by OBC.

OBC decided that the United Kingdom would be the lead market for another skin care product. Because North America was a priority for the Forever Young brand and Canada was "clean" (that is, OBC was not testing other products in Canada at that time), Canada became the new primary test market for Forever Young. In addition, Canadians' personal skin care habits and the distribution process for skin care products were more reflective of overall Western practices (i.e., the Western world) than were those in other potential test markets. Taiwan became the secondary test market for Asian consumers. These choices were consistent with OBC's interest in global brand validation.

In keeping with OBC's team structures, LB maintained the global brand team in London and formed satellite teams in Toronto, Canada, and Taipei, Taiwan, to manage material execution in their local markets. It was up to the LB Toronto and Taipei offices to determine their members in the Forever Young satellite teams. In Taipei, Cathy Lee, an account director who was particularly interested in the assignment, took the lead on local agency activities. In Toronto, Geoff Davids, an account supervisor from the direct

Exhibit 4: Brand Development Chronology

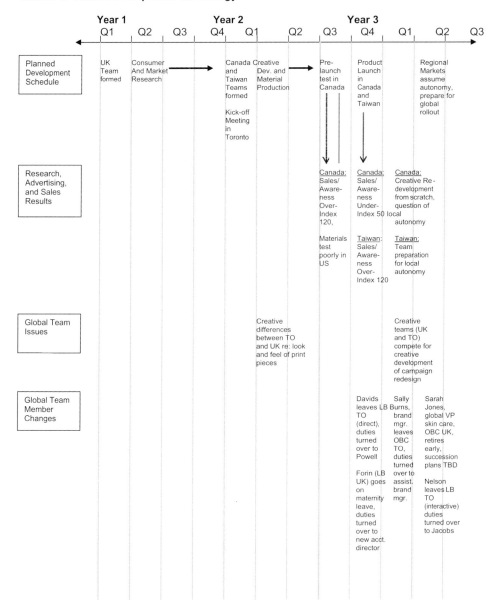

	Year 1 Q1	Q2	Q3	Year 2 Q4	Q1	Q2	Year 3 Q3	Q4	Q1	Q2	Q3
Planned Development Schedule	UK Team formed	Consumer And Market Research		Canada and Taiwan Teams formed / Kick-off Meeting in Toronto	Creative Dev. and Material Production		Pre-launch test in Canada	Product Launch in Canada and Taiwan		Regional Markets assume autonomy, prepare for global rollout	
Research, Advertising, and Sales Results							Canada: Sales/Aware-ness Over-Index 120, / Materials test poorly in US	Canada: Sales/Aware-ness Under-Index 50 / Taiwan: Sales/Aware-ness Over-Index 120	Canada: Creative Re-development from scratch, question of local autonomy / Taiwan: Team preparation for local autonomy		
Global Team Issues					Creative differences between TO and UK re: look and feel of print pieces				Creative teams (UK and TO) compete for creative development of campaign redesign		
Global Team Member Changes							Davids leaves LB TO (direct), duties turned over to Powell / Forin (LB UK) goes on maternity leave, duties turned over to new acct. director	Sally Burns, brand mgr. leaves OBC TO, duties turned over to assist. brand mgr.	Sarah Jones, global VP skin care, OBC UK, retires early, succession plans TBD / Nelson leaves LB TO (interactive) duties turned over to Jacobs		

marketing group, was assigned to lead the Toronto team. The global brand team and the two satellite teams now formed the LB side of the global advertising and communications team for Forever Young (see Exhibit 5).

Kick-off Meeting

A face-to-face kick-off meeting took place in Toronto with the intent to bring all senior members of LB's and OBC's London, Toronto, and Taipei teams onto the same

Exhibit 5: The Global Forever Young Team

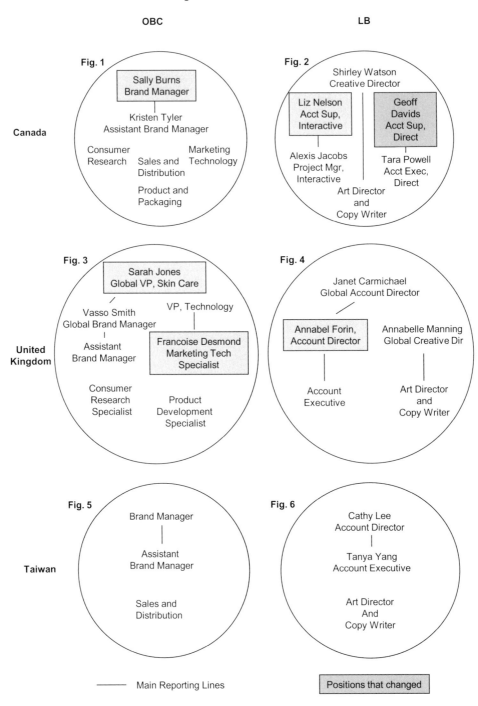

page regarding the new brand and the status of the launch process. One or two senior representatives from OBC London, Toronto, and Taipei participated in the meeting. From LB, the complete London team participated, along with Geoff Davids and a senior agency representative from the Toronto office, and Cathy Lee and a senior agency representative from the Taipei office. Carmichael and her U.K. team members shared their initial brand creative concepts, which had already garnered admiration throughout the LB network, and their knowledge about the product and target audience.

It was decided that Davids and Lee would serve as the main links to LB's London-based global brand team. Specifically, Davids and Lee reported to Annabel Forin, Carmichael's account director in the United Kingdom. Forin then reported to Carmichael and OBC's London team. Besides Forin, Carmichael's primary contacts would be Annabelle Manning, the global creative director at LB United Kingdom, and Sarah Jones, OBC's global vice-president of skin care in London. All work produced by LB's satellite teams would require approval from LB's London team.

The Creative Assignments

The creative assignments for the Canadian and Taiwanese teams were slightly different from each other. Normally, the global team would produce a creative template for a brand (meaning the design of the advertising and communications materials), which would then be passed to the satellite teams to be adapted for the local market.

In the Taiwanese market, this would be the case. The Taiwanese LB team would be responsible for adapting the advertising materials, which would include re-filming the television ad to star an Asian actress, as well as retaking photos for the print ads, again, to demonstrate product benefits on Asian skin. The brand message (meaning the

text in print ads and the vocal message in television ads) would be adapted to appeal to the Taiwanese audience.

In Toronto, however, the assignment broke from this traditional format. The LB team in London would produce English television and print advertising, which would be used in the Canadian market. The LB team in Toronto would design and produce the direct marketing and website materials because the London office did not have strong in-house capabilities in these areas. While the Toronto office would have control of the design of these communication pieces, the U.K. office would require that certain elements be incorporated into the design (for example, specific photos and colors), in order for the pieces to be visually consistent with the print advertising.

Events Leading up to the Launch

LB's Taipei Office

After returning to Taipei from the kick-off meeting, Lee formed her local team, which consisted of an account executive (Tanya Yang) and a creative team (one art director and one copy writer). In co-operation with OBC's Taipei team, Lee and her team focused first on recreating the television ad. The ad followed the original creative idea developed in the United Kingdom but used a popular Taiwanese actress in the lead. The character differentiation was necessary to demonstrate the product's benefit for Asian skin because the original ad featured a blond, Caucasian actress as the lead. The team moved on to adapt the brand's print advertising and direct marketing pieces, and developed a public relations campaign to meet local market needs. These communication elements were visually and strategically consistent with the television ad as they incorporated photos of the same Taiwanese actress.

Throughout this process, the Taipei team regularly updated LB's and OBC's London teams about its progress. Although all work required U.K. approval, the Taiwanese team worked with a significant amount of autonomy because of the cultural differences present in its market. Carmichael and Manning occasionally travelled to Taiwan to meet with the team and approve its creative work, which they generally received well. In addition, the Taipei team communicated with the London offices through videoconference calls and e-mail. The LB Taipei and Toronto teams had contact with each other only during the global team videoconference meetings, held every two months.

LB's Toronto Office

After the kick-off meeting, Davids, with the approval of LB's Toronto management, assigned representatives from the direct marketing group and the interactive marketing group to the brand team. This included account management (Tara Powell, account executive for direct; Liz Nelson, account supervisor; and Alexis Jacobs, project manager for interactive) and creative staff (Shirley Watson, creative director; and one copy writer from each of the direct and interactive groups).

In co-operation with OBC's Toronto team, the LB Toronto team was responsible for developing a full communication plan for its local market. Along with running the television and print ads developed in the United Kingdom, the team would focus on producing the brand's below the line materials (i.e., direct mail, website). These communication elements served as the education pieces that supplemented the TV ad. Davids conducted an internal team debrief, outlining the information he had received at the kick-off meeting. From this, the team developed a communications plan that, in Carmichael's opinion, was "on-brief" (i.e., consistent with the original brand strategic

direction) and included some very innovative thinking.

Next, the team began determining a creative look and feel for the direct mail pieces. The look and feel could be different from the television creative but had to be consistent across all of the paper-based (print ads, direct mail pieces and in-store materials) and online communication elements. The creatives on LB's Toronto team developed the direct marketing materials, and, simultaneously, the creatives on LB's U.K. team developed the print advertising. The two sides' creative work evolved in different directions, but each side hoped that the other would adapt their look and feel. Eventually, however, LB's Toronto team told its London counterpart to "figure it out," and they would follow London's lead. Communication between the two sides mostly flowed through Davids and Forin to Carmichael. Carmichael, however, had received a copy of the following e-mail from Watson to Davids:

Geoff, as you know, it's always a challenge to work with someone else's art direction. I don't think the model that London chose is right for this market, and the photography we have to work with doesn't have as contemporary a feel as I would like.

This would be easier if I could connect directly with Annabelle [Manning] but she's on the road so much of the time it's hard to catch her. We weren't asked for our opinion initially and, given the timing constraints at this point, we don't have much choice but to use what they've sent us, but could you please convey to Annabel [Forin] that in the future, if possible, we'd like to have the chance to input on the photography before it's taken? It will help us develop good direct mail creative.

For now, though, I think we'll be able to do something with what they've sent us. Thanks.

There had been other challenges for LB's Toronto team. Davids described an incident that had occurred when his direct marketing team tried to present its creative concept to the team in the United Kingdom during a videoconference meeting:

Our direct mail concept was a three-panel, folded piece. We sent two flat files to the United Kingdom via e-mail, which were to be cut out, pasted back-to-back [to form the front and back of the piece] and then folded into thirds. It took us *so* long to explain how to do that—somehow we just weren't getting through! Our colleagues in London cut and folded and pasted in different places, and what should have been a simple preliminary procedure took up 45 minutes of our one-hour videoconference meeting! By the time we actually got around to discussing the layout of the piece, everyone on the call was frustrated. That's never a good frame of mind to be in when reviewing and critiquing a new layout. It's too bad our clients were on that call as well.

A greater challenge came when the team was behind schedule in the development of the website after encountering difficulties with OBC's technology standards. The budgeting for the website development came out of the global budget, not the local budget. This meant that the members of LB's Toronto team who were responsible for the website development ("interactive marketing") received directions from OBC's London team. The budgeting for direct marketing, however, came out of the local budget, and the members of LB's Toronto team who were responsible for the development of the direct marketing materials dealt with OBC's Toronto team. The instructions from these two OBC teams were often inconsistent. Compounding matters, the two OBC client teams repeatedly requested changes of the Web and direct marketing materials, which made these materials even more different from each other and forced the LB Toronto team into extremely tight timeframes.

Carmichael learned about this sort of difficulty mostly through the direct supervisors of the team members. She frequently received calls from LB Toronto's Interactive Marketing Group and Direct Marketing Group senior managers. Carmichael repeatedly had to explain the basic project components to these senior managers and wished that the members of LB's Toronto team would just follow the team communications protocol and forward their concerns to Davids, who would then take up matters as necessary with the U.K. team.

Canadian Pre-Launch Test

Despite these challenges, LB's Toronto team produced the materials in time for the Canadian pre-launch test. The pre-launch test was a launch of the complete communications program (TV ad, newspaper inserts, distribution of trial packs, direct mail, and a website launch) in a market whose media could be completely isolated. A small town in the interior of British Columbia, Canada's most westerly province, met these conditions. In terms of product trial and product sales as a percentage of market share, the test indexed 120 against its objectives, which had a base index of 100. Subsequently, OBC and LB decided to move immediately into research to test the advertising in the U.S. market. The global OBC and LB teams worked with their Canadian counterparts to conduct this research, the results of which were very poor. As a result, OBC London required that LB's London and Toronto teams revised the advertising materials even before the Canadian launch.

Canadian National Launch

The days before the launch were panic-filled, as LB's London and Toronto teams scrambled to revise the advertising. In February 2001, the campaign was launched in Canada with the following elements:

- One 30-second TV ad;
- One direct mail piece;
- The English website;
- Product samples available from the web, from direct mail piece, and from an in-store coupon;
- Specially designed in-store displays;
- Trial-sized package bundles (one week's worth);
- A public relations campaign; and
- Five print ads in national magazines.

Research following the national launch showed that the brand did not perform well among Canadian consumers. It indexed 50 against a base index of 100. Because of the success of the Canadian pre-launch test, OBC and LB were surprised. The Forever Young global advertising and communications team attributed the discrepancy between the pre-launch test and national launch, in part, to the fact that the pre-launch test conditions were not replicable on a national scale. The audience penetration in the small B.C. town, the pre-test site, was significantly greater than it was in the national launch. OBC decided that the results of the Canadian launch were below "action standards," meaning that OBC would not even consider a roll-out into the U.S. market at the current time.

The tension levels on both LB's side and OBC's side of the Forever Young global advertising and communications team were high. LB's future business on the brand was in jeopardy. The OBC side was under tremendous pressure internally to improve brand trial and market share metrics, and already planned to decentralize the local teams for the global product rollout. Despite numerous revisions to the advertising, it never tested well enough to convince OBC that a U.S. or European launch would be successful.

A Different Story in Asia

In Taiwan, the product launch was successful. Test results showed that the brand was indexing 120 per cent against brand objectives. Research also showed that Taiwanese consumers, in contrast to Canadian consumers, did not perceive some of the advertising elements as "violent." Moreover, in Taiwan, overall research scores in terms of "likeability" and "whether or not the advertising would inspire you to try the product" were higher, leading to higher sales. The Taiwanese team was ready to take on more local-market responsibility and move into the post-launch phase of the advertising campaign. This phase would involve creating new ads to build on the initial success and grow sales in the market.

Recovery Plan for Canada

LB needed to take drastic measures to develop a new Forever Young campaign in order to improve the brand's performance in the Canadian marketplace. Whereas, before the launch, there had been a clear division of responsibilities (with the United Kingdom developing the television and print advertising and Canada developing direct marketing, in-store and website communications), now the global LB team in London decided that it would be necessary to have all hands on deck. New creative teams from the mass advertising department in the Toronto office, as well as supplementary creative teams from the London office, were briefed to develop new campaign ideas. Each team had only three weeks to develop their new ideas, less than half of the eight weeks they would normally have, and the teams had to work independent of each other. The London and Toronto creative teams had to present their concepts to the entire global OBC and LB teams at the same time. Subsequently, the results of market research would determine the winning creative concept. Squabbling between the offices began over which team would present first, which office received what compensation for the development, and whether or not overall remuneration packages were fair. Moreover, the communication between the account services members of LB's London and Toronto teams, which was the primary communication channel between the two agencies, became less frequent, less candid and more formal. The presentations took place in Toronto. Watson, the creative director in Toronto, commented:

> This process has been exciting, but we're near the ends of our collective ropes now. We have a new mass advertising creative team [who specialized in TV ads] on the business in Toronto, and they're being expected to produce world-class creative results for a brand they've only heard about for the past few days. They don't— and couldn't possibly—have the same passion for the brand that the direct marketing creative team members have after working on it for so long. I'm having a hard time motivating them to work under these tight timelines.
>
> We're even more isolated now in Toronto. Our connection to the creative teams and the global creative director in London was distant at best, and now it's non-existent. And our relationship with the local OBC client feels very remote, too. Still, we're moving forward with our work. We're trying to learn from the Taiwanese experience and are considering what success we would have with a nationally recognized actress starring in our television ads.

Evolution of the Forever Young Global Advertising and Communcations Team

Personnel Changes

Numerous personnel changes in the Forever Young global advertising and communications team occurred (see Exhibit 5). In LB's London office, Forin, the U.K. account director, had been replaced following her departure for maternity leave. In OBC's London office, Sarah Jones, the global vice-president for skin care, took early retirement without putting a succession plan in place. In LB's Toronto office, Davids, the Toronto brand team leader, had left the agency. Tara Powell, who had reported to Davids, took on his responsibilities, but she had not met most of the global team members. Liz Nelson, the account supervisor for interactive, left LB's Toronto office to return to school. Alexis Jacobs, who had managed the website development, took over her responsibilities. Powell and Jacobs did not have close relationships with their international counterparts. At OBC Toronto, Sally Burns, the local brand manager who had been LB's main contact in the local market and had been with the brand since inception, left OBC. LB's and OBC's Taiwanese teams remained stable over time. Cathy Lee worked with a team that was nearly identical to her initial team.

Communications

Early on, after the kick-off meeting, Carmichael had orchestrated frequent face-to-face meetings to ensure clarity of communication and sufficient information sharing. In the following months, the team relied on videoconferences and phone calls, with visits back and forth between London and Toronto on occasion. Later, the team had relied increasingly on e-mails and telephone calls to communicate. Carmichael noted that the communication had become more formal, and she had lost the feeling of being part of a global team. She wondered if giving the LB's Toronto team more autonomy to develop the brand in their market would help the brand progress. Working together as a smaller team might improve the Toronto group's team dynamic as well. Carmichael was concerned that the current discord between LB's London and Toronto offices would negatively affect the relationship to OBC.

Budget Problems

The extra creative teams assigned to the redevelopment of the brand's television advertising and the unexpected changes to the Forever Young communication materials had meant that LB's costs to staff the project had been higher than originally estimated and higher than the revenues that had been negotiated with OBC. Since OBC did not want to pay more for its advertising than had been originally budgeted, LB faced tremendous internal pressure to finish the project as soon as possible. This situation created conflict between LB and OBC in the United Kingdom, who was responsible for negotiating LB's overall fees. Because all fees were paid to the global brand office (in this case, LB's London office) and then transferred to the local satellite teams, this situation also created conflict between LB's London and Toronto teams, who had both expended additional staff time to revise the advertising materials and wanted "fair" compensation.

What Next?

In three days, Carmichael had to leave for Toronto to sit in research sessions to test the recently presented new creative concepts. In the meetings that followed, she would present to the team her recommendation for how to move forward with the brand. Carmichael reviewed the brand events and team interaction of the past two years (see Exhibit 4) to determine the best global team structure for salvaging the Forever Young brand and maintaining the relationship between OBC and LB.

Carmichael felt torn in her loyalties. On the one hand, she was Canadian and knew LB's Toronto office well—she knew that LB's Toronto brand team worked hard, and she wished them every success. On the other

hand, she had now worked in LB's London office for several years, and she had always liked the creative that the U.K. team had initially produced. If she maintained the current form of centralized control of the team, either creative concept might be chosen; however, if she decentralized team control, the Toronto team would almost certainly choose their own creative concept for the television ads. Since the creative direction chosen now would become the brand's advertising in most North American and European markets, it needed to be top calibre. Carmichael thought this posed a risk if the creative development was left to the new Toronto-based mass advertising creative team. It would be a shame to lose the U.K. team's original creative concept.

In making her decision on whether to decentralize the team, Carmichael considered the following:

1. Where was the knowledge necessary to create a competitive advantage for the brand in Canada? Would it be in the Canadian marketplace because they understood the market, or would it be in London because they had more in-depth knowledge of the brand?
2. Where was the client responsibility, and where should it be? Now that the London-based global vice-president of skin care was retiring, the client was considering creating a virtual global team to manage the brand, headquartered in the United States but composed of members of the original United Kingdom OBC team, in preparation for a U.S. launch. If the client team had its headquarters in North America, should LB also structure its team this way?
3. If Carmichael decentralized the brand and gave the Toronto team greater autonomy, who would lead the brand in Toronto now that Davids had left the agency?

How would the necessary knowledge be imparted to the new leader?

4. If they remained centralized, would the team make it through before it self-destructed? How much would this risk the client relationship? To what extent would it strain the already tight budget?

Carmichael had to make a decision that was best for the brand, LB and OBC.

🛡IVEY | Publishing

SOPHIA TANNIS: THE EUROPEAN TRANSFER

Kanina Blanchard wrote this case under the supervision of Professor Gerard Seijts solely to provide material for class discussion. The authors do not intend to illustrate either effective or ineffective handling of a managerial situation. The authors may have disguised certain names and other identifying information to protect confidentiality.

This publication may not be transmitted, photocopied, digitized or otherwise reproduced in any form or by any means without the permission of the copyright holder. Reproduction of this material is not covered under authorization by any reproduction rights organization. To order copies or request permission to reproduce materials, contact Ivey Publishing, Ivey Business School, Western University, London, Ontario, Canada, N6G 0N1; (t) 519.661.3208; (e) cases@ivey.ca; www .iveycases.com.

Copyright © 2013, Richard Ivey School of Business Foundation

Version: 2013-07-31

Introduction

Imagine day one in a new job, in a new business, in a new country. In fact, you are on a new continent. Now imagine that you have just met your most important internal business partner, who greeted you with this opening salvo:

> So you are the one? The one who is supposed to replace Antonio Vella? You know the man speaks seven languages? He is a good friend. He knows the business completely after 20-some years. He knows everyone... . So tell me, how do you plan to replace him, dear?

Well Sophia Tannis didn't need to imagine it – the words remained etched in her memory. It had been in 2002, on the first day of her European assignment.

Tannis was the first senior female leader to be moved by her company to its European headquarters in Switzerland. And she had a dual career and two young children. It was a dream location, a make-or-break assignment and a professional chance of a lifetime. It was her opportunity to fly high or flop in front of the entire organization.

Corporate Context

In 2002, Tannis worked for CPA Solutions (CPA), a Fortune 100 company with more than $20 billion[1] in annual sales. CPA was a leading global industrial company that offered a wide array of chemical, plastic and agricultural products and services. Employing approximately 40,000 people worldwide, CPA manufactured its products at more than 100 sites in dozens of countries across the globe.

As a company operating across national and political boundaries and regulatory regimes, CPA faced the ongoing challenge of balancing the need for a strong, consistent global corporate brand with the imperative of being locally relevant to customers and other stakeholders, including governments, non-governmental organizations (NGOs) and other decision makers. This challenge presented itself in almost all aspects of company activity, including researching and developing products; marketing, sales and service; policies relating to human resources

---

[1] All currency amounts are in U.S. dollars unless otherwise noted.

and information technology; stakeholder outreach initiatives and advocacy efforts on key issues, ranging from taxation to legislation.[2]

Tannis's new role was about leading change and recalibrating that very balance in relation to one of the company's biggest and most impactful businesses. It meant changing some long-held beliefs and ways of doing things, such as how key issues and decisions would be made. It also meant recalibrating the power base, which meant some big challenges ahead – and strong opposition.

Tannis's Task

Tannis was, at the time, the first woman to join the exclusively male-dominated energy business run out of Europe. She was charged with revitalizing the business culture, which, although very successful based on financial metrics, had become entrenched and operated as a stereotypic "old boys' club." The culture wasn't in line with the broader company culture, and issues around attraction and retention of women and minorities had become a growing issue.

Her first challenge, though, was to create and establish a more collaborative way for the entire organization internally (in Europe and globally) to develop and implement consistent strategies, policies and lobbying

efforts related to energy policy and associated issues.

Thus far, CPA had empowered its European-led energy business to develop the company approach on energy policy and associated issues. With Europe having been the center of action on the issues for more than a decade, the approach had been sound. The work done had been thoughtful, analytical, and technically focussed. Decisions on company positioning were made at the highest levels in Europe and were professionally conveyed in Brussels, either directly or through trade associations. The organizational culture at the time, however, did not encourage information sharing, brainstorming, transparency or garnering buy-in to ensure consistency of positions and messages across geographies and businesses. As a result, although consistent messages were being shared at the highest levels in the European Union, company leaders in European member states and business leaders in other geographies (e.g., Canada and Brazil) worked essentially independently to convey their views at the local level.

By early 2000, however, CPA management had started to envisage how political, legislative and regulatory decisions on energy and related issues globally would start to affect the bottom line. By 2002, the company decided it needed someone with a proven track record to work across boundaries, both physical and cultural, to deliver comprehensive and big-picture positions and solutions to enable a one-company voice on such key issues. That someone was Tannis.

Why Tannis?

Tannis had joined the multinational company 11 years earlier and had steadily moved up, achieving higher profile roles and responsibilities. The company, well known for providing career development opportunities, had yet to disappoint Tannis in her pursuit for challenge and growth.

---

[2] Global companies regularly deal with these "balancing act" challenges. Examples include but are not limited to situations where corporate strategies on critical matters such as pandemic planning conflict with national priorities, information security laws in one jurisdiction contravene corporate policy, one nation legally requires a unique level of engagement with unionized workforces that relies on significant resource commitments, company practices around gift giving are viewed as offensive to some nationalities and cultures, and NGOs expect global companies to offer commensurate benefits regardless of country of employment. Such realities require flexibility but also create risks for high-profile multinational organizations.

Tannis had demonstrated her skills and ability to take on complex and challenging assignments across a variety of functions, businesses, and geographies. In her first global role after only four years in the company, she had been assigned to re-haul a key business process, working with two dozen tenured and established professionals around the world. She had accepted the assignment, which required her to deliver the new process within a year and to do so without any formal control or authority. In some ways naive, she hadn't balked at being told to use influence and persuasion to have her colleagues realize their jobs were redundant and that the work they had been doing for years needed a complete change!

After not only succeeding in that role but being recognized, along with her team, in industry publications and even through an international best practice award, Tannis had gone on to lead a multifunctional team to build the company's first Internet and intranet sites. By 1996, she was in every major web-focussed publication, talking about ecommerce and was even highlighted in the *Wall Street Journal* as Miss.CPA.com.

In less than a decade, Tannis had successfully navigated the company's complicated, matrixed organization. She had been recognized for her ability to deliver in high-stress, high-profile situations and to lead and inspire people to go above and beyond. She had put her family on airplanes to fly to safety and had led emergency teams through hurricanes. She had left home for weeks at a time to help lead others through natural disasters, fires, explosions, and even bomb threats. Tannis had balanced corporate, public, and employee interests during issues and crises and had consistently demonstrated strategic business acumen even through major downsizings and business restructurings.

Known as a workhorse and nicknamed "Little Tiger" during an assignment in Hong Kong, she had changed jobs seven times in her first 11 years at CPA; had successfully transitioned to working in three countries (Canada, United States, and Hong Kong) in six different locations and had built a strong reputation as a relationship builder who could get the job done!

Prior to the transfer to Europe, Tannis had led a major transformational initiative in the southern United States, which included designing and implementing significant cultural, policy, and staffing changes and playing a lead role through a major merger/acquisition. Despite encountering many of the barriers synonymous with working in the southern states, including gender, culture, nationality (Tannis being Canadian), and religion (with her not being Christian and having a mixed ethnic background), Tannis had delivered strongly and had built a capable team to sustain the changes she initiated. Tannis had also been recognized for her efforts in several crisis situations, including a perceived cancer cluster issue in a local community and a significant fire and explosion that left employees severely injured and a community reeling.

Handpicked but not the Obvious Choice

Two corporate vice presidents had worked to position Tannis for the new European role. Her most recent professional success (in the southern United States) and the skills she demonstrated had convinced the executive wing that she was the ideal candidate for the strategic work needing to be addressed in Europe. As the new energy policy leader, she would need to deliver significant results in a short time frame (approximately six months). If successful, a director's position would be her reward.

Tannis was seen at the corporate level as being not only capable to deliver but also as "neutral" as possible (i.e., as a Canadian with years of experience in multiple geographies, businesses, and functions) and without allegiances to any of the existing networks, cliques, positions, businesses, or geography. Some wanted to see her succeed; others assumed she would fail; and yet others were simply curious whether recruiting an outsider would work!

On the ground in Europe, she was an unknown quantity and did not appear to be the obvious choice. Even before arriving at the Zurich-area office, the hallway talk had three strikes squarely against her: she wasn't a man, she wasn't European, and she was seen as being "corporate."

Eyes Wide Open

Job transitions and changes were nothing new to the 32-year old Tannis or her family, but this assignment posed more than the usual challenges. Although a European assignment was widely seen in the company as an opportunity of a lifetime, Tannis had her eyes wide open. Not one to forget that "with great opportunity comes great responsibility," she had known that the potential rewards of such an assignment would also be accompanied by risks and stress.

Tannis brought to the role not only her international work experience with the company but also a lifetime of navigating diverse and often conflict-ridden waters. Tannis was a child of mixed heritage, having been left to the child care system and ultimately raised in an Asian household. Tannis spoke multiple languages and had developed the ability to move seamlessly among people from varied cultures, organizations, languages, and religions. She was comfortable being in the minority, or the odd one out, which had served her well in her extensive travels as a child, when she had been exposed to many social and economic realities around the world. She could blend in when needed and could empathize with the needs and concerns of others.

Tannis also recognized that, more so than with past transitions, her success or failure in Europe would affect not only herself but also others. As a people leader and mentor, her many female colleagues believed her anticipated success would influence the organization to provide more geographic opportunities for women with dual careers and families. Tannis herself also had a family to consider. Thus, after transplanting her two young boys halfway around the world, and with her husband having to change his career path to transfer as a dual career, excitement and a healthy dose of nerves flowed through her veins as she had readied herself for her first day in the office.

Understanding the Game

Years earlier, one of her mentors had given Tannis sage advice. "When you get that chance of a lifetime opportunity ... watch out because there's a lot more going on than they are telling you," Frank Menske had said. "When they want to make the big investment in you ... they're expecting you to score a touchdown, they just don't tell you that the ball is in the other guys' possession." Menske was a trusted colleague and coach and, for years, had been there to give her the straight talk. This time was no different. He had said, "Get out there and do what it takes to figure out the game plan early or just know you're gonna get sacked when you least expect it!"

Right after saying "yes" to the offer of the European role, Tannis mapped out the realities she needed to deal with. Menske had been right. Taking the time to strip away emotion and conjecture and look analytically at the situation was helpful in mapping out her initial game plan. A pretty complex set of dynamics were at play:

- Tannis would report to three different and powerful leaders: a functional vice president, a geographic vice president, and a business vice president, each with distinct agendas.
- Tannis was expected to get everyone (the business, the various geographies, corporate headquarters, etc.) working together to develop and play by the same strategy. She needed to get the entire organization sharing the same company-wide

positions on some of the most contentious issues for the organization, energy policy.[3]

- Using a consistent playbook meant changing the status quo in terms of decision making, information sharing, and power recalibration. It meant the loss of autonomy and new expectations around collaboration and changed accountability.
- Personally, Tannis faced opposition internally. She was seen by many as an outsider taking one of the few and valued leadership roles in Europe as a non-European. Tannis was also seen as a change agent being forced or thrust on the organization.
- She also needed to establish trust and credibility with external stakeholders who had long and tenured relationships and shared similar educational, political, and social priorities.[4]

After accepting the European role, Tannis also followed Menske's advice and challenged her new bosses in candid and courageous conversations to ensure she understood their individual perspectives and unwritten expectations.

The Real Deal

As a result of her discussions with her three new bosses, Tannis came into the role knowing who wanted what and their individual expectations and demands. Tannis also got a flavour for the anticipated level and the nature of support she could expect.

Key for Tannis was that both Richard Markus and Nico Zinkweg, the geographic

and business vice presidents respectively, recognized the changes she needed to initiate. They committed to support her but set the expectation that they would be seen to maintain their autonomy and the ability to strongly influence any decision or action that could affect their respective areas of responsibility.

Markus specifically told Tannis that she needed to be careful to not try to Americanize the European approach and to be mindful of relationships that had been established over time. He was thoughtful in sharing this advice and counsel, even providing examples of how others had tried and failed to establish themselves in the region, let alone having any real influence. "This is Europe, and you must remember they [the external partners] want what is best for Europe – not for our company bottom line and not for the U.S."

Zinkweg, the business vice-president was explicit in his expectation that he maintain independent authority over issues affecting his business and with relations at the level of the European Council and the European Commission. He was willing to provide support to placate the corporate entity, but made it clear that Tannis needed to ensure his position externally was not undermined by her actions or those of the corporate entity. His tenure, experience, and knowledge were well recognized and were absolutely critical for the company to have a voice on these issues on a European and global stage; therefore, his support and personal engagement were fundamental in achieving Tannis's deliverables.

Day One: Staff

On day one, Tannis started by meeting her new global team. Some joined in person, some by phone, some even through video conferencing – but all seemed very curious about her, both personally and professionally. Compared with her past experiences with new staff "meet and greets," the intensity of interest and focus seemed heightened.

---

[3] For example, would the company support a "cap and trade" system? If they would support it in Europe, would they also support it in the United States?

[4] As did most companies, CPA not only worked to develop its own positions and plans but worked with third parties and associations to influence politicians and decision makers. Therefore, building a recognized and valued brand as an individual was imperative to succeed, both internally and externally.

While encouraged by the open dialogue, Tannis recognized that her arrival brought to an end months of chit chat and hallway talk about who she was, what she was like and how she would tackle the challenges ahead.

Tannis had not only studied up on the new business but she had also tried to learn about the individuals in her team and other stakeholders (companies, business leaders, and lobbyists). She had talked to knowledgeable colleagues, looked at best practices and sought out some cultural coaching. She already knew that culture and nationality were significant factors in how Europeans did business, and their significance was confirmed in the questions she was asked. Within an hour, it was clear that the new staff had done their homework on her. While many had asked the standard questions about plans and priorities, the conversation had quickly shifted to the following:

- How would she establish credibility with the powerful businessmen she would now be interacting with?
- How would she handle being the only woman?
- Would she deal with issues of attraction and retention of women in this business?
- Would she try to make the team more connected to the corporate way?
- Would she force them to become "corporate," or did she support maintaining their uniqueness, as part of the energy business, in their unique geographies?

The questions were frank and direct, and they provided some significant insight into the challenges ahead.

Day One: A Long Day

Following her two-hour staff meeting, Tannis took a few minutes to reflect on the discussions and to prepare to meet with some key internal partners, including the director of energy. At the working and collegial level, his partnership and support had been flagged as critical. Apprehensive about lobbying and interacting with government himself, his thought leadership and extensive relationships inside the business and within the industry could make the difference in terms of constructing and working through key business-related arguments and messaging. With his support, she hoped to create a working group to gather broad input, develop more coordinated and comprehensive approaches, and drive toward stronger positioning on key issues.

Tannis walked along the pristine glass and marble hallways. Bare white shelves in the offices illustrated the workplace's minimalistic and impersonal style and provided the starkest possible contrast to offices in the southern United States where she had last been assigned. There, wood panelling was ubiquitous. Shelves were muddled with memorabilia, diplomas, and family photos. Religious crosses were displayed prominently and with pride. Occasionally, one could spot a boudoir photo of someone's wife and the proudly displayed and coveted prizes from "gator hunting." She reflected on how something as simple as décor could reinforce difference and how she needed to be mindful of the subtle cues around her.

"Andre, I am Sophia, pleasure to meet you!" With a strong stretched-out hand, she smiled.

"Well well. So you are Sophia," noted Andre van het Hof.

"Yes, I am," responded Tannis, as she entered his office, which boasted a picturesque view of the lake.

"So you are the one! The one who is supposed to replace Antonio Vella?" A long deep pause stretched between them.

"You have met Antonio?" he continued. "You know the man speaks seven languages? He is a good friend. He knows the business completely after 20-some years. He knows everyone in Brussels – they call him 'the silver-haired fox,' you know? He is a man of refinement and culture and, of course, he is European. So tell me, how do you plan to replace him, dear?"

The Power of Being Present

In the days that followed, Tannis settled in and slowly made some headway building relationships with staff and with her internal colleagues. She took the advice she had been given – to begin by listening more than she talked. She demonstrated her interest in understanding others' perspectives and passions. She was the minority, and she opened herself to learn. By doing so, she realized what others wanted from her – not the "right answer" but a frank and candid answer to questions. Being politically correct was not seen as being honest or transparent, and being Canadian as opposed to being American opened doors for some important discussions, such as how the American approach to relationship building was alienating some potential business partners in the Middle East and how American companies in Europe needed to develop a real appreciation for European institutions and approaches, not just pay lip service.

Tannis recognized that others appreciated her answering questions without mincing words, addressing stereotypes and misinformation candidly, and being open to criticism (both personal and of a corporate nature). Unlike in Texas and other parts of the United States where she had previously lived and worked, the hot topic was not religion but issues around nationality and culture. She became mindful that her actions, reactions, and comments served to instantaneously reinforce concerns or to slowly create the opportunity to work collaboratively.

"Corporate doesn't trust us" was a common theme and frustration expressed by staff in the office. While not unlike perceptions of "headquarters" she had heard working in other locations, the emotion around the comment was different.

Through discussion, she realized that, for her new staff and colleagues, the corporate way was often interpreted as the "right" way, which, by default, meant their way was "wrong." The level of pride in the European way became increasingly apparent, and Tannis recognized that her efforts to build better coordination and collaboration would need to consider this reality.

The Silver-Haired Fox

Respecting the European way was nowhere more important than in her interaction with the man who had previously held her current position. Antonio Vella, "the silver-haired fox," was elegant, sophisticated, gracious, and charming. Always dressed and coiffed immaculately, he was subtle, yet formidable in his presence.

Vella knew that Tannis's role was to change things – those things he himself had created and worked with for a long time. He acknowledged that times were changing, that the time had come for both a fresh approach and a drawing in of global perspectives. Yet, understandably, his legacy and reputation were his priority. His 20 years in the business and 30 years in the company had earned him a reputation he was proud of. Thus, the symbolism of his job now being filled by a non-European, relatively young woman without the education or pedigree he had brought to the table was, in his mind, a slight of sorts.

Tannis had come to describe her assignment as a high-wire act. Balancing such divergent needs and interests required a combination of courage and finesse – the slightest misstep or misstatement seemed to trigger doubt and shake confidence. Vella, with his subtle yet persuasive mannerisms seemed able to effortlessly balance or destabilize the taut wire. It was a skill Tannis needed to learn – and quickly.

Brussels at Last

A couple of weeks had passed and Tannis and Vella were on their way together to Brussels. The trip was to be her first of many to work with external colleagues and the European trade association on lobby efforts related to energy policy. She took the time to decompress from the intensity at the office and the steep learning curve and to further process new insights into what she needed to do to help her team and drive success!

During their travel, she realized she also felt torn about her relationship with Vella. She had spent hours, in fact days, with him. She had listened, learned, asked questions, and tried to internalize the big picture and the realities on the ground. His growing support and endorsement of her as a quick study had both calmed those who had doubts about her and opened the door for further constructive conversations with Andre van het Hof and her geographic and business vice-presidents (Markus and Zinkweg). Yet an undercurrent remained – she had a long way to go before no longer being considered what the Swiss referred to as an *auslander*, an outsider.

While travelling from the airport to the offices of the trade association, where the large meeting with company and national association representatives awaited them, Vella provided Tannis with insights into the individuals and their positions on the debates scheduled for the day. Vella knew each person at a deeply personal level, and the strength of those relationships came to life as they entered the conference room. While eyes glanced in her direction, everyone engaged Vella directly, congratulating

him on his impending retirement and his plans to keep busy. "The silver-haired fox will not be able to stay away from the world of Brussels or energy policy," they quipped.

Vella was animated and charismatic talking about his plans, yet the quick glance between him and Tannis acknowledged the unspoken. His departure was not completely by choice but was part of the planned restructuring and strategy to address organizational culture.

Once the greetings were done, the packed room, including key thought leaders, PhDs, and highly successful businessmen, meandered back to their chairs. It was then that Vella turned to Tannis, and, with his always graceful style, he introduced her by name to his colleagues. Polite but mostly disinterested glancing eyes fell upon her, before Vella could articulate that Tannis was his replacement and their new colleague. Then, an individual abruptly thanked her for coming and noted his appreciation for her getting coffees for the leaders so they could start the day's activities.

A lengthy pause ensued. Tannis took a deep breath. She stepped forward and, with a smile, declared in a jovial tone, "I am more than happy to do so, as long you promise to get mine at our next meeting."

The room fell silent. All eyes refocused on Tannis as Vella clarified that he meant to proudly introduce her as his replacement. Looking around, Tannis noted the looks of confusion, the glimmer of disbelief, and some embarrassment.

"She is replacing you, Antonio?"

The Ivey Business School and the Ian O. Ihnatowycz Institute for Leadership gratefully acknowledges the generous support of Bill and Kathleen Troost in the development of this case.

🛡IVEY | Publishing

School of Business
D'Amore-McKim
Northeastern University

SELECTING A COUNTRY MANAGER FOR DELTA BEVERAGES INDIA

Professors Paula Caligiuri and Henry W. Lane wrote this case solely to provide material for class discussion. The authors do not intend to illustrate either effective or ineffective handling of a managerial situation. The authors may have disguised certain names and other identifying information to protect confidentiality.

This publication may not be transmitted, photocopied, digitized or otherwise reproduced in any form or by any means without the permission of Ivey Publishing, the exclusive representative of the copyright holder. Reproduction of this material is not covered under authorization by any reproduction rights organization. To order copies or request permission to reproduce materials, contact Ivey Publishing, Ivey Business School, Western University, London, Ontario, Canada, N6G 0N1; (t) 519.661.3208; (e) cases@ivey.ca; www.iveycases.com.

Copyright © 2015, Northeastern University, D'Amore-McKim School of Business   Version: 2015-06-22

Five Candidates' Notes from the Succession Planning Meeting

To prepare for today's meeting, you reviewed the materials from the past year's performance review and succession planning meetings. This activity has surfaced five possible candidates for the role of country manager, India. Your notes on these candidates are as follows.

1. Anika "Ani" Navithar
   Navithar has been with Delta for the past 15 years. She joined Delta immediately after completing her MBA at Northeastern University, joining us in the supply chain functional area. She has moved up the ranks quickly to director-level positions in both supply chain and customer service. While based in Boston, Navithar has successfully completed several short-term projects internationally, and for the Indian subsidiary specifically. Navithar has never been a country manager. She speaks English, Hindi, and Telugu. Part of Navithar's leadership development plan is an international assignment. Navithar is American.

2. Carlos Delgado
   Between his experience at Delta and with his previous employer (Delta's major competitor), Delgado has had three international assignments over the past 18 years. Delgado began his career with Delta at your Boston headquarters and is currently reporting to you as the country manager in South Korea. He is highly regarded as a global leader and, as the succession plan indicates, he was on the slate of candidates for your current role. Prior to becoming the country manager in Korea, Delgado was the Argentinean country manager for Delta and in supply chain role in Poland with his previous employer. Delgado speaks Spanish and English. He is a Mexican national.

3. Haziq Tengku
   Tengku reports directly to you and is currently the country manager for Malaysia, where he has been extremely successful. He has been serving in that role for the past six years and is ready

for a promotion, according to the succession plan. With the exception of one three-month orientation at the Boston headquarters when he first joined Delta 10 years ago, he has spent his tenure at Delta within the Malaysian subsidiary. Prior to joining Delta, Tengku worked for the Malaysian subsidiary of a U.S.-based fast-food chain. Part of Tengku's leadership development plan is to be a country manager for a larger market. He speaks Malay and English and has a degree in business from University of Malaya. Tengku is a Malaysian national.

4. Lucas Hansson

Lucas was appointed as the vice president for Delta's Europe, Middle East, and Africa (EMEA) region one year ago. In this current role, he is living and working in Delta's EMEA headquarter location of Basel, Switzerland. Prior to his current role, he was country manager in Germany (four years) and has led a variety of functional positions in the International Division from headquarters in Boston, including a two-year global quality initiative. Hansson speaks Swedish, English, French, and German. He is a Swedish national.

5. Pranav Subramanium

Subramanium is the vice president of the Indian subsidiary, reporting to Xiao Zhang, the recently re-assigned country manager of India. Subramanium joined Delta three years ago, after spending five years at a consulting firm in Delhi. The succession plan states that his performance has been exemplary, and he is considered in the top rank of the regional talent pool. Subramanium has an MBA from the Institute of Advanced Management and Research in Ghaziabad. Part of Subramanium's leadership development plan is a short-term assignment in the Boston headquarters. Subramanium speaks English, Hindi, and Urdu. He is an Indian national.

Your Personal Reflections

You know all of these candidates personally, some better than others. Here are the mental notes you recall about each.

Anika "Ani" Navithar

You know Navithar well and have been extremely impressed with her. She is intelligent and authentic, rising to every leadership role in which she has been placed across multiple functional areas. Last summer at the Delta company picnic, you enjoyed meeting her family, her husband (who is a university professor in Boston) and their nine-year-old twin girls. Also, when Navithar did her short-term project in India, Xiao Zhang said she was very effective. Navithar's husband used their short-term experience in India to conduct some research and work with colleagues at Delhi University. You learned at the picnic that he now has a joint appointment at Delhi University.

Carlos Delgado

If you were hit by a bus tomorrow, Delgado would likely be asked to step into your role. He has really proven himself at Delta, with the trajectory of success. He and his family have been willing to relocate to Korea, although the demands they made regarding housing for their family, a cost-of-living allowance, and education for their teenage children seemed, in your opinion, a bit excessive. Delgado would probably enjoy the expatriate community in Delhi but you wish he was more willing to integrate and acculturate and, at least, would attempt to learn the host country's national languages.

Haziq Tengku

Tengku has clearly proven himself in Malaysia and is probably ready for the next step in the Asia region. Six months ago when you were in Malaysia, Tengku was on a short leave of absence to support his wife and care for their two small children while his wife was undergoing cancer treatments. Last month, you heard that Tengku's wife is doing well.

Lucas Hansson

Hansson and his family seem to "bloom wherever they are planted," becoming part of the local community in every host country where they have lived. At the last leadership offsite, you and Hansson spoke about whether he would be interested in accepting the position as president of EMEA in the future, becoming your counterpart in EMEA. He noted that he's always looking for the next exciting opportunity – but feels as though he needs more experience running a country in emerging markets. You thought he was being exceptionally humble but appreciated his self-awareness, which probably makes him such a great international assignee. At one of the social events, Hansson also shared with you that he and his wife began to discuss whether they should retire in a few years and move back to Sweden to be with their elderly parents.

Pranav Subramanium

Subramanium is a solid performer but seems as though he needs a few more years as the second-in-command. However, this opening could be exactly the stretch challenge Subramanium needs to launch a global leadership career at Delta.

Exercise 2

Still working alone, continue to prepare for your meeting with the leadership team by considering the strengths and weaknesses of each of these five leading candidates for the job. Decide which candidate is best suited for the job.

PART III

Executing Strategy and Performance

7 Executing Global Strategy: Foundations

> However beautiful the strategy, you should occasionally look at the results.
>
> Sir Winston Churchill

Strategy Execution Is Embedded in Context: Know Your Assumptions

As a global leader, cultural understanding and good intercultural skills are important competences. However, to be successful you will need more than intercultural skills. You also have to understand how the cultural context of a host country may affect your company's strategy, structure, administrative systems, and operations. The formulation and implementation of a strategy require understanding market demands, competitors, and external constraints, such as government policies. In addition to choosing, for example, markets and manufacturing sites, important organizational actions include choosing structures, work systems, and administrative mechanisms to motivate employees toward the desired goals.

Since a company's knowledge and practices are not completely documented or explicit, a great deal of implicit or tacit knowledge is required to manage effectively (Nonaka and Takeuchi, 1995). Executives need to be aware of the implicit knowledge or assumptions underlying their firm's strategy, structure, systems, and practices. These practices are influenced by both organizational culture and national culture. Culture, the "shoulds" and the "oughts" of life and business that people often have difficulty articulating, is acquired through a socialization process that creates common experiences, shared mental models, and accepted ways of operating. Using domestic strategy, systems, or practices, unmodified, in another country may lead to unforeseen negative consequences. Therefore, global executives need to understand how their assumptions about organizing and managing may differ in an international market from those in their company's home country.

As a company expands globally, top managers may need to recalibrate their cultural lenses. The experiences, tacit knowledge, and explicit policies and practices shared by a top management group create the operational and cultural lenses to interpret and understand context-rich information. With accurately interpreted information, global executives can make mindful strategic decisions about the design and implementation of culturally appropriate organizational structures and systems to achieve strategic goals.

Aligning the Organizational System for Performance

Up to this point, the book has focused primarily on people and culture. In this chapter, we move to the organizational level. We start by introducing a tool, the alignment framework, to identify and analyze the organizational elements to be aligned – the people, work tasks, coordination structures, and administrative systems (Lane, 1980). We also provide an overview of strategy and the need to consider realignment as strategies change. Although this is not a book about strategy, it is impossible to discuss implementing strategy without briefly discussing strategic choices.

Organizations as Aligned Socio-Technical Systems

Organizations are socio-technical systems, meaning that they have both social and technical components, and need to be understood as such. In practical terms this means that what happens in one part of the organization impacts other parts. The "technical" component is the numerous technical and/or functional tasks of the business. These include acquiring inputs such as capital and raw materials, as well as using specific technology and work processes to create finished products or services. Each of the major functional areas of an organization – such as production, marketing, sales, or finance – also is a system within the larger "technical" organizational system. Each has a set of tasks and operations necessary to the effective functioning of the entire organization.

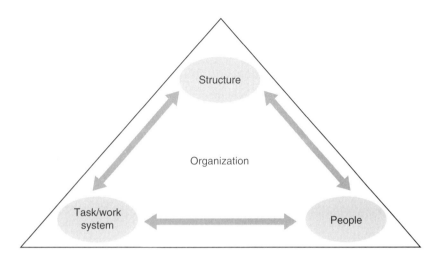

Figure 7.1 Organizational alignment model: internal alignment

The "social" component is the human element, the people and groups, with their skills, needs, feelings, expectations, experience, and beliefs, who carry out the tasks and operations. Through the use of structures and systems, managers connect and align the interdependent social and technical elements of a company to achieve the organization's goals. The basic components of the organizational alignment model are shown in Figure 7.1.

Although identifying the discrete components of the system is important, understanding that alignment or "fit" is the force that binds them together for performance is just as important. Christopher Alexander, in writing about the process of design of physical objects such as buildings or transportation systems, commented on the need for fit or alignment:

Every design problem begins with an effort to achieve fitness between two entities: the form in question and its context. The form is the solution to the problem; the context defines the problem. In other words, when we speak of design, the real object of discussion is not the form alone, but the ensemble comprising the form and its context. (Alexander, 1964)

We can think of the context as the organization's strategy. The context (strategy) makes demands on the form (people, task, structure, systems). The form is the result of decisions that managers make about how to structure and coordinate tasks, whom to hire, how to evaluate and reward them, and so on. Meeting the demands of the strategy is "fitness" or alignment.

Before looking at the detail of the model more closely, we begin with an example from a company we were involved with and whose experience shows the dynamics of the overall model.

Aligning the Organization: The Case of Global Multi-Products Chile

An international example of organizational and strategic alignment and change is the experience of Global Multi-Products in Chile (see Lane and Campbell, 2007; although this is a disguised case, the company is real and is a Fortune 100 company). Global Multi-Products' strategy was the continuous introduction of new, innovative products based on proprietary technology that had high margins. Approximately 30 percent of its sales came from products introduced in the previous few years. Historically, its value proposition for the customer was: buy our products because they are the best quality, based on the latest technology, and they are reliable.

To deliver on this strategy, it excelled in R&D, where the new products originated, and it had a formal program of R&D with multiple technology platforms that were the seedbeds of the company's new products. It distributed its products through separate product-related strategic business units (SBUs). We could characterize the company's business model as investing in R&D; developing proprietary technology and high margin products; manufacturing them efficiently; and continually introducing these new products.

The competitive environment in Chile changed. Small sole proprietorships were largely replaced by big American retailers and local retailers developing similar superstore models. Previously, superstores represented approximately 60 percent of retail sales. The superstore segment, local and international, grew quickly to represent over 90 percent of the company's business, and power shifted from the manufacturer to the large retailers. The level of sophistication among customers' purchasing managers increased. They were concerned with return on investment and they demanded more from their suppliers, such as more advertising and lower prices. Products that traditionally had margins averaging around 80 percent for Multi-Products now had margins not very different from those of competitors. Finally, customers wanted to reduce the number of Global Multi-Products' sales representatives with whom they were dealing. They wanted to see one face representing the manufacturer.

At the time that one of the authors was involved with Global Multi-Products in Chile, it was in the process of transitioning from a best product strategy to a customer solutions strategy, which had been forced on it by the shift in power to large retail customers. The new strategy was to sell "solutions" to its customers by understanding in detail their processes where Multi-Products' offerings were, or could be, used. Multi-Products would make money by helping customers decrease costs while selling more products at lower margins.

Internally, this change meant that more integration was required among business units and that employees had to work in teams horizontally across the organization to analyze customer operations in order to provide solutions and recommend products for them. This program sought to reorient the sales and marketing effort around the needs of customers, instead of the company's product groups. Global Multi-Products also developed a program of strategic relationships with customers to conduct joint R&D to develop new products that could benefit the customer and that could be turned into products for their wider market. The company was now competing on the basis of its total organization, as well as its technology, to provide solutions for its customers.

Many of the companies we have worked with have wanted to follow the customer solutions strategy also. However, like Multi-Products, they usually did not appreciate what the change meant internally. To compete on the basis of creating value to the customer by providing "solutions," companies have to learn to leverage all of their capabilities more effectively by working horizontally across the organization. Corporate culture, entrenched interests, and existing evaluation and reward systems were among the barriers to change. In Global Multi-Products Chile, it was not a simple change to implement.

Organizational Realignment in Chile. There were a number of barriers in the way of necessary changes. These barriers can be organized using the alignment framework in the following categories:

- *Organizational structure*: SBUs, product groups, hierarchy, and functional "silos" worked against cooperation. Teams had to work laterally across them.
- *Organizational culture*: heads of functions had a great deal of autonomy and it was almost a "feudal" system.
- *Top management team*: Executives didn't have skills with group/team processes. They were concerned with their authority, and there was resistance to change.
- *Society/national culture*: Status was important to executives, reflecting Chile's status conscious culture.
- *Political history*: Although the Pinochet era was long in the past, a legacy of distrust and not speaking out continued to exist. There was little trust among the executives.
- *People*: The sales representatives' status, lack of required new skills, title, education, and age/seniority all worked against their success in the new environment. Sales reps were not high-status jobs and the people in them did not have the necessary skills and training to interact with the new, sophisticated

purchasing executives of the "big box" stores. The company had to find new sales reps, provide them with new titles, and improve training.

- *Rewards*: The reward system did not encourage selling other SBUs' products or working together in teams. The new behavior required of sales reps was to continually introduce new products and not simply to push the old ones, which the reward system did not encourage.

It took the managing director a number of years to implement the organizational changes necessary to realign the Chilean organization with its new business model. Global Multi-Products provides an example of changes in the entire strategic and organizational alignment model. The change in strategy created a need to realign the management systems that were aligned to the old strategy. For best performance, there should be a fit, or *alignment*, between the people and their new job demands.

We will now look at the different parts of the model. We do not intend to deal with particular systems in depth. Our aim is to explore how, when used effectively or ineffectively, such systems can create fits or misfits between people and their jobs, or between people and the organizations in which they work. You should be able to use this diagnostic tool to help you analyze a situation to detect misalignments that need correcting.

Tasks Are the Building Blocks

Global organizations employ many people for distinct jobs or tasks that contribute to overall organizational performance. Tasks and their coordination are the foundation for creating organizational structure. These tasks have different characteristics requiring different skills, which means employing people with different educational backgrounds, knowledge bases, and competences. Think of the differences between accounting, marketing, R&D, and manufacturing, for example. There are usually patterns of systematic variances between people in these various functional departments. Functions within a company are organized for specific tasks and some people seem more appropriate for some jobs than others based on education, experience, and attitude. This is the concept of differentiation or the "difference in cognitive and emotional orientation among managers in different functional departments" (Lawrence and Lorsch, 1969). This concept encompasses the specialized knowledge required for the tasks, as well as the differences in attitude and behavior of the people in the jobs. As complexity in organization increases, differentiation likely increases as well. As this happens, the potential for departments to pursue their own particular goals increases, as does the likeli-hood for potential conflict. Therefore, it is important to coordinate these functional areas, which is not always easy in large corporations since people may be separated physically and attitudinally by their personal predispositions and orientations.

In complex, differentiated organizations, integration is needed. The concept of integration includes the coordination of tasks and interrelationships, includ-ing conflict resolution, and depends on the level of task interdependence.

What is the Level of Task Interdependence?

To ensure the proper coordination, managers also must be aware of how each area is dependent on the others to achieve its goals. There are three basic types of internal interdependence in organizations, and most complex organizations exhibit all three (Thompson, 1967). The simplest is **pooled** or **simple interde-pendence**. This means that each part of an organization can pursue the achieve-ment of its goals relatively independently from other parts and still contribute to the overall objectives of the organization, as shown in Figure 7.2. This is a situ-ation in which each part contributes to the whole and each is supported by the whole. For example, in a department store, personnel from the furniture depart-ment do not necessarily have to interact with people from sporting goods for each to fulfill their objectives. They can contribute, independently, to the goals of the store. Each however, is supported by the HR department and the account-ing department, for instance. Similarly, a McDonald's restaurant in Seattle does not need to interact with a McDonald's in Boston for the corporation to succeed.

Higher up on the complexity scale is **sequential interdependence**, mean-ing that there is a predetermined and ordered progression by which tasks must proceed. As the name implies, one group must accomplish its task before the next one can begin. In the manufacture of a relatively standard product, one can see a progression from the design department to engineering to purchasing to production scheduling and then to manufacturing. On the assembly line of

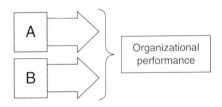

Figure 7.2 Task interdependence: pooled or simple

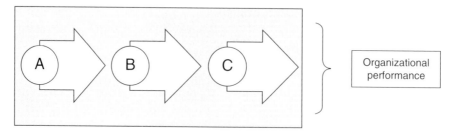

Figure 7.3 Task interdependence: sequential

an automobile, for example, the car's frame and axles are assembled before the engine and the body are attached. A specific task, "A," must be accomplished before the next task, "B," is begun and so forth. This is depicted in Figure 7.3.

A situation of **reciprocal** or **complex interdependence** between tasks means that "the output of each becomes the input for the others." Rather than having discrete linear relationships between groups and tasks, the relationships are continuous and almost circular in nature. For example, in creating sophisticated technology systems, production must understand what the researchers have developed, and the development engineers must understand the constraints on manufacturing. Similarly, both the researchers and the engineers must understand the customers' needs in order to accurately forecast delivery dates. As can be inferred from this simple example, reciprocal interdependence creates an iterative process in which the required level of inter-group communication is high and the potential for conflict increases dramatically. Think of an advertising agency working on a new account. Copywriting, photography, art, production, finance, and the account executive constantly meet to decide on the latest iteration of the ad. Each has to understand the constraints on the others. And if, when the customer sees the ad, changes are required, the interactive process starts all over again. Reciprocal interdependence is depicted in Figure 7.4.

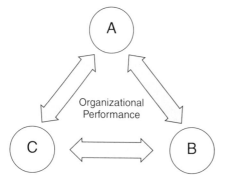

Figure 7.4 Task interdependence: reciprocal

Coordination Mechanisms and Conflict Resolution

As the complexity of organizations increases, the need to coordinate and control the activities of diverse groups of individuals also increases, and formal control mechanisms, such as accounting, auditing, and management information systems, are important. Most organizations systematically collect, analyze, and disseminate information on production, finances, and personnel. Budgets are developed, refined, and monitored. Like other mechanisms, these provide messages about what is required or valued.

For example, requiring manufacturing to concentrate on costs and sales on customer satisfaction could in some circumstances produce high levels of dysfunctional conflict. Manufacturing would want long production runs to minimize downtime and re-tooling costs, while sales might want runs stopped to meet a valued customer's urgent need for another product. Both need to understand the other and act in a coordinated fashion if either is to satisfy their objectives.

The managerial issue is how to best coordinate interdependence. At the simplest level, for example, with pooled interdependence, standardization by rules and budgets can be used. A department is given a budget, a set of operating procedures, hours of operation, and a set of well-defined tasks, and is measured on its results against set objectives. With sequential interdependence, coordination is usually also accomplished by also adding plans and schedules.

However, at the level of reciprocal interdependence, special structural integrating roles such as project teams or product managers may be employed, and coordinating mechanisms such as taskforces are often used. Direct, face-to-face communication or coordination through mutual adjustment, usually is required as well. In Global Multi-Products, the shift in strategy and away from product-focused selling within SBUs to team-based selling across SBUs increased the interdependence among units that previously had little, if any, interdependence.

These mechanisms are summarized in Table 7.1.

Particularly in situations of reciprocal interdependence where there is a lot of interpersonal engagement, the potential for conflict arises. This is an area where intercultural skills are important.

People in different cultures tend to prefer different ways of solving this interdependence conflict. Stella Ting-Toomey's research shows that cultural variability (individualism versus collectivism, power distance and high versus low context communication patterns) provides "lenses" through which conflict is viewed: individualists use an outcome-oriented model while collectivists follow a process-oriented model (Ting-Toomey, 1999). Where Americans and other individualistic, low context cultures may embrace conflict as potentially beneficial,

Table 7.1 **Interdependence, coordination, and task alignment**

Interdependence	Coordination	Task environment characteristics
Pooled (simple)	Standardization: rules, regulations	Relatively simple, static, certain, predictable, unchanging (stability)
Sequential	Plans: schedules, budgets, milestones	Multiple interrelated components, frequent but manageable changes (complexity)
Reciprocal (complex)	Mutual adjustment: constant communication; often face-to-face	Multiple interrelated components, rapidly changing, unpredictable, multiple interpretations, cause and effect uncertainty (dynamic complexity)

collectivistic, high context cultures may seek to avoid open conflict and may prefer hierarchical cultures with more clear responsibilities. Ting-Toomey states:

For individualists, effective conflict negotiation means settling the conflict problem openly and working out a set of functional conflict solutions conjointly. Effective conflict resolution behavior (e.g., emphasizing the importance of addressing incompatible goals/outcomes) is relatively more important for individualists than is appropriate facework behavior. For collectivists, on the other hand, appropriate conflict management means the subtle negotiation of in-group/out-group face-related issues – pride, honor, dignity, insult, shame, disgrace, humility, trust, mistrust, respect, and prestige – in a given conflict episode. Appropriate facework moves and countermoves are critical for collectivists before tangible conflict outcomes or goals can be addressed. (Ting-Toomey, 1999)

We have provided an in-depth way to think about tasks here because we find that managers tend to jump straight from strategy to structure and people without analyzing the requirements of the tasks that will be organized and executed. The nature of interdependence required is the most fundamental task characteristic that affects decisions around organizing and executing.

The Right People: Selection and Development

The first, extremely important fit is between the tasks to be performed and the skills of the people who perform them. The people brought into an organization through its recruitment and selection systems affect organizational alignment. The most obvious effect is on the pool of knowledge, skills, and attitudes.

Selection is the mechanism by which a pool of candidates is narrowed to the number of job vacancies. Several sources of assessment error can enter these decisions. The one most frequently described is the "just like me" error in which the successful candidate is the one who is closest in skills and personality to those making the decision. Although it might augur well for the fit between the person and his or her boss, this type of decision might not provide the required congruence between person and task. Selection, like recruitment, involves a careful analysis of both the job and the organization to determine the right type of person.

Rarely does a selection decision alone provide a perfect person-task (P–T) or person-organization (P–O) fit. P–T fit is the traditional focus of employee selection, the skills and abilities to do the job; while P–O fit is concerned with a person's compatibility with broader characteristics of the organization, such as culture, values, and colleagues.[1] If it is only to find out how things are done in the company, most employees need some form of training or development to make them effective performers. So even if the fit is perfect, it is not likely that condition will last for long. Continual development is needed as conditions change.

In Global Multi-Products, the existing sales reps did not have the requisite skills for the new sales task. They were accustomed to relationship selling with customers with whom they had dealt over the years. Now they had to contend with purchasing agents who cared about ROI and expected professional presentations. New reps were needed and some existing sales reps required training and developmental experiences to perform the new task.

Chapter 6 focused entirely on selecting, preparing, and moving people – now we can see those decisions and actions as part of aligning for execution.

Structure

The people, and the tasks they are working on, are organized using various divisions of labor and structures to achieve coordination, efficiency, and effectiveness. Structure is the set of formal relationships between people in an organization and is one mechanism that communicates to organization members what behavior is expected of them, what tasks to work on, what not to do, what goals to work toward, with whom to work, whom to obey, and whom to direct. This includes such things as hierarchy, teams, and rules

[1] For a review of this literature see Sekiguchi (2004).

and procedures. Structures also are used as integrating mechanisms. These may include taskforces, teams, liaison people, product or project managers, product management departments, and matrix organization designs. Organizational structures are not free from the influence of culture. Each structure carries with it identifiable assumptions about the legitimacy of certain practices and relationships and defines the locus of authority, responsibility, and bases of power differently. Each legitimizes a different pattern of communication and interaction. In addition to "fitting" better with certain competitive situations or product characteristics, some structures may be more acceptable than others in a given culture. For example, the matrix organization, a structure in which a person has two bosses, has cultural assumptions built into it. It violates the principle of unity of command that some hierarchical cultures may believe is correct, and because of the existence of potentially competing interests, it can force conflict into the open, which some cultures may avoid.

Chapter 8, which looks at specific applications of executing strategy, will identify a host of structural options for organizations.

Aligning the Organization: The Critical Role of Systems

Organizations should be designed to elicit the behavior needed by its strategy. All too often, procedures are imposed without due consideration of the task at hand, simply because, de facto, they just "have become company policy." In such situations, the administrative heritage of the company may become the controlling factor, with the jobs and the people forced into the existing systems, when it should be the other way around.

Managers use administrative systems to create the alignment between people and tasks. The systems send employees messages about what is expected of them. These social-relational tools channel the activities of employees. And their signals are important. Care must be taken not to mix messages. This can happen when a strategy changes. Managers may expect that employees will automatically adjust their behavior, but the systems may tell them to continue as before. Different systems send different messages or signals. Ineffectiveness often results when individuals cannot reconcile those different messages. They often pay attention to the messages of one system to the exclusion of messages coming from another.

Encouraging Performance: Performance Appraisal and Rewards

Two of the most talked about and studied management systems are **performance appraisal** and **rewards**. Appraisal processes are seen in many forms and
administered in many ways. However, at the core, there are several common
purposes:

- communicate expectations or standards of performance;
- provide feedback on how well one is doing against expectations or standards;
- identify areas of developmental need and develop a plan of remedy;
- provide information and documentation for decisions about salary, promotion, or discipline.

Rewards come in different forms and in different ways for different people. One
person's reasons for working are different from another's. Basically, rewards
fall into one of two categories: intrinsic, those that come from doing the job
itself or being directly part of the work environment, and extrinsic, those that
are more tangible. More job autonomy is an example of the former, while getting a raise is an example of the latter.

Rewards have different meanings for different people. Some rewards (particularly the financial reward) have instrumental value, helping us get other
things of importance such as food and shelter. Rewards often serve as a signal that one's contribution or presence is valued: a form of recognition. They
can serve as a signal to others of one's value, thereby enhancing self-esteem.
Individual needs determine which of these meanings are most important at any
one time and which reward will have the desired effect.

In designing and administering reward systems from the employee's perspective, several issues are important. From the organization's perspective, it is
important to ask the following questions about rewards:

1. Are they competitive? Can the organization attract the people it wants vis-à-
   vis its competitors? Are the rewards commensurate with what the employee
   brings to the job in terms of skill, knowledge, and aptitude?
2. Are they sufficient? Do employees get enough of the right things to satisfy
   their needs? Is the sum of both the intrinsic and extrinsic rewards enough to
   motivate, and retain employees?
3. Are they equitable? Is the internal distribution of rewards fair? Are they commensurate with the required attitude and effort?
4. Do they motivate the right task behavior, or do they create a disincentive? Do
   they motivate for a sustained period of time?

Evaluation and reward systems help to create alignment with the strategy. In Global Multi-Products, the compensation system was changed to reflect not only the sales reps' individual goals, but also the performance of their team and the company. The evaluation and reward systems also changed from primarily individualistic to a combination of individualistic and collectivistic.

As another example, let's look at a firm with which we worked that we will call ABC Financial Printing. ABC had long provided transaction services for companies' Initial Public Offerings (IPOs), mergers and acquisitions, such as completing and filing required documents with government regulators. This highly customized service was based on relationship selling by a sales force and had very high margins. The sales representatives who were hired to sell transaction services were aggressive self-starters who liked the substantial salary, bonuses, and glory that came from being successful in the high margin, relationship-oriented transaction business.

In 2002, the Sarbanes-Oxley Act required firms to file numerous routine, standardized periodic reports that were time consuming to prepare. As a result, companies like ABC, pushed by competitors that were offering low cost "do it yourself" computer programs and Internet products, introduced a compliance service for their customers to meet the requirements of Sarbanes-Oxley. The compliance service was a lower margin offering than the transaction service. However, in terms of company revenue, it was growing to become a very important part of the firm's business.

ABC developed a range of products, including computer programs, to address this market. However, it had difficulty motivating sales representatives to sell compliance products. They did not have the technical skills to sell the new products. There also was a misfit between the characteristics of the salespeople and the reward and evaluation systems with the new products. ABC struggled to meet the demands of the new market and the needs of compliance customers.

Responsibility Centers and Evaluation

Earlier in the chapter, we referred to the practice of using budget systems to manage task interdependencies. Identifiable parts of an organization, such as departments, divisions, or subsidiaries, usually are established as responsibility centers to manage financial resources and to account for revenue and expenses. The three basic types of responsibility centers are cost, profit, and investment. The heads of these centers have differing responsibilities and accountabilities. Cost center managers are responsible for managing expenses within the budgets that they are allocated. Profit center managers are responsible for the expenses of their units and also for the revenue that they generate. Investment center managers control expenses, revenue, and assets.

These managers have authority to run their operations in a manner that they think is best to achieve their goals and they are evaluated on their results. For our purposes, the important point is that the responsibility systems of a firm directly influence the behavior of executives and contribute significantly to alignment. A change in strategy may create conflict with existing control systems and responsibility centers, necessitating realignment.

Organizations Have Cultures Too

Organizations also have cultures that may facilitate or hinder the work of the company, and management is responsible for fostering the culture of the organization. A set of values and philosophy will develop in every organization, whether it is created explicitly with careful forethought, or whether it happens implicitly without specific guidance. The result may be positive or negative. Management's values can encourage a culture of trust, problem-solving, and adaptation or create mistrust, obedience, and domination. In Chapter 2, we saw the examples of the toxic cultures of Uber and Wells Fargo (see p. 40). In Chapter 9, you will read about IBM's conservative, paternalistic culture and its "religion of decentralization" that presented challenges to Lou Gerstner when he took over as CEO (see p. 294).

Many books have been written about organizational culture and numerous consulting companies offer tools for assessing corporate cultures. Our intention is not to replicate that material, but to make the point that organizational culture is an important element in the success of a company.

Zappos is reputed to be a company with a positive culture. It regularly shows up in rankings of top corporate cultures. It is known for terrific customer service and a unique culture where everyone is a brand ambassador and enjoys working there. Robert Richman is the former culture strategist at Zappos and author of *The Culture Blueprint* (Richman, 2015). Two of his principles of culture are that it is co-created and that it consists of systems. No single person is in charge of creating a company culture, but rather it is the outcome of the continuing daily interactions of the people in the organization and the feelings that they create at work (Richman, 2015). As we have said in this chapter, the administrative systems send messages to employees about how to behave. Regardless of what a company says about its culture and values on the posters on its walls or the pages on its website, it is the behavior created by the employees, the systems, and the tone set by top management that becomes the culture.

Organizational culture is a variable that needs to be taken seriously in creating alignment, which is why it is included in the model. The quote, "Culture eats strategy for breakfast," is attributed to Peter Drucker. The quote highlights the importance of culture in the hierarchy of organizational ingredients needed for success. Similarly, Lou Gerstner in a 2002 Harvard Business School speech about the renewal effort he led at IBM said, "The thing I have learned at IBM is that culture is everything."

Aligning the Organization with Systems: Each Part Affects the Others

In summary, people are selected for certain skills and attitudes, trained and educated (developed) to improve these skills, evaluated on how they do their jobs, and rewarded. Evaluation and reward systems, development, budgets, and control systems are also used to motivate people. To make sure that the tasks of the organization are coordinated and carried out in the best possible way, companies use various structures. Too often decisions about the administrative systems are made as a result of unexamined assumptions about motivation, rather than an understanding of the organization in its context.

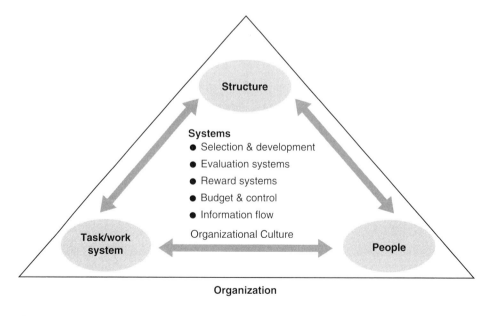

Figure 7.5 Organizational alignment: systems to shape internal alignment

Managers must comprehend that if they make a change in either the task or the people, their action may impact other parts of the system, with potentially unintended implications for overall results. This is one of the properties of a system; a change in one part affects other parts. Therefore, a systemic and integrated perspective of organizations is essential in diagnosing problems and considering courses of action. The internal organizational alignment model with systems is shown in Figure 7.5.

Aligning the Organization with the Environment

A global organization's context comprises social, political, economic, and technological influences. The social, political, and economic institutions in a host country may be very different from those in the home country. Also, the (national) cultural assumptions about "how things should be done" or the "right way to manage" may differ as well.

Global leaders must function in these complex systems. The complexity and responsibility faced by a manager vary by job and by level within the organization. People at the highest levels generally are more concerned with forces outside of the organization and linking the organization to its external environment, while people under them are more concerned with internal operations. However, with globalization people at all levels now are being exposed to the complexities of how other cultures affect their work.

Culture influences assumptions about management systems and practices. Managers must judge the potential effectiveness of their home country management systems and practices in relation to host country cultural assumptions. For example, in the conduct of domestic business, North American companies tend to decide about strategy, structure, and systems with the use of rational, economic cost–benefit analyses. Decisions may be based on discussions that reference and build upon implicit sets of shared cultural assumptions; all managers of the domestic companies are assumed to share such assumptions (although they don't necessarily). Yet, these assumptions of common viewpoints must be challenged and questioned when a manager operates in multiple national markets.

"Theories reflect the cultural environment in which they were written," explained Geert Hofstede. He further asked, "To what extent do theories developed in one country and reflecting the cultural boundaries of that country apply to other countries?" He questioned whether management theories developed primarily in the USA were applicable to other cultures. Management concepts and practices are explained by theories regarding organization, motivation, and leadership. Therefore, theories of management and the derived management systems and practices may work well in the culture that developed them, because they are based on local cultural assumptions and paradigms about the right way to manage.

An organization's management systems and processes have cultural assumptions incorporated into them. Although there is some debate about the ways that cultures around the world are converging or diverging, there is no doubt that, in the realm of systems and practices preferred in a given country, culture influences preferred behavioral style and the management systems that are acceptable or even desirable. The practices of one country, such as hiring friends and relatives, are often unacceptable or even ridiculed in another.

Earlier chapters provided numerous examples of how culture influenced management systems and processes. The alignment model can be used by any executive formulating and implementing strategy in his or her home market. Unless they are operating in a very multicultural domestic context, they don't necessarily give much thought to cultural influences in their domestic operations. But they must learn to do so when crossing cultural borders both within and between nation states. When firms start operating in different cultural environments, the ability to create alignment can change – often dramatically.

Administrative systems should be adaptable to changing conditions and workforces and not be ends in themselves. Furthermore, the fit that they create needs to be dynamic. This means that as strategies, competitive environments, or geographic locations change, structures, systems, and policies also need to be reevaluated and modified.

The cultural assumptions underlying administrative systems may not be immediately obvious. If you are experiencing problems in an international location, it might be easier to conclude that workers are the problem, instead of examining the assumptions underlying a reward or evaluation system, for instance. Types of questions you could ask in such a situation include: What would be the effect of a highly individualistic or independent compensation system in an interdependent culture? What are the cultural assumptions underlying practices such as empowerment, self-directed work teams, and 360-degree feedback? How would they work in status-oriented versus egalitarian cultures?

Counter-examples exist of managerial systems that are successful despite their lack of alignment with the local culture. It is important to remember that cultures are not monolithic and that there is a distribution of values, beliefs,

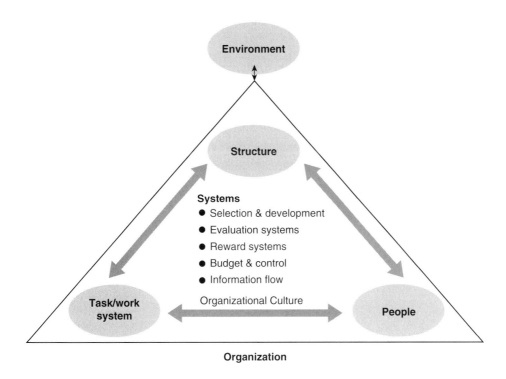

Figure 7.6 Aligning the organization with the environment

and ways of doing things in each one as we discussed in Chapter 3. Executives must decide whether existing practices, systems, and management styles can be transferred from one culture to another, or whether they must be changed and adapted when they appear to conflict with the norms of another culture.

Alignment to the environment is shown in Figure 7.6.

Can You Transfer Practices Directly? Should You Adapt to the Culture or Not?

Can existing practices, systems, and management styles be transferred or adapted? The answer is, "It all depends." It is not necessary to always change the system, even if it is different from the host country. In Rome, you do not always have to do as the Romans do! Sometimes people in another culture simply need to be trained to use a system (remembering, of course, that the best training format may be influenced by the culture). However, to assume that training is all that is required is also usually a mistake. Each response has a proper time and place.

The decision regarding transferring, adapting, or possibly even creating a new hybrid practice should be the result of careful, informed judgment based on understanding the cultural biases of management systems and the cultural norms of the country in which the operations are located. Are there rules? Not really, but careful analysis can help sort out the issues and help managers solve the problem. First, one must remember that cultures are not monolithic or deterministic. Also, if certain cultural values or practices are a critical part of an organization's model for success, then managers can use their selection system to find employees who display these characteristics.

Questions such as "How important is it that we do it identically to the way it's done at home?" can guide your decisions. Following procedures the same way may not be as important as achieving results. Just because headquarters does it one way does not mean that it is right for a different cultural environment.

What Does the Business Need?

The first important questions are around the business imperatives: tasks that must be done well for the firm to create value.

For example, a customer-centric strategy requires a lot of interfaces with the customer. If the customer is in a dynamic industry, customer-facing employees will need to make decisions on their own about how to adapt to the customer's needs. These business imperatives suggest a more egalitarian rather than a status-oriented decision-making structure, no matter what the national culture prefers. A company that relies on deep technology development must put a lot of resources into R&D. Rather than scattering those around the world, they may need to centralize with some big capital purchases. This implies a less egalitarian way of managing R&D resources, even in an egalitarian country culture.

In Chapter 2 we referred to Professor Paula Caligiuri's concept of culturally agile professionals who, "succeed in contexts where the successful outcome of their jobs, roles, positions or tasks depends on dealing with unfamiliar sets of cultural norms or multiple sets of them." They achieve success by being able to draw on three different behavioral responses: cultural minimization, cultural adaptation, or cultural integration. These three responses also describe the spectrum of adaptation responses for strategy execution.

Keep Your Own Practices ("Cultural Minimization")

Take the experience of a Canadian bank, the Bank of Nova Scotia, in Mexico. When the Mexican banking system was about to collapse after the economic crisis in 1994, the Mexican government put up for sale most of the Mexican banks. The Bank of Nova Scotia bought Inverlat. In 1982, Mexico's banks had been nationalized and they remained essentially government institutions for many years. Mexican banks stagnated, despite substantial innovations in the global banking industry. Many Inverlat managers claimed that their bank had generally deteriorated more than the rest of the banking sector in Mexico, and overall had failed to create a new generation of bankers who understood and reflected the changed conditions and times. The bank had been lending primarily to the government, and managers were unfamiliar with the challenges of lending to the private sector, and therefore failed to collateralize their loans properly or to ensure that covenants were being maintained. The existing managers did not have the knowledge or the capacity to manage the critical credit assessment function.

Whose practices should be followed? Banks make money by lending money, and the credit function is critical, or what we think of as a business imperative. The Canadians were the experts in this situation, and their practices should dominate.

Adapt to Your Partner ("Cultural Adaptation")

A different situation faced an American auto parts company that entered into a joint venture in North America with a Japanese company to learn about just-in-time manufacturing, a technique in which the Japanese company was a leader. The American company had a short-term orientation to cost control, and as the joint venture progressed, it became uncomfortable with the Japanese partner's longer-term orientation and wanted to institute tighter controls, which, however, interfered with its original objective for the joint venture – learning. In this situation, whose way should be followed? The Americans wanted to learn from the Japanese, who were the clear experts. The Japanese way should take precedence.

Create a New Way ("Cultural Integration")

When Renault attempted its rescue of Nissan in 1999, they appointed Carlos Ghosn, a Brazilian-born French-Lebanese engineer who had managed several turnarounds. Because Nissan was in crisis, people in the company assumed that

Ghosn would bring in French/Renault management methods and restructure in a non-Japanese way. In fact, Ghosn did change a lot of Japanese characteristics of the company. In a culture of lifetime employment, seniority, clear departmentalization, and interlocking supplier and customer business relationships, he eliminated 21,000 jobs, closed plants, introduced bonuses and stock options, had younger people managing older ones in cross-functional teams, and reduced the interdependency with suppliers in the keiretsu. At the same time, he deeply valued other aspects of Japanese culture: patience, discipline and conscientiousness, attention to detail, commitment to continuous improvement, and commitment to the goals of the organization. By combining what he saw as the strengths of Japanese culture with the systems needed to run a business that creates value, Ghosn led the turnaround of the business to become profitable within two years and decrease the debt to acceptable levels a year later. Reflecting over a decade later, Ghosn and senior Nissan and Renault executives agreed that Renault and Nissan both learned from each other, with some of the Nissan discipline transferring to Renault as well. Nissan retained its Japanese identity, but with a different way of working and going to market than other Japanese auto manufacturers (Ikegami, Maznevski, and Ota, 2017).

Aligning Dynamically Requires Judgment

We encourage you to use the alignment model as an analytic tool, remembering that organizations and their environment are both dynamic. The model simply provides an initial analytic tool to help global leaders adapt their organizations. There is no simple formula for choosing effective structures and systems. Use judgment in assessing the likely impact of systems on employees and in adjusting the systems to support job achievement and organizational results. Successful implementation means finding the right combination of strategy, structure, and systems that motivates people to strive for high performance.

Strategy in Global Organizations

Recalling the observation by Christopher Alexander referred to earlier that, "Every design problem begins with an effort to achieve fitness between two entities: the form in question and its context," we turn now to a brief discussion of strategy.

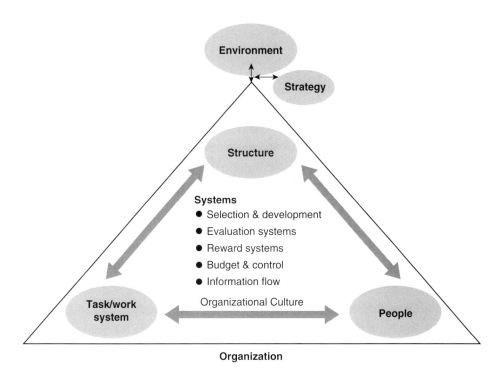

Figure 7.7 Complete alignment model

Strategy (form) defines the way an organization chooses to position itself in its competitive environment (context). It encompasses such things as the firm's segment in its industry and the control of critical factors for competing successfully in that segment. The complete alignment model, including strategy, is shown in Figure 7.7.

To be successful in a business or industry there are certain activities that an organization must do well. For example, if you are producing a commodity product, it might be critical to have a secure source of supply and efficient production or processing operations so you can be the low-cost producer. If you are producing highly differentiated products, advertising, marketing, and product development are likely the critical activities. If you are in the aerospace industry, your R&D capability and the ability to manage contracts to produce on time and within budgets may be key success factors.

You have to understand the critical success factors and you must recognize that these factors typically vary from industry to industry. Although one could say "you have to do everything well," that truism would not reflect the specific competitive situation within an industry. All firms need finance, production, marketing, sales, and human resource capabilities, but the relative emphasis or importance of each is determined by the nature of the business. Once you understand how you have to compete in your business, you can translate this into the tasks to be performed within the organization. Once you know what tasks need to be done and how they should be done, a structure and set of administrative systems can be implemented to get the jobs done properly.

Business Strategy: The Most Fundamental Business Decisions

Although this chapter is not about formulating strategy but, rather, executing strategy, a basic understanding of a firm's strategy (or any planned changes to a strategy) is needed to evaluate its alignment, or misalignment, with the internal structure and systems, and with the skills and abilities of employees.

There are multiple levels and types of strategy: corporate, business, international, and functional strategies. Corporate strategy, in a diversified company, is about deciding what businesses the company engages in; where in the world it should operate; and how these businesses should be managed to create value. Both business and corporate strategy tell you what the company does and, just as importantly, what it doesn't do. It also tells executives where to put resources. Peter Drucker said strategic management is "analytical thinking [formulation] and a commitment of resources to action [execution]" (Drucker, 1974).

We will focus mostly on business strategy: the level of strategy that must be aligned for successful execution. In a single business or in a business unit of a diversified company, business strategy, also called competitive strategy, refers to how a company creates competitive advantage by offering better customer value than its competitors. There are multiple frameworks, and our intent is not to explain all of them, but rather to present three that we have found particularly useful as we work with managers.

Porter's Generic Competitive Strategies for Product Focus

Probably the best known and most widely used competitive strategy framework is Michael Porter's (Porter, 1980). He identified three generic strategies: cost leadership (low cost), differentiation, and focus. Cost leadership requires keeping costs (and, therefore, prices) low through an emphasis on tight cost control, efficient operations, low overheads, and leveraging the benefits of a well-managed supply chain. Industries that produce products such as sugar, microchips, or other commodity-like offerings, usually fit in this category. In retailing, companies like Wal-Mart and IKEA come to mind.

Differentiation means creating distinct products or services for which customers are willing to pay a premium. Differentiation can be created in multiple ways, such as through prestige or brand image, proprietary technology or state of the art product features, or outstanding service networks. In examining prestige or brand image, one can think about automobiles: Mercedes stands for quality engineering; BMW for the driving experience; and Volvo for safety.

Focus, or market segmentation, means choosing a niche in an industry and tailoring a strategy to serve clients in this niche (Dess, Lumpkin, and Taylor, 2005). However, even this strategy requires a choice between cost leadership and differentiation. Southwest Airlines, Ryanair, and IKEA are examples of strategy focused on cost leadership and Ferrari on differentiation.

Today, companies are finding that they must move beyond simply offering products, and they must compete on the basis of customer solutions. This has become a common phenomenon in global companies. In some cases, companies even work closely with customers to develop the solutions together – this is referred to as co-creation. We believe that researchers such as Jay Galbraith, Arnoldo Hax, and Dean Wilde have described this contemporary change in the strategic posture of companies well. We begin with what Galbraith identified as the rise of the **customer dimension**.

Galbraith's Rise of the Customer Dimension

Jay Galbraith identified five factors that gave rise to the customer dimension in most industries (Galbraith, 2001):

1. Globalization of customers.
2. Customers' preference for partnerships or relationships.
3. Customers' desire for solutions.
4. The rise of e-commerce.
5. The continuing increase in the power of buyers.

As a result many companies created customer-facing organizational units but experienced implementation challenges because their structures remained oriented to SBUs, countries, and functions; and internal alignments that favored business as usual. He saw differences in the mindset, cultures, and organizational characteristics of product-centric versus customer-centric companies as shown in Table 7.2.

Table 7.2 **Comparison of product- and customer-centric organizations**

The product-centric company	The customer-centric company
Best product for customer	Best solution for customer
Creates value through cutting-edge products, useful features, new applications	Creates value through customizing for best total solution
Divergent thinking: How many possible uses of product?	Convergent thinking: What combination of products is best for this customer?
Manage through product profit centers, product reviews, product teams	Organized by customer segments, customer teams, customer P&Ls
Most important process: New Product Development	Most important process: Customer Relationship Management
Measures • Number of new products • % revenue from products less than two years old • Market share	Measures • Customer share of most valuable customers • Customer satisfaction • Lifetime value of a customer • Customer retention
New product culture – open to new ideas, experimentation	Co-creation culture – open to new ideas, experimentation, together with customer
Most important customer is advanced customer	Most important customer is most profitable, loyal customer
Priority-setting around portfolio of products	Priority-setting around portfolio of customers, customer profitability
Highest reward is working on next most challenging product	Power to people with in-depth knowledge of customer's business
Manage creative people through challenges with a deadline	Manage creative people through exposure to customer insight and customer problem-solving challenges
Power to people who develop products	Personalized packages of service, support, education, consulting
On the side of the seller in a transaction	On the side of the buyer in a transaction
Price according to market	Price according to value and risk share

Source: Galbraith (2001).

Hax and Wilde's Delta Model

Hax and Wilde argued that Porter's framework does not capture all the ways in which companies compete in a dynamic, networked economy (Hax and Wilde, 2001). Their framework includes Porter's emphasis on product characteristics, but they go beyond a product orientation to focus heavily on creating customer

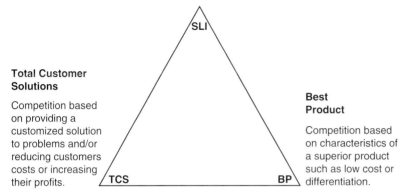

Systems Lock-In

Competition based on total system economics, network effects based on market dominance through "complementor" lock-in, competitor lock-out or proprietary standards.

SLI

Total Customer Solutions

Competition based on providing a customized solution to problems and/or reducing customers costs or increasing their profits.

Best Product

Competition based on characteristics of a superior product such as low cost or differentiation.

TCS

BP

Figure 7.8 Hax and Wilde's Delta Model for customer-centric strategy
Adapted from Hax and Wilde (2001), reprinted with permission of Palgrave Macmillan; and Hax (2010).

value. Companies must shift their thinking from "developing, making, and distributing standardized goods and services to [creating] a bundle of competencies that can be packaged into a well-integrated portfolio of products and services" that provide exceptional and unique value for their customers. The Delta Model is summarized in Figure 7.8.

In a networked economy it is important not to focus simply on competitive advantage but to achieve **customer bonding**, which creates a beneficial relationship for the company and its customers. Hax and Wilde propose three strategic options: best product, total customer solutions, and system lock-in. The first two are relatively straightforward. **Best product (BP)** competition is essentially low cost or differentiation based on product economics. **Total customer solutions (TCS)** competition is based on customer economics; the challenge is to reduce customer costs or increase their profits.

System lock-in (SLI) competition is based on system economics or network effects and economies. This means that companies may bundle products and services and customize them to the needs of their customers or do joint product development. They try to lock in "**complementors**," lock out competitors, or develop proprietary standards. This means considering all the meaningful players in a system that contribute to the creation of economic value. Customers, suppliers, and complementors should be included as important contributors to thinking about strategy.

What is a complementor? An easy way to think about complementors and SLI competition is to think about the software industry. Microsoft, for example, provides its Windows operating system and there are a number of companies that develop applications for Windows. These companies are complementors and, because of their involvement and products, they contribute to the value of the total system and to the value of Microsoft. Similarly, app developers for Apple's iPhone are complementors.

Complementors also exist outside of high-tech industries. An example in North America is the ubiquitous K-Cup used in the Keurig brewing systems for coffee, tea, and hot cocoa. Well-known brands such as Starbucks, Celestial Seasonings, Wolfgang Puck, Caribou Coffee, Gloria Jean's, Swiss Miss, Twinings of London, and Dunkin' Donuts all use K-Cups to package their products. The more name brands that package their products in this format, the greater the value the system creates for Keurig and the more difficult it becomes for competitors to gain market share.

There are many models for making strategic choices, and we encourage you to use the ones that make most sense for your industry and competitive context, while taking the time to question your assumptions from time to time as the environment changes.

Business Models: Making the "How" Choices

Business, or competitive, strategy refers to a company's way of creating a competitive advantage by offering better customer value than competitors. Three questions to ask about strategy are *who, what,* and *how*: who are our customers, what is our product or service, and how is it delivered?

A business model is how a firm creates and captures value and earns a profit in a competitive environment. Simply stated, it is how a firm delivers its value proposition to customers and how it makes money. An example should help in understanding the concept of the business model.

Think about retail booksellers in the late 1990s. Barnes & Noble Booksellers was founded in New York in 1917 and by 1987 had become a national chain in the USA. In the late 1980s and early 1990s, it evolved the concept of the suburban superstore, which generated 96 percent of its retail sales. The company offered a comprehensive selection of books and music (the *what*) using experienced staff in spacious stores, complete with cafés that sold Starbucks coffee (the *how*). It became a destination for people, a sort of town meeting place, but its business model was to deliver its products and services to its customers in bricks and mortar stores that were open during certain hours. Although it opened its first online book superstore on America Online in 1997, Amazon.com is generally considered the developer of this new industry business model.

Founded in 1994, Amazon.com went public in 1997 and by 1999 it generated over US$1.6 billion in sales. Amazon.com turned the retail bookselling industry upside down. Its business model was to sell books to customers anytime and anyplace, using the Internet. It created an online community of customers by allowing people to write their own book reviews and share them. This example shows how companies in the same industry, selling the same products, can have vastly different business models to deliver their products and services. And the people, skills, and systems for each model to function are vastly different.

Another example is the movie rental business. Blockbuster was founded in 1985 when the market was dominated by local "mom & pop" shops. These outlets required a deposit for bulky VHS or Betamax tapes. Blockbuster introduced the membership model, opened stores across the USA, and members could rent videos from any of its stores. Like its competitors of the time, it charged late fees. By 1999 it was the largest video rental company in the world. Its business model and scale replaced that of the local shops.

The introduction of DVDs in the mid-1990s made videotape technology obsolete and contributed to Blockbuster's demise. Even though Blockbuster rented DVDs, Netflix had arrived with a different strategy and business model. It delivered movies by mail from a central location, eliminating the need for bricks and mortar stores. However, Netflix itself eventually faced competition: video streaming services like Amazon Video on Demand, Hulu, and Apple iTunes. Redbox, which offered extremely cheap video rentals from kiosks in convenient, high-volume traffic locations such as supermarkets captured 25 percent of the rental market by 2010. Blockbuster filed for bankruptcy in 2010, and in 2011 it was bought by DISH Network.

This example also shows that a company does not need to have a technologically sophisticated business model like Amazon to displace existing companies and be successful. However, technology has become a critical tool and asset in disruption. Ride sharing services like Uber and Lyft, for example, used technology to disrupt the taxi industry and Airbnb has done the same with hotel accommodation.

Companies Are Becoming More Customer-Focused

It is easy to talk about globalization and being customer-centric, but it is not easy to put these ideas into practice. It has been the authors' experience over the past years working with a number of companies in various industries such as defense, financial printing, telecommunications, financial services, fast-moving consumer goods, construction and development, and even law enforcement that they all were experiencing the need to provide "solutions" and to develop organizations that were customer-centric. This need to behave differently was driven in all cases by changes in the organizations' external environment. For some, it was the appearance of new competitors with new products and business models that sparked the need to coordinate across functional or business areas. For others, firms in financial services like accounting for example, the consolidation of the global players into the Big Four and increased regulation (Sarbanes-Oxley and other changes) affected their customer orientation. For law enforcement agencies, it was the appearance of new criminal or terrorist network organizations posing new threats that drove the change.

However, the characteristic that they all had in common was that to become customer-centric and provide solutions, they had to work horizontally across the organization to coordinate information and activities in order to improve performance in the new environments that they faced. They all struggled to do this effectively.

Culture's Influence on Strategy

It takes a deep understanding of a company's strategy and management systems and an understanding of the history and culture of the host country to execute a global strategy properly. And it takes time.

What happens when a company takes its strategy "on the road" so to speak – when it begins implementing it in another country? What appears to be obvious and straightforward in a firm's home market or in another international location may not work in a new country. What executives take for granted at home may not apply abroad.

Consider the TJX Companies, the world's leading off-price retailer of apparel and home fashions, operating multiple businesses through four divisions: The Marmaxx Group (TJ Maxx and Marshalls), Sierra Trading

Post, and HomeGoods in the USA; TJX Canada (Winners, HomeSense, and Marshalls); and TJX Europe (TK Maxx and HomeSense). At the end of its 2017 fiscal year, it operated more than 3,800 stores in nine countries and three e-commerce sites. Its revenue exceeded US$33 billion and it employed approximately 235,000 "Associates." We learned about the company's globalization journey in a conversation with Ted English, the CEO at the time they entered Europe.

TJX's value proposition was to deliver a rapidly changing assortment of fashionable, quality, brand name merchandise at 20–60 percent below regular department and specialty store prices. It was able to do this because it relied on opportunistic buying, disciplined inventory management, and a low expense structure. Its stores are located in community shopping centers and are flexible spaces with no permanent, fixed store features. Its target market is value-conscious customers across wide income levels and demographics.

Customers entering the TJ Maxx Store in Newport, Rhode Island, for example, would encounter this business model by driving to a shopping mall, parking their car in a spacious parking lot, and taking a shopping cart as they entered the store, which they would push to hold all the merchandise they selected in their "exciting treasure-hunt shopping experience." This is a straightforward, common experience in the United States in this type of retail store. However, this mode of operating has a number of built-in, culturally influenced assumptions which include:

- Customers can and will drive to the mall where there is plenty of parking.
- Customers will need and use a shopping cart in order to purchase many items.
- Customers can identify the value inherent in their purchases because they can recognize the brand name and its reduced selling price in the store.

When TJX opened its first European stores in the UK and the Netherlands, it discovered that many of its customers only bought one or two items. Also, the idea of using a shopping cart was foreign to them, and they initially refused to use them. In the Netherlands, there were more obstacles to overcome than in the UK, including language and culture. TJX was not able to replicate the brand/value proposition in the Netherlands, as customers did not easily recognize the value offering – the brand versus price trade-off. The business model did not work there as it did in the USA.

Executing Global Strategy: The Importance of Mindful Leadership and Adaptation

Amazon.com has continued to modify its business model and has morphed into being more of a technology company than a bookseller. Although it owns companies outside the retail industry, most visibly it continues its disruption of retail industry segments such as shoes with the purchase of Zappos and grocery by buying Whole Foods. It exemplifies the basic premises of strategic adaption that apply domestically or globally.

1. *The environment is always changing.*

   The retail industry has gone through what some observers refer to as "Retail Darwinism," meaning survival of the fittest (or more accurately survival of the best adapted to the environment). Family stores (so-called "mom and pop" stores) were essentially the retail industry in the USA in the 1800s and into the 1900s. In the 1900s chains that had coexisted with the family stores in major city centers expanded regionally aided by the development of suburbs, an increase in automobile ownership, and shopping malls. Also around the mid-1900s many of the chains located in the malls and city centers declined in importance for the retail trade. Then came the "big box" stores like we saw in the Global Multi-Products case. More recently came companies like Amazon that created another inflection point, *e-commerce*, and traditional retailers are struggling to react.

2. *Strategies need to change or firms need to find market niches to remain in alignment with their environment.*

   A classic example of failure to successfully adapt is Sears (formerly Sears, Roebuck and Company) that at one time it was the largest retailer in the USA. It has been called the Amazon of the early twentieth century because it was a very innovative company for its time, starting as a distance retailer with its famous mail-order, Sears Catalog, in the late 1800s. It failed to update its retail model to remain in sync with the changing tastes and fashions and faced industry competitors such as Wal-Mart, Home Depot, and Amazon. Speculation continues about its ability to survive.

3. *Execution is key.*

   Sears entered businesses that it had no experience with such as real estate and financial services. It developed many well-known product brands that it no longer owns and had to sell off in order to stay in business. These products could have contributed to its success in the twenty-first century if they had been managed well, but it was unable to capitalize on them. It was even an early mover in using the Internet. Along with CBS and IBM, it created Prodigy, which eventually became a part of Telmex and currently is a major Internet Service Provider (ISP) in Mexico. Sears could not turn innovative ideas into sustainable businesses. As Thomas Edison is reported to have said, "Vision without execution is just hallucination."

In this chapter, we have identified key elements that managers should keep in mind as they implement strategy. We shared a model of internal alignment within the organization, including the task, the people, structure, and administrative systems. We examined the relationship between organizational alignment and the environment, including the role of strategic choices and business models. Although we have provided some tools, principles, and ways of thinking based on research and experience, you will need to provide the requisite judgment component by combining your learning and experience with the principles as you develop into a mindful global leader.

Reflection Questions

This chapter's reflection questions lead you through applying the alignment framework to your own organization. The intention is to increase mindfulness about how your own organizational system works, allowing you to compare it with others you encounter. We will refer to your "business," but you can adapt the questions to a not-for-profit organization, to a business unit or department within a larger business, or any other organizational unit.

1. Internal alignment
   a. Structure: What are the key elements of your structure? How much hierarchy is there? How centralized is decision-making? Who has power (which positions or roles)?
   b. Tasks/Work Systems: What is the main set of tasks or work system? How is this work organized? For example, what kind of interdependence is required, and how complex are the tasks? What professional skills and knowledge do they require?
   c. People: What are the main skill sets and areas of expertise that people currently have? What are some patterns of personal values? Think about the key people in power and decision-making roles – what are their likely motivations and priorities?

     d. Culture and Systems: How would you characterize the organizational culture? What are some dominant guiding values? How strong is the organizational culture? On what basis is performance measured and rewarded? What other systems are particularly important in guiding decision-making and action?

     e. Alignment: How well-aligned are the elements of the organization? Where are the strongest alignments, where are there gaps? What's the cause of the gaps (e.g., labor shortage, new regulations for tasks, organizational restructuring, new business planning system for the company ...)?

2. External alignment
   a. Environment: What are the key characteristics of the external environment that affect your business? This could be a long list, but try to prioritize the main effects of customer demands, competitive pressures, and your industry's business model.

   b. Strategy: How would you describe your business's strategy and business model? Who are your customers, what do you deliver to them, and how do you do it? Again, this could be a long and comprehensive exercise. For these purposes focus on the key elements that most affect your decision-making and how you and others work together.

   c. Alignment: How well-aligned is the strategy with the external environment for your business? Does your strategy take into account changes happening now in the environment?

3. Total alignment
   a. Alignment is a moving target, and often the internal alignment of an organization is aligned with a *past* business environment and strategy, but less with the *current* business environment and strategy. How would you assess the match between internal and external alignment in your company? Does the alignment among structure, task/work systems, and people match the alignment between strategy and the environment?

   b. How does this alignment explain patterns of performance? Your areas of lower performance are likely related to areas of misalignment. What could be changed to increase alignment?

   c. To what extent do you think your business's alignment choices might be affected by the culture you're embedded in? The culture of the headquarters? In what ways does this enable or hinder performance in your current environment?

We will address the change management process itself in Chapter 9.

Further Resources

The organizational design framework and analytic model have been adapted from a number of writers on the contingency theory of organizations. Some classic sources that still provide important perspectives today include:

Galbraith, J. R. (1977). *Organization Design.* Addison-Wesley.
Lawrence, P. R. & Lorsch, J. W. (1969). *Organization and Environment.* Richard D. Irwin.

Two excellent resources on modern organizations are:

Galbraith, J. R. (2009). *Designing Matrix Organizations That Actually Work.* Jossey-Bass.
Kates, A., & Galbraith, J. R. (2007). *Designing Your Organization.* Jossey-Bass.

The Delta Model is described in a summary article:

Hax, A. C., & Wilde, D. L. (1999).The Delta Model: Adaptive Management for a Changing World. *MIT Sloan Management Review*, 40, 11–28.

An updated and extended version of the original book is Hax's *The Delta Model: Reinventing Your Business Strategy* (2010).

Some of the better-known corporate culture assessments are the following:

- Competing Values Framework (Quinn and Rohrbaugh, 1983). www.ocai-online.com/about-the-Organizational-Culture-Assessment-Instrument-OCAI
- Denison Culture Model (Denison Consulting). www.denisonconsulting.com/
- Organizational Culture Inventory (Human Synergistics). www.humansynergistics.com/
- CultureIQ Survey. https://cultureiq.com/

Bibliography

Alexander, C. (1964). *Notes on the Synthesis of Form.* Harvard University Press.
Dess, G., Lumpkin, G., & Taylor, M. (2005). *Strategic Management.* McGraw-Hill/Irwin.
Drucker, P. (1974). *Management: Tasks, Responsibilities, Practices.* Harper.
Galbraith, J. (2001). Building Organizations around the Global Consumer. *Ivey Business Journal*, September/October.
Available at: https://iveybusinessjournal.com/publication/building-organizations-around-the-global-customer/
Hax, A. (2010). *The Delta Model: Reinventing Your Business Strategy.* Springer.
Hax, A., & Wilde, D. (2001). *The Delta Project.* Palgrave Macmillan.
Hofstede, G. (1980). Motivation, Leadership, and Organization: Do American

Theories Apply Abroad? *Organizational Dynamics*, 8, 42–63.

Ikegami, J., Maznevski, M., & Ota, M. (2017). Creating the Asset of Foreignness: Schrödinger's Cat and Lessons from the Nissan Revival. *Cross-Cultural and Strategic Management*, 24, 55–77.

Lane, H. W. (1980). Systems, Values, and Action: An Analytic Framework for Intercultural Management Research. *Management International Review*, 20, 61–70.

Lane, H. W., & Campbell, D. (2007). *Global Multi-Products Chile.* Ivey case no. 9A98C007. Ivey Publishing.

Lawrence, P., & Lorsch, J. (1969). *Organization and Environment.* Richard D. Irwin.

Nonaka, I., & Takeuchi, H. (1995). *The Knowledge Creating Company.* Oxford University Press.

Porter, M. (1980). *Competitive Strategy.* Hill & Wang.

Quinn, R., & Rohrbaugh, J. (1983). A Spatial Model of Effectiveness Criteria: Towards a Competing Values Approach to Organizational Analysis. *Management Science*, 29, 363–77.

Richman, R. (2015). *The Culture Blueprint.* Culture Hackers.

Sekiguchi, T. (2004). Person–Organization Fit and Person–Job Fit in Employee Selection: A Review of the Literature. *Osaka Keidai Ronshu*, 55. Retrieved March 21, 2013 from: www.osaka-ue .ac.jp/gakkai/pdf/ronshu/2004/5501_ ronko_sekiguti.pdf

Thompson, J. (1967). *Organizations in Action.* McGraw-Hill.

Ting-Toomey, S. (1999). Constructive Intercultural Conflict Management. In S. Ting-Toomey, *Communicating Across Cultures.* Guilford Press.

8   Executing Global Strategy: Applications

> I don't think architecture is only about shelter, is only about a very simple enclosure. It should be able to excite you, to calm you, to make you think.
>
> It is insufficient for architecture today to directly implement an existing building typology; it instead requires architects to carefully examine the whole area with new interventions and programmatic typologies.
>
> Zaha Hadid, architect

What's the Best Organizational Form for Executing Strategy? What Kind of Leadership Does It Require?

Organization design is to business action and decision-making as architecture is to the design of physical spaces for living and working in. And just as the architecture of buildings and cities has evolved with our way of living, organizational forms have evolved for new requirements of doing business.

As we established in Chapter 7, executing strategy requires aligning tasks, people, and the structure with the external environment and a business strategy that creates value in the target arena. Within these alignment parameters, there is a plethora of ways to organize, and the implications can seem overwhelming. In this chapter we identify the most frequent ways of organizing to execute strategy in global business, and we highlight the alignment and leadership implications for each. By the end of this chapter, you should be able to identify the main elements of most international business forms, diagnose their alignment, and develop insights about the type of leadership they require. We begin by examining the tensions of global integration and local responsiveness. We turn to the general organization of large multinational enterprises (MNEs), and then look at different organizational vehicles for growth. Next we look at small companies that manage to be global without scale. We also consider some important emerging trends and organizational mechanisms for coordinating.

The Classic Dilemma: Global Integration versus Local Responsiveness

How global companies organize themselves is a consequence of factors or business needs that push them toward either **global integration** (globalization) or pull them toward **local responsiveness** (localization) (Bartlett & Ghoshal, 2002; Prahalad & Doz, 1987). Global integration is centralizing decision-making and formalizing procedures for one way of doing things globally, applied the same everywhere, without redundancies. Local responsiveness is decentralizing decision-making and having fewer formal procedures, such that each geographical region determines its own way of doing business.

Factors that favor **global integration** include the need to align under a specific **stakeholder interface**, such as a global brand. Another factor is the need to **reduce costs** through global efficiencies, such as leveraging scale for bulk purchasing of supplies, decreasing labor costs, or centralizing large investments such as R&D costs or large manufacturing plants. Global integration drivers require companies to control activities centrally and to minimize duplication of functions. A company with high global integration can centralize decisions for aligned implementation throughout the globe, enabled by today's fluidity of transporting goods and information across borders. This configuration allows the company to place specific value chain activities in one or several locations around the world, such as locations with less expensive labor, specifically trained workforces, access to particular raw materials, or other resources. At the extreme, companies can locate each activity in a region from which the firm could best serve the rest of its global activities. Whatever the distribution of activities, global integration requires high levels of centralization and standardization in the structure, with associated alignment implications for tasks, people, and systems.

The requirement for **local responsiveness** appears when a company has to adapt its products and services, tailor its business model, or realign its administrative systems to meet the needs of a specific national market. The three main factors driving local responsiveness are differing **local customer** needs for the products or services, **local cultural norms** for effective organizing, and **local**

regulations for business operations or products and services. Today's information and digital technologies enable localization in new ways, for example by making smaller-run manufacturing feasible and less costly. To achieve local responsiveness, an organization adopts a structure, set of tasks, characteristics of people, and alignment systems that are consistent with the local operation. This may mean flatter or taller hierarchical structures, more or less team-based manufacturing, different professional backgrounds for salespeople and technical service, and so on.

In addition to balancing globalization and localization, a successful global organization engages in global learning, that is, the transfer and sharing of new ideas and knowledge among units. A new production technology, marketing strategy, or product feature designed for one market often can be transferred to other markets. The challenge is to be able to identify synergistic links among units and to transfer knowledge and skills effectively. The proper organizational structures and systems, as well as the right individuals, play an important role in facilitating global learning.

Generic International Organizational Forms

All companies that operate globally are subject to the pressures of global integration and local responsiveness. The degree to which a company must respond to these forces depends heavily on the characteristics of the industry in which it competes and influences its multinational strategy. One common classification scheme, based on the integration-responsiveness framework, identifies four structures, each related to a specific type of strategy: the global, the multi-domestic, the international, and the transnational. This is shown in Figure 8.1.

Figure 8.1 Generic international organizational forms

First, a company that follows a strategy that is highly dependent on global integration for most of its value chain activities and is locally responsive for only a few of them needs a **globally standardized organization**. Such a company usually is characterized by a high degree of complex interdependencies among its subsidiaries and has a governance structure that is tightly and centrally controlled. Coca-Cola has a globally standardized organization for its branding, and Royal Dutch Shell has a globally standardized organization for its oil production.

Second, a company that follows a strategy that is minimally dependent on global integration but highly dependent on local responsiveness for many of its value chain activities needs a **multi-domestic organization**. These companies may operate differently in each country; in an extreme case, each country or region would have its own manufacturing, marketing, and R&D. These companies can be thought of as a confederation of loosely coupled organizations with strong local control and weak central control. The managers of multi-domestic subsidiaries often function as independent "feudal lords" who may or may not be expatriate managers depending on the company's administrative heritage. Traditionally, some large consumer goods companies such as Unilever and Nestlé were organized this way, although they are moving toward being transnational organizations now (see below). Companies in the building materials and construction industries, including cement and concrete firms such as Lafarge (now part of LafargeHolcim) and construction and development firms such as Vinci tend to be multi-domestic organizations.

Third, a multinational company that depends minimally on global integration and minimally on local responsiveness needs an **international organization**. Essentially, it replicates its home market systems in each of its foreign subsidiaries. These companies are very centralized and their subsidiaries are simply outlets for headquarters' decisions. In today's global economy there are few industries left where an international organization works well. The product categories most suitable to such a strategy would include commodities. For example, grain businesses (AMD, Cargill) are large organizations that deal with commodity products that are traded around the world on the basis of price; however, even in these companies it is only a small set of operations that are conducted using international organizations.

Finally, a company that is simultaneously globally integrated and locally responsive needs a **transnational organization**. This organizational structure distributes the global responsibility for specific activities to the leaders who manage the subsidiary to which the activity has been assigned. Each country manager may report to different people with different worldwide activity responsibilities. The local responsiveness is achieved by managing each distributed value chain activity with enough flexibility so that the local manager can make the essential compromises necessary to achieve as high a local market fit as possible. The transnational organization is costly to implement and requires managers who are cross-culturally and interpersonally skilled and flexible. Few – if any – truly transnational corporations exist, but many are aspiring and progressing in that direction, including Nestlé, Shell, and Matsushita. However, as we will see in the specific examples below, the trend toward customer-centric strategies has led to an increase in companies attempting to deliver in a transnational organization.

   In the sections below, we'll see how companies with different strategies adapt these generic organizational forms to achieve alignment according to different needs.

Large MNEs: The Benchmark for Global Organizing

The vast majority of MNEs began as companies that produced for and sold in their local national market, then grew over time through a combination of acquisitions and organic growth. Often these companies started their international expansion with a business unit (BU) called "International," and only after many years did they incorporate non-home markets into the rest of the organization. The large consumer products companies, for example, followed this path, such as Procter & Gamble, Unilever, and Nestlé. MNEs tend to be organized first by geography, then by product or service area.

Multi-Divisional Structures

Most MNEs are organized in many divisions, with each having responsibility for its own profits and losses. Divisional leaders can make decisions about most operations, including investments, within the parameters of global coordination at the top. Profits go to the global organization, and may be redistributed to other divisions or directly to shareholders, or they may be applied to global investments. These organizations tend to prioritize either global integration or local responsiveness for each activity, although there may be units focusing on global integration and local responsiveness across the company. For example, Skanska, a multinational construction and development company, is based in

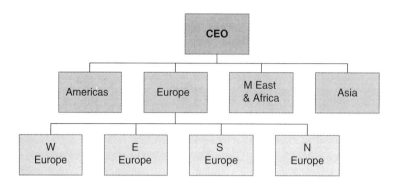

Figure 8.2 Generic multi-divisional structure with geography-based business units
Note: Americas, Middle East and Africa, and Asia would also have regions, not shown here.

Sweden with operations in the Nordics, Eastern Europe, the UK, and the USA. Because construction projects are essentially local, their dominant mode of organizing is multi-domestic by geography: first organized by country, then by region within the country. On the other hand, Bombardier, a Canadian aircraft and transportation manufacturer, is organized by product groups: business aircraft, commercial aircraft, transportation (such as public transit and railway), and services. Each of these businesses relies first on core technology and global value propositions, and second on adaptation to local markets. A generic geography-based multi-divisional structure is shown in Figure 8.2.

Multi-divisional structures have been the mainstay for global organizing since its inception. The separation of work into divisions allows efficiency and focus within the division on the key value proposition parameters (global integration), while the separation of different divisions allows for adaptation to different market segments (local responsiveness). Because the divisions are clear, it is possible to grow by adding a division or sub-division, or through acquisition, without affecting the whole organization. Although these organizations are large, the specialization of divisions means it is fairly straightforward to align task, structure, and people within a division. Headquarters is usually large enough to provide strong systems to support alignment, such as performance management, compensation, and development. Leading in a multi-divisional structure requires seeing a systems view of the organization – understanding how the parts fit together to make a whole, and how one division's or sub-division's decision affects others.

A multi-divisional structure has several negative forces that must be counter-balanced. These organizations have a tendency toward internal focus and bureaucracy – they are coordinated through rules and procedures, and they can get so focused on these systems that they lose sight of the customer and/ or the larger organization. They often replicate effort and create inefficiencies without coordination – for example, several parts of the company may develop protocols for particular problems or situations, without knowing that the others are doing the same thing. Leaders at the top must constantly keep themselves informed about what's happening in the different divisions, and enable coordination knowledge and information transfer to "cascade" back down. Skanska faces these challenges for developing expertise in particular kinds of projects, such as hospitals and schools, tunnels and shopping malls. Bombardier faces these challenges for interacting with customers. In both these organizations, they balance the multi-divisional structure with multiple coordination mechanisms, such as centers of excellence (which will be discussed below).

The Quiet Return of the Matrix

A matrix organization has two (or more) organizing principles that are equal or almost equal in strength. For example, geography and product organization could have equal weight. There is a head of each geography, and also a head of each product area. Someone working on product type X in geography Y would report to two ultimate bosses, one each for product type and geography. The matrix is the structure most MNEs invoke, at least in part, to move more toward their ideal of transnational organization.

In the 1980s most MNEs experimented with the matrix with great enthusiasm. We worked with one company that even had a six-dimensional matrix, with each person in the organization reporting equally to six bosses! Leaders found that the matrix was too complex – most people had two or more bosses with equal power, and a lot of effort was spent resolving conflicts or identifying gaps or redundancies. In status-oriented cultures, the matrix violates cultural norms of having clear hierarchy, and it was particularly rejected in these cultures. Even in egalitarian-oriented cultures, the added coordination time and effort were deemed not worth the effort for a gain in knowledge and information distribution. By the 1990s, most companies had moved back to a multi-divisional structure with some informal coordination mechanisms.

However, two trends have led to a quiet return of the matrix: the tendency toward customer-centric strategies means local responsiveness is more important to all firms, and the extreme competition and volatility of the business environment since the early 2000s mean that all firms need to focus on integrating globally for cost and efficiency. In the current situation, most companies find they *must* counter the downsides of multi-divisional structure by giving clear authority and priority to multiple sets of organizing criteria. The main difference from the 1980s is that today's matrix organizations are usually limited to two or at most three dimensions, and, importantly, they tend to clearly (if slightly) prioritize one dimension over others. Even firms from status-oriented cultures like Tata Motors in India and Toyota Trading Company in Japan are now organized with a matrix.

In Figure 8.3, you see a generic version of a modern matrix organization. The relationships indicated by the solid line, that is, the primary ones, are geographic. But product groups are also important, and there is a clear organizational structure around product groups. This secondary organization is indicated with dotted lines. Within the organization, each person reports to both a geography leader and a product-area leader. Companies tend to signal the relative priority through systems alignment – for example, compensation may be based 60 percent on a leader's geography results, and 40 percent on the same leader's global product results. Note that the dimensions could be any of geography, product or service, function (e.g., marketing, manufacturing, finance), customer segment (e.g., government, corporate), or other dimensions important to the firm's strategy and alignment.

It is particularly easy to see the matrix organization in consumer goods firms. For example, Nestlé is organized by geographic zones, with country and zone

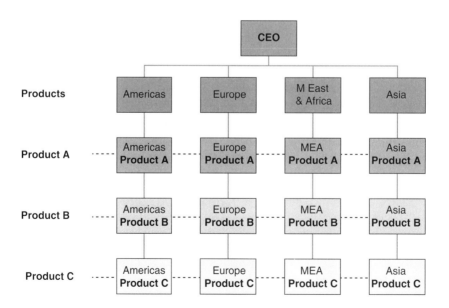

Figure 8.3 Generic matrix structure with geographies primary and products secondary

managers having profit and loss responsibility for their geographies. At the same time, strategic product groups are managed globally: Nutrition, Waters, Nespresso, and some brands such as Nescafé and KitKat. Unilever is organized both by geographic zones and by products groups such as Personal Care, Home Care, Foods, and Refreshment. Likewise, Procter & Gamble (P&G) is organized by geographic regions and product areas such as Baby, Family, Fabric, Grooming, and Hair.

Today's matrices are still complex; managers have accepted that some level of complexity is necessary for optimizing. Alignment, in particular, provides ongoing challenges. Main business units tend to be aligned according to the needs of that dimension (e.g., geography), but with adjustments made for maximizing the matrixed functions. For example, product quality may require that each plant have an expert in a particular quality process, such as six sigma. If the skills are not available locally, the local business unit may have to bring in an expatriate.

MNEs organized by the matrix find that they can leverage their scale strengths for global brands, innovating, and supply chain. They can develop a portfolio of expertise and have people work on projects wherever they're needed, and at the same time they can develop and execute the best plans for each market they operate in.

Central Services and Aligning MNEs

Most MNEs, whether "simple" multi-divisional or matrixed, also have some kind of business services unit that provides support for all parts of the organization. This unit could include finance and audit, human resources, technology, investor relations, and other functions that are important to support the organization as a whole. Country or product areas may have business services members assigned to them, such as a Human Resources Business Partner or a local Chief Financial Officer (CFO). Even in a simple multi-divisional organization, these business services units tend to be organized as a matrix, often with the functional leader reporting first to the function (Human Resources, Finance) and second to the geography.

As the discussion above shows, developing alignment of tasks, people, structure, and systems across an MNE is a daunting challenge and an ever-moving target. The potential benefits are clear – the possibility of delivering more comprehensive and sustainable value for customers. For this reason, companies continue to aspire to these forms, adapting and adjusting as the environment changes while still maintaining stability for employees, customers, and suppliers. This discussion also makes it clear why global leadership competences are increasingly important for anyone working in an MNE. With current organizational configurations, whatever their balance of global integration and local responsiveness, leaders who are mindful of the global context will be able to coordinate better across the organization.

Growing through Acquisitions, Alliances, and Joint Ventures

MNEs commonly grow internationally through organic means (growing the current operations across borders) or inorganic means (acquiring or allying with another enterprise). **Organic growth** adds to the organization incrementally, and does not usually require a separate form of aligning or organizing. Inorganic growth can confront the organization's alignment, and require responses in shaping organizational structures. In this section we'll consider two common ways to execute inorganic growth, both of which have important implications for alignment and leadership: acquisitions and alliances.

International Acquisitions

Companies make **acquisitions** to fill a strategic gap in their products, people, or capabilities, to enter a new geographic market, or some combination of these reasons. This is a very common method of growth, and an enormous body of research has been conducted on how MNEs select their acquisitions. Here our focus is on the organizational alignment and execution issues. In this respect, the most important decision for acquisitions is how tightly to integrate. Should the newly-acquired company be held at arm's length, almost as institutional investors would? Or should it be integrated into the parent company? If the latter, how much, and in what ways? Most global expansion strategies integrate the acquired company at least lightly.

   The Tata group has expanded internationally by acquiring big companies in many markets, including motor companies Jaguar, Land Rover, and Daewoo Commercial Vehicles, steel companies Corus, NatSteel, and Millennium Steel, hot beverage companies Tetley Tea and Eight O'Clock Coffee, and IT company Tyco Global Network. Tata follows a general practice of **light touch integration**. All acquired companies are required to sign up to the Tata values and some key practices, including the Business Excellence Model and the Code of Conduct. Senior Tata executives encourage collaboration around these values. However, acquired companies are left to themselves to determine strategy and run the business (Kale, Singh, and Raman, 2009).

Most of the big technology companies, on the other hand, are more likely to engage in tight integration. Google, Cisco, and Amazon buy services or applications that they bring directly into the core business. At Google, for example, senior executives at the acquired company are offered roles in the parent company, and inducements to stay. The strategy of the acquired company is integrated into the overall picture of Google, and the acquired company's products and services fold into the existing Google structure (Luckerson, 2015). Cisco's strategy execution depends so strongly on aligning and integrating the acquired organization tightly, that many of CEO John Chambers's criteria for identifying potential acquisitions predict easy alignment: sharing a vision, matching corporate cultures, key people being willing to join Cisco, and being geographically close to Cisco (Bort, 2014). This is an explicit acknowledgment that international acquisitions are challenging to integrate.

Aligning and Leading International Acquisitions

Light integration makes it easier to maintain internal alignment of both the acquirer and acquired, and it is often applied when the acquirer wants to learn from the acquired company about new products or markets. Whether you are leading at the acquired or acquiring firm, it is helpful to be proactive about learning across boundaries. Asking questions and offering information in the ways outlined in the Map–Bridge–Integrate model (see p. 138) will provide quicker synergies for both companies.

Tight integration requires change from both the acquirer and acquired company (see Chapter 9), and the process can be painful. Once accomplished, it can greatly benefit customers as well as other stakeholders. Leaders engaged in tight integration of acquisitions should aim to create synergies, rather than equalize value with shared ground or just invoking the dominant way. This means leading with all cross-cultural competences, at a high level of mindfulness. The main danger of tight integration is the promise of timelines to investors – these timelines are often unrealistic for integrating across differences well, and forcing the tight timelines leads to destroying value rather than creating it.

Non-Equity Alliances and Joint Ventures

"Alliances" is the term for the broad category of formal agreements to collaborate, in order to create joint value. Most strategic alliances are structured with investment-, cost-, and/or revenue-sharing agreements, licensing, or royalty payments. If they include the deeper commitment of equity sharing, they become the special case of "joint ventures." Alliances can be a way to try out a new partnership or direction, and successful alliances may become joint ventures or acquisitions.

Pharmaceutical companies' traditional model of conducting all research in-house has proven to be inefficient. Yes, some breakthrough medications develop this way, but chances are that university or other labs will develop new advances more quickly, such as gene-based therapy or new delivery mechanisms. Moreover, research in other industries may be more likely to develop technology that facilitates drug therapy research more quickly. Most pharmaceutical companies now engage in many different types of alliances in order to develop new therapies while promoting the innovation that comes from decentralized idea generation.

Eli Lilly (Lilly), for example, has built a strong competence in alliance management over two decades. Lilly partners with universities, start-up biotech firms, distribution companies, and firms that build technology such as analytic or simulation capabilities. They openly invite interested groups from around the world to approach them for alliances. Their alliance in India with Lupin, for example, markets and distributes oral anti-diabetes medications.

Joint ventures are alliances in which two or more parties create a new entity, sharing ownership equity. Joint ventures are probably the most challenging method of inorganic growth. In an acquisition, the acquiring company has power to determine strategy and direction. In non-equity alliances, the lack of ownership commitment reduces the potential for conflict. Joint ventures, because they share equity and hence formal and legal commitment among entities that are very different from each other, create a context ripe for conflict. So why do companies create so many international joint ventures? Joint ventures are used for many reasons. The most common is that local regulations often restrict the amount of foreign ownership of local companies, or offer strong financial incentives for increased local ownership. Other reasons include sharing financial risk, securing access to natural resources, acquiring particular technical skills, gaining local management knowledge and experience, or obtaining access to markets and distribution systems.

Telecommunications companies often engage in joint ventures to access local markets, where regulations require local ownership. MTN, a multinational telecom company headquartered in South Africa, has engaged in major joint ventures in Botswana, Swaziland, Nigeria, and Iran. They identify joint ventures and partnerships as one of their four most important keys to growth. Most of these joint ventures are for infrastructure or licensing. For example, they have partnered with IHS Towers, a Nigerian company, to provide infrastructure in several African countries. On a different path, MTN recently began a joint venture with financial services company MMI to provide micro-insurance products across a number of African countries. Neither MTN nor MMI could build this business on their own, and the joint venture has potential for positive impact on millions of people without insurance.

Companies in resources industries often engage in joint ventures with local companies, including Indigenous companies in countries with histories of colonization. These joint ventures are formed partly for access to the resources, and also to develop partnering relationships with local communities, with the community having adequate power in the relationship. Sometimes this is regulated by governments, but more and more frequently it is initiated by companies as a practice that leads to sustainable, synergistic results. For example, in Canada, Indigenous communities and mining companies are increasingly developing partnerships and formal joint ventures to mine and service mines in ways that are sustainable for the social communities and more responsible to the environment.

In establishing joint ventures, managers often make some common mistakes. There can be a tendency to concentrate on the end result and desired outcome and not to think carefully and critically about the process through which these results will be obtained. Executives need to build the personal relationships that are essential to create a joint venture and commit the time and effort necessary to make the venture successful. They need to think more clearly about joint venturing, which is a process orientation. There are many operational issues beyond the legal and economic ones that may not be given enough careful forethought and may be left to be resolved as problems arise, which often is too late. The "invisible," "intangible," or "non-quantifiable" components of a venture, like trust, commitment, and partners ' expectations, often are overlooked or ignored, possibly because they may not be part of a manager's prior training or mindset.

Aligning and Leading International Alliances and Joint Ventures

Perhaps the most critical decision to be made in establishing an international alliance or joint venture is the choice of a partner, as Geringer explains:

Selecting partners with compatible skills is not necessarily synonymous with selecting compatible partners ... Although selecting a compatible partner may not always result in a successful [joint venture], the selection of an incompatible partner virtually guarantees that venture performance will be unsatisfactory. (Geringer, 1988)

How does one choose a partner? Where does one look? What characteristics should a partner have? What are one's expectations? What are the potential partner's expectations? There are a number of criteria that should be considered, including relative power in the relationship (such as size, resources, financial capabilities, need for each other), complementarity of strategies and policies, ability to communicate, and so on.

The role of relationships in strategy and international joint ventures is worthy of special comment, recalling our discussion in Chapter 3 on cultures that prioritize the task or the relationship (see p. 62). Often in Anglo countries, relationships are viewed as instrumental, as means to ends, if they are thought of at all in a business context. In contrast, much of the world outside the Anglo countries values relationships in and of themselves. They form a basis of trust and linkage upon which a business activity may be built. Relationships are a major determinant of strategy, if not part of the strategy themselves. Given such striking differences in outlook on relationships, it is not surprising that partnership problems are one of the most frequently cited reasons for alliance and joint venture failure (Beamish, 2013).

Executing strategy through alliances and joint ventures has important implications for alignment and leadership. Both (or multiple) parties enter the alliance with their own way of leading tasks, structure, and people, aligned with organizational systems and culture. Bringing the two (or more) together means that at least one party must change. If possible, it's easiest to select a partner that is as similar as possible; however, this may defeat the purpose of learning from or doing something new and innovative. A partner who is doing something different from you – whether it's a different business model or a different market – is very likely going to be aligned differently. Most inexperienced alignment leaders underestimate the importance of realigning the alliance, so the first leadership advice is to apply the alignment tools carefully, practicing the Map–Bridge–Integrate skills, and to adjust timing expectations to allow for this. In the process of developing a new alignment for the alliance, it's important to remember that employees in the alliance also need to interface with their "home" enterprises, both to draw on them for resources, and to return to after their time in the alliance. Leaders tend to focus on customers and suppliers, but you must take into account the **inter-organizational interfaces** too.

Also critical in leading alliances is focusing on learning. The Renault–Nissan Alliance is a very complicated alliance. Both companies have shareholdings in each other, but the relationship between the companies is run with the philosophy of an alliance – neither company can compel the other to do something based on ownership. They develop common platforms and technologies, and they purchase almost all supplies through the alliance; both of these activities provide cost savings and revenue opportunities, an estimated €5 billion in annual synergies by 2016. However, leaders at the Renault–Nissan Alliance state that an equally important benefit of their alliance is the ability to learn from each other (Ikegami, Maznevski, and Ota, 2017; Nissan Motor Corporation, 2017). The two companies compete head-to-head in many markets around the world. The Alliance encourages this competition as experimentation, then each company can learn quickly from its own and the other's experiences.

Alliances always provide opportunities for learning, but it takes mindful global leaders to make the learning happen. The Renault–Nissan Alliance has been practicing this kind of leadership since 1999, Lilly has been systematically developing alliance expertise since about the same time, and MTN has developed expertise in cross-cultural interaction and is building on that to enhance its alliance management. Developing mindful global leadership competence can take many years for an organization; the good news is that the capabilities can be applied in so many contexts that they are well worth the investment.

Small Enterprises Can Be Global, Too

Most of the common knowledge and research about international management takes place in large MNEs, but there is growing recognition of the importance of smaller enterprises. Normally we think of start-ups and entrepreneurship as local, and most such companies are. But with today's globalization and technology, many small businesses are either "born global" or globalize very quickly without becoming large enough for multiple divisions and matrices, and it's important to recognize this phenomenon.

Born Global

Some small companies start global because they happen to sell a product or service internationally. Platforms such as eBay, Etsy, Alibaba, Tencent, and PayPal have made the transactions simple, and the global logistics industry has made physical transfer of goods straightforward. These companies may not have a global strategy, that is, they are not trying to serve specific international markets, but they do need to develop more complex alignment systems than purely domestic small companies. For example, they need access to people with foreign exchange expertise, tax jurisdiction knowledge, and international shipping insurance.

Other small companies deliberately craft their strategy to serve international needs, right from their founding.

Tony Jamous, a French-Lebanese telecom engineer working at a technical start-up in the UK, entered an MBA program to gain a qualification that would help him move to a larger company. However, when he graduated he saw an important unmet need for global digitally-driven businesses, such as Airbnb, Uber, and Tencent. These companies needed a single technology for connecting their software with phone networks, one that would work equally well with early generation mobile phones in emerging markets, as with smart phones in developed markets. His company, Nexmo, was born in 2010 with a global strategy. Organizationally, too, it was global: it opened with headquarters in London, San Francisco, and Hong Kong; and investors from Germany, USA, and Korea. Nexmo's customers' headquarters were mainly in the USA, UK, and East Asia, but *their* customers were all over the world, working with different infrastructures and different mobile carriers. Nexmo's employee team quickly grew to comprise over 50 nationalities, and they built strong relationships with more than 500 networks in different countries.

One of the most important challenges for Jamous and his team, and for any born global company with a global strategy, was developing a unified company culture. The company was spread out over the globe long before the founders had a chance to establish a culture to launch and disseminate. Jamous and the other senior leaders met extensively with people in local markets, traveling to communicate in person about why and how to do things, training in everything from technical expertise to customer relations. According to Jamous, "We had to embed being global as one of our values, and live it. No time zone was *the* time zone." One important initiative for creating the culture was the requirement that every new employee, no matter how senior, must work on the customer helpdesk solving tickets until they have the highest satisfaction rating.

The company continues to leverage its born global character, for example by innovating to leverage new regulations and compliance requirements as competitive advantages. They were ahead of most competitors on compliance for the EU data privacy regulations, and, unusually, they acquired telecom carrier licenses for their own platforms in some key jurisdictions. Jamous reflects that by starting off thinking and acting globally, the company has been able to create unique value.

That value has been reflected in the growth of the firm: its revenues grew to over US$100 million in five years. Having raised US$30 million in venture capital (VC) funds to start, it was acquired by Vonage in 2016 for over US$250 million. Being born global may be a challenging way to start an organization, and even with a good business idea, success is not guaranteed. Jamous's mindful global leadership was key to the company's growth and value creation for customers in this specialized technology space.

Global Small- to Medium-Sized Enterprises

There are many well-established small- to medium-sized enterprises (SMEs) that offer targeted products or services globally, without developing the scale of an MNE. Many of these enterprises offer specific technologies or technical solutions. For example, the German *Mittelstand*, mid-sized companies, make up over a third of the German economy and two thirds of its exports (Weber, 2016). Most of these companies are family-owned, with 5000 or fewer employees, and focus on specialized niche products or services in business-to-business (B2B) relationships, such as precision manufacturing machinery, solar panels, and components. For these companies, growth is less important than excellence and ambition with a particular set of customers. Many are very global, generating far more revenue from outside Germany (or even Europe) than from inside. For example, Sennheiser started making headphones and microphones in 1945 for professionals, and has grown to become an important manufacturer of these products globally for B2B and consumers. They now have just under 3000 employees, about half in Germany and half abroad, with manufacturing in Germany, Ireland, and the USA. Around half of their revenue comes from Europe, the rest from outside Europe. They are structured with two main divisions: consumer and professional. Sennheiser is now larger than the vast majority of the more than three million SMEs in Germany, but its roots and strategy are very representative.

Aligning and Leading in Smaller Global Enterprises

The alignment of tasks, people, structure, strategy, and the environment can be simpler in a smaller enterprise than in a large MNE: there are generally fewer people and fewer tasks than in an MNE. However, because of the smaller size and fewer resources, it's more important for the fewer people in leadership to be able to cover a broad range of capabilities themselves, and to structure in a way that shares knowledge and roles fluidly. It is no coincidence that successful global SMEs focus on people development – recruiting, retaining, developing, coaching, and so on – as much as they do on strategy or business development.

Leaders in these firms must recognize the importance of their own global leadership competence to their strategy execution. As smaller players, these firms do not inherently have the power of size and resources. Their power comes from their ability to provide something very specific and to do it well; which in turn relies on the execution of mindful global leadership practices.

Emerging Forms and Processes for Organizing

We think it's important briefly to point out some current trends in organizing. They stem from the three drivers identified earlier in different parts of this book: the environmental driver of high complexity and volatility (discussed throughout Chapter 1), the business driver of customer-centric strategies (described in Chapter 7), and the enabling driver of digital technology (identified in Chapter 1 and described in Chapter 5 with its effect on virtual teams). We will discuss two trends: organizing for digital transformation and lateral collaboration across MNEs. All managers are likely to be exposed to these ways of organizing, and you should feel prepared to decide the extent to which you adopt them, and under what conditions. We will also identify the organizational conditions which are most conducive to executing these newer forms and trends, and describe a framework to help develop them.

Organizing for Digital Transformations

Digital transformation is the shift to business models that rely on the combination of digital technologies and the Internet of Things (IoT) to deliver more value for customers (Wade, 2017a). These technologies can transform the value proposition in three ways: cost value (decreasing the cost of delivery), experience value (increasing the quality of the customer experience), and platform value (providing enhanced cost or experience by leveraging a networked platform, such as crowd sourcing or big data analytics) (Wade et al., 2015). Different industries are affected by digitization in different ways and at different rates. For example, media and entertainment, technology, telecoms, retail, and financial services industries are experiencing high levels of disruption already, with content and services online and traditional companies struggling. Real estate, healthcare and pharmaceuticals, and energy and utilities are affected less, but "less" is not "none": the IoT and digital data availability are affecting R&D greatly in the latter two, and consumer sales in real estate.

The Global Center for Digital Business Transformation, an alliance between Cisco and the IMD business school, found three sets of organizational capabilities for thriving through the digital business transformation. **Hyperawareness** is constantly scanning both internal and external environments for opportunities and threats. **Informed decision-making** is the obsessive use of data – widely available through the company – to make evidence-based decisions. **Fast execution** is the ability to move quickly, often valuing speed over perfection (Loucks et al., 2016). Loucks and colleagues highlight the story of McLaren, the Formula 1 auto racing team, to illustrate the organizational transformation. Because the cost of running a Formula 1 team makes the enterprise inevitably unprofitable, McLaren set up a separate group, McLaren Applied Technologies, to leverage their technology capabilities in other industries. They developed offerings of data collection, modeling, and simulation services for customers facing rapid change across a wide range of industries. They created new partnerships and shaped new internal operations for delivering the value. Their Formula 1 culture and internal systems already fit the new alignment they created, but they became refined over time with different types of expertise in the new group (Wade, 2017b).

Digital Transformations: Implications for Alignment and Leadership

Organizing for digital transformation follows the same alignment principles as any other kind of strategy execution: tasks, people, and structure must be aligned to each other with systems and organizational culture, in a way that also aligns with the value proposition or strategy of the company. More specifically, though, the digital transformation compels an alignment that includes a structure of broad information-sharing and with decision-making authority as low as possible for speed. On the surface this implies an independent, egalitarian culture, but it also helps to have the clarity of roles consistent with status cultures, and the interlocked communication of interdependence-oriented cultures.

In a separate study, the Center for Digital Business Transformation identified four characteristics for agile leaders, those who lead digital transformation well. Agile leaders are **humble** (open to feedback and ideas from others), **adaptable** (accept that changing with new information is a strength), **engaged** (propensity to listen, interact, and engage with interest and curiosity), and **visionary** (clear sense of long-term direction) (Neubauer, Tarlking, and Wade, 2017). The first three of these characteristics are very similar to what we've identified as global leadership characteristics, because the global business environment and the digital business transformation are similar in their context of volatility. The good news is that global leaders should be well placed to lead digital business transformations, and vice versa.

Lateral Collaboration

A second important trend in global organizing is the increase in planned and facilitated collaboration across boundaries, such as collaborating across different parts of an MNE, or collaborating in association or alliances with other organizations. We referred to this trend earlier in the section on MNEs, and in Chapter 5 looking at networks. Here we would like to emphasize it as an organizing pattern and look at the alignment and leadership dynamics.

Formal Team-Based Lateral Collaboration

Team-based lateral communication is when a group of people is formally identified to achieve a specific joint outcome, working across different parts of the organization. The most common form of team-based lateral collaboration is the global key account team. Most firms that sell products globally identify their largest global customers and assign a global key account manager (KAM) to the accounts. In each country where the customer is present, someone is assigned to the account team. This becomes a form of matrixed relationship – a salesperson or technical service person in Vietnam reports both to the company's head of Vietnam regarding overall country sales, and to the global KAM (who could be sitting at the company headquarters or somewhere else in the world, such as the customer's headquarters city) regarding this one customer. The KAM role is to advocate for the customer within the enterprise, communicate leading edge innovations and even shape innovations for the customer, enable and facilitate technical service to the customer around the world, and negotiate prices to the customer for products and services.

The challenge in lateral collaboration is resolving the tension when local market needs are different from global customer needs, both for the customer and for the supplier. For example, one of our alumni, we'll call her Ellen, is a global KAM for a large MNE in the specialty chemicals industry, which we'll refer to as ABChem. When she first took over the account, she spent months coordinating with her team members around the world, organizing R&D projects, aligning a suite of products to cater to the next generation of needs for the customer. She met with representatives of the customer and her own company's sales and technical service staff around the world, for a better understanding of the different local market needs. Then she worked directly with the customer's global purchasing office over a period of several weeks to negotiate a multi-year agreement.

After the agreement was completed but before it was signed, Ellen got a phone call from a friend in another ABChem division, informing her that one of Ellen's country-based account managers had just signed a supplier contract with the local branch of the customer, for a much higher price. The people at the customer's headquarters were going to be furious with Ellen and the ABChem team for not coordinating their global purchase contract! The local customer was going to be furious with ABChem and the local supplier for not offering the global price they knew was coming! Ellen wondered what was going on. Drawing on her extensive network inside ABChem, she discovered that the ABChem operation in the local country was behind on its sales targets for the year, and the country manager was asking employees to do everything they could to hit the sales targets. He was threatening to eliminate bonuses and even fire salespeople who did not step up. To the local salesperson, the opportunity to get a sale and guarantee a job and income was more important than complying with a global headquarters agreement that had not yet been formalized.

Ellen resolved the issue by leveraging her network with ABChem country managers and at the customer's firm. She was able to implement a clause with lower prices for volume that satisfied both the country and the client. Perhaps more importantly overall, she used the opportunity to build deeper relationships with the country manager, the local account manager, and the customer. In the first year of implementing the new contract, she worked more closely with the team of account managers from around the world, to help them learn from each other and to develop new ways to win with the customer. Her approach with the team worked so well that her next role was to develop a new global industry segment for ABChem.

There are many other forms of lateral teams. In MNEs, they include matrixed functions, such as audit, quality control, or human resources across a company. In alliances, they may connect the formal members of the alliance with the most important stakeholders in the parent organizations. High-performing lateral teams are ones that work well across divisions of the MNE, or across different organizations such as an alliance. At their best, they transfer best practices, align the organization for efficiency and better customer interfaces, and drive extensive value-creating innovation.

Less Formal Collaboration

While teams are an identifiable group of people with a joint deliverable, organizations are also developing many forms of organizing that are much less formal. Two common ones are **centers of excellence** and **communities of practice**. Centers of excellence are usually small groups of people within an organization who specialize in a particular type of expertise. They identify and share best practices, case studies, and recommendations with others in the organization who need the knowledge. They are often located virtually, with members embedded in different parts of the organization. Communities of practice are larger groups of people who are involved in similar kinds of work across the organization, and who share and develop knowledge together (Wagner, 1998). These communities are also often located virtually.

IBM was one of the pioneers of less formal collaboration, and uses both centers of excellence (CoEs) and communities of practice (CoPs) extensively. Some of the CoEs include Software (and many sub-centers, both across and within geographies), Cyber Security, and Analytics. These core operations of each center are located in different places; for example, Cyber Security is in Haifa, Israel, and India has a strong Software Center of Excellence. They produce white papers and recommendations for people throughout IBM and externally, and they provide support to practitioners within IBM. IBM supports CoPs for many of its software and hardware systems and applications such as Business Process Manager and Rational Application Security, for market segments such as health and human services, for new innovations such as Watson, and so on. IBM supports these forms of collaboration with good alignment – participation in these communities and centers is expected, with a culture and systems of people reaching out to contribute and learn from each other. Centers and communities are aligned with the tasks that people are undertaking, and they provide a complementary structure to the main divisions of IBM.

Lateral Collaboration: Implications for Alignment and Leadership

Our research suggests that all of these forms of collaboration rely on a set of underlying social dynamics. If the social dynamics are already in place, then it is much easier to build alignment quickly and lead adaptively when needed. If the social dynamics are not in place, then alignment and adaptation are painful, and the social dynamics must be addressed before the collaboration can perform.

A useful framework for diagnosing the social dynamics is the TACK framework: Trust, Ambition, Cohesion, and Knowledge. Each of these elements must be shared among a group of people before collaboration will yield results. For each of these elements there are two levels: a basic level, which will provide enough collaboration to enable people to begin working well together, and an advanced level, which is important for deeper collaboration in challenging situations or adaptive collaboration in changing situations (Maznevski and Dhanaraj, 2017).

Trust is a positive belief about others that they will look after your needs when you are vulnerable or need to rely on them. Trust is the most fundamental dynamic for collaboration in any situation. The two levels of trust we identify are based on seminal research on two types of trust: cognitive and affective (McAllister, 1995). Cognitive trust is like reliability – do I believe you'll do what you said you are going to do? That you are capable and will honor the commitment? Affective trust is more values-based – do I believe that you will look out for me, in a situation of potential conflict?

Ambition motivates collaboration. While a common goal is always necessary for a team (see Chapter 5), this common goal only gets collaboration to a basic level. Common ambition, a stretch goal with a higher purpose, motivates collaboration further. Often, to be motivating across a broad range of stakeholders, a compelling ambition is directly related to creating important value for customers or other external stakeholders such as society as a whole, rather than simply achieving organizational targets.

Cohesion is necessary at a basic level for successful collaboration. As we implied in Chapter 5, it is not necessary for people to like each other to collaborate. However, it is important that they respect each other and appreciate each other's contribution to the work, and that they are committed to helping each other out. This is the basic level of cohesion needed for collaboration. The more advanced level of cohesion is based on our social need for identity with a group (McAllister, 1995). When we identify with others as a strong and positive group identity, we are more willing to go out of our way to help each other. We define our personal success with respect to the success of the group as a whole: I can only succeed if the group succeeds. This deeper cohesion is important for more advanced collaboration.

Trust	Cohesion
Level 1: Do we believe that others will fulfill their commitments to the collaboration and the organization? Level 2: Do we believe that others will act in the best interests of the collaboration and the organization, even in the absence of clear guidance?	Level 1: Do we help each other out, do we appreciate working together? Level 2: Do we really go out of our way for each other, do we truly believe "my success is your success"?
Ambition	Knowledge
Level 1: Do we all buy into a common, stated goal, and are we willing to work toward it? Level 2: Do we stretch to high ambitions, and are we committed to those ambitions, individually and together?	Level 1: Do we share a common idea about what we are doing, and why it is important? Level 2: Do we share deeper understanding of each other's contexts and the implications of our collective tasks?

Figure 8.4 TACK: organizational conditions for collaboration

Shared knowledge at some level is necessary for collaboration. On the other hand, collaboration is necessary for organizational performance because different collaborators have different knowledge, and it is also important to leverage that. The basic level of shared knowledge need for collaboration is a common idea about the reason for collaboration. The more advanced level is shared knowledge about each other's context. This is directly related to Decentering as part of Bridging, in the MBI model. Consistent with our research about interpersonal interaction, we've found that mindful contextual knowledge is critical for high-level collaboration.

The TACK model is summarized in Figure 8.4.

Executing Strategy: Organizing for Effectiveness at the Point of Action

Chapter 7 presented a logic for organizing and a framework for analyzing organizational alignment for effective strategy execution. This chapter provided a tour of the most common and important forms of organizing for executing strategy. The MNE is the most visible form, and most large organizations today are structured in this way, with some matrixed components. Leading in MNEs requires being comfortable with the complexity of multiple types of relationships and spanning many types of boundaries. However, it is important not to assume that the MNE is the only way to organize for international strategy execution.

Small firms can be very global, and these forms have their own advantages, challenges, and leadership requirements. They can be nimble and focused, and require leadership at the top that is both mindful and high on global leadership competences. In this chapter we also looked at two trends that affect organizing at least to some extent in every industry and geography: digital business transformation and lateral collaboration. These two trends pose challenges and offer opportunities for companies and leaders, with specific implications for aligning and leading.

When we work with organizations around the world, we appreciate the variety of organizational forms we see. Within the patterns of alignment and strategy execution and these basic forms, there are infinite ways of implementing them. Mindful leaders can shape the organization that best suits the needs of the enterprise and takes advantage of the different knowledge bases and experiences of different parts of the global enterprise.

Reflection Questions

This chapter's reflection questions help you develop your own repertoire of organization examples, developing mindfulness about organizations and their contexts. The more examples and models you are familiar with, the better you can assess your own company's organizational options and effectiveness. We refer to "company," but we encourage you to incorporate into your repertoire not-for-profit organizations, quasi-government organizations (e.g., police forces), or any other type of organization that's of interest to you.

1. Think about the company you work for now, or one that you're very familiar with. Applying the categories in this chapter, how would you describe the company's organization type? Which different forms has it had through its history? In what ways does the organization type take into account the complexity of the global business environment?
2. List five to ten companies you admire. You might like their products or use their services, you might appreciate their reputation for growth or innovation, you might know people who work there and enjoy their work. Try to identify companies with a range of sizes and geographic scopes. Look them up and try to identify the main characteristics of their organizational types.
   a. Did they cover the range described in this chapter? Which types were most common, and why?

b. In what way is the company's organizational design influenced by the country culture of its headquarters?

c. For the companies whose organization changed over time, what was the trajectory (e.g., multi-divisional to matrix, alliances and acquisitions)?

3. Which are the organization types you are most attracted to work in? Why?

Further Resources

For the classic work on global integration and local responsiveness, see Bartlett and Ghoshal's, *Managing Across Borders* (2002). The organizational implications are well articulated in Prahalad and Doz's *The Multinational Mission* (1999).

The field's understanding of alliances and joint ventures has been developed mainly by Paul Beamish and colleagues. Beamish has published a comprehensive summary of this work in his *Multinational Joint Ventures in Developing Countries* (2013).

For more on mergers and acquisitions, see the following review article:

Haleblian, J., Devers, C. E., McNamara, G., Carpenter, M. A., & Davison, R. B. (2009). Taking Stock of What We Know about Mergers and Acquisitions: A Review and Research Agenda. *Journal of Management*, 35, 469–502.

For a good review and study on the role of cultural differences in international mergers and acquisitions, see:

Stahl, G. K., & Voigt, A. (2008). Do Cultural Differences Matter in Mergers and Acquisitions? A Tentative Model and Examination. *Organization Science*, 19, 160–176.

The annual research series *Advances in Mergers and Acquisitions*, edited by Sydney Finkelstein and Cary Cooper (Emerald Group) provides leading edge insights on many international topics.

IMD's Center for Digital Business Transformation, sponsored by Cisco, is conducting a multi-year investigation into how businesses integrate the effects and opportunities of digital and Internet technologies. They publish reviews, research, and recommendations with regular updates at www.imd.org/dbt/digital-business-transformation/.

Bibliography

Bartlett, C. A., & Ghoshal, S. (2002). *Managing Across Borders: The Transnational Solution*, 2nd edn. Harvard Business School Press.

Beamish, P. W. (2013). *Multinational Joint Ventures in Developing Countries*. Routledge.

Bort, J. (2014). *Cisco's John Chambers: What I look for before we buy a startup*. Retrieved 12, 2017, from Business Insider: www.businessinsider.com/cisco-john-chambers-acquisition-strategy-2014-7

Geringer, J. M. (1988). Partner Selection Criteria for Developed Country Joint Ventures. *Business Quarterly*, 53, 55–62.

Ikegami, J. J., Maznevski, M., & Ota, M. (2017). Creating the Asset of Foreignness: Schrödinger's Cat and Lessons from the Nissan Revival. *Cross-Cultural and Strategic Management*, 24, 55–77.

Kale, P., Singh, H., & Raman, A. (2009). Don't Integrate Your Acquisitions, Partner with Them. *Harvard Business Review*, 87, 109–115.

Loucks, J., Macaulay, J., Noronha, A., & Wade, M. (2016). *Digital Vortex: How Today's Market Leaders Can Beat Disruptive Competitors at Their Own Game*. DBT Center Press.

Luckerson, V. (2015). How Google Perfected the Silicon Valley Acquisition. *Time*, April 15. Retrieved December 2017 from *Time*: http://time.com/3815612/silicon-valley-acquisition/

Maznevski, M., and Dhanaraj, C. (2017). *Leading Collaboration in Global Organizations: How to Build a House without a Hammer*. Retrieved December 2017 from IMD: www.imd.org/research/insightsimd/leading-collaboration-in-global-organizations-how-to-build-a-house-without-a-hammer/

McAllister, D. J. (1995). Affect and Cognition-Based Trust as Foundations for Interpersonal Cooperation in Organizations. *Academy of Management Journal*, 38, 24–59.

Neubauer, R., Tarlking, A., & Wade, M. (2017). *Redefining Leadership for a Digital Age*, March Retrieved December 2017 from IMD Research: www.imd.org/dbt/whitepapers/redefining-leadership/

Nissan Motor Corporation (2017). *Making the Most of Cultural Diversity*. Retrieved 12 2017 from Nissan-Global: www.nissan-global.com/EN/COMPANY/DIVERSITY/CULTURE/

Prahalad, C. K., & Doz, Y. L. (1987). *The Multinational Mission: Balancing Local Demands and Global Vision*. The Free Press.

Wade, M. (2017a). *The Digital Vortex in 2017: It's Not a Question of "When."* Retrieved December 2017 from IMD: https://hbr.org/2016/08/germanys-midsize-manufacturers-outperform-its-industrial-giants

Wade, M. (2017b). *Standing Ovation: McLaren Puts the Digital Orchestra into Action*. Retrieved December 2017 from IMD: www.imd.org/dbt/articles/standing-ovation-mclaren-puts-the-digital-orchestra-into-action/

Wade, M., Loucks, J., Macaulay, J., & Noronha, A. (2015). *New Paths to Customer Value: Disruptive Business Models in the Digital Vortex*. Retrieved December 2017 from IMD: www.imd.org/dbt/whitepapers/new-paths-to-customer-value/

Wagner, E. (1998). *Communities of Practice*. Cambridge University Press.

Weber, W. W. (2016). Germany's Midsize Manufacturers Outperform Its Industrial Giants. *Harvard Business Review*, August 12. Retrieved December 2017 from Harvard Business Review Online: https://hbr.org/2016/08/germanys-midsize-manufacturers-outperform-its-industrial-giants

9 Leading Change in Global Organizations

> "Would you tell me, please, which way I ought to go from here?" Alice asked the Cheshire Cat.
>
> "That depends a good deal on where you want to get to," said the Cat.
>
> "I don't much care where –" said Alice.
>
> "Then it doesn't matter which way you go," said the Cat.
>
> Lewis Carroll, *Alice's Adventures in Wonderland*

This chapter[1] deals with the implementation of **global organizational change** that we define as strategically aligned alterations in patterns of employee behavior within organizations operating across national borders. As the competitive environment changes, which it does continually, companies have to adapt and may have to reformulate their strategy; realign how employees do their work; and revise organizational structures and/or systems to support the new behaviors and the new strategy.

IBM: A Model of Successful Strategic Change

In the 1960s and 1970s, the computer technology industry was vertically integrated. IBM's core business was manufacturing and selling mainframe computers and the software that ran on them, which was primarily for transaction processing applications like accounting and payroll, or word processing and email.

---

[1] We dedicate this chapter to the memory of Al Mikalachki who taught us about organizational change over two decades at the Ivey Business School in London, Canada and on whose work this chapter builds.

IBM experienced a "perfect storm" of disruption. Technology, competitors, and customers all changed. Mini-computers reduced the size and cost of computers making them affordable for more companies. The PC revolution decentralized computing and ushered in the client–server computing model where mainframes were often re-purposed as servers. Large companies, IBM's target market, adopted client–server systems no longer wanting the mainframes and bundled software. They started buying hardware from multiple vendors and third-party software from companies like Oracle and SAP.

A new breed of Chief Information Officers (CIOs) appeared. They were "web-focused, e-business aware, and didn't demonstrate the vendor loyalty that characterized his or her predecessors – the 'career customers' who would buy equipment and software only from IBM" (Meyer, 2007). Over time, customers became disenchanted with what IBM referred to as "piece-part technologies" or purchasing different pieces of software and hardware from various vendors and integrating these components themselves. They again wanted comprehensive integrated solutions that worked across their organizations, regardless of size or geographic location (Palmisano, 2003).

When Lou Gerstner became CEO in April 1993, the company's annual net losses were US$8 billion. Gerstner ignored the calls to break up the company. IBM had been organized to sell products (mainframes) developed on the basis of strong R&D. Gerstner decided to offer customers comprehensive solutions focused on solving problems rather than just selling products. He explained:

Once again, customers were focused on integrated business solutions – a key IBM strength that combined the company's expertise in solutions, services, products, and technologies ... and would be the company's overarching strategy.

Gerstner aligned the resources of the company behind the Internet as a medium for real business and in 1997 IBM announced its new *e-business* strategy (Gerstner, Jr., 2002).

There were a lot of changes that had to take place to implement this new strategy. The complex organizational structure – twenty separate business units with independent and different systems – presented a challenge. IBM's "religion of decentralization" had led to autonomous country general managers who reported to powerful regional executives. Country managers grew their business based on local responsiveness, but at the cost of collaboration. Non-US employees considered themselves to be working for their own home country company.

IBM's global customers complained about interacting with different mini-IBMs in each country. They wanted to see one face for IBM globally. Gerstner believed that customer-focused, global teams that transcended national borders would allow seamless responsiveness to global customers. To do this he had to integrate IBM's US and overseas operations.

A new structure of twelve customer groups (e.g. banking, government, and insurance) and one small and medium-sized company group would take over all IBM accounts, including responsibility for budgets and personnel. Most employees in non-US operations were reassigned to industry groups under the global leaders of their group instead of their country general manager.

The reaction from country general managers was overwhelmingly negative claiming that it wouldn't work and would destroy the company. Some ignored the new structure and one reportedly blocked all communications with Gerstner.

Company units were internally focused and competed with each other. Gerstner changed the compensation system based on individual performance toward one based on the overall performance of IBM instead of division, unit, or geography. He also increased the amount of executive compensation given as stock and options, set quotas for how many customer calls each executive had to make, and relentlessly pushed coordination among IBM's many divisions. At a talk at the Harvard Business School in 2002, he said, "We needed to integrate as a team inside the company so that we could integrate for the customers on their premises."

He also had to contend with IBM's strong company culture. There was a dynamic, highly motivated, and successful sales culture. Employees shared a belief in hard work and ethical behavior. There was also the famous strict dress code (dark suits and white shirts), an exemplar of the Organization Man ethos (Whyte, 1956/2002). Gerstner came to see the culture as the "company's DNA – from the paternalism to the stingy stock option program; from the no-drinking at corporate gathering policy to the preference that employees be married" (Gerstner, Jr., 2002).

He felt that many of the values on which IBM had been founded had ossified into hard and fast rules that, in fact, failed to represent Watson's real views. It took three years of a "painful and sometimes tumultuous process" to implement his changes. Only after shifts in resources and changes to systems and processes – as well as the removal and replacement of numerous country managers who could not or would not make the transition – did the new structure take hold. Gerstner said:

Changing the attitude and behavior of thousands of people is very, very hard to accomplish. You can't simply give a couple of speeches or write a new credo for the company and declare that a new culture has taken hold. You can't mandate it, can't engineer it. What you can do is create the conditions for transformation, provide incentives. (Lagace, 2002)

At his talk at Harvard, he summarized the importance of culture, "The thing I have learned at IBM is that culture is everything."

Gerstner met with IBM's top 400 executives and told them that they would all need to become change agents within the company.

We don't execute, because, again, we don't have the perspective that what counts outside [the company] is more important than what happens inside. Too many IBM'ers fight change if it's not in their personal interest. (Gerstner, Jr., 2002)

He continued, "Those of you who are uncomfortable with it, you should think about doing something else. Those of you who are excited about it, I welcome you to the team, because I sure can't do it alone."

Lessons about Implementing Strategic Change

IBM's example highlights a number of important insights or "lessons learned" about strategic change and our orientation to the topic.

1. Adapting to changes in the environment is essential to remaining competitive and successful. Our "law" of change states that the environment will always win.
2. All change is behavioral. A new strategy may require employees to assume new roles, develop new skills (technical and interpersonal), assume new responsibilities or build new relationships.
3. Employees need to understand that the old way of doing business is no longer sustainable and to see the benefits of the new way.
4. Change often brings discomfort and possibly resistance.
5. Effective communication is essential. "Telling" is not communicating or executing. Employees may "see" and interpret the same situation differently. Executives need to understand what others "see" and work to create a shared frame of reference or common understanding.
6. Organizations don't change; people do. The final result of a successful change effort may look and act like a changed organization.
7. Strategic change is a process and not just an outcome. It may take a long time to complete.

8. Executives need to work not only with people (individuals and groups) but also to realign the organization. Existing systems, structures, practices, and/ or cultures may need to change in order to reinforce and support the new required behaviors and tasks.

9. Leaders need a way of thinking about the process – a framework.

This chapter presents a three-phase framework for strategic change that managers can use as a guide – a checklist before starting off on the journey.

Strategic Organizational Change and Renewal

There are at least three change scenarios companies may face depending on their current performance: anticipatory, reactive, and crisis, as shown in Figure 9.1.

Ideally companies would like to **anticipate** environmental shifts and make changes through a process of continuous learning to follow the path of renewal. This is not always easy to do when performance is still good and there are no real indicators that there is trouble ahead. Not everyone in the company will be looking out into the future or be sensitive enough to important environmental

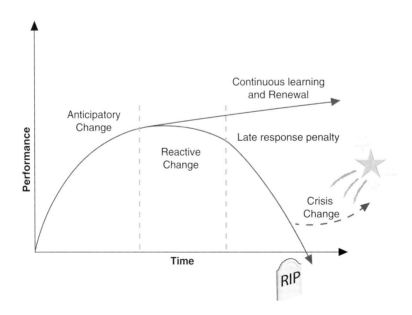

Figure 9.1 Strategic change and renewal
Note: This diagram was adapted from our colleagues Peter Killing, Nick Fry, Rod White, and Mary Crossan at the Ivey Business School and at IMD.

shifts. The management challenge at this stage is education – educating people about the potential dangers and convincing them of the possible threat. **Anticipatory change** generally proceeds at a slow pace.

In the **reactive stage**, as performance begins to suffer, more managers see the warning signs but they very likely may interpret them differently depending on their roles or functional perspectives. Change initiatives may move faster now, as more people acknowledge the potential threats. The management challenge at this stage is creating a cohesive picture of the future and achieving agreement on it.

In the **crisis stage**, the problems are clear for everyone to see and crises generally encourage and permit rapid change. Indeed, organizations may require it to survive. History is littered with examples of companies that resisted change or that did not respond fast enough to major changes in their industries. Polaroid missed the shift to digital photography. About the same time, the Boston area was the center of the mini-computer industry that included companies like Digital Equipment, Wang, Prime, and Data General; none of these survived the personal computer revolution. In the American automobile industry, General Motors, in particular, is a good example of the late response penalty. It took the US government to bail out General Motors (GM). The CEO was fired; the Pontiac Division was shut down; Hummer, Saturn, and Saab were sold; and something like 35 percent of the executives in the USA were let go. Critics had said for years that GM needed to do things like this, but executives were never able to muster the will to do them.

More recently, we see examples of company efforts to adapt to changing environmental conditions such as Wal-Mart's purchase of Jet.com in 2017. However, we are also witness to the collapse of numerous retailers (e.g., Macy's, Sears, and JCPenney) in the face of online competitors. The taxi industry is another sector that is struggling to adapt in the face of dramatic disruption by companies like Uber and Lyft and the prospect of driverless taxis.

Process Orientation: The Foundation of Strategic Organizational Change

Mindful global leaders are process-oriented, not simply goal and outcome fixated. There are many "noisy" signals and much extraneous information coming from the complex global environment and decision-makers need a way of determining what is, or isn't, important. Engineers use filters to remove unwanted noise from signals. The change model presented in this chapter can act as a filter to block out noise to focus the attention of change agents on mission-critical variables; and to serve as a guide and checklist for implementing successful change.

IDEO, one of the preeminent design firms in the world, states, "Thinking like a designer can transform the way organizations develop products, services, processes, and strategy." The firm has used its process to design services, spaces, and even school systems in addition to consumer products. Tim Brown, CEO of IDEO, states, "Design thinking is a human-centered approach to innovation that draws from the designer's toolkit to integrate the needs of people, the possibilities of technology, and the requirements for business success" (Brown, 2017).

In thinking about implementing strategic organizational change and requiring employees to behave differently, one realizes that it is a human-centered activity focused on designing new processes or systems for accomplishing organizational goals. We attended a conference at the Stanford Design School where we were introduced to the **design thinking process** and took a field trip to IDEO. We quickly realized the potential of the design thinking process to inform our understanding of, and approach to, managing strategic change and we have incorporated it into our framework.

Design Thinking

The design thinking process as defined by IDEO and the Stanford Design School consists of five steps: empathize, define, ideate, prototype, and test (Platner, 2017). For the purpose of this chapter, we translate and expand these steps to understand the specific activities to be undertaken.

1. **Empathize** means to observe and understand the situation or problem from the end user's point of view. Earlier in the book we referred to Alfred Korzybski's remark, "the map is not the territory," which means to us that you have to have a first-hand understanding of the situation as it exists on the ground and in reality, not simply in theory.
2. **Define** the problem correctly. Remember that the presenting problem or the initial assessment of a situation may not be the problem, but only a symptom of the problem.
3. **Ideate** means developing potential solutions – get user feedback – and repeat. You are looking for validation of ideas and possible acceptance of solutions. Jointly explore and formulate some possible options; build allies and coalitions that will support the change.
4. **Prototype** means experimenting with various solutions or what designers refer to as rapid prototyping. Develop some alternatives; evaluate and refine them.

5. **Test** means creating pilot projects, or what Kotter refers to as short-term wins (Kotter, 2012). Implement these in a strategically selected location or location(s) with personnel who are supportive of the change.

The model that follows recognizes that change occurs in a larger organizational context. New strategies or changes to strategies usually are devised at headquarters by executives who often pay attention to only half the challenge that they face, which is strategy formulation. They focus on the big picture – the new product, service, or business model. However, they tend not to spend as much time or effort on the process of change – how the actual implementation will take place in the field. Think back to the insights of Jesús Sotomayor referred to in Chapter 2: "Nobody ever lost money on a spreadsheet" (overestimation of benefits and underestimation of costs) and "If you torture the numbers long enough, they will confess." This is another way of expressing that the map is not the territory and executives need to take the time to observe and understand the situation in order to define the problem correctly.

Phase 1: Appraising the Readiness for Change

An organization's readiness for change can be determined by analyzing several factors that affect the support of, or resistance to, a change initiative, such as the visibility of the need for change, the organization's management style, the past history of change processes, and the timing of the change.

Is the Need for Change Visible?

When an organization is doing well and engages in anticipatory change, managers and employees will not necessarily see the need for change. "If it ain't broke, don't fix it," or "Why should we change something that works well?" are common comments that can be heard in organizations. If, however, the environment has already shifted and the organization engages in reactive change, managers and employees will more easily recognize why the organization's strategy and employees' behaviors have to change.

Diagnosing the visibility of the need for change is important because (1) employees will not embrace the change unless they see the need for it; (2) the more the need for change is visible to employees, the faster managers can accelerate the change process.

What is the organization's management style? Employees may be used to a management style that differs from the management style needed to lead the change effort. Many change practitioners in the West in countries like Canada and the USA advise a participatory approach to managing change that involves the employees. In many cultures, however, employees may be used to an authoritarian management style and might be confused if they had suddenly a voice in the change process.

What is the history of change processes? If change processes went awry in the past, employees may mistrust new change efforts. In the foreign subsidiaries of global organizations, often expatriates come in for limited term assignments, unleash a major change effort, and then leave after a couple of years, independent of the completion of the change process. This leaves local employees distinctly uncomfortable with the next change initiative.

What is the timing? Managers have to assess the timing of the change effort. If the resources of the organization are already stretched to the limit, it does not make sense to launch an anticipatory change effort that will further stretch resources. Such situations can arise during recessions, peak seasons, or when changes occur concurrently with other change efforts (e.g., a product launch).

Top Management Support and Commitment

Change agents need to ensure top management support for the proposed changes or build support for it as necessary. Top management can provide both direction and resources (e.g., funds), and have the power to remove obstacles. More importantly, top management support signals the importance of the change effort. An important way for top management to support the change is to be visibly involved and, in conjunction with the change agent, be the initial communicators of the change effort.

Employees evaluate the sincerity of a change effort in large part because of top management support and commitment. Hence, the visibility of top management support is critical for implementing change successfully, especially in the early stages of the change process. Employees will be more likely to engage the change effort enthusiastically if top managers make the effort to explain the goals and reasons for the change and the change process. In addition, top management signals the importance of an organizational change through the allocation of resources. Top management support alone will not elicit a change in employee behaviors. However, the absence of top management support might result in resistance or indifference among employees.

Who Will the Change Agent(s) Be?

In selecting a change agent, managers need to ask three questions:

- **Does the change agent have power to implement the change?** Power can be positional, expert, or personal, all relating to the credibility of the change agent. But note that different cultures emphasize different aspects of the bases of power. If employees do not have confidence or trust in the change agent, it will be difficult to motivate them to change.
- **What are the change agent's personal motivations?** The change agent must support the change and act as a positive example.
- **What are the management knowledge, skills, and abilities of the change agent?** The change agent should have communication, management, and conflict resolution skills to carry out the change effort. And the more cultural boundaries that the change crosses, the greater the need for cross-cultural skills.

Depending on the size and global scale of a company and the magnitude of a change program, implementing a strategic change in multiple countries will likely require a team of change agents. The three questions above still need to be asked of team members.

Who is the Target Group for the Change?

The key players in a change process include the obvious, immediate employees who will have to engage in new behaviors. However, less obvious stakeholders such as unions, suppliers, or customers whose business, systems, or behavior may be affected need to be considered. Managers need to think about the organization as a social system and the target group(s) in the broadest possible terms by considering interdependencies between the immediate target group and others with whom they may interact.

If a global organization embarks on an organization-wide change effort, both headquarters and foreign subsidiaries are affected. Subsidiaries may differ regarding effective change processes, depending on local cultural differences, proximity to headquarters, and the relationship between headquarters and subsidiaries. Hence, managers of global change must understand local differences to determine the processes needed to motivate the expected change in employee behaviors.

In assessing the readiness of employees to change, two questions are critical.

First is the **ability** question. Can they do it? What knowledge, skills, abilities, and resources do employees need to perform the new behaviors? Even if they are supportive, they may not be able to behave appropriately. Worry about an inability to perform the new behaviors often leads to anxiety and can undermine support for a change. If employees cannot perform the new behaviors, the change process will have to include education and/or training. Provision of other resources (e.g., computers or equipment) may be needed as well. A lack of resources will lead to frustration.

Second is the **motivation** question. Will they do it? What is the predisposition of employees toward the change? Will they support or resist it? This is an important question to assess the organization's readiness for change because high motivation leads people to acquire the needed skills and to exert the extra effort that contributes to success. Managers need to identify opponents as well as supporters and analyze the reasons for the resistance or support (Strebel, 1997). This analysis provides information about how opposition may be turned into support. If employees resist because, for example, they do not see the need for change, managers need to explain the links between the new strategy, the new behaviors, and the resulting improvements for the organization and the employees.

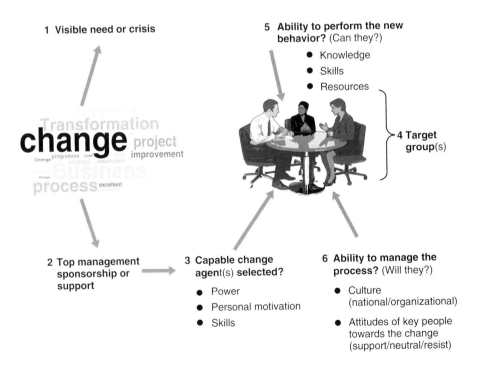

Figure 9.2 Phase 1: assessing the readiness for change

Are there preemptive problems like previous failed change efforts and a lack of trust that will discourage employees from engaging the change effort? If so, then these issues need to be addressed before moving forward.

Here is where cultural differences potentially are important and managers need to understand employees' expectations about the appropriate role for managers in the change process. Knowledge of local ways of expressing agreement and disagreement are very important. Figure 9.2 is a summary of Phase 1.

Applying Design Thinking

Phase 1 can be viewed as a gap analysis and checklist to assess an organization's and its employees' readiness to enact a new strategy. Our advice is that if any of the answers to the questions asked in Figure 9.2 are "no," then it is important to stop and work to turn those answers into "yes." The gap analysis can help managers create an initial change plan but how do they really get the answers to the questions?

This is a time in the process when we believe design thinking can be a useful tool in a manager's toolbox. The design thinking process might go as follows:

1. Get out of your office and visit subsidiaries to observe and understand first-hand what is going on there.
2. Based on step 1 you may consider redefining your initial analysis and change plan.
3. Meet the people who will be involved in the change. This can be beneficial in multiple ways:

   - It can give you an understanding of capabilities and possible resource needs.
   - The visits may generate ideas that you had not considered.
   - It can provide insight into personal motivations.

4. You can do a preliminary *test* of your initial solutions; assess who might be allies in the change program; and identify possible locations for pilot programs.

Phase 2: Initiating Change and Adopting the New Behavior

Leading strategic change is a full-time effort and requires intimate knowledge of the organization, which is why in most cases the change agent is a capable and respected insider. A capable change agent is one who has the requisite power, motivation, and change management skills. These skills include analysis, communication, conflict resolution, and, in global organizations, cultural intelligence. Once chosen, he or she needs to initiate the change by making sure the right people are in place for the new tasks and by building support for the change effort.

Training and Selection

To perform new behaviors, employees must be able to do so. If the change calls for behaviors that current employees do not have the potential to perform, managers must either provide training or select new employees. If current employees have the potential to perform the new behavior, but do not yet possess the ability to do so, the change agent must find a way to get them the necessary training. Selection and/or training should occur early because any inability to perform the new behaviors will cause employees to be frustrated, leading to resistance or lowered efforts.

We want to be clear about our use of the terms "selection" or its opposite, "deselection." We do not necessarily mean firing a person. They may be transferred to another job or department, for example. It is important to have alignment between employees and tasks that need to be done. If new tasks are a necessary part of the strategic change, then it is important to have in place people who can do these tasks.

Building Support for the Change

Change agents need to establish the need for change; build commitment and a winning coalition to support the change; and devise and communicate a road-map to all stakeholders. This chapter focuses on anticipatory change and early stage reactive change in which educating employees is critical to the success of the change effort. It is important to recognize also that every change situation is different. If you are dealing with a union, negotiations will be required. If it is a crisis, then rapid top-down decision-making may be appropriate.

Establish the need for change. This is an educational process. In anticipatory change and even reactive change, resistance is most likely a result of different interpretations of the company's situation. The challenge is to establish the most accurate interpretation and to educate employees. It is essential to convince the

target group that the change and associated new behaviors will lead to benefits, such as improved performance for their organization, recognition for them,
or, possibly, monetary rewards. Some companies we have worked with have
used the "burning platform" metaphor for this activity. This business jargon
is intended to convince employees of an impending discontinuity, significant
change, or potential crisis.

Learning new behaviors can be stressful and at first glance seem costlier
than sticking with old habits. It is imperative that managers convincingly show
that, after a suitable adjustment period, survival and success will follow. Since
change is a complex undertaking that involves many different people and possibly different cultures and many different interpretations of the situation, it
is usually difficult to convince people of the need to change with just words, a
memo, or an email. In addition to being on the lookout for the "If it ain't broke,
why fix it?" attitude, change agents need to be alert to the "What's in it for us?"
attitude.

We encourage you to use as many different media and types of data as possible. Personal visits by senior executives, video recordings, financial and market data, comparisons with competitors, and first-hand customer or supplier
data all can help to make the case for change.

The initiators of the change and the target groups may have different cultural backgrounds. Thus, the change agent has to take into consideration the
perspectives of various groups of employees with regard to their knowledge of
the change and their preferred mode of communication. Remember, this is the
Bridging (B) part of the MBI model (see p. 117).

Devise and communicate a roadmap. A good roadmap shows the destination
and a route to get there. This is the new strategy, objectives, task behaviors,
and possible new organizational structures and systems that appear necessary.
The roadmap describes the path toward these goals to include education, skill
training to learn the new behaviors, and resources to be provided. The roadmap
serves as a starting point and the change agents update it through the application of the design thinking process.

The communication strategy should include feedback opportunities such
as meetings (town hall and small group), surveys, or suggestion boxes.
Depending on the cultural background, employees will react differently to
feedback modes. For example, indirect feedback through a trusted third party
may be the local way of disagreeing upwards, while simultaneously seeming

to agree publicly with a superior. This can be confusing to a manager from a culture where disagreement is openly and directly expressed regardless of different status levels.

Establishing effective dialogue takes time, something that managers do not have in crisis change. Instead, they must act quickly. It may be tempting to push through with a change process by creating crises. We do not recommend the use of such a tactic, as employees may lose faith or call the manager's bluff or the organization will be exposed to unnecessary risks.

Obtain commitment. A clearly communicated and a data-driven new strategy will build commitment as will a diligent assessment of the readiness for change. However, it is of utmost importance that the target group is involved in the change process. The application of the design thinking process is helpful in this regard. Involvement breeds ownership of and commitment to the solution and to the change process.

Involvement requires skillful leadership, as people may initially resist a change effort. It also takes time and, hence, is hardly feasible in crisis-driven change management.

Maintain participation in the change effort. The change agent must ensure that the target group stays involved throughout the change process. This involvement has to give the employees a voice through, for example, meetings, suggestion boxes, and one-on-one conversations. An effective change process typically includes joint discussions between the target group, the change agent, and top management. If the change yields negative outcomes for employees, such as job loss, outside facilitators may join the discussions to assist handling potential hostility.

The benefits of involving the target group are obvious. Employees will know more about the change process and their task-related knowledge is relevant in particular for determining new behaviors. As mentioned before, the most important benefit is a sense of ownership. It also becomes easier for this group to convince their peers to join in the change effort.

In obtaining commitment and gaining participation of employees in the change effort, the mode of involvement needs to be appropriate to the cultural norms of the situation. But it is equally important that the assessment of the appropriate mode not be based on stereotypes or assumptions based on partial or inaccurate information.

Figure 9.3 is a summary of Phase 2.

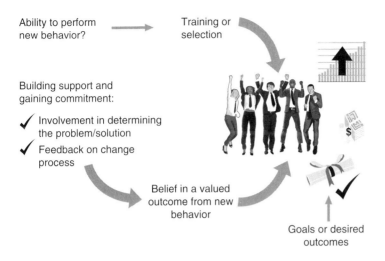

Figure 9.3 Phase 2: initiating the change

Phase 3: Reinforcing the Change

A change and the associated new behaviors are sustainable only if the organization supports and rewards them. We have seen many companies that have sent executives to management programs to develop general management skills and learn new techniques, but have failed to reinforce the new lessons and ideas when they return. To facilitate the performance of the new behaviors, we recommend that senior executives do two things – plan for and showcase the small wins and adjust the alignment model as necessary.

Small Wins

Our first recommendation is that outcomes you told the target group to expect actually do occur. Many writers on the subject of change would argue in favor of the "theory of the small win." It is the small, incremental changes that stand the best chances of success (Quinn, 1980). Unless forced by a crisis into making major, system-wide changes, you may be wise to start small and let the change mature and grow. The diffusion of change beyond its initiation depends in large measure on perceived success – continuation of change is fueled by such success and, unless early success is apparent, the chances of realizing your goals are slim.

Recognizing that it is not feasible to control all variables in a change process or that trying to change an entire global company at once may not be feasible, we suggest eating the elephant one bite at a time. This is where the theory of the small win plays an important part. If you design your change plan to incorporate small wins, then you have some control over positive reinforcement that supports the change. Employees will continue to engage in the new behaviors if the rewards (both tangible and intangible) match their expectations. They must see that their behaviors advance the organization's goals and serve their self-interests.

Small wins are not necessarily small, but rather they are intermediate steps on the road to a larger strategic change. Keep in mind that they are real and visible success stories that validate your decisions and actions. They build credibility, commitment, and allies and reduce the power of critics. Our recommendation in planning a change effort is to make sure you have designed in some small wins. Showcasing or celebrating successes is vital, because employees appreciate being part of a winning team, which in turn increases commitment and breeds confidence. As important as it is to showcase small wins, it is equally important not to confuse achieving interim goals with final success – in other words, not declaring victory too soon (Kotter, 2012).

Realignment

If the existing systems, structures, and culture are not aligned with the new required behaviors, managers must adjust them. A potential new alignment model should be a part of the change plan, but modifications may be necessary based on insights gained during the design thinking process.

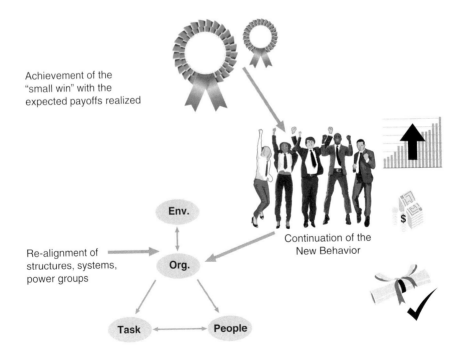

Figure 9.4 Phase 3: reinforcing the change

This step is critical. Employees respond to signals sent by reward and evaluation systems, for example. It does no good to train employees in new behaviors and then put them back in an organizational system that inhibits these new behaviors. Figure 9.4 is a summary of Phase 3.

Organization Renewal

Organizational change efforts are not one-time events. They are processes that require discipline and communication. Skipping a part of the change process can result in failure of the change initiative. The change model focuses on issues that managers should consider in change efforts and suggests actions that they can take. The model, in particular, centers on enabling and motivating employees to engage in the new behaviors.

Although the change model suggests a process for completing one change, it should not be interpreted to suggest that change is a one-time effort. It is more meaningful to think about change as a continuous process that can be broken into meaningful phases.

Ideally organizations should try to build a culture for change that becomes part of the organizational mindset – organizational cultures that create "nimbleness"; allowing for agility, flexibility, and adaptation to changing environmental conditions, on the one hand, while fulfilling the traditional task of creating stability and predictability on the other hand (Worley and Lawler, 2006).

As discussed in earlier chapters, organizational structures and management systems have generally been viewed as means of reducing the variability and increasing the stability of human behavior, and programs like total quality management or Six Sigma, for example, do that. Global corporations, however, do not operate in stable and predictable environments. Trying to manage a global company with models and processes designed to reduce variation in an environment that is characterized by dynamic complexity will probably be ineffective or possibly work only in the short term, if at all. Responding to dynamic complexity means that organizations have to find the right people and to manage the complexity and execute action plans.

Change can be a challenge in any culture, but when trying to make changes in a global company in multiple countries, the challenge can be compounded by different cultural understandings. The MBI framework (Chapter 4), organizational alignment framework (Chapter 8), design thinking, and change model are tools that will help provide mindful global leaders with the confidence and skills to negotiate the challenge.

Reflection Questions

For these questions, we suggest you reflect on a change going on in your company right now, or to think about a required change, for example one that comes out of your reflection to Chapter 7 on organizational alignment.

1. Appraise the readiness for change. Is there a visible need? Does the change have top management support and commitment? Is there a ready and engaged change agent (maybe this is you!)? Is there a good understanding of the target group for the change?
2. In initiating the change and influencing people to adopt the new behavior, how well-defined are the implementation mechanisms?
   a. Select people with particular skills and attitudes.
   b. Train for new skills and knowledge.
   c. Communicate to establish the need for change.
   d. Build a roadmap with a clear process.
   e. Develop commitment from stakeholders.
   f. Ensure continuous participation from target group.

   Which could be improved? How?

3. What is being done to reinforce the change?
   a. How are small wins acknowledged, celebrated, and communicated?
   b. How are realignment needs monitored and responded to?
   c. How is the company supporting the need for continuous change and organizational renewal?
4. If you are not familiar with design thinking, we suggest you try the technique on a current challenge you are facing. It can even be applied to personal and small group change. Go to the Stanford Design School and IDEO links suggested below. Start by applying the techniques to a relatively small challenge or question you are facing, then reflect on how else the tools could be used. https://dschool-old.stanford.edu/sandbox/groups/designresources/wiki/36873/attachments/74b3d/ModeGuideBOOTCAMP2010L.pdf www.ideou.com/pages/design-thinking

Further Resources

Two excellent books on change management are:

Brown, T. (2009). *Change by Design: How Design Thinking Transforms Organizations and Inspires Innovation*. HarperCollins.

Spector. B. (2013). *Implementing Organizational Change: Theory Into Practice,* 3rd edn. Pearson.

For more on IBM's change story, the most comprehensive explanation is still Louis Gerstner Jr.'s *Who Says Elephants Can't Dance?* (2002).

If you would like to know more about the burning platform metaphor and where it originated, here are two websites that tell the story: http://gardner.utah.edu/_documents/ outreach/articles/pp-burning-platform.pdf and www.connerpartners.com/frameworks- and-processes/the-real-story-of-the-burning-platform

Bibliography

Brown, T. (2017). *Design Thinking is a Process for Creative Problem Solving.* Retrieved November 2017 from Ideou: www.ideou.com/pages/design-thinking

Gerstner, Jr., L. V. (2002). *Who Says Elephants Can't Dance? Inside IBM's Historic Turnaround.* Harper Business.

Kotter, J. (2012). *Leading Change.* Harvard Business Review Press.

Lagace, M. (2002). *Changing Culture at IBM : Lou Gerstner Discusses Changing the Culture at IBM.* Retrieved November 2017 from Harvard Business School: https://hbswk.hbs.edu/archive/ gerstner-changing-culture-at-ibm- lou-gerstner-discusses-changing-the- culture-at-ibm

Meyer, M. (2007). *The Fast Path to Corporate Growth.* Oxford University Press.

Palmisano, S. (2003). *Our Values at Work: On Being an IBMer.* Retrieved July 2017 from IBM: www.zurich.ibm.com/pdf/hr/ Our_Values_at_Work.pdf

Platner, H. (2017). *An Introduction to Design Thinking: Process Guide.* Retrieved November 2017 from Institute of Design at Stanford: https://dschool-old.stanford .edu/sandbox/groups/designresources/ wiki/36873/attachments/74b3d/ ModeGuideBOOTCAMP2010L.pdf

Quinn, J. (1980). Managing Strategic Change. *MIT Sloan Management Review,* July 15.

Sernovitz, G. (2016). *What the Organization Man Can Tell Us about Inequality Today. The New Yorker,* December 29. Retrieved July 2017 from: www.newyorker.com/ business/currency/what-the-organization- man-can-tell-us-about-inequality-today

Strebel, P. (1997). The Politics of Change. *IMD Perspectives for Managers,* 2.

Whyte, W. (1956/2002). *The Organization Man.* University of Pennsylvania Press.

Worley, C., & Lawler, E. (2006). Designing Organizations that Are Built to Change. *MIT Sloan Management Review,* 48, 19–23.

IVEY | Publishing

CUSHY ARMCHAIR

Professor Brian Golden prepared this case solely to provide material for class discussion. The author does not intend to illustrate either effective or ineffective handling of a managerial situation. The author may have disguised certain names and other identifying information to protect confidentiality.

This publication may not be transmitted, photocopied, digitized or otherwise reproduced in any form or by any means without the permission of the copyright holder. Reproduction of this material is not covered under authorization by any reproduction rights organization. To order copies or request permission to reproduce materials, contact Ivey Publishing, Ivey Business School, Western University, London, Ontario, Canada, N6G 0N1; (t) 519.661.3208; (e) cases@ivey.ca; www .iveycases.com.

Copyright © 2001, Richard Ivey School of Business Foundation

Version: 2013-08-08

Cabletronica U.S. is a large, prosperous cable and wireless company based in upstate New York. In order to expand the scope of operations, it has recently targeted several strategically related industries in which to take a greater stake. Specifically, its research on changing demographic and cable viewing patterns concluded that reclining armchairs would be a growth business over the next 20 years. Cabletronica thus moved their minority investment position in Cushy Armchair (CA), based in Hong Kong, to a position of total equity and operating control. Cabletronica had just completed the acquisition of WorldFurniture, also based in New York.

Cushy Armchair is a recognized leader in the global reclining chair business, with fully autonomous business groups in 17 countries. This decentralized model evolved as a result of the substantial communication and logistics challenges facing multinationals in 1962, the year it was founded. And since economies of scale had been inconsequential, while national market differences were substantial, this model had been sensible and had paid off handsomely. National differences could be seen, for example, in the U.S. division's recent introduction of reclining chairs that offered drink-holders and coolers built into the chair armrests. The Scandinavian market had introduced a "tingling fingers" massage chair, and although successful in that market, it was shown to have minimal attractiveness elsewhere. Other differences across the world included fabric preferences, as well as size requirements (to accommodate varying torso characteristics, as well as differing housing space constraints). Although historically a sleepy industry, the recliner industry is expected to heat up as a result of consolidation, new materials and technology, and shortening design cycles. In addition, competitors founded in the past few years have built global (centralized), rather than multidomestic (decentralized) businesses. This further enhances their potential cost and cycle-time advantages.

As part of Cabletronica's attempts to breathe new life into Cushy Armchair, the company dispatched Alison Sampson to take the helm of CA in Hong Kong, replacing the well-regarded founder, Frances Wong. Cabletronica's chief operating officer announced this appointment like all Cabletronica senior personnel changes, through a global e-mail message. Sampson's appointment was to begin March 14th, the busiest time of year as most of the businesses ramped up design and manufacturing for strong end-of-year holiday sales. Sampson's immediate goals were to reduce costs, speed product design and improve technology transfer. Specifically, production, design (fabric and style), sales and distribution (advertising), and procurement would be her focus in the short term. Sampson came to this with a successful background integrating numerous acquisitions for Cabletronica, mainly in the cable industry. She had risen through the finance ranks, and was looking forward to the challenge of moving into a manufacturing setting and working for the first time with line managers. Wong would serve as a consultant to Sampson for the next six months, in an effort to ensure a smooth transfer of control. Sampson, after careful examination of industry trends and competitor analysis, was keen to hit the ground running. After two weeks on the job, she drafted the following e-mail memorandum to the executives responsible for purchasing, sales and design in each of the 17 countries.

> **To:** National Purchasing, Marketing, and Design managers
> **From:** Alison Sampson, C.A., M.B.A.
> **Date:** April 1
>
> As you know, our industry is changing dramatically, and although virtually all of our national businesses have been very successful these past years, that is going to change unless we change. I know you share my observations and concerns for the future of Cushy Armchair, and I trust that you will welcome these changes as I move to consolidate operations. We will begin with some small steps, all involving greater centralization in order to achieve economies of scale and scope. Specifically, from the first of next month onwards, I would like to request the following of all purchasing, marketing and design managers:
>
> 1. All purchasing managers should ensure that all chair glide-mechanisms, as well as fabric orders in excess of HK$1 million be contracted through WorldFurniture's procurement division in New York.
> 2. Advertising campaigns will in the future be co-ordinated through New York, where we have an expert group of advertising specialists. Therefore, all interest in launching new advertising campaigns should be cleared by our New York staff.
> 3. The New York staff should approve any substantial design and feature changes.
>
> Though I haven't yet had the opportunity to meet with most of you, I look forward to doing so over the next three months to discuss the impact of these policy changes and the changes ahead.
>
> A. Sampson, C.A., M.B.A.

Before sending this e-mail, Sampson asked Wong for his reaction. Wong suggested that e-mail was perhaps not the most effective way to deliver this message. While Sampson appreciated the advice, she felt e-mail was most expedient, given the urgency to change in time for next season's rush.

Two months later, in a casual conversation with the head of procurement for WorldFurniture, Sampson learned that no orders from any of Cushy Armchair's divisions had yet been received. It didn't take long for Sampson to learn that either all of her policy changes had been ignored *or* that no actions or decisions by purchasing, design or marketing had yet met the criteria set out by Sampson in her e-mail memo of April 1st.

IMD

MAGDI BATATO AT NESTLÉ MALAYSIA (A): INTRODUCING TEAM-BASED PRODUCTION

Tom Gleave and Professor Martha Maznevski prepared this case as a basis for class discussion rather than to illustrate either effective or ineffective handling of a business situation.

Copyright © 2011 by **IMD – International Institute for Management Development**, Lausanne, Switzerland (www.imd.org). No part of this publication may be reproduced, stored in a retrieval system or transmitted in any form or by any means without the prior written permission of **IMD**.

In June 2005, Magdi Batato, executive director of production for Nestlé Malaysia, was frustrated. He had spent the last four months trying to convince the Nestlé Malaysia Production Management Committee to adopt a new approach to organizing production improvement: team-based management with goal alignment across teams and increased team autonomy. However, the committee had yet to reach a consensus on whether or not to endorse such an initiative.

Batato was a 14-year Nestlé veteran with an excellent track record in leadership and production in several countries. He had been transferred from South Africa in September 2004. Soon after arriving, Batato concluded that his biggest challenge was to ensure the long-term sustainability of the seven local factories, despite their above average performance compared to other Nestlé factories. His experience and research convinced him that this approach was the best way to make the next performance leap. He did not face active resistance, but there was a seemingly endless parade of reasons to "examine the options further," to "wait for better conditions."

Working in semi-autonomous teams required internal motivation and initiative, so forcing the Committee to move might backfire. Some of their reasons for delay – for example, that people here were not used to working this way – suggested moving slowly. Besides there was no urgent need to turn productivity around. But Batato knew that implementation took time. He had already been in Malaysia for nine months of what was likely a maximum five-year assignment. In South Africa his production improvements looked like they were losing ground, and Batato believed this was because he had been transferred away before he had had a chance to institutionalize them.

He wanted to push ahead, but how could he do so without jeopardizing the effectiveness of the changes? Maybe he should just be more patient.

Overview of Nestlé S.A.

Nestlé S.A (Nestlé) traced its roots to the 1860s when Henri Nestlé, a German pharmacist living in Vevey, Switzerland, developed a formula for babies who were unable to breastfeed. The product was an immediate success and was quickly sold throughout continental Europe and the UK. Nestlé built on this success by developing an increasing number of branded food products, such as Milo and Nescafé, that were sold in a growing number of countries. After World War

II the pace of growth quickened, in part through the acquisition of a wide range of branded category leaders.

The company organized the bulk of its activities around product-based strategic business units (SBUs), including baby food, coffee and beverages, breakfast and infant cereals, chilled dairy, chocolate, and ice cream. Each SBU was supported by operations, sales and marketing, finance, innovation and technology, and R&D functions, all of which cascaded down from the corporate headquarters to the "market" (country) level, from where they were again cascaded down to individual factories, field sales offices and laboratories. The company's overseas operations enjoyed a great deal of operating autonomy, particularly with respect to the products it developed so that local factories could better meet local market preferences.

By 2005, Nestlé had become the world's largest manufacturer and marketer of foods, with worldwide revenues topping CHF 86.8 billion and earnings before interest, tax and amortization (EBITA) of CHF 11 billion.[1] Of the 250,000 people who worked for the company, the majority were employed at some 500 factories spread across more than 80 countries. Many of these employees spent the bulk of their careers at Nestlé, as evidenced by the fact that the average tenure of service upon retirement was 27 years.

Magdi Batato's Journey: From Knowledge Expert to Practice Expert

The Early Days

Magdi Batato was born in Cairo, raised in Lebanon and moved to Switzerland, where he graduated from the Ecole Polytechnique Fédérale de Lausanne with a mechanical engineering degree and a multidisciplinary PhD that combined thermodynamics with

human physiology. Batato then worked for a consultancy before joining Nestlé's headquarters in Vevey in 1991, where he was initially a corporate advisor on energy- and environment-related matters. Batato was quickly recognized there as a strong leader with potential for operational responsibilities. He was invited to join a high profile group of "centrally based expatriates," the members of whom were viewed as key talents within the company's global management development pipeline.

In 1995 Batato was transferred to Germany where, as the newly appointed head of production, he was expected to bolster the 225-person seasonings and soup factory's operational capabilities. Batato's predecessor, a 50-year Nestlé veteran who had spent the past 30 years working at the factory, was due to retire. Batato was expected to bring innovation and process improvements to the factory.

Off to Lebanon …

After two years in Germany, Batato had achieved a number of improvements in the factory's key performance indicators (KPIs) with relatively straightforward incremental innovation. He was then transferred to Lebanon, where Nestlé Waters held a minority stake (49%) in a local bottled water factory. As the factory manager, he found his new assignment a challenging one. Batato recalled:

Most of the employees in Lebanon had taken on a "survival mindset." They were trying their best to serve the customer with high quality, but they were distracted by a variety of factors. This wasn't surprising when you consider that multiple races and multiple religions had been living side-by-side in an environment that had been fraught with conflict for years. So I set out to develop a more performance driven and customer-focused mindset, starting

---

[1] Figures are for fiscal 2004. Source: Nestlé 2004 Annual Report.

with the natural leaders whom the other employees respected. For example, one engineer was our "Mr. Fix-It" guy whenever any operational issue arose. But he was working a lot of overtime and putting himself and others under pressure because he was fixing so much for us. I promoted him to a manager, with a large enough salary that it compensated for his lack of overtime pay. I helped him learn to coach others to fix things so he would not have to do so much himself. The arrangement worked well because he gained the esteem of colleagues and he helped other workers become more productive. In Lebanon I really learned the importance of getting people on board for performance and the customer, even to make production changes.

… And Then to South Africa

After four years of implementing such mindset changes and performance improvements, the Nestlé Waters joint venture was performing better. In 2001 Batato was posted to Estcourt, South Africa where, as factory manager, he was expected to turn around the once high-performing coffee and beverages factory. The factory comprised six mini business units (MBUs), one each for the separate processing and filling/packing functions related to the three main product lines: spray dried coffee, Milo and Nesquik. Each MBU ran three shifts. In the past, the factory was considered a "best-in-class" operation. After the dissolution of apartheid in 1994 its performance began to suffer. At that time, people's roles and responsibilities across South African society shifted, creating confusion, inefficiency and heightened emotions in plants like Nestlé's.

Batato's predecessor had developed a program called "Pulling Together" to facilitate the employees' relations with one another and to focus on performance. Batato built on Pulling Together with a program "Working Together" to cultivate a more businesslike mindset among the employees, focusing on business performance and customer requirements. He hoped this would eventually replace the emotional mindset that pervaded the operation. He encouraged employees to analyze situations in a methodical and dispassionate manner, and he helped staff see the problems in terms they could relate to. For example, he showed one group of employees that financial losses of a certain number of units of spray dried coffee equated to so many lost South African rand (R) which, by extension, equated to the value of so many cows a local tribesperson could buy or sell. Because he took this approach with many different aspects of the business, employees began to dub him "Mr. Fact," a nickname he did not mind because "the employees became more businesslike and dispensed with much of the emotional baggage that had been undermining their performance."

In addition, Batato tried to align the reward system with performance. He identified top performing MBUs and awarded them prizes valued up to R30,000 (around US$3,333 at the time), to divide among the people in the unit. As he later discovered, however, the process underlying the drive for operational performance improvements was too unstructured and the rewards were not as well received as he had originally envisioned. He needed to find another way to put mindset and practice together to increase performance.

Discovering Semi-Autonomous Work Teams

Around this time, Batato was introduced to the idea of semi-autonomous work teams by a consultant.[2] This was a system of

---

[2] The consulting firm was Competitive Dynamics International, www.cdi.biz, which has implemented its Mission-directed Work Teams program in many companies globally, in addition to multiple Nestlé sites.

empowering production teams to set goals and improve their own performance, within a structure of goal-alignment interlocked throughout the plant. The key was to link motivation, group accountability and competences with business performance in a complete socio-technical system. "I jumped at the opportunity," Batato remembers.

In this system, the measurement, reporting, analysis, and continuous improvement aspects of production are supported by *semi-autonomous work teams* (SAWTs). SAWTs are frontline production teams who are aligned with the management of the company and the plant, but who determine their own goals and directions for improvement. They are held accountable for results and rewarded based on meeting their own goals and their contributions to the overall goals of the plant. Through coaching and empowerment, they are encouraged to take initiatives to enhance performance whenever possible, and are supported with training and resources for self-management. To achieve their goals, SAWT members must develop competences in production and problem-solving continuous improvement

techniques to increase consistency and reliability and eliminate waste. They must also learn to work together in a collaborative way to identify targets for continuous improvement, and to accomplish those targets.

Batato and the consultant began in November 2003 by training the department heads in the main ideas behind SAWTs. Because of the importance of coaching in the model, these department heads then trained lower level production supervisors and frontline workers. Over the next six months, the Estcourt management and staff focused on aligning the goals of each MBU to those of the factory, the market office in Johannesburg, and the customers. Teams initiated service-level agreements between themselves and their value stream partners to align goals vertically and horizontally, to maximize overall performance of the MBU and the factory, and to reinforce a customer mindset among everyone (*refer to* Exhibit 1, *Goal Alignment in Coffee Production*).

SAWT offices were created on the production lines, which in turn reported to their respective production business units. Each team office tracked the agreed-upon KPIs

Exhibit 1   Semi-autonomous Work Teams and Goal Alignment at Nestlé Estcourt Example: Coffee Production

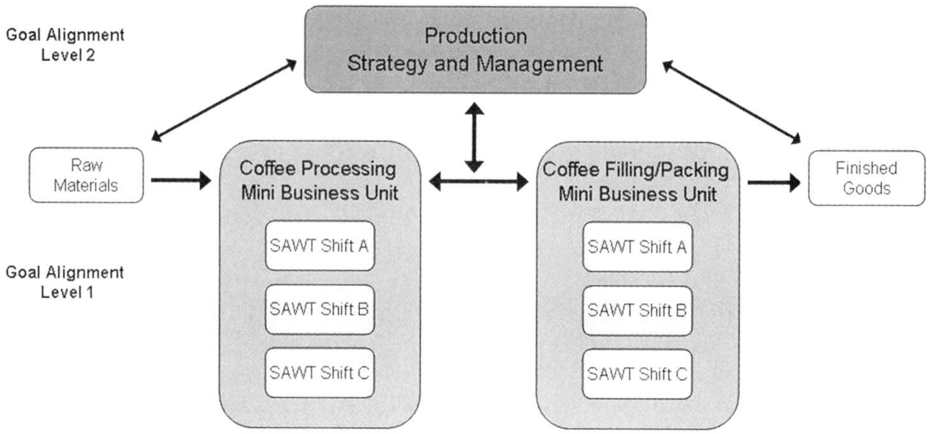

Source: Company information

and prominently displayed them. Teams updated KPI displays on a daily, weekly or monthly basis. They identified key production problems, proposed solutions, and tracked indicators until problems were solved.

Once Batato and the consultant were satisfied that employees had adopted the routines and social systems for SAWTs, they introduced the more rigorous manufacturing and problem- solving techniques of continuous improvement. These included deep cause-effect analysis, pareto analysis, flow charts, check sheets, histograms, process control charts, and so on.

Supervisors became coaches rather than authoritarian leaders; they met regularly with their SAWTs to monitor their progress, facilitate their improvements, train them in new methods, communicate regarding alignment, and reinforce empowerment and the teams' taking responsibility for their performance. These responsibilities and improvements were "cascaded up" through management, while coaching was "cascaded down" with each successive layer coaching the layer below regarding manufacturing processes and performance focus.

Batato also revised the factory's reward systems. Earlier he had offered relatively large cash payouts to a few teams that had achieved large improvements in performance, consistent with his original goals. Now, to be aligned with the philosophy of SAWTs and continuous improvement, he offered a larger number of soft rewards (such as public recognition and product vouchers) to more teams that had achieved smaller incremental gains. He also sponsored various parties and barbecues for the winning teams, which he learned was very motivating to them. At the same time he developed a more formal performance management system that supported specific individual- and team-based goals. The strong workers' union at the factory made it difficult to discipline underperforming employees without such a

system, and in addition the system was now aligned with the SAWT philosophies.

Ten months after introducing SAWTs to the Estcourt factory, Batato and his team saw improvements across quality, speed, service, and people-focused measures. Batato was impressed with the combination of tools. People working in the factory were much more customer- and business-focused. The continuous monitoring and coaching meant that problems were identified and resolved quickly. The reward systems "struck a good balance between having carrots and sticks to encourage performance."

Batato's Journey Continues to Malaysia

In August 2004, just when he was beginning to see results in Estcourt, Batato was transferred to Nestlé Malaysia. Nestlé's Malaysian operations dated back to 1912 and had since grown to employ some 4,000 people, the majority of whom worked in the six multi-product factories based in Malaysia proper as well as one multi-product factory based in Singapore. As executive director of production, Batato assumed responsibility for the seven factories, producing a wide range of food items for the domestic market and several markets throughout Southeast Asia and the Middle East. Unlike the operations he had encountered when he first arrived in Germany, Lebanon, and South Africa, Nestlé's Malaysian operations were running smoothly, with all seven factories achieving between 75% and 90% of their target KPIs. This performance was grounded in a strong management team, sound product development and branding policies, and strong IT support. Batato also found that local management had nurtured a very positive relationship with employees. This was partly through maintaining open communication and policies that tried to prevent negative impacts during times of adversity. For example, in 2000/2001 Nestlé Asean had implemented an industrial structure, strategically shifting production among plants so that ingredients and products were each produced in larger batches in fewer plants. As a result, Nestlé Malaysia had shut down some operations in two factories and increased volumes in other operations. The company offered its employees transfers to other operations to minimize permanent layoffs. This and other actions helped the company develop a reputation for being a "trusted employer" not just by the employees themselves, but by other workers in the country who aspired to work there as well.

Despite Nestlé Malaysia's operational success, Batato believed there was room for improvement in operational performance, particularly for those production lines with KPIs hovering around the 75% range. This view was reinforced after his initial visits to the factories. He found that two long-simmering issues had not been sufficiently addressed by previous management. On the one hand, many frontline employees had given Batato the impression, through indirect hints and veiled references, that their supervisors and managers did not understand the difficulties they often encountered on the front line. On the other hand, many supervisors and managers maintained a belief that the abilities and predispositions of the frontline employees limited the performance potential of the factories. Clearly there was room for improvement!

Introducing SAWTS in Malaysia?

In February 2005, at the monthly meeting of the Production Management Committee (PMC),[3] Batato introduced the idea of SAWTs as a possible means for tackling these issues.

[3] The 15 member PMC was composed of Batato, senior managers from key support functions (including industrial performance, innovation and technology, and R&D), as well as the seven factory managers. The group typically met once per month to discuss high priority issues related to production.

Most PMC members were intrigued by the new concepts and were cautiously positive about the ideas when the consultant came and addressed them. They acknowledged the initial results that Batato had achieved in South Africa. But many members were reluctant to endorse a similar initiative in Malaysia. One reason was that, even though plenty of positive improvements had been realized, the progress made at the Estcourt factory had not lived up to original expectations. Batato acknowledged this concern, and believed the main reason for the slow progress was his transfer to Malaysia at a time when the reforms still had not fully taken root.

The PMC members also expressed a lack of urgency for change in Malaysia. Existing performance levels at the factories were already high compared with all factories in Asia, Africa and Oceana. PMC managers were worried about "change fatigue" setting in with frontline employees and their supervisors, given that they had implemented separate worldwide IT system and cultural change initiatives driven out of head office in recent years. These initiatives, coupled with Nestlé Malaysia's 2000/2001 consolidation activities, made some managers skeptical about the ability or desire of the employees to absorb further changes.

PMC members also observed that implementing these practices would face different challenges in different factories. On the one hand, four factories were running smoothly and were not expecting any new plant and equipment upgrades in the coming years. Moreover, since these factories were performing well already, introducing these practices here where they were not urgently needed would increase the performance gap with the other factories. Leading improvement there would mean working against a lot of resistance. Shouldn't they address the more problematic factories first? On the other hand, two factories suffered from capacity constraints and needed new investment. This could present an opportunity for change, but it meant adding another layer of complexity on top of the already constrained workforce. Wouldn't it be better to add the new capacity first, then worry about improvement?

Finally, the overall social context of Malaysia raised concerns among several PMC members. As a multiracial, multireligious society comprised of a majority Malay community (50%), along with Chinese (24%), indigenous (11%), and Indian (7%) communities, Malaysia's working environment was inherently diverse across cultural, religious and linguistic dimensions.[4] This resulted in differences in attitudes and behaviors toward the role of work in people's lives, as well as how work should be managed. For example, while all of Malaysia's main ethnic groups had strong family orientations and a high degree of respect for parental authority, variations in degree existed across the groups. This had important implications for the nature of the relationships formed between the subordinates and their supervisors. As a consultant explained:

> Malaysia has one of the highest hierarchy scores anywhere in the world as well as relatively high scores on collectivism. The result is a well-established deference to hierarchy between subordinates and their superiors, and a commitment to not standing out in a group. At a practical level, these front line workers prefer to wait for orders before doing anything. They are also not naturally expressive when solicited for new ideas on how to improve things. This clearly goes against what we try to do with SAWTs in manufacturing – we want the shop floor to take ownership of their work and become proactive in identifying operational improvements and innovations.

The situation is a considerable contrast to South Africa, where hierarchy scores are relatively moderate.

There were also apparently large differences in attitudes and behaviors exhibited by employees who worked at the five urban factories compared with those who worked in the two rural factories. According to a number of PMC members, the urban factories were staffed by employees who were more willing to accept changes than their counterparts working at the rural factories. Adnan Pawanteh, factory manager of Shah Alam, on the outskirts of Kuala Lumpur, explained:

> The operating environment in Malaysia is complex. The dominant Malay population is conservative in nature and perhaps more paternalistic than the Chinese or Indians. They tend to have strong rural roots, as the "balik kampung" phenomenon shows. This is when millions of Malays return to their small hometowns – or "kampungs" – during holidays and festivals, leaving the cities like ghost towns. By contrast, the overseas Chinese come from an immigrant legacy. The early arrivals had to survive as a minority in a country with different cultural, linguistic and religious norms. This led them to congregate mainly in the cities where they could then trade with each other. The same is true for the Indians. They, too, are descendants of immigrants and have had to adapt to survive, be they Muslims or Hindus. At the same time, they carry on some traditional values, including some vestiges of the old caste system, which can mean some people they feel they are predestined to assume certain roles in society.

It had been four months since Batato first suggested to his PMC colleagues that Nestlé Malaysia implement a new approach to production management based on SAWTs. Most

---

[4] The World Factbook, Malaysia. Central Intelligence Agency. https://www.cia.gov/library/publications/the-world-factbook/geos/my.html

of the PMC members had seen the potential benefits such approaches could provide, as shown by the initial positive results achieved at Estcourt as well as at other Nestlé factories in South Africa. At the same time, many members continued to express reservations about the suitability of SAWTs for Nestlé Malaysia's operations. There was a lack of urgency for such changes, the changes might create further performance gaps among existing operations, and the new management approaches would not fit well within the sociocultural context of the Malaysia working environment.

Considering the Options

Sensing he had reached an impasse, Batato needed to decide what to do next.

One option was simply to cease advocating the implementation of SAWTs and focus on other ways to improve the company's operating performance. Another option was to persist in trying to persuade those who remained unconvinced of the merits and suitability of such an initiative in Malaysia. He also considered pushing his ideas more forcefully and directing the implementation more authoritatively. He did not actually need the PMC's approval if top management agreed with the direction.

Moving too quickly could sabotage the whole implementation by going against its basic principles, but moving too slowly could be just as dangerous by not giving the time for and attention to implementation. In either case, the long-term sustainability of Malaysia's operations would be at risk and Batato's reputation as a "rising star" within the company would be affected. A wrong move would come back to haunt Batato and his colleagues.

PART IV
Integrity and Sustainable Performance

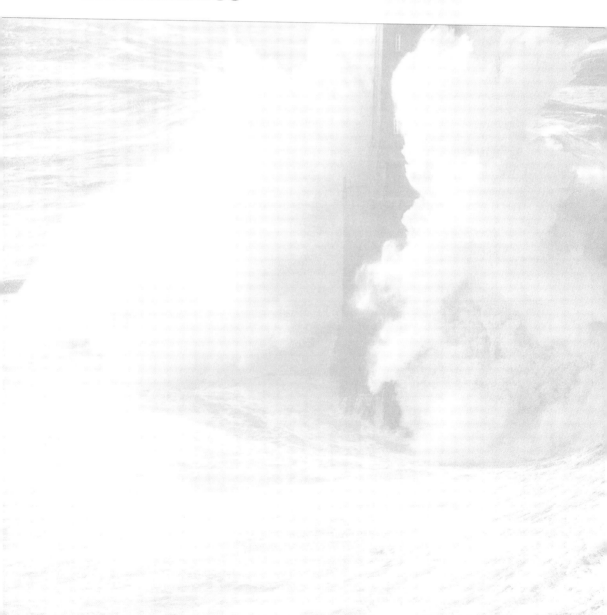

10 Competing with Integrity: Personal Integrity

The supreme quality for leadership is unquestionably integrity. Without it, no real success is possible.

Dwight D. Eisenhower

One of the truest tests of integrity is its blunt refusal to be compromised.

Chinua Achebe

Overview: Competing with Integrity

This chapter examines the issues of personal **ethical behavior** that you, as a manager, may face in your career. We focus on personal integrity in this chapter, because we believe that issues of **individual responsibility** and **ethics** do not always receive the attention that they deserve in business courses.

The objective is to challenge you to consider your responsibilities as a business leader more broadly rather than simply from a financial perspective. There can be social consequences from your decisions as well as financial ones. The human and social impact of decisions should be considered at the time these decisions are being made. And it is not just the consequences for some faceless group of people in some far away land that you need to consider. There can be personal consequences from your decisions.

Following on from the global mindset framework presented in Chapter 2 (see p. 31), we discuss these issues at the individual level (ethical behavior) in this chapter and at the organizational level (**corporate sustainability**) in Chapter 11. What is the difference between personal integrity or ethics and corporate sustainability? To us, the distinction is between the decisions and behavior of an individual or a small group of people and the formal social responsibility initiatives of an organization (Table 10.1).

Table 10.1 **Global mindset framework applied to ethics and corporate sustainability**

	Individual/Personal	Organizational
Self	Clarify and understand my beliefs about ethical behavior.	Clarify and understand my organization's approach to corporate sustainability.
Other	Clarify and understand other beliefs about ethical behavior in the context of other cultures and principal theories of moral philosophy.	Clarify and understand other corporate approaches to sustainability in the context of other industries, other cultures, and principal codes of conduct.
Choice	Belief in and commitment to a set of ethical principles.	Belief in and commitment to an approach to corporate sustainability.

Corporate sustainability decisions and programs may involve potential ethical considerations. However, if there are no clear guidelines it is left to each executive to decide. As companies develop sustainability initiatives and define their approach to corporate sustainability more clearly, the guidelines provide employees with counsel regarding their behavior and decisions about social (people), environmental (planet), and business (profit) trade-offs.

This chapter explores the distinction between ethical and legal behavior as well as the differences in major ethical frameworks or theories of moral philosophy, such as **consequential** (results focused), **rules–based** (universal), and **cultural relativism**. We believe that this discussion can help you develop your own perspective and position on competing with integrity.

Personal Integrity

What is integrity? Professor Glen Rowe from the Ivey Business School describes integrity as "consistency among what you believe in your heart; think in your head; what you say with your mouth; and what you do – your behavior and actions" (Rowe, 2012).

De George advises executives to act and compete with integrity in international business. Acting with integrity is the same as acting ethically, but the word integrity does not have the negative connotation, the moralizing tone, or the sense of naïveté that the word "ethics" carries for many people. According to De George: "Acting with integrity means both acting in accordance with one's highest self-accepted norms of behavior and imposing on oneself the norms demanded by ethics and morality" (De George, 1993).

Competing with integrity means that corporate executives should compete in a way that is consistent with their own highest values and norms of behavior. Although these values and norms are self-imposed and self-accepted, they cannot be simply arbitrary and self-serving; but neither is there a requirement to be perfect.

The least clear aspect of managerial responsibility may be in the domain of ethics, which is the "moral thinking and analysis by corporate decision-makers regarding the motives and consequences of their decisions and actions" (Amba-Rao, 1993). Ethics is the study of morals and systems of morality, or principles of conduct. The study of ethics is concerned with the right or wrong and the "should" or "should not" of human decisions and actions. This does not mean that all questions of right and wrong are ethical issues, however. There is right and wrong associated with rules of etiquette – for example, in which hand to hold your knife and fork, in the use of language and rules of grammar, and in making a computer work. Holding a fork in the wrong hand or speaking ungrammatically does not constitute unethical behavior.

The ethical or moral frame of reference is concerned with human behavior in society and with the relationships, duties, and obligations between people, groups, and organizations. It is concerned with the human consequences associated with decisions and actions, consequences not fully addressed in the pursuit of profit, more sophisticated technology, or larger market share. In this concern for human outcomes, it differs from other perspectives, such as financial, marketing, accounting, or legal. An ethical perspective requires that you extend consideration beyond your own self-interest (or that of your company) to consider the interests of a wider community of stakeholders, including employees, customers, suppliers, the general public, and even foreign governments. It also advocates behaving according to what would be considered better or higher standards of conduct, not necessarily the minimum acceptable by law.

Ethical decisions do not necessarily arise separately from finance, marketing, or production decisions, because problems in the real world do not come with neat labels attached: here is a finance problem; here is a marketing problem; and now, an ethical problem. Managers may categorize issues by functional area or break up a complex problem into components, such as those mentioned. Usually policy issues and decisions are multifaceted and simultaneously may have financial, marketing, and production components. They also may have ethical dimensions that managers should consider. However, in considering a typical complex problem with more than one dimension, the ethical dimension may be overlooked.

If situations did come with labels on them, a person could apply the techniques and concepts he or she had learned, such as net present value to a financial problem or market segmentation to a marketing problem. What would happen if a problem labeled "ethical dilemma" arrived? A manager probably would be in a quandary, lacking a way of analyzing, let alone resolving, this type of problem.

The decision-making tools for this type of situation probably would be absent. Business schools, traditionally, did not emphasize the teaching of ethics as rigorously as they did the teaching of finance or marketing. Nor were students trained to think about ethical issues in the same way as they were trained to think about the frameworks and techniques for functional areas of specialization.

However, after numerous scandals in the USA (e.g., Enron, Tyco, WorldCom, Bernie Madoff's Ponzi scheme) and in Europe (e.g., Parmalat in Italy, Barclay's Libor manipulation in the UK, VW's Dieselgate and Siemens bribery in Germany), this has changed, as business schools moved to address the issue of managerial ethics.

Ethical versus Legal Behavior

A question always arises as to the distinction between legal and ethical behavior. If one acts legally, in accordance with laws, is that not sufficient? Not all of society's norms regarding moral behavior have been codified or made into law. There can, therefore, be many instances of questionable behavior that are not illegal. Acting legally is the minimum required behavior for executives. However, society relies on more than laws to function effectively in many spheres of endeavor. In business, trust is essential.

Henderson has provided a useful way to think about the relationship between ethical and legal actions (Henderson, 1982). He created a matrix based on whether an action was legal or illegal and ethical or unethical, similar to that shown in Table 10.2. Assuming that executives want to act legally and ethically (quadrant 4) and avoid making decisions (or acting in ways) that are illegal and unethical (quadrant 2), the decisions that create dilemmas are the ones that fall into quadrants 1 and 3.

Table 10.2 **Framework for classifying behavior**

	Illegal	Legal
Ethical	1 Illegal & Ethical	4 Legal & Ethical
Unethical	2 Illegal & Unethical	3 Legal & Unethical

For example, consider the decision of a chemical company manager who refuses to promote a pregnant woman to an area of the company where she could be exposed to toxic chemicals that could harm her child. In the USA, or Canada, the manager probably would be acting ethically, but illegally (quadrant 1). Maybe, the problem could be solved by delaying the promotion, if possible. This simple example illustrates a decision that can be ethical, but not legal; there also may be solutions that allow a win/win outcome in which the decision is legal and ethical, because of the way it is made.

In quadrant 3, there will be situations like the marketing of infant formula in developing countries. Infant formula, which was misused in many countries with poor sanitation and polluted water and where people were illiterate and could not read directions, was blamed for the deaths of hundreds of thousands of babies each year. This activity was not illegal, but the United Nations considered it unethical and criticized companies for unethical marketing practices (UNICEF, 2005).

An interesting twist to this example is that, although breastfeeding has been shown to be the healthiest option, it is recommended that mothers who are HIV positive, on certain medicines, or who have drug or alcohol addictions should not breastfeed. UNICEF estimates that about one third of HIV positive pregnant women will pass the infection to their babies during pregnancy and that up to 20 percent of infants could contract the virus if breastfed for two years (Choe, 2012). Infant formula may be a way to combat the transmission of HIV, but it will require companies to be involved in educational outreach to ensure that formula is mixed with clean water and not diluted. This example demonstrates that society's notions of ethical behavior may change with the times, and with new conditions and knowledge.

Ignoring human rights in global supply chains or manufacturing and selling cigarettes that kill through normal use may be other examples of legal but unethical behavior. In 2008, the deregulation of the banking industry in the USA and the excesses that developed in subprime mortgage lending led to a global financial crisis. Subprime mortgage lending is not illegal, but it became predatory and unethical when mortgage brokers targeted the elderly or low-income people who would never be able to pay their mortgages or borrowers who did not understand the transactions. Employing child labor in some countries might be legal, but generally would be considered unethical. Some other situations that may be legal but unethical include the unequal treatment of women in some countries; laws prohibiting assisted suicide for terminally ill people; or prohibiting the use of medical marijuana by people with epilepsy or multiple sclerosis.

It should be recognized that not all laws are moral; an example would be apartheid in South Africa, which was legal but clearly not moral. This historical example raises the question about whose laws and values should be followed when conflicts arise. Although it might seem that we are avoiding answers, we believe that these are questions each person and company need to answer for themselves. The challenge is to find ways of operating that are consistent with local laws and high standards of conduct. We believe that this goal is attainable with thorough analysis and carefully considered action. In those situations, where a win/win outcome is not possible, there is always the option of choosing not to operate in that environment.

The decision to walk away and lose the business may seem naïve, but we have met and interviewed executives of very successful companies that have done just that. One CEO described how his company turned down a $50 million contract in a Latin American country because there was no way to avoid paying a bribe to a government official. Another explained that, in his experience, if a company developed a reputation for acting ethically, usually it was not subjected to unethical demands. Each person has to make their own decision and live with the consequences of their actions.

Integrity issues arise in many areas of a business: the type of products produced, marketing and advertising practices, business conduct in countries where physical security is a problem, requests for illegal payments to secure contracts or sales, and protection payments to prevent damage to plants and equipment or injury to employees. Some products are controversial in themselves, such as tobacco or the abortion pill, since they facilitate behavior that some people would consider unethical. Other products, such as jeans or rugs may not be as controversial, but their production may raise ethical questions.

The United Nations Global Compact is a set of principles to which almost 13,000 organizations around the world have become signatories. These principles provide a framework of ethically responsible business practices that:

at a minimum, meet fundamental responsibilities in the areas of human rights, labour, environment and anti-corruption. Responsible businesses enact the same values and principles wherever they have a presence, and know that good practices in one area do not offset harm in another. By incorporating the Global Compact principles into strategies, policies and procedures, and establishing a culture of integrity, companies are not only upholding their basic responsibilities to people and planet, but also setting the stage for long-term success. (United Nations, n.d.)

The following sections provide some examples from the areas covered by the UN Global Compact.

Human Rights and Labor

There are potential ethical issues in managing supply chains when products are manufactured by or purchased from contractors that abuse workers. Monitoring a company's supply chain for potential abuses and taking action to correct them is increasingly being recognized as a management responsibility for the contracting company and has become a serious concern for corporations.

Clothing

Levi Strauss and Company (LS & Co.) stopped purchasing from subcontractors in Myanmar and China because of practices such as using child and prison labor to manufacture products. In 1991, the company developed a set of Global Sourcing and Operating Guidelines (GSOG) to (a) improve the lives of workers, establish standards addressing workplace issues for its partners and subcontractors, and (b) to aid in the selection of countries for sourcing products. It was the first apparel company to establish a comprehensive ethical code of conduct for manufacturing and finishing contractors. The company's terms of engagement (TOE) were aimed at its business partners and primarily based on the United Nations Universal Declaration of Human Rights. Since then the GSOG has been expanded and modified over time based on feedback from NGOs. It addresses ethical standards, legal requirements, environmental requirements, and community involvement; and specifically addresses issues of child labor, forced labor, disciplinary practices, working hours, wages and benefits, freedom of association, discrimination, and health and safety (Levi Strauss & Co., n.d.; The Economist, 1995).

The original TOE were based on a philosophy of compliance and "do no harm," but in 2012 the company decided that compliance, monitoring, and reporting progress were not sufficient to really make a difference in the lives of the suppliers' workers and their communities, so the company pioneered a development-oriented approach, the Worker Well-Being initiative focusing on financial empowerment; health and family well-being; and equality and acceptance. This program was featured as a reason that the company was ranked 11th out of 50 companies on *Fortune*'s 2017 "Change the World" list. LS & Co. has made its program publicly available.

Rugs and Furniture

In the 1980s, attention was drawn to the illegal use of child labor in the hand-woven rug industry by the International Labor Organization (ILO), the US Department of Labor, and human rights groups. In 1994, the RugMark Foundation was established by Kailash Satyarthi, with a coalition of NGOs, businesses, government entities, and multilateral groups, like UNICEF, to combat child labor. The first carpets bearing the RugMark label were exported from India at the beginning of 1995, mainly to Germany. Later, countries promoting the RugMark label grew to include the UK, the USA, Canada, and Nepal. RugMark is now known as GoodWeave International. To date, more than 11 million carpets bearing the GoodWeave label have been sold in Europe and North America (GoodWeave, n.d.).

What is a company's responsibility toward ensuring that its suppliers are not using child labor? Some people would argue that children are better suited to making rugs because of their greater dexterity than adults, and that their families, who need the money, would be worse off if the children were not working. Opponents, however, point out that many of the children were found to be victims of debt bondage or forced labor, practices banned by the United Nations and condemned as modern forms of slavery.

Is participating in GoodWeave the only way to counter child labor? Is it ever acceptable to use child labor? Ethical issues, by definition, are never simple. The issue about manufacturing rugs is not as simple as "do not use child labor." We spoke at length with a small business owner who exports rugs from Pakistan and Afghanistan. She visits her manufacturers regularly and encourages community development around the making of rugs. There were many girls as young as eight years who were working in her craft shops:

If I did not hire these girls, they would not be in school. They would be in the fields. Their life expectancy would be shorter; they would be working alone. In the workshop, they sit together with women of three or more generations, they learn a skill, and they learn about their culture. Because they are in my workshop, I can provide good meals and people and materials to provide at least some education and social support for them. Am I doing the right thing? According to the press and many consumers, definitely not! But I do believe that, in this case, hiring these girls and trying to provide a better environment for them is the right thing.

IKEA also recognizes that child labor abuses exist in countries where its products are manufactured and it has created a code of conduct for suppliers called IWAY and a separate code and program to prevent child labor based on the United Nations Convention on the Rights of the Child, the "IKEA Way on Preventing Child Labour." In addition, it now supports projects to eliminate child labor by addressing its root causes, such as poverty or lack of education and safety. The following incident experienced by a group from IKEA touring factories in India illustrates the complexity of the issue.

Some time ago, our team went out to India to monitor how things were happening in the field. The team's host, the owner of a local factory, was taking them to see conditions there. They were in his car, and suddenly he stopped, jumped out of the car and went to talk to a young boy, who was hanging out on the side of the road with some other kids.

When the factory-owner returned, he explained: "That kid used to work in our factory. Now, because of IKEA's strict policies prohibiting child labor, we let him go and he's on the streets selling drugs." This was a real aha moment for the group, when they decided to go beyond child labor to address the root causes of child labor. (Cohen, 2012)

One could debate whether or not the factory owner was living up to his responsibility to children or if strict policies prohibiting child labor are the answer. IKEA's shift in emphasis would imply that there are better-informed policies and more effective programs to address the problem.

Prior to apparently addressing the child labor issue responsibly, it had issued apologies for some of its suppliers having used forced prison labor in East Germany in the 1980s and for removing images of women from its catalogs sent to Saudi Arabia. In the former instance, the company was criticized for not monitoring its supplier network two decades earlier, and in the latter case for its "medieval" approach to gender inequality. The IKEA examples clearly illustrate that operating with integrity globally is complicated and as soon as one issue dies down another appears to take its place.

Food

Haribo, the German maker of the popular Gummy Bears candy, was the focus of a German broadcasting network documentary in 2017 that accused it of being "unknowingly complicit in both modern-day slave labor and animal abuse" (Fantozzi, 2017). Workers on plantations in Brazil from where its carnauba wax came were subject to cruel and inhuman treatment, and at the pig farms where it sourced its gelatin the pigs had open sores; the pens were covered in feces and in some cases were littered with pig carcasses. As we were writing this edition, Haribo had begun an investigation into the situation. It said:

We would like to emphasize that we are extremely concerned by some of the images shown on the consumer program 'HARIBO-Check' on German TV channel ARD last week ... The conditions on the pig farms and the Brazilian plantations shown are insupportable. Our fundamental attitude in this respect is: Social and ethical standards are indivisible and non-negotiable. (Fantozzi, 2017)

Apparently the conditions on some plantations in this poor, northeastern region of Brazil are so bad that police occasionally conduct raids in order to free the workers.

In 2015 a class action lawsuit was filed against Nestlé in California for allegedly using fish caught by slave labor in its cat food. Nestlé commissioned an independent study by Verité, a "global, independent, non-profit organization that conducts research, advocacy, consulting, training, and assessments with a vision that people worldwide work under safe, fair, and legal conditions" (Verité, n.d.). The company focuses on the issues of child labor, forced labor, human trafficking, and gender discrimination. Nestlé publicly announced the results of the study and committed itself to eliminating forced labor in its supply chain. One year into the program, more than 99 percent of the seafood Nestlé sources from Thailand is traceable to fish farms or catch vessels. Furthermore, Nestlé partnered with the Thai government to educate Thai fishers on workers' rights:

In Thailand specifically, we embarked on a dedicated project to eliminate human rights violations and encourage sustainable fishing. One year into the program, more than 99% of the seafood ingredients that Nestlé sources from its seafood supply chain in Thailand are traceable back to farms and catch vessels. Additionally, Nestlé, its seafood supplier, and Verité, an NGO whose mission is to enhance human rights on a global basis, continue to work closely with the Royal Thai Government, Thailand's Department of Fisheries, and the Southeast Asian Fisheries Development Center to develop a practical training program to educate vessel owners, boat captains, and crew members on living and working conditions aboard a fishing vessel and on worker's rights in Thailand. (Nestlé, n.d.)

Bribery and Corruption

Other dilemmas that executives may encounter are requests for bribes or even extortion. For example, mobsters threatened the Otis Elevator company that they would firebomb its operation in Russia if it did not pay protection money (Drohan, 1994). How should this situation be handled? Otis had a code delineating its view of right and wrong behavior that all executives sign each year. Its response was not to give in to the extortion, but to pay more for security. The Otis example took place in the early 1990s but according to Fey and Shekshnia, writing a decade later, corruption is omnipresent in Russia (Fey and Shekshnia, 2008). Their counsel, that managers need to understand their own ethical standards as well as the reality and risks they face, is good advice.

Over the years, there have been many examples of legal and ethical lapses by executives from many companies and many nations. Some examples included Xerox, which in 2002 admitted that its subsidiary in India had made "improper payments" to win government contracts over a period of years.

The Norwegian state-run oil group, Statoil, was involved in a bribery scandal with Iran in 2003 (International Petroleum Finance, 2003). Statoil's internal auditors uncovered secret payments of US$5 million to Horton Investments, a Turks and Caicos Islands registered consultancy believed to be run by the son of a former Iranian president. According to Statoil, Horton Investments was hired to provide insight into financial, industrial, legal, and social issues associated with business development in Iran. But the Iranian government said that the secret US$15 million contract between Horton and Statoil was used to channel bribes to unnamed government officials. Statoil settled with the USA, accepted a fine of US$10.5 million for violating the US Foreign Corrupt Practices Act, and accepted responsibility for the bribery, as well as for accounting for those payments improperly; and for having insufficient internal controls to prevent the payments. The company also paid a fine of US$3 million to Norway for violation of Norway's law.

In 2007 Chiquita Brands International, the banana company, pleaded guilty to providing US$1.7 million in illegal protection payments from 1997 to 2004 to Autodefensas Unidas de Colombia (AUC) or the United Self-Defense Forces of Colombia, a right-wing paramilitary group.

Unfortunately, some executives apparently have not received the message from these examples or learned from others' mistakes, and similar transgressions have continued. In 2010, BAE Systems pleaded guilty to making false statements about its accounting practices in a corruption and bribery scandal related to arms deals in Saudi Arabia and Africa. A culture of bribery developed in Siemens over the years. It was a way of doing business and until 1998, under German law, it was not illegal. Peter Solmssen, who was board member and general counsel of Siemens explained, "It was largely a failure of leadership. It seems employees believed that they had to pay bribes in order to get business" (Solmssen, 2012).

In 2008, Siemens pleaded guilty to violating the Foreign Corrupt Practices Act and agreed to a fine of US$1.6 billion to American and European authorities for bribes and kickbacks in countries such as Argentina (identity cards), Venezuela (transportation projects), and Bangladesh (cellphone network).

In 2012, Wal-Mart was involved in a bribery scandal in Mexico. An executive of the company in Mexico allegedly paid US$52,000 to have a zoning map redrawn of the area around the Teotihuacan pyramids so that it could build a store where one would not have been previously permitted and this, apparently, was not the first instance of such behavior.

In 2017, Deutsche Bank was fined US$7.2 billion for misleading investors back to 2008 about the "toxic" mortgage-backed securities it was selling and then another US$41 million for failing to maintain adequate controls against a Russian money laundering scheme.

Of course, not all legal and ethical lapses involve bribery. Between 2011 and 2016, Wells Fargo employees, driven by its evaluation and reward system and fearing being fired, created over 1.5 million fake customer accounts; in 2015 VW was found to have created emissions cheating software to circumvent emissions checks in the USA and Europe; in 2017, Uber revealed that a year earlier it paid hackers $100,000 to remain silent about the theft of personal data on 57 million customers.

The ubiquitous occurrence of bribery has led to efforts to curtail it. In addition to the UN's Global Compact, other examples include the OECD's Anti-Bribery Convention and the UK's Bribery Act 2010. The Foreign Corrupt Practices Act in the USA is another example.

The Foreign Corrupt Practices Act

In 1977, the United States Congress passed into law the Foreign Corrupt Practices Act (FCPA) in response to investigations that discovered that over 400 US companies had made questionable or illegal payments to foreign government officials, politicians, and political parties for a range of reasons. Twenty years later, the USA and thirty-three other countries signed the OECD Anti-Bribery Convention (officially Convention on Combating Bribery of Foreign Public Officials in International Business Transactions).

Under the FCPA it is illegal for a US citizen, as well as foreign companies with securities listed in the USA, to make a payment to a foreign official to obtain or retain business for or with, or directing business to, any person or company. Since 1998, the rules also apply to foreign firms and persons, while in the USA.

Specifically, the law prohibits:

any offer, payment, promise to pay, or authorization of the payment of money or any-thing of value to any person, while knowing that all or a portion of such money or thing of value will be offered, given or promised, directly or indirectly, to a foreign official to influence the foreign official in his or her official capacity, induce the foreign official to do or omit to do an act in violation of his or her lawful duty, or to secure any improper advantage in order to assist in obtaining or retaining business for or with, or directing business to, any person.

The FCPA does contain an exception for "facilitating or expediting payments" for "routine governmental actions" such as processing permits, licenses, work orders, or visas. These are situations where an official does not have the discretionary power to award business or ignore violations of law or regulations.

The law requires companies whose securities are listed in the USA to make and keep records that accurately reflect the transactions of the corporation and to maintain an adequate system of internal accounting controls. Companies that have been found to violate the Act tend to plead guilty to accounting lapses and pay a fine rather than pleading guilty to bribery. In addition to criminal and civil penalties, they may be barred from doing business with the federal government. Debarment from public procurement is being used a weapon to combat bribery, and numerous countries besides the USA have adopted it.

Bribery and corruption are global problems that are not limited to public officials in a few developing countries. Executives of global corporations head-quartered in developed countries are affected and some have been implicated in scandals. Global executives should not be smug about assuming that the locus of the problem is elsewhere. There is an old saying, "It takes two to tango."

Transparency International

One NGO that has been established to combat the problem of bribery and cor-ruption is Transparency International.

Since 1993 when it was founded, Transparency International (TI) has become the leading NGO combating national and international corruption. TI has devel-oped chapters in over 100 countries and works with numerous intergovern-mental organizations like the OECD, World Bank, the Organization of American

States (OAS), and the European Union to develop and monitor anti-corruption legislation and treaties. It analyzes corruption by measuring its occurrence through surveys, and it has created resources and tools used by people around the world in the fight against corruption.

These tools include the Corruption Perceptions Index, Global Corruption Barometer, Global Corruption Report, Bribe Payers Index, and the latest anti-corruption information on TI's website. TI's Bribe Payers Index (BPI) evaluates the likelihood of firms from the world's twenty-eight largest economies to bribe. Companies from the wealthiest countries generally rank in the top half of the Index, but still routinely pay bribes, and TI saw no improvement from its previous report in 2008 and its latest report in 2011. There is no country that is entirely clean. The Netherlands and Switzerland are the "cleanest" and Mexico, China, and Russia are at the bottom of the list.

The **Corruption Perception Index** ranks 176 countries by their perceived levels of corruption, as determined by expert assessments, opinion surveys, and thirteen different data sources from twelve different institutions that capture perceptions of corruption within the previous two years. The score ranges between 100 (highly clean) and 0 (highly corrupt). The ten countries that scored the highest (highly clean) on the 2016 Index were Denmark, New Zealand, Sweden, Finland, Singapore, Switzerland, the Netherlands, Norway, Germany, and Canada. The UK was tied tenth with Luxembourg and the USA was eighteenth. Over two thirds of the countries had scores of lower than 50 indicating serious corruption problems. The countries that scored the lowest (highly corrupt) were Somalia, Sudan, Yemen, North Korea, and Syria.

Other Examples

Not all ethical problems fall into the categories established by the UN Global Compact.

Employee Security

Situations in which the physical security of employees could be a problem may present ethical issues for managers. Consider a situation in which British expatriate women working in the Middle East training center of a North American-based bank found themselves. They were en route to conduct a training program in Lagos, Nigeria, and were supposed to be met by one of the bank's local staff who would assist them through difficulties in customs at the airport. When the local staff member failed to appear, the women felt forced to pay bribes to bring legitimate training materials and equipment into the country. Soon after paying the money, their taxi was stopped at the darkened perimeter of the airport and uniformed men pointed guns at them. The women were subject to a shakedown again and felt very vulnerable, particularly with no foreign currency left. After repeatedly showing their documents and denying that they were violating any laws, they were finally permitted to pass. The women were deeply shaken by the experience and vowed never to travel into that country alone again.

What responsibility did the local management bear for abandoning them? And what was the ethical responsibility of the experienced managers for whom the women worked who sent them into such a situation so ill-prepared? What is a manager's responsibility regarding the implementation of his or her decisions, particularly when the specific action has to be taken by another person?

Unfortunately, in recent years the world has become a more dangerous place and situations in which physical security is a managerial concern are becoming more common for global companies. As recently as 2013, one of the current authors was involved in a training program for a European-based company and learned that travel to and in Lagos for its executives remained a security priority. This company developed elaborate safety procedures for its executives traveling there.

In 2013, a sophisticated, large-scale terrorist attack took place in Mumbai, India that left more than 170 people dead. Deccan Mujahideen claimed responsibility for the attack and it was learned they had received training from Lashkar-e-Taiba, a group fighting to bring independence to Muslims in the Indian Kashmir. An American, David Headley, who admitted to helping plan the attack, was sentenced in January 2013 to thirty-five years in prison. News reports at the time suggested that they were apparently searching for and targeting foreigners, although many more Indians died in the attack than foreigners. *The Telegraph* reported that the "Mumbai terrorist attacks nearly wiped out top management at Unilever" when the CEO, CEO elect, and entire board of the subsidiary were dining at the Taj Mahal hotel (Hope, 2009).

Many companies currently operate in countries where there are personal security concerns and political violence and terrorism may be issues. On March 11, 2004, terrorists bombed a train in Madrid, killing 191 people and injuring 2000 others. In late May 2004, terrorists killed twenty-two people in oil company office compounds and in an expatriate housing compound in Saudi Arabia and took over forty hostages, including Americans and Europeans. In January 2013, terrorists seized an Algerian gas field for four days until the Algerian army liberated it and killed over thirty terrorists. In the process, however, the terrorists killed more than twenty hostages from numerous countries. In 2015, terrorists killed twelve people in Paris in an attack on the offices of Charlie Hebdo, a satirical newspaper.

It may be tempting for you to say that the examples above come from industries that you won't be working in or occurred in countries where you won't be working. However, you don't have to be working for a global engineering company, a global oil company, or other natural resource industry companies in remote and difficult areas to be at risk. You could be a banking or consumer goods executive or a consultant managing a project in Lagos, Mumbai, Madrid, or Paris or you might only be visiting these cities on business.

Global companies continue to look for ways to grow and new markets to enter. Where is future growth going to come from? The answer, most likely, is from emerging markets. What is a company's ethical responsibility associated with assigning an employee to one of these countries? What should it do regarding training and security for employees who work in difficult areas? What is the responsibility of individuals who agree to work there?

Managing in Difficult Markets

Emerging markets are the fastest growing markets and represent about 70 percent of the world's population. The IMF predicts that real GDP growth for 2022 in the emerging markets and developing economies will be 5 percent, compared to only 1.7 percent for developed countries. Global companies undoubtedly will be looking to increase business in these areas and aspiring global leaders will likely be working in these countries or be responsible for people in them. We identified the CIVETS and the Next 11 in Chapter 6. The Chief Economist at Goldman Sachs, Jim O'Neil, who coined the acronym BRIC and identified the Next 11 future major economies also identified Mexico, Indonesia, South Korea, and Turkey (MIKT) as being the most promising (Moore, 2012).

Most likely the reader has knowledge about the economic reality of the BRIC countries, but are you familiar with the CIVETS and the Next 11 or MIKT (Moore, 2012)? It was the Economist Intelligence Unit that identified the set of nations collectively known as the CIVETS (Colombia, Indonesia, Vietnam, Egypt, Turkey, and South Africa).

The authors do not have an opinion about which of those countries are the likely economic powerhouses of the future, but we do know that many of them can be difficult places in which global leaders will be working. The Fund for Peace has created an interactive Failed States Index, which can be found on its website. On the Index, all of the countries included in the CIVETS and Next 11 fall into a "Warning" or higher category, with the exception of South Korea, which is rated as "Stable." If these are the countries where growth is likely to come from, what are companies doing to attract, train, and manage executives who can function effectively, and safely, there?

Responding to Ethical Problems

How might managers respond when they encounter ethical problems such as the examples that we have just seen or work in countries where corruption is rampant and where they may encounter requests for bribes? One of the first things they may do is avoid the ethical dilemma through the process of rationalization. They may focus on some other aspect of the problem. They may transform the ethical problem into a legal or accounting problem, for instance. The reasoning seems to be that, so long as one is behaving legally or in accordance with accepted accounting practices, for example, nothing else is required. As we said earlier, compliance with laws and professional regulations is a minimum requirement for responsible managers.

Another avoidance behavior is to see the problem as only one small piece of a larger puzzle and to assume that someone higher up in the organization must be looking after any unusual aspects, such as ethical considerations. Alternatively, the decision-maker might try to make it someone else's problem – perhaps a customer, supplier, or person in higher authority – with the comment: "I was following my boss's orders" or "It was my customer's instructions." When a customer asks for a falsified invoice on imported goods for his or her records, with the difference deposited in a foreign bank, and you provide this "service," is it only the customer's behavior that is questionable?

Rationalizing one's behavior by transforming an ethical problem into another type of problem, or assuming responsibility for only one specific, technical component of the issue, or claiming that it is someone else's problem, gives one the feeling of being absolved from culpability by putting the burden of responsibility elsewhere.

Who is responsible for ensuring that managers act ethically? We believe that corporations have a responsibility to make clear to their employees what sort of behavior is expected of them. This means that executives in headquarters have a responsibility, not just for their own behavior, but also for providing guidance to subordinates. Many companies have corporate codes to do just this. However, an issue that global executives need to consider carefully is whether codes of conduct are effective. Donaldson found that effective codes of conduct meet three criteria (Donaldson, 2000):

1. Senior management must be committed to ethical behavior and the codes of conduct; and the codes must affect "everyday decisions and actions."
2. External or "imposed" codes are not generally effective. Companies must develop their own and take ownership of their codes.
3. Various important stakeholders (employees, customers, suppliers, NGOs) must be involved in shaping the development and implementation of the codes.

Although a company has a responsibility to outline what behavior it expects from an employee, the person on the spot facing the decision is ultimately responsible for his or her own behavior, with or without guidance from headquarters. Through the cases that are discussed in this chapter, consider how you would develop your own stance on the issues. We encourage you to think carefully about the problems to develop reasoned positions. You may find yourself in a similar situation someday, and you will have to make a critical decision. We hope that, by working through the decisions in these cases now, you will be better able to deal with similar decisions later.

As we personally encountered ethical dilemmas or talked with others who had experienced them, we wrote cases and developed a managerial framework for thinking about and analyzing the problems to guide ourselves and to teach our classes. We make no claim that the framework to be presented is a complete or definitive treatment of the topic of ethics. However, we think it does provide a practical and managerial way to think about the topic.

Ethical Frameworks

Moral philosophers have developed theories for thinking about moral issues and for analyzing ethical problems, but these generally were not included in international business curricula. There are various approaches for analyzing ethical problems and there are conflicting positions and prescriptions among them. We have observed that people advocate actions representing the major theories, but without understanding the foundations or the strengths and weaknesses of their positions. Consider the following discussion:

Person X: "If we don't pay what he is asking we will lose the contract and people back home will lose jobs. Is that ethical when people can't feed their families?"

Person Y: "I don't care. What you are suggesting is absolutely wrong."

Person Z: "Now hold on, it doesn't seem to be against the rules there. It is a different culture. Everyone is doing it. They need the extra money to support their families. Besides, we should not impose our system of morality on other cultures."

You may have heard or have taken part in similar exchanges. The people in the conversation above may not realize it, but they are engaged in a discussion of moral philosophy. However, it is the type of discussion that tends to excite emotions and generate heat and argument, rather than provide insight or a thoughtful course of action.

Since you will likely take part in similar discussions (or arguments) at some time in your career, we think that knowledge of these three frameworks will be useful. The intent is to help you link some everyday reasoning and the positions you might espouse to the ethical frameworks underlying them. In the brief exchange above, one sees elements of Kant's categorical imperative, utilitarianism, and cultural relativism. These are commonly invoked frameworks, which is why they were chosen. Each represents a different ethical map and moral calculus.

The main categories of ethical theories can be divided into: **consequential** (or **teleological**) theories, which focus on the consequences, outcomes, or results of decisions and behavior; **rule-based** (or **deontological**) theories, which focus on moral obligations, duties, and rights; and **cultural** theories, which emphasize cultural differences in standards of behavior. These are discussed briefly here.

Consequential Theories

Consequential theories focus on the goals, end results, and/or consequences of decisions and actions. They are concerned with doing the maximum amount of "good" and the minimum amount of "harm." Utilitarianism is the most widely used example of this type of moral framework. It argues for doing the best for the greatest number of people or acting in a way that provides more net utility than an alternative act. It is essentially an economic, cost–benefit approach to ethical decision-making. If the benefits outweigh the costs, then that course of action is indicated.

The limitations of this approach are that it is difficult or impossible to identify and account for all the costs and benefits, and, since people have different utility curves, it is difficult to decide whose curve should be used. In real life, how do you compute this utility curve? Finally, to weigh the costs and benefits, one relies on quantitative data, usually economic data, and many important variables that should be considered are not quantifiable and, therefore, are often ignored.

Rule-Based Theories

Rule-based theories include both absolute (or universal) theories and conditional theories. The emphasis of these theories is on duty, obligations, and rights. For example, if an employee follows orders or performs a certain task, management has an obligation to ensure that the task is not illegal or harmful to that person's health. People in power have a responsibility to protect the rights of the less powerful. These theories are concerned with the universal shoulds and oughts of human existence – the rules that should guide all people's decision-making and behavior wherever they are.

One of the best-known absolute theories is the categorical imperative of Immanuel Kant. Whereas utilitarianism takes a group or societal perspective, the categorical imperative has a more individualistic focus: individuals should be treated with respect and dignity as an end in itself; they should not be used simply as a means to an end. A person should not be done harm, even if the ultimate end is good. The criteria should be applied consistently to everyone. One of the questions to ask is: "If I were in the other person's (or group's or organization's) position, would I be willing for them to make the same decision that I am going to make, for the same reasons?"

A variation on absolute theories is fundamentalism. In this case, the rules may come from a book like the Bible, Koran, or Torah. In these systems, one is dealing with an authoritative, divine wisdom that has been revealed through prophets. Difficult questions arise when considering which book or prophet to follow and whose interpretation of the chosen book to use. Priests, ministers, mullahs, or rabbis who may reflect the views of an elite segment of society, or possibly an isolated group, usually interpret the books. There can be conflicting interpretations within the same religion as well. Also, the interpretations may be inconsistent with current social and environmental circumstances, as well as with the beliefs of large segments of a society. The rules that people follow can also be secular as well as religious, as was the case in Nazi Germany.

One shortcoming of these types of prescriptions is that they allow you to claim that you are not responsible for your own behavior: "I was just following orders" is a common excuse. The end result may be the same – you do not have to think for yourself or make a moral judgment, but rather you can avoid it by claiming to be following a higher authority. However, the war crimes trials after World War II established that following orders is not an acceptable legal defense for committing atrocities.

Cultural Theories

With cultural theories, local standards prevail. **Cultural relativism** is interpreted to mean that there is no single right way; in other words, people should not impose their values and standards on others. The reasoning behind the argument usually is that we should behave as the locals behave. The familiar expression tells us: "When in Rome, do as the Romans do." One problem, however, comes from the fact that the local people we are encouraged to emulate may not necessarily be the most exemplary. In your own culture, you know that people exhibit different standards of behavior. Does that mean we should advocate that business people coming to the USA act like the people at Wells Fargo, for example, just because those people were Americans? Or should expatriate managers working in Germany follow the example set by VW executives, because they were German? Adopting this philosophy also can encourage denial of accountability and the avoidance of moral choice. Using arguments based on this philosophy, the morality of bribes or actions of repressive regimes, for example, do not have to be examined very closely. These theories are summarized in Figure 10.1.

Perry has described a perspective that provides more insight into relativism arguments that managers may find useful – a process of intellectual and ethical development (Perry, Jr., 1970). Although we should recognize that Perry's ideas reflect a cultural bias toward individualism and were derived from a narrow part of the US population, his ideas can help managers think about their positions on this issue. In his full scheme there are nine stages. We have chosen to use only the three major positions in the scheme. The first category is **dualism,** in which a bipolar structure of the world is assumed or taken for granted. According to

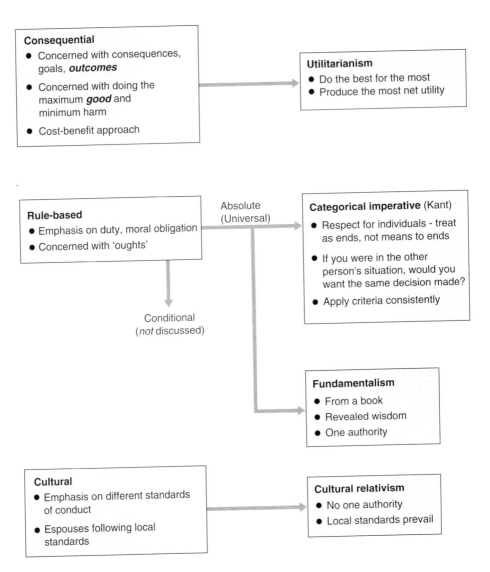

Figure 10.1 Analytical frameworks for ethical decision-making

this perspective there is a clear right and wrong, good and bad, we and they. These positions are defined from one's own perspective based on membership in a group and belief in or adherence to a common set of traditional beliefs.

   The next category, posited by Perry as a more developed perspective, is **relativism**, in which the dualistic world-view is moderated by an understanding of the importance of context, which helps a person to see that knowledge and values are relative. As we have seen through earlier parts of this book, different people in different parts of the world think and believe differently, and a relativistic mode of making ethical judgments recognizes this fact. As originally observed by Blaise Pascal, Hofstede notes in the preface to his book, *Culture's Consequences:* "There are truths on this side of the Pyrenees which are false-hoods on the other."

In Perry's scheme, the third "level" of development is **commitment in relativism**, in which a person understands the relativistic nature of the world, but makes a commitment to a set of values, beliefs, and a way of behaving within this expanded world-view. The goal is to arrive at the point where you assume responsibility for your own actions and decisions based upon careful consideration and the application of the essential tools of moral reasoning – deliberation and justification.

Perry suggests that progression to this stage is not automatic or guaranteed and that people may become "delayed" in their development or even "stuck" in the earlier stages. People who adhere to a set of absolute rules, however, may reject this notion of a hierarchy of development.

Our inclusion of Perry's ideas is not meant to judge others' choices in this regard, but rather to encourage self-awareness and recognition that simple cultural relativism is not the highest end point of moral development. Underlying our perspective throughout this book are (1) the assumption that you are interested in developing a relativistic understanding of the world, and (2) the encouragement for you to decide about your own commitments within this relativistic framework. We understand that voicing this position reflects our own values.

Universalism, Relativism, and the "Asian Values" Debate

The previous brief discussion of different theories in moral philosophy provides a context for understanding the underlying ethical positions of what has been termed the "Asian values" debate. This was a 1990s political ideology that went dormant, but has reappeared in 2017. At one level, it is the age-old debate in moral philosophy about universalism versus relativism. Is there a universal set of rules that should be followed or are morals and ethics relative depending on the culture? Are one culture's beliefs, values, and practices superior and preferable to those of another? Whose laws, values, or ethics should be followed if and when a disagreement develops, a different course of action is proposed, or a conflict arises? This theoretical debate became more tangible when it turned into an international debate about human rights and economic growth.

In 1948, the United Nations adopted the Universal Declaration of Human Rights. Since that time, there have been discussions and disagreements over which of the human rights specified in its thirty articles are universal and which are culturally influenced. China, long criticized by the West for human rights violations, issued a White Paper on Human Rights in China in November 1991. Although it supported the development of the international human rights regime it argued that human rights were a matter of domestic jurisdiction. This proclamation of cultural sovereignty was followed by other pronouncements made by some Asian leaders.

In 1993, the Bangkok Declaration was signed by more than thirty Asian and Middle Eastern countries. It presented the view that universal human rights represented statements of Western values and that they were at odds with "Asian values" and not applicable to Asia. This theme was later reiterated by notable Asian leaders.

The imposition of Western values as a form of **cultural imperialism** was alleged by Singapore's first Prime Minister Lee Kuan Yew in 1994, when he stated: "It is not my business to tell people what's wrong with their system. It is my business to tell people not to foist their system indiscriminately on societies in which it will not work" (Zakaria, 1994). In this interview, he described some of the differentiators that he saw between East and West:

The fundamental difference between Western concepts of society and government and East Asian concepts – when I say East Asians, I mean Korea, Japan, China, Vietnam, as distinct from Southeast Asia, which is a mix between the Sinic and the Indian, though Indian culture also emphasizes similar values – is that Eastern societies believe that the individual exists in the context of his family. He is not pristine and separate. The family is part of the extended family, and then friends and the wider society. (Zakaria, 1994)

Although he admired parts of the American system, he was critical of other parts.

As an East Asian looking at America, I find attractive and unattractive features. I like, for example, the free, easy and open relations between people regardless of social status, ethnicity or religion ... a certain openness in argument about what is good or bad for society; the accountability of public officials; none of the secrecy and terror that's part and parcel of communist government.

But as a total system, I find parts of it totally unacceptable: guns, drugs, violent crime, vagrancy, unbecoming behavior in public – in sum the breakdown of civil society. The expansion of the right of the individual to behave or misbehave as he pleases has come at the expense of orderly society. In the East, the main object is to have a well-ordered society so that everybody can have maximum enjoyment of his freedoms. This freedom can only exist in an ordered state and not in a natural state of contention and anarchy. (Zakaria, 1994)

In 1996 at the 29th International General Meeting of the Pacific Basin Economic Council, Dr. Mahathir Mohamad, Prime Minister of Malaysia, continued to defend cultural relativism when he said that there was a belief among many in the West that their values and beliefs were universal – that too much democracy could lead to violence, instability, and anarchy; and that the West was using ideals such as democracy and human rights as tools to re-colonize parts of Asia.

In the remarks of Lee and Mohamad one can see the primary values that are in conflict in this debate.

- The East values community and family (interdependence or collectivism) while the West values the individual and independence. In the East, responsibility toward family and community takes precedence over individual interests and privileges. In the East, people have duties and obligations while in the West they have rights.
- The East values order and harmony while the West values personal freedom, individual initiative, and competition. In the East, this is reflected in respect for age, leaders, persons in authority, hierarchy, and institutions. In the West, it is reflected in democracy, the rights of individuals, and capitalism.
- The West believes in universalism, while the East practices particularism. Universalism emphasizes rules, laws, and generalizations, while particularism emphasizes exceptions, circumstances, and relations. Particularism often is expressed in the East in practices like *guanxi* (the use of interpersonal relationships) in China, which also can be interpreted from a Western perspective as corruption or bribery.

Not all Asian political leaders and academics see "Asian values" as different from, and as an alternative to, Western cultural beliefs. Asia is not a monolithic, homogeneous area. Critics dismiss the idea that a common set of distinctively Asian principles exists, given Asia's immense cultural, religious, and political diversity. There are regional differences between East, Southeast, and South Asia, and these nations have highly varying historical and religious backgrounds, such as Hindu, Muslim, Confucian, Shinto, and Buddhist.

The former president of Singapore Devan Nair has stated, "Human rights and values are universal by any standard, and their violation anywhere is a grievous offence to men and women everywhere."

Nobel Laureate Amartya Sen also disagreed with the proponents of "Asian values" and those who believe that human rights are an artifact of solely Western culture. He disputed the "grand contrast" between Asian and Western values and said:

The so-called Asian values that are invoked to justify authoritarianism are not espe-cially Asian in any significant sense. Nor is it easy to see how they could be made into an Asian cause against the West, by the mere force of rhetoric. The people whose rights are being disputed are Asians, and no matter what the West's guilt may be (there are many skeletons in many cupboards across the world), the rights of the Asians can scarcely be compromised on those grounds. The case for liberty and political rights turns ultimately on their basic importance and on their instrumental role. This case is as strong in Asia as it is elsewhere. (Sen, 1997)

Echoing Sen, critics argue the debate is not so much about cultural values but about maintaining political power and an excuse for autocratic governments that suppress individual rights and dissidents. Human Rights Watch and Amnesty International called China's White Paper a "whitewash."

In May 2017, the Asian Law Institute held a conference at the University of the Philippines. The topic was "A Uniting Force? 'Asian Values' and the Law." The keynote speaker was Judge Raul C. Pangalangan of the International Criminal Court who expressed surprise at the longevity of this 1990s political ideology. He noted that variations of this theme were used by authoritarian regimes to support the way they governed and to denounce Western detractors for their criticism and interference.

Some events in 2017 give credence to Sen's and Pangalangan's observations that political regimes use "Asian values" to counter Western criticism.

When we wrote the seventh edition of this text, we used the example of Aung San Suu Kyi, Burmese democracy and human rights advocate and winner of the 1991 Nobel Peace Prize, who was a critic of the Asian values thesis. At that time, we quoted her saying:

Human rights are relevant to all human beings. Those [authoritarian regimes] who wish to deny us certain political rights try to convince us that these are not Asian values ... This is something that we cannot accept.

However, in 2017, as the head of the governing National League for Democracy, she appeared to reverse her stance on the issue as she came under intense criti-cism for her government's handling of (or ignoring the military's role in) the Rohingya crisis. Over 400,000 ethnic Rohingya fled the country to Bangladesh in what has been described as a campaign of ethnic cleansing that has included murder, rape, and the burning of villages. Whether she reversed her beliefs or was afraid to speak out against the military is open to debate. Nevertheless, the world expected more from her.

In November 2017, Justin Trudeau, Prime Minister of Canada, criticized Philippine President Rodrigo Duterte's record on human rights and his war on drugs in which, by some estimates, extrajudicial killings have claimed 7000 victims (CBC News, 2017). Duterte told Trudeau, "It angers me when you are a foreigner you do not know exactly what is happening in this country."

An article in the *Manila Times* said:

President Rodrigo Duterte's war on drugs mirrors Singapore Prime Minister Lee Kuan Yew's campaign for "Asian values" vs Western values that became an intense polemic between Singaporeans and Americans. Those who thought that the Asian values debate died with Lee Kuan Yew should think again. The old debate is coming back in a different form courtesy of DU30's drug war and the wide-ranging quarrel over "human rights" that it has provoked. (Makabenta, 2017)

Some academics have argued that "academic moral theory is useless" and the Asian values debate tends to lend credence to that view since the debate does not lead to actionable decision criteria without embracing the beliefs of one side or the other (Peerenboom, 2003). There does not seem to be any way to cut through the arguments to find the "truth." One is left with either having to impose one's beliefs and values on the other through coercion or allowing the conflicting parties to agree to disagree.

We think that it is important for managers to be able to recognize the basis for their moral and ethical decisions and to be aware, for example, if they are shifting from one theory to another as a way of avoiding tough decisions. Global executives must make decisions and take action, and they do not have the luxury of simply debating the issue. How do they decide? How do they choose among mutually conflicting moral theories? We believe Integrative Social Contracts Theory may help find a path forward.

Integrative Social Contracts Theory: A Way to Avoid Ethical Paralysis?

Integrative Social Contracts Theory (ISCT), developed by Donaldson and Dunfee, is one approach for resolving conflicting ethical viewpoints (Donaldson and Dunfee, 1999). We believe that ISCT is a useful tool when making decisions and determining a course of action. However, before showing how to apply this theory, it is helpful to put it in context with the theories previously discussed. On a continuum with extreme relativism at one end and extreme universalism at the other end, ISCT is a pluralistic theory and probably is closer to the relativism end of the continuum as shown and described in Table 10.3.

Table 10.3 **Integrative Social Contracts Theory in context**

Theory	Position
Extreme relativism	No ethical view, regardless of source or basis, is better than any other.
Cultural relativism	No ethical view held by one culture is better than any other view held by another culture.
ISCT (Pluralism)	There exist a broad range of ethical viewpoints that may be chosen by communities and cultures. The possibility exists that conflicting ethical positions in different communities are equally valid. There are, however, circumstances in which the viewpoint of a particular culture will be invalid due either to a universally binding moral precept or to the priority of the view of another culture or community.
Modified universalism	There exists a set of precepts expressible in many different ethical languages that reflects universally binding moral precepts and that captures many issues of global ethical significance. These precepts rule out the possibility of two conflicting ethical positions in different cultures being equally valid.
Extreme universalism	There exists a single set of precepts expressed only in a single ethical language that reflects universally binding moral precepts and that captures all issues of global ethical significance. These precepts rule out the possibility of two conflicting ethical positions in different cultures being equally valid.

ISCT essentially says that local communities and cultures can determine ethical norms for members of that society but that these norms must be based on the rights of individual members to exercise "voice" and "exit." However, to be legitimate, these local norms or principles must be compatible with macro-level norms, "hypernorms," which are universal precepts. If there is a conflict, the hypernorms take priority.

The challenge, therefore, is to know if a principle has hypernorm status. Donaldson and Dunfee offer eleven types of evidence that support the existence of hypernorm status. The more types of supportive evidence, the stronger the case for hypernorm status.

1. Widespread consensus that the principle is universal.
2. Component of well-known global industry standards.
3. Supported by prominent NGOs such as the International Labor Organization or Transparency International.

4. Supported by regional governmental organizations such as the EU, OECD, or OAS.

5. Consistently referred to as a global ethical standard by the global media.

6. Known to be consistent with precepts of major religions.

7. Supported by global business organizations such as the International Chamber of Commerce or the Caux Round Table.

8. Known to be consistent with the precepts of major philosophies.

9. Generally supported by a relevant international community of professionals such as accountants or engineers.

10. Known to be consistent with the findings of universal human values.

11. Supported by the laws of many different nations.

One such set of hypernorms would be the Universal Declaration of Human Rights, which can be found at the United Nations website.

Competing with Integrity: Some Guidelines to Consider

Managers have multiple interests that they must consider because they are embedded in a complex network of relationships. The interests, goals, and values of the various actors in any situation can potentially conflict. Identifying these relationships helps in structuring an analysis. To assist in analysis and to promote rational discussion of ethical dilemmas, a series of diagnostic questions and some recommendations are presented below that we hope can serve as a guide for you in the future.

Prepare for Ethical Dilemmas

1. Develop relationships, but with care.

To the extent possible, enter strong, trust-based relationships with customers and suppliers. These relationships will allow you to assess the impact of "requests" and you will be less likely to be pushed into behaviors that you believe are unethical or irresponsible.

Enter dependent relationships with care. If you increase dependency on a particular customer or supplier, be certain about the relationship and make certain you retain enough power to maintain your standards.

Don't wait until you are in a crisis situation to reach out to important industry, community, regulatory, and possibly religious groups in a country. Build relationships and social capital with multiple stakeholders as early as possible to enhance your reputation and develop support, to increase your leverage to follow your own standards if the need arises.

2. Get the best information possible.

Take the time to get the facts, all of them. Avoid fuzzy thinking. Avoid using or being swayed by hearsay or unsubstantiated assertions. These are statements that have no specifics to go with them: "Everybody is doing it," "We'll lose business if we don't do it," or "It's a normal practice." Unsubstantiated assertions like these, parading as analysis, are often "red flags" that should push you to seek more details.

Identify the Impact on Stakeholders

3. Identify all stakeholders.

Remember that a company has multiple groups of stakeholders: shareholders, the home country government, host country governments, customers, suppliers, employees, and unions. There are probably others that could be added to that list, but the point is to comprehensively identify the stakeholders and their interests. It can be easy to ignore some of them, particularly when they may be thousands of miles away and may not be able to stand up for their interests and rights. Ethical managers do not avoid them or pretend that they do not exist.

4. Assess your responsibilities and obligations to these stakeholders.

Identify the responsibilities that your organization may have to external stakeholders as well as to stakeholders (e.g. employees) in your own organization. Be clear about your responsibilities and obligations to these groups. For example, a decision about whether to shut down operations in a country may involve both external and internal ethical issues.

Take the situation of an insurance company with which one of the authors and his colleague were involved. The company was selling life insurance in Uganda during a period of civil war. Years earlier, the company's operation was nationalized and now was having its ownership restored. The branch in Uganda was not profitable, and a financial analysis showed that it should be shut down.

From a profit-and-loss perspective, the decision may have been easy to make. But what were the company's responsibilities to the managers who ran the company in their interest after it had been nationalized and who were concerned about possible violence to field personnel and to themselves if the company closed its operations? And what were its obligations to its policyholders? The issue may not be whether the company should shut down, but how it should handle its responsibilities, obligations, and commitments to its employees and customers, and shareholders as it shuts down.

Assess and Select Options

5. Identify a broad range of options.

Some options will jump up immediately, such as pay the bribe or don't pay the bribe. Are there options that have not been identified? In trying to identify possible action, avoid characterizing decisions using false dichotomies – either/ or characterizations. Alternatives and options do not have to be win/lose positions. For example, the statement "We need to pay the bribe or lose the business" portrays the situation as win/lose, but it may not be. These positions often develop because the initial analysis was not as complete as it could have been. This mindset can limit the action possibilities open to the manager. Strive for a win/win situation. Is there a way to solve the problem that satisfies all parties and allows you to fulfill your obligations?

6. Analyze the assumptions behind the options.

What assumptions are being made? What ethical framework is being invoked? Whose utility is being maximized? Whose values are being used? Consider multiple (including opposing) viewpoints, but examine them carefully. Weigh the costs and benefits to all stakeholders.

7. Select an option and develop an action plan.

If you have followed the steps above, you will be in a better position to develop an action plan. Some decision criteria to consider include: do the best for all involved stakeholders; fulfill obligations; observe laws and contracts; do not use deception; and avoid knowingly doing harm (physical, psychological, economic, or social).

Consider Your Own Position Carefully

In conducting objective, arm's length analyses, it is easy to take ourselves – the ones who make the decisions – out of the picture. Remember that there can be personal consequences associated with your decision. People have lost their jobs because someone higher in the organization needed a scapegoat, and others have gone to jail for the actions of others. Don't just think about the decision in terms of your role as a manager. Consider your roles as community leader, spouse, parent, or global citizen. Ask yourself if you will be acting in accordance with your own highest set of values and norms. Certainly, look after the interests of your company in your role as manager, but also look after your own interests. You may be the only one that does!

8. Make decisions that are your responsibility.

Do not avoid making ethical decisions on issues that are your responsibility by passing the responsibility on to someone else or waiting until the problem passes.

9. Don't let people put the monkey on your back.

Do not accept responsibility for decisions that are *not* your responsibility. Some people will try to find a scapegoat to make a particularly difficult, possibly illegal or unethical decision. Do not let them use you. How do you protect yourself? You can ask for the decision or directive in writing or suggest an open meeting with other people present to discuss it.

10. Do not use "culture" as an excuse for improper actions.

Just because the local company does not treat its toxic waste properly does not mean that it is acting as a role model for that culture. Beware of confusing culture and an individual's personality and character. If a person is asking for something that is illegal or unethical, that tells you something about that person's character, not necessarily about his or her culture.

11. Act consistently with your own values.

Consider the "billboard" or the "light-of-day" tests. When you drive to work in the morning, would you be happy to see your decision or action prominently announced on a large billboard for everyone to read? Or alternatively, would you be willing to discuss your actions in a meeting where you would be subject to questions and scrutiny? Could you justify them? Would your actions look as reasonable in the light-of-day as they did when the decision was made behind closed doors?

A Final Word

As you progress through your career as a global leader, we encourage you to maintain high standards. We suggest that you follow an adage that we have modified, "When in Rome don't do as the Romans do, but rather do as the *better* Romans do."

Ask yourself, and answer honestly, if you are behaving up to your highest values and expectations of yourself. Are you happy with your answer? If not, you know what to do!

Reflection Questions

These questions suggest that you think about various ethical dilemmas and how you would face them, reflect on situations you've faced, and learn from others. Increasing mindfulness about these situations will help you manage them effectively when you do face them.

1. This chapter offered many examples of ethical dilemmas. When you read them, you most likely had different personal reactions to different examples.
   a. Which examples seemed simple to you – you didn't see a dilemma, it was obvious what to do and why?
   b. Which examples seemed more difficult to you – if you put yourself in the situation, would it be hard for you to know which path to take?
   c. What does this reflection tell you about your own values and priorities? How have these been shaped by your life experiences?
2. What ethical dilemmas have you faced in the past? Looking back, would you deal with it the same way if you knew then what you know now? What do you learn about yourself from this reflection?
3. Scan your favorite international business news source and identify an example of a company facing an ethical dilemma today, in an international context (e.g., a company with headquarters in one country facing a dilemma in a different country). Learn about how the company's managers perceive the dilemma, and what they are doing about it. How would you categorize their perceptions and responses – consequential, rule-based, culturally relative, or some combination? How could they see it from other perspectives, and how might this resolve the dilemma?
4. Interview an experienced global leader, someone who has worked in many countries in different decision-making contexts. Ask them about some of the ethical dilemmas they've faced, and how they managed them. What do you take from this for yourself, in your own career?

Further Resources

See the website of the Caux Round Table which states: "The Caux Round Table (CRT) is an international network of principled business leaders working to promote a moral capitalism ... The CRT Principles apply fundamental ethical norms to business decision-making." See www.cauxroundtable.org/index.cfm?&menuid=2.

An influential book on ethics in an international context is Peter Singer's *One World: The Ethics of Globalization* (2002).

Donaldson and Dunfee's book *Ties That Bind: A Social Contracts Approach to Business Ethics* (1999) explains the role of social contracts. We would like to thank Sheila Puffer and Dan McCarthy of Northeastern University for introducing us to this perspective.

Bibliography

Amba-Rao, S. (1993). Multinational Corporate Social Responsibility, Ethics, Interactions and Third World Governments: An Agenda for the 1990s. *Journal of Business Ethics*, 12, 553–572.

Beaver, W. (1995). Levi's is Leaving China. *Business Horizons*, March–April, 35–40.

Cassel, D. (1995). Corporate Initiatives: A Second Human Rights Revolution. *Fordham International Law Journal*, 19, Article 10.

CBC News (2017). Duterte Tells Leaders to "Lay Off" after Trudeau Raises Human Rights in Philippines. *CBC News*, November 14.

China White Paper (n.d.). *International Human Rights Activists*. Retrieved from: www.china.org.cn/e-white/7/7-L.htm

Choe, K. (2012). *Infant Formula Contributes to Malnourishment – UNICEF*. Retrieved November 2017 from Newshub: www .newshub.co.nz/world/infant-formula-contributes-to-malnourishment–unicef-2012110608

Cohen, E. (2012). *Banning Child Labor: The Symptom or the Cause?* Retrieved November 2017 from CSRwire Talkback: www.csrwire.com/blog/posts/547-banning-child-labor-the-symptom-or-the-cause

De George, R. (1993). *Competing with Integrity in International Business*. Oxford University Press.

Donaldson, T. (2000). *The Promise of Corporate Codes of Conduct*. Retrieved November 2017 from Human Rights Dialogue: www.carnegiecouncil.org/publications/archive/dialogue/2_04/articles/896

Donaldson, T., & Dunfee, T. (1999). *Ties that Bind: A Social Contracts Approach to Business Ethics*. Harvard Business School Press.

Drohan, M. (1994). To Bribe or Not to Bribe. *The Global and Mail*, February 14, p. B7.

Fantozzi, J. (2017). *A New Documentary Claims Haribo Gummy Bears Are Made Using Slave Labour In Brazil*. Retrieved November 2017 from Business Insider: www.businessinsider.com/investigation-into-haribo-alleges-slave-labor-2017-10

Fey, C., & Shekshnia, S. (2008). *The Key Commandments of Doing Business in Russia*. INSEAD Working Paper. Also in: *Organizational Dynamics*, 40 (2011), 57–66.

Fortune (2017). *Change the World*. Retrieved November 2017 from *Fortune*: http://fortune.com/change-the-world/list/

Fragile States Index (n.d.). *Fund for Peace*. Retrieved February 2013 from: http://fundforpeace.org/fsi/

GoodWeave (n.d.). *Standards Development*. Retrieved November 2017 from GoodWeave: http://goodweave.org/proven-approach/standard/development/

Henderson, V. (1982). The Ethical Side of Enterprise. *MIT Sloan Management Review*, 23, 37–47.

Hope, C. (2009). How Mumbai Terrorist Attacks Nearly Wiped Out Top Management at Unilever. *The Telegraph*, November 26. Retrieved November 2017 from: www.telegraph.co.uk/news/worldnews/asia/india/6645178/Revealed-how-Mumbai-terrorist-attacks-nearly-wiped-out-top-management-at-Unilever.html

International Petroleum Finance (2003). Statoil Still Afloat Despite Losing Man Overboard. *International Petroleum Finance*, October 8.

Levi Strauss & Co. (n.d.). *Sustainability*. Retrieved November 2017 from *Sustainability Guidebook:* www .levistrauss.com/sustainability/sustainability-guidebook/

Makabenta, Y. (2017). Dopey Drug War Recalls Asian Values Debate. *The Manila*

Times, May 13. Retrieved November 2017 from: www.manilatimes.net/dopey-drug-war-recalls-asian-values-debate/326982/

Moore, E. (2012). CIVETS, BRICS and the Next 11. *Financial Times*, June 8. Retrieved November 2017 from: www.ft.com/content/c14730ae-aff3-11e1-ad0b-00144feabdc0

Nestlé (n.d.). *Responsible Sourcing*. Retrieved from: www.nestleusa.com/socialimpact/responsible%20sourcing/home

Peerenboom, R. (2003). Beyond Universalism and Relativism: The Evolving Debates About "Values in Asia". *Indiana International & Comparative Law Review*, 14, 1–85. Retrieved from: https://journals.iupui.edu/index.php/iiclr/article/view/17786/17969

Perry, Jr., W. (1970). *Forms of Intellectual and Ethical Development in the College Years: A Scheme*. Holt, Reinhart & Winston.

Rowe, G. (2012). Statement Made in Class During International Week of the EMBA at IPADE. Mexico City.

Sen, A. (1997). *Human Rights and Asian Values*. Retrieved from Carnegie Council: www.carnegiecouncil.org/publications/archive/morgenthau/254

Singer, P. (2002). *One World: The Ethics of Globalization*. Yale University Press.

Solmssen, P. (2012). Siemens Changes Its Culture: No More Bribes. NPR Radio, May 1 (S. Inskeep, interviewer). Transcript available at: www.npr.org/2012/05/01/151745671/companies-can-recovery-from-bribery-scandals

The Economist (1995). Human Rights. Retrieved from: www.economist.com/topics/human-rights

Transparency International (n.d.). www.transparency.org/research

Transparency International (2016). *Corruptions Perceptions Index*. Retrieved November 2017 from: www.transparency.org/news/feature/corruption_perceptions_index_2016

UNICEF (2005). *HIV and Infant Feeding*, January 13. Retrieved November 26, 2017 from: www.unicef.org/nutrition/index_24827.html

United Nations (n.d.). *The Ten Principles of the UN Global Compact*. Retrieved November 2017 from: www.unglobalcompact.org/what-is-gc/mission/principles

United States Department of Justice (n.d.). *Foreign Corrupt Practices Act*. Retrieved February 2013 from: www.justice.gov/criminal-fraud/foreign-corrupt-practices-act

Verité (n.d.). *About*. Retrieved November 2017 from: www.verite.org/about/

Zakaria, F. (1994). Culture is Destiny: A Conversation with Lee Kuan Yew. *Foreign Affairs*, 73, 109–126.

11 Competing with Integrity: Corporate Sustainability

> Although we are in different boats, you in your boat and we in our canoe, we share the same river of life.
>
> Chief Oren Lyons, Onandaga Nation

> The best time to plant a tree was twenty years ago. The second best time is today.
>
> Chinese proverb

Introduction

The concept of "sustainable development" came into common usage when the UN General Assembly's World Commission on Environment and Development issued its 1987 report *Our Common Future.* The report defined sustainable development as "development which meets the needs of current generations without compromising the ability of future generations to meet their own needs" (United Nations, 1987). To many people this concept became synonymous simply with protecting the environment or being "green." However, it encompasses more than a focus on the physical eco-system and includes concern for economic and social development.[1]

Defining Corporate Sustainability and Tracing Its Importance

There are hundreds of definitions of "sustainability" and "sustainable development." As it relates to business, sustainability has become the prevailing term for finding the overlap between business's interests and society's interests and

---

[1] The authors gratefully acknowledge Andrew Savitz for his contributions to this chapter.

we are adopting that convention in this edition. Some writers and companies include ethics in their definitions of corporate sustainability. As we said in Chapter 10, we think it's helpful to distinguish between the decisions and behavior of individuals or a small group of people, and the policies and practices of an organization that most likely uses corporate resources to achieve its ends.

Corporate governance, narrowly conceived as the corporation's relationship with shareholders, may also be included in an understanding of sustainability, especially when it includes well-defined shareholder rights, effective control, transparency and disclosure, and an independent, empowered board of directors. In this case, sustainability refers to the longevity of a firm. Some people consider sustainability to be the same as corporate social responsibility (CSR). More recently, people talk about environmental, social, and governance (ESG) criteria as the best way to implement sustainability and to evaluate business behavior. All these terms or concepts address the broad notion of aligning companies' activities with society's interests.

Sustainability is not simply philanthropy – providing funding for environmental projects or communities in developing countries, for example – no matter how beneficial these programs may be. This philanthropy may be a component of a corporation's sustainability efforts but philanthropy alone is not sustainability. Sustainability programs and projects are usually discretionary. They are usually not required by law, and their effect on the business itself tends to be indirect and difficult to measure. *Sustainability is not about how a company spends its money but rather about how a company makes its money* (Perez, 2015).

As we continue to address the domains of the global mindset, this chapter focuses on the organizational column, focusing on increasing awareness of the responsible decision-making of your own and other organizations, as shown in Table 11.1. This contrasts with the individual focus of Chapter 10.

The Evolution of Corporate Sustainability

As recounted by Spector (2008), the history and ideology of Western corporations having social responsibility as an explicit management theme can be traced back to 1927. At that time Wallace Donham, Dean of the Harvard Business School, advocated greater corporate social responsibility as a way of "aligning business interests with the defense of free-market capitalism against

Table 11.1 **Global mindset framework applied to ethics and corporate sustainability**

	Individual/Personal	Organizational
Self	Clarify and understand my beliefs about ethical behavior.	Clarify and understand my organization's approach to corporate sustainability.
Other	Clarify and understand other beliefs about ethical behavior in the context of other cultures and principal theories of moral philosophy.	Clarify and understand other corporate approaches to sustainability in the context of other industries, other cultures, and principal codes of conduct.
Choice	Belief in and commitment to a set of ethical principles.	Belief in and commitment to an approach to corporate sustainability.

what was depicted as the clear and present danger of Soviet Communism." Starting in 1946, another Dean of the Harvard Business School, Donald K. David, became a "persistent and consistent voice on behalf of expanding the role of business in American society" (Spector 2008), a view also supported by the *Harvard Business Review*. Serious discussion of the topic in North America increased in 1953 with the publication of Bowen's *Social Responsibilities of the Businessman* (Bowen, 1953; Carroll, 1979). The discussion became a debate with strong disagreement from Harvard Business School professor Theodore Levitt, who in 1958 published a critique in the *Harvard Business Review* on "the dangers of social responsibility" (Levitt, 1958). Milton Friedman asserted that a company's only social responsibility was to make a profit for its stockholders. Friedman said:

there is one and only one social responsibility of business – to use its resources and engage in activities designed to increase its profits so long as it stays within the rules of the game, which is to say, engages in open and free competition without deception or fraud. (Friedman, 1970)

However, the rules of the game have changed since Friedman wrote those words. So too has the role of business in society. Starting in the 1960s, Rachel Carson and Ralph Nader initiated new dialogue in North America. Carson's book *Silent Spring* spoke to the dramatic impact of pesticides on humans and the environment, and Nader's book *Unsafe at Any Speed* alerted the public to the importance of paying attention to product safety (Carson, 2002; Nader, 1966). These authors sparked movements that gained momentum over the next decades. Savitz's book *The Triple Bottom Line*, first published in 2006, consolidated the movement and pointed a way forward with the monitoring and measurement of a company's impact on People, Planet, and Profits. Lately, social responsibility and sustainability have become central ideas with strong support among business leaders (Savitz, 2013). The Economist Intelligence Unit's 2017 report on *Global Resource Challenges* found that most companies they researched faced significant resource constraints and shortages related to previous generations' lack of focus on sustainability (e.g., natural resources, labor shortages) – to the extent that they estimated an average decrease in revenues of 9 percent related to resource challenges (Economist Intelligence Unit, 2017). Sustainability is no longer just "nice" for future generations, it is now acknowledged as a business imperative.

In short, society's expectations of businesses have changed over time, as summarized in Figure 11.1. Concerns that were once primarily seen as the responsibility of government have become areas in which businesses are now expected to show leadership.

Our purpose here is not to provide a complete treatment of the topic of corporate sustainability, as there are entire books devoted to it. Rather, as in previous chapters, our purpose is to raise questions about management's responsibility,

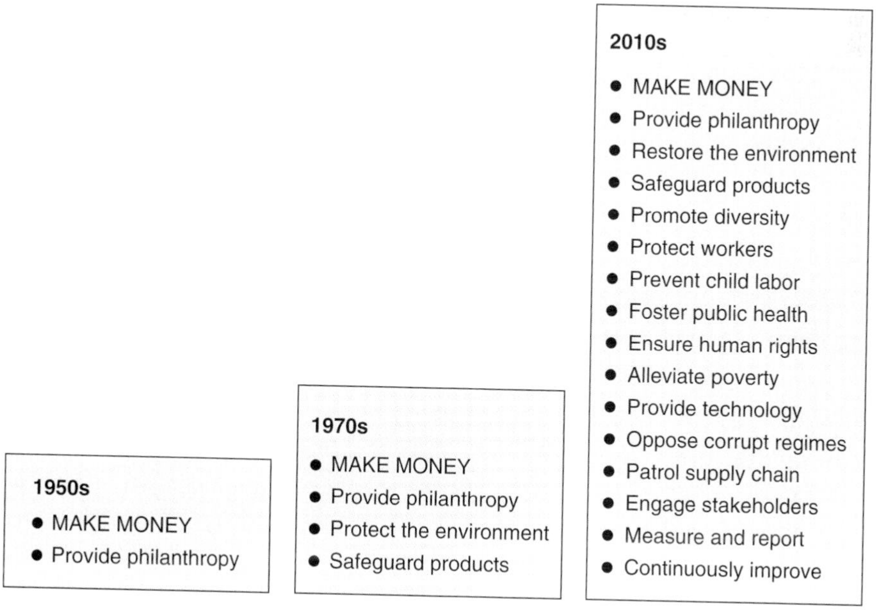

1950s
- MAKE MONEY
- Provide philanthropy

1970s
- MAKE MONEY
- Provide philanthropy
- Protect the environment
- Safeguard products

2010s
- MAKE MONEY
- Provide philanthropy
- Restore the environment
- Safeguard products
- Promote diversity
- Protect workers
- Prevent child labor
- Foster public health
- Ensure human rights
- Alleviate poverty
- Provide technology
- Oppose corrupt regimes
- Patrol supply chain
- Engage stakeholders
- Measure and report
- Continuously improve

Figure 11.1 The rise of corporate accountability
From Savitz (2013), reprinted with permission.

provide some examples, and offer some ways of thinking about the issues that we have found helpful and we hope you will find useful.

Corporate Sustainability Frameworks

Just as there are numerous definitions of sustainability, similarly there are many organizations, public and private, focusing on sustainability. Numerous international accords and sets of principles have been formulated, adopted, and endorsed in the latter half of the twentieth century that provide a base for the development of a transcultural standard of how corporations should behave in the global economy. These documents include: the United Nations Universal Declaration of Human Rights (1948), the European Convention on Human Rights (1950), the Helsinki Final Act (1975), the OECD Guidelines for Multinational Enterprises (1976), the International Labor Office Tripartite Declaration of Principles Concerning Multinational Enterprises and Social Policy (1977), the United Nations Code of Conduct for Transnational Corporations (1983), and the United Nations Global Compact (2000). These accords and principles address the following issues:

- **Employment practices and policies.** For example, multinationals should develop nondiscriminatory employment practices, provide equal pay for equal work, observe the rights of employees to join unions and to bargain collectively, give advance notice of plant closings and mitigate their adverse effects, respect local host country job standards, provide favorable work conditions and limited working hours, adopt adequate health and safety standards, and inform employees about health hazards. They should not permit unacceptable practices such as the exploitation of children, physical punishment, female abuse, or involuntary servitude.
- **Consumer protection.** MNCs should respect host country laws regarding consumer protection, safeguard the health and safety of consumers through proper labeling, disclosures, and advertising, and provide safe products and packaging.
- **Environmental protection.** MNCs should preserve ecological balance, protect the environment, rehabilitate environments damaged by them, and respect host country laws, goals, and priorities regarding protection of the environment.
- **Political payments and involvement.** MNCs should not pay bribes to public officials and should avoid illegal involvement or interference in internal politics.

- **Basic human rights and fundamental freedoms.** Multinationals should respect the rights of people to life, liberty, security of person, and privacy; and freedom of religion, peaceful assembly, and opinion.
- **Community responsibility.** MNCs should work with governments and communities in which they do business to improve the quality of life in those communities.

The UN Global Compact, the Global Reporting Initiative (GRI), and the Dow Jones Sustainability Index (DJSI) are three global organizations that currently lead different aspects of corporate sustainability and have comprehensive frameworks and programs that we find helpful; together, they provide a broad set of lenses for diagnosing and discussing corporate sustainability. The UN Global Compact is a quasi-governmental international organization and links corporate practices with human rights and international law. The GRI is a non-profit, network-based organization that develops standards for reporting, monitoring, and comparing sustainability initiatives. The DJSI is a private company that develops indices of sustainability performance for the use of the financial industry, for creating sustainable funds and other financial instruments.

The UN Global Compact

The Global Compact was formally launched in July 2000. It is the world's largest corporate sustainability initiative. Its focus is not regulatory but, rather, transparency and disclosure to achieve public accountability. Companies sign up to the Global Compact, and in doing so they agree to commit to adhering to the UN's ten principles on human rights, labor, environment, and anti-corruption. Starting in 2016 with the establishment of the UN Sustainable Development Goals (SDGs), companies in the Global Compact also commit to advance these goals. By the end of 2017 almost 10,000 companies had signed up, from more than 160 countries. The *UN Global Compact Progress Report* provides annual updates of the extent to which goals are being addressed or met (United Nations, 2017). The Global Compact organization facilitates collaboration and best practice sharing among members, and facilitates innovation through research and encouragement of new company initiatives.

The ten Global Compact Principles are as follows (United Nations, 2018):

Human Rights

- Principle 1: Businesses should support and respect the protection of internationally proclaimed human rights; and
- Principle 2: make sure they are not complicit in human rights abuses.

Labor

- Principle 3: Businesses should uphold the freedom of association and the effective recognition of the right to collective bargaining;
- Principle 4: the elimination of all forms of forced and compulsory labor;
- Principle 5: the effective abolition of child labor; and
- Principle 6: the elimination of discrimination in respect of employment and occupation.

Environment

- Principle 7: Businesses should support a precautionary approach to environmental challenges;
- Principle 8: undertake initiatives to promote greater environmental responsibility; and
- Principle 9: encourage the development and diffusion of environmentally friendly technologies.

Anti-Corruption

- Principle 10: Businesses should work against corruption in all its forms, including extortion and bribery.

An impact study of the Compact by Accenture traced the evolution of the Global Compact's effect on business (Accenture, 2016). The 2016 study found that "frustrated ambition has given way to optimism as CEOs see a mandate to solve societal challenges as a core element in the search for competitive advantage." They report that the adoption of the SDGs by the UN and the Global Compact organization has created a more tangible framework for pursuing sustainability.

Do companies participate in the Global Compact simply to bolster their image? Yes, greenwashing is alive and well. In the years since its inception, more than 7000 companies have been delisted for failing to communicate progress. However, an analysis of the expelled companies indicated that about 65 percent were SMEs who could not fulfill all the reporting requirements, reinforcing a criticism that the Compact is primarily for large companies that can support the reporting requirements (Global Compact Critics, n.d.). In addition to expelling companies, in 2011 the Compact introduced a differentiation framework of participants sorting them under their level of disclosure on progress made in integrating the Global Compact principles and contributing to broader UN goals. These levels are Learner, Active, and Advanced; the Advanced level includes a Leadership category. Even among companies that are communicating good progress, the principles related to labor and working conditions are being addressed at a much faster pace than social, community, and environment principles. In other words, companies seem to be focusing on the principles which are easiest for them to control, but not necessarily those that relate to the greatest need in their environments. Current activism around the Global Compact is aimed at increasing the activity around the latter sets of principles.

Global Reporting Initiative

The GRI believes that: "A sustainable global economy should combine long term profitability with social justice and environmental care ... sustainability covers the key areas of economic, environmental, social and governance performance" (Global Reporting, 2018a). GRI created a non-financial reporting (NFR) system that covers corporate economic, environmental, and social performance indicators. The system has become the world's preeminent global, voluntary sustainability reporting system (Levy, Brown, and de Jong, 2010).

GRI Reporting Standards focus on Economic Performance including direct and indirect economic impact and procurement practices; Environmental Aspects to include such items as materials, energy and water usage, biodiversity, emissions and waste; and Social elements which include sub-categories of labor practices and decent work, human rights, society and product responsibility. A complete listing of the Guidelines and detailed explanations of all the categories can be found on the Global Reporting Initiative's website. The Sustainability Disclosure Database has a list of almost 12,000 organizations that have filed sustainability reports, with links to their reports (some of which are compliant with GRI's standards) (Global Reporting, 2018b).

It would be naïve, however, not to acknowledge that companies can be hypocritical in their support of sustainability, social responsibility, and ethical behavior in the areas indicated. Endorsing codes such as the GRI or the Global Compact is easy to do, but this act alone does not mean that a company is committed to implementing them or managing by them.

Dow Jones Sustainability Index

Sustainability, its definition, management guidelines to promote it, and outcomes are no longer only the concern of international, quasi-governmental organizations or NGOs, but are now also the concern of some private investment companies. The Dow Jones Sustainability Indexes (DJSI) are a product of

RobecoSAM Indexes and S&P Dow Jones Indices, who track the performance of the world's leading companies in the area of sustainability (RobecoSAM, 2018). DJSIs are based on the belief that corporate sustainability leaders "create long-term shareholder value by ... gearing their strategies and management to harness the market's potential for sustainability products and services while at the same time successfully reducing and avoiding sustainability costs and risks ... [and that] the opportunities and risks deriving from economic, environmental and social developments can be quantified and used to identify and select leading companies for investment purposes."

S&P Dow Jones Indices LLC is a subsidiary of The McGraw-Hill Companies and is a source of data and indices such as the S&P 500 and the Dow Jones Industrial Average. RobecoSAM is an asset manager and investment specialist in sustainability located in Zurich and Rotterdam. The indexes track the stock performance of the world's leading companies in terms of environmental, social, and governance criteria. They serve as benchmarks for investors who integrate sustainability considerations into their portfolios, and provide an effective engagement platform for companies who want to adopt sustainable best practices. The partnership between the two organizations has created an important source of sustainability analysis and information for the investment community.

Each year the world's 3000+ largest companies in terms of market capitalization are invited to participate. Questionnaires are completed by these companies regarding their sustainability efforts and then evaluated according to specified criteria, scored, and the data verified. The top companies in each sector are then included in the indexes. Not all companies are eligible to be included. For example, companies that generate revenue from following list of activities and products are excluded from the index participation: Adult Entertainment, Alcohol, Armaments, Cluster Bombs, Firearms, Gambling, Landmines, Nuclear (power plants, uranium mining), and Tobacco.

Unlike the UN Global Compact or the GSI, the DJSI takes into account financial materiality. It identifies the sustainability factors that drive business value and have an impact on the long-term valuation assumptions used in financial analysis, and focuses on their impact. Each industry is therefore assessed differently according to its specific value drivers (RobecoSAM, 2017). For example, the economic dimension is measured in all industries, but it accounts for 43 percent of the weight in banks (including measurement of anti-crime policy and systemic financial risk) and 31 percent of the DJSI weight in electric utilities (including measurement of supply chain management). Environmental dimensions, on the other hand, are weighted higher for electric utilities at 40 percent (including measurement of water-related risks and biodiversity) and lower for banks at 23 percent (including measurement of operational eco-efficiency and climate strategy). RobecoSam continually updates the criteria used to measure sustainability based on new research and societal perspectives. For example, in 2017 new assessments were added on human rights, water-related risk, and policy influence.

Summary: The Triple Bottom Line – People, Planet, Profits

Although there may be some differences in the specific categories, dimensions, or values that the three organizations use, it is clear that there is convergence around the idea that corporate sustainability encompasses continued, strong economic performance, a broad concept of social justice, and a concern for environmental quality; and recognizes the interdependence between the three areas. John Elkington, founder of SustainAbility, coined the concept and term "triple bottom line" in his 1994 book, *Cannibals with Forks* (SustainAbility, 2018). Sustainability is about performance and progress on the three pillars of sustainability – people, planet, and profits – and the triple bottom line is a way of measuring and reporting this performance (Savitz, 2013).

Some Examples

Let's look at three examples of what some leading global companies in very different industries and countries are doing: a technology company headquartered in the USA, a nutrition company headquartered in Switzerland, and a multi-industry conglomerate headquartered in India. All three are committed to the UN Global Compact, report according to the guidelines of the GRI, and are members of the DJSI.

Microsoft

Microsoft was ranked in 2017 by Forbes as the top US company for CSR reputation among consumers, in a comparison of 170,000 companies. The ranking looks at consumers' perceptions of company governance, influence on society, and treatment of employees. Microsoft is well-respected for several elements of its approach to business, from the company's focus on making education and training accessible globally, to the open platform for software development. The company reputation also benefits from the important work of the Bill & Melinda Gates Foundation.

Microsoft focuses its CSR around three key principles that are fundamental to its own business relationship with society: human rights, privacy and data security, and responsible sourcing. With respect to human rights, Microsoft's work revolves first around the role of technology in both respecting and promoting human rights. For example, they identify that access to technology is increasingly perceived as a human right. They are active in providing services and new technology for addressing slavery and human trafficking; they participate in several multi-lateral initiatives to protect vulnerable groups such as children, women, and people with disabilities; and they are conducting extensive research on the relationship between human rights and the use of artificial intelligence.

Microsoft recognizes that privacy and data security is an arena in which technology companies have particular responsibilities and skills. The company practices six key privacy principles:

1. Control – putting users in control of their privacy.
2. Transparency – about data collection so users can make informed decisions.
3. Security – protecting data through strong security and encryption.
4. Legal protections – respecting local laws and fighting for the protection of users' privacy as a fundamental human right.
5. No content-based targeting – Microsoft does not use personal content, such as email or files, to target ads.
6. User benefits – ensuring that all collection of data is used only to benefit users and users' experience.

In more specific initiatives, for example, Microsoft says it is very supportive of and well-prepared for the European Union's new General Data Protection Regulation (GDPR) requirements. It is proactively incorporating GDPR compliance into cloud services and partnerships. Microsoft is also very active in advocating for international agreements to protect civilians' privacy and data security.

Microsoft extends its approach to CSR through its responsible sourcing. This is a set of principles and agreements for working with suppliers and partners. Beyond holding suppliers accountable, Microsoft also invests in capacity building with its suppliers. For example, Microsoft has an extensive development program for training its suppliers in Social and Environmental Accountability

(SEA). In the sourcing of raw materials for its hardware, Microsoft extends its reach to human rights, health and safety, environmental protection, and business ethics in the production of its devices and packaging around the world. This includes collaboration with associations of extractive industries, such as the Initiative for Responsible Mining and the Alliance for Responsible Mining. A good example of this is the "Children Out of Mining" program in the Democratic Republic of Congo (DRC), which is aimed at reducing and eventually eliminating child labor in mining. The program is multifaceted with different elements addressing policy, education, economic alternatives, social norms, and child protection. Between 2014 and 2016 the program reported a 77–97 per cent reduction in children working in the mines. The project is continuing with an increased focus on the most vulnerable segments of children. Microsoft also participates actively in initiatives to source "Conflict-Free Minerals," that is, minerals mined from facilities from which the profits are not funding armed conflict. They have increased their number of conflict-free smelters gradually over the years, and have made progress in working with suppliers and advocating actively for industry programs.

Microsoft is also committed to creating shared value by empowering stakeholders throughout its business value chain. For example, it has important programs for increasing the amount it spends with suppliers owned by ethnic or racial minorities and women in the different countries in which it operates. Microsoft helps suppliers extend empowerment programs to their own suppliers, such as YouthSpark computer training for local community members in fourteen countries, and life skills and career training for community members and specific target groups such as migrant parents and underprivileged women.

Microsoft is a good example of a company that focuses its CSR around its business model, both in content (the role of technology) and in the value chain (with suppliers and partners). This focus helps both external observers and employees understand the initiatives more clearly, and incorporate them into the everyday running of the business. This is critical for CSR that has powerful results beyond a set of initiatives in a specific part of the company.

Nestlé

This Swiss-headquartered global food and nutrition company recently adopted a strategy of Nutrition, Health, and Wellness, and has been gradually shifting its acquisitions and divestments in the direction of creating a healthy future. In itself, this is evidence of a shift in their view of the relationship between the business and society. While chocolate and coffee continue to be developed, Nestlé focuses more and more of its resources on products like healthy cereals, chilled and frozen foods, and dairy products such as yogurt.

This strategy helps to direct their CSR, which Nestlé refers to as "Creating Shared Value" (CSV). CSV has three main pillars for different stakeholder groups, with specific goals to achieve for 2030 (aligned with the UN Sustainable Development Goals):

• For individuals and families: Help 50 million children to lead healthier lives.
• For communities: Help to improve 30 million livelihoods in communities directly connected to our business activities.
• For the planet: Strive for zero environmental impact in our operations.

With respect to individuals and families, most of Nestlé's initiatives are around increasing health and nutrition, through education, product development, marketing, and contributing to biomedical science. Interestingly, Nestlé has decided to self-regulate its marketing to children. In 2017 they rolled out training to all marketing teams on the new Policy on Marketing Communication to Children, which mandates that all communication to children is limited to foods and beverages that meet a nutritional profile. In 2018 they plan to be implementing this policy across the globe.

Nestlé focuses on the communities of its supply chain for many of its community initiatives. For example, Nestlé's activities in Côte d'Ivoire, a major cocoa-growing country, are affecting more than 1,100 families. In the communities, many women suffer from the effects of social and economic marginalization. Nestlé helps them receive income and develop skills for running their own businesses. Nestlé's activities also help households earn enough income to send their children to schools rather than have them work on cocoa farms. In the Philippines, Nestlé created the annual "Women Movers" program to identify, recognize, and support important female role models who may not be visible leaders. The program raises the profile of these women employees both within Nestlé and in the community, and has had a strong impact on empowering the women recognized by the awards and their work in the community.

With respect to the planet, Nestlé focuses a great deal of effort on its supply chain, particularly water and waste. They work closely with NGOs such as the WWF to improve water stewardship. Nestlé chairs the 2030 Water Resources Group, and complies with a pledge for safe water, sanitation, and hygiene for all employees. The company also works actively to support water conservation and water security actions for places with water shortages. Nestlé also engages in many initiatives for reducing packaging. For example, in Thailand they changed the packaging for their Maggi sauces. This initiative alone created an annual net saving of 64 tonnes of plastic and 43 tonnes of paper. Similar projects are under way in all of Nestlé's operations.

Nestlé's CSR has evolved a long way since it irresponsibly marketed baby formula in developing countries in the late 1970s and early 1980s, and even since its business relied on chocolate and coffee in the late 1990s and early 2000s. It provides an example of how a company can evolve through pressure, dialogue, learning, and its own difficult internal conversations about values, principles, and future strategies.

Tata Group

The Tata Group is a conglomerate of over 100 companies, headquartered in India. Their major divisions include steel, automotive, power, chemicals, beverages, technology and consultancy, and hotels. Many of their companies are among the top in the industry, including Tata Motors, which has a range from the company's famous Nano city car to Jaguar Land Rover's luxury vehicles.

Tata Group was founded by Jamsetji Tata in 1868, and the company is strongly influenced by his values and principles. The Group's mission is "To improve the quality of life of the communities we serve globally, through long-term stakeholder value creation based on Leadership with Trust" (Tata Group, 2018). Tata has a strong reputation within its home country for providing social, educational, and other services for the communities in which it operates. From Tata's point of view, this is simply good business – the only way to have employees and customers is to look after the community.

As the company grew globally, Tata had to learn how to translate this philosophy to companies from other countries. All Tata companies are encouraged to engage in a set of best practices, selected from a menu provided by Tata Group and with support from the Group. However, all Tata companies *must* adhere to the Group's code of conduct. The first three principles of this code dictate moral and ethical standards, good corporate citizenship, and contribution to the economic and social development of the communities the Group companies operate in.

Tata's CSR initiatives begin with the assumption that "the most successful, respected, and desirable businesses exist to do much more than make money; they exist to use the power of business to solve social and environmental problems." Their CSR initiatives are guided by ten core principles:

1. Beyond Compliance
2. Impactful
3. Linked to Business
4. Relevant to National & Local Contexts
5. Sustainable Development Principles
6. Participative & Bottom-up
7. Focused on the Disadvantaged
8. Strategic and Built to Last
9. Partnerships with Local Institutions
10. Opportunities for Volunteering

In a typical example, at Tata Chemicals' soda ash factory in Magadi, Kenya, plant managers worked closely with the local community leaders and community-based organizations over a decade to help the township's residents with poverty reduction efforts. The company set up multi-party relationships and supported the development of strong town governance, even when the governance was not in agreement with the company. While the initiatives did not protect the factory from the competitive need to cut costs and become more efficient, the partnerships developed helped the community diversify and become more stable in its development (Valente, 2015).

In 2014 Tata set up the Tata Sustainability Group to work with Tata companies around the world on sustainability initiatives. For example, the STRIVE program addresses the need for employment skills for India's underprivileged young people. Tata is able to apply its understanding of business and multi-disciplinary resources to tackle multifaceted challenges that are difficult for smaller organizations to address, such as upskilling facilitators and instructors, decreasing attrition at entry level jobs, developing soft skills, and developing entrepreneurs. Another example is Tata Engage, a global initiative to connect employees, their family members, and retired employees to communities in need. The Sustainability Group has also set up a Disaster Management initiative to bring together professionals, resources, and volunteers to respond quickly and effectively to earthquakes, hurricanes, and typhoons, and other natural disasters in their communities.

The Tata Group challenges Western assumptions that companies from developed countries are more advanced in their CSR efforts than companies from emerging economies. In fact, in part because its business was built with a strong set of principles about community growth in markets with extreme poverty, Tata's own assumption is that business and CSR must grow hand-in-hand.

No One's Perfect

All three of these companies have been criticized for different aspects of their corporate social responsibility. Microsoft has been accused regularly of tax avoidance with its global holdings practices, and of treating long-term contract employees unethically by denying them the benefits of full-time employment while requiring full-time responsibilities. Nestlé found in 2015 that Thai suppliers in its seafood supply chain were fishing with people forced into labor and slavery. Nestlé immediately engaged the not-for-profit labor rights watchdog Verité to conduct an independent audit and is working to implement the recommendations, but the resolution of a large supply chain is not easy. At Tata, the 2016 change in leadership was mired in accusations of fraudulent transactions and potential corruption; the Tata family owners express confidence that the new CEO, Natarajan Chandrasekaran, represents a return to the "Mr. Clean" reputation of Ratan Tata.

The three companies – and many others – have in common their ongoing commitment to improving the communities and physical environment in which they operate. Sustainability may be viewed as a naïve ideal. For these companies, it is seen as good business practice that creates a competitive advantage in business processes, produces environmentally friendly products or solutions, and possibly assists in recruiting capable, motivated employees wishing to join companies with which they can identify.

Does Corporate Sustainability Pay?

The three companies highlighted above show that sustainability is much more than a naïve ideal. But a question remains: Does sustainability pay? There is evidence that there is a benefit at least in the long term and across companies and industries. Most meta-analyses have concluded that there is a positive association between corporate social performance (CSP) and corporate financial performance (CFP), as well as between corporate environmental performance (CEP) and CFP, although the correlations are often quite low. Most research now focuses on the conditions under which sustainability pays, such as company size (Does it only "pay" for larger companies, compared with their competitors?) or economic environment (Does it only "pay" when times are relatively stable?).

In two reports from the Harvard Business School and MIT, a study compared nineteen High Sustainability firms with a matched set of Low Sustainability ones. The authors found that "High Sustainability firms ... pay attention to externalities and this is manifested in their relationships with stakeholders such as employees, customers, and NGOs representing civil society." The study also examined the financial performance of these firms over an eighteen-year period:

the High Sustainability firms dramatically outperformed the Low Sustainability ones in terms of both stock market and accounting measures [such as ROI, ROE, etc.]. However, the results suggest that this outperformance occurs only in the long-term. (Orlitzky, Schmidt, and Rynes, 2003; see also Margolis and Elfenbein, 2008; Dixon-Fowler et al., 2013)

Perhaps the most interesting answer to the question "Does sustainability pay?" is that the question itself is becoming less relevant. In 2008, the Economist Intelligence Unit's (EIU) research, reported in *Doing Good: Business and the Sustainability Challenge*, found that "sustainability does pay," but 80 percent of senior executives in their survey said they believed that any change in profit would most likely be small (Economist Intelligence Unit, 2008). In 2010, the EIU report *Managing for Sustainability* found that only 24 percent of the 200 executives in its survey felt that there was a correlation between sustainability and financial performance – in the short term. However, 69 per cent said that the link was stronger in the long term (Economist Intelligence Unit, 2008). The EIU's 2017 report *Global Resources Challenges*, as we discussed earlier, does not ask the question of whether sustainability pays. Instead, its respondents focused more on how *unsustainability* had affected their financial business results negatively.

Creating Sustainable Value

Arguments about the role of sustainability, corporate citizenship, creating shared value, or other terminology for the initiatives tend to pit business against society and moral actions against profitable ones. One of the major debates is to whom and for what are the management and board of directors of a company primarily responsible – the shareholders or other stakeholders. Unfortunately, this argument, much like the ones we discussed in the previous chapter, generates more heat than light. Positioning shareholders against other stakeholders creates a false dichotomy. Shareholders are a subset of stakeholders, and management should be trying to do the best they can for all groups – aiming for the upper right quadrant of Figure 11.2. Let's take a look at some examples of companies represented in the quadrants. As we'll see, companies can shift from one quadrant to another as they learn to engage with stakeholders over time.

Shareholders benefit and other stakeholders lose (unsustainable, lower left). This happens often in supply chains. Monitoring activities of suppliers in a global supply chain can be an enormous and complicated task; and is viewed as the "weakest link" in the sustainability initiatives of companies. Anglo American, the mining company, has 40,000 suppliers and Coca-Cola has over 100,000. How do companies ensure that their sustainability codes of conduct are adhered to with so many suppliers spread around the world in countries with very different cultures and standards of what are acceptable practices?

Two of the more salient sustainability dimensions related to a global supply chain are potential environmental degradation and human rights abuses. For

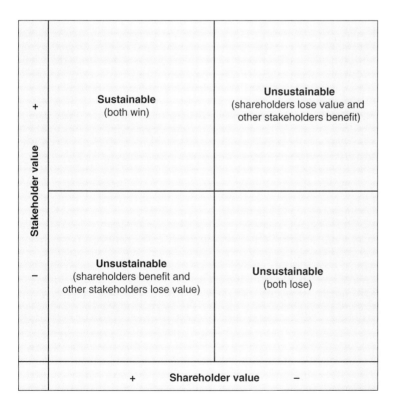

Figure 11.2 Sustainable value framework

example, Wal-Mart has well over 100,000 suppliers and in 2012 was criticized for selling clothes made by two of its suppliers in a factory in Bangladesh where 112 workers died in a fire. Wal-Mart had previously taken the factories off its authorized list, but the main contractor used them anyway, without Wal-Mart knowing. The factory had a record of previous fire violations, including barred windows that prevented workers from escaping the 2012 blaze (Greenhouse, 2013). As a result of the criticism Wal-Mart has toughened fire safety standards for its suppliers and requires them to pre-authorize factories they intend to use. Although it is commendable to react to events like the fire to improve surveillance and tighten standards, companies have to be more proactive in policing suppliers and taking preventive measures in order to avoid tragedies such as the building collapse in 2013 in Bangladesh that killed over 1000 workers (BBC, 2013) – shortly after Wal-Mart and other companies vowed to become better.

Sometimes the visibility of being in this quadrant leads to changes in the company. A classic and still important example is Nike. In the 1990s, Nike was often used as a prime example of all that was wrong with globalization as "greedy" companies eliminated jobs in the USA and took advantage of workers in other countries. It moved production out of the USA into low-wage places such as Korea and Taiwan. When wages increased there and unions became more powerful in Korea, it encouraged suppliers to move again into places such as China, Vietnam, and Indonesia. It was seen as "the 'poster child' of corporate *ir*responsibility in a global economy" (Spector, 2013).

At first Nike's shareholders benefited from its unsustainable operations. In 1977 Nike started producing shoes in Korea and Taiwan and it became a public company in 1980. Its revenue in 1980 was US$270 million and its earnings per share were US$.39. In 1986, two years after signing Michael Jordan to a sponsorship contract, revenue reached US$1 billion for the first time. In 1998, at the height of the sweatshop scandal, revenue reached US$9.6 billion and earnings were US$1.35 per share in what looked like a classic transfer of value from stakeholders to shareholders. At the time it was accused of numerous transgressions such as using toxic, carcinogenic materials, worker abuse, child labor, and low wages. There were numerous anti-Nike protest groups, like Team Sweat, that organized against the company to publicize and condemn its activities and held demonstrations at its stores. In 1998, Phil Knight, Chairman and one of Nike's founders, admitted at the National Press Club that, "the Nike product has become synonymous with slave wages, forced overtime, and arbitrary abuse" (Canizares, 2001; Sterling, 2012).

But that is not the end of the story. In 2000 Nike became active in the UN Global Compact. It participates in the GRI and in 2012 was invited to participate in the DJSI. That same year it received the SAM Silver Class Designation for companies in the Clothing, Accessories and Footwear Sector (KPMG & SAM, 2012). The Sector Leader and Gold Class designation went to Adidas AG from Germany, and a Silver Class distinction means that Nike scored within 1–5 percent of Adidas AG.

Nike can be considered a sustainability turnaround story. Sustainability offenders can change, and companies discussed as falling into any of the four quadrants in Figure 11.2 represent only a snapshot at a particular point in time. However, it is not simple to turn a company around and requires more than creating a department, as Nike learned. Sustainability must become integral to corporate strategy; and people and systems, in addition to structures, must be aligned with the new strategic thrust as was discussed in Chapter 7.

Shareholders lose value and stakeholders benefit (unsustainable, upper right). The most visible examples of this quadrant are boycotts of products; however, although sales may dip slightly, most boycotts do not affect sales or shareholders in the long term (Diermeier, 2012). An interesting example to illustrate this category is toy manufacturer Mattel in 2007. A lack of attention to its suppliers' practices in China created the need for a large recall, due to lead paint being used and small strong magnets in the products that could be unsafe for children. Then it emerged that the vast majority of the product recalls (17.4 million of the 19.6 million recalled toys) were due to the Mattel design flaw of the magnets, not the Chinese suppliers (Blanchard, 2007). As suppliers of Mattel, the Chinese firms received value from the Mattel business and customers may have benefited from lower prices for toys made in China. But the result of Mattel not coordinating its global supply chain effectively ultimately took value from the Mattel shareholders. From May 1, 2007, before the recall, until a year later, Mattel's share price declined by 34.4 percent. Meanwhile its major competitor, Hasbro, gained 11 percent in the same period. Mattel apologized publicly for its errors, and focused on fixing its supply chain; the company recovered all the value of its share drop by the end of 2010.

Both lose (unsustainable, lower right). The most recent high-profile example of this quadrant is British Petroleum (BP) and its Deepwater Horizon oil spill in the Gulf of Mexico on April 20, 2010. Between January 4 and April 19, 2010 BP's share price, adjusted for dividends and splits, fluctuated between US$53.43 and US$54.14 with average sales volumes ranging from 4.5 to 10.5 million shares. From April 26 to June 21, 2010 the adjusted share price ranged from a high of US$47.15 down to US$24.84 on average volumes of sales of 37.5 to 147.2 million shares. BP shareholders lost a lot of value. For the period June 26, 2010 to December 31, 2012, share prices stabilized in a range of US$26.98–45.94 fluctuating mostly in mid-to-high US$30 dollar to low US$40 dollar range. By the end of 2017 BP shares had not yet recovered their pre-Deepwater Horizon price.

Who else lost? Just about everyone except maybe the lawyers involved in the case. Eleven men were killed. The oil spill, the largest in US waters, lasted for 84 days and was estimated at 206 million gallons or 4.9 million barrels (Ramseur and Haggerty, 2015). Beaches, fisheries, and wetlands were damaged and thousands of people's livelihoods were threatened. In January 2013, a federal judge approved the agreement between the Justice Department and BP in which it pleaded guilty to fourteen criminal charges and paid a fine of US$4 billion (Krauss, 2013). Although this agreement settled the criminal case for BP, in early 2018 the company still faced civil penalties resulting from numerous law suits. In 2016 BP said the final total cost of the Deepwater Horizon explosion was US$61.6 billion (Financial Times, n.d.). In addition to the monetary costs, two BP officials were charged with manslaughter and a former vice president was charged with obstruction of Congress and making false statements.

Depending on one's perspective, BP can be viewed as a villain; or as a cautionary tale of trying to do too much too soon without changing the organizational culture first; or as a possible example of green spin or greenwashing (Lewis, 2010; Savitz, 2013). BP participates in the GRI but some observers claim that its reporting just "veiled core weaknesses in how the company managed pivotal issues of maintenance and safety" (Lewis, 2010). Prior to the Gulf crisis in 2012, BP developed a reputation for trading off maintenance and safety in favor of cost savings. Examples of this include the fire and explosion at the Texas City refinery that killed fifteen workers in 2005, and the Prudhoe Bay (Alaska) oil spill of 2006, which was linked to not inspecting and cleaning two pipelines for a period of years. However, BP's Sustainability Reports to the GRI presented a very different and positive picture of their sustainability efforts and culture.

It is not enough for companies to talk the talk, they also must walk the talk. Where companies want to aim for is in the upper right hand quadrant: win/win.

Both win (sustainable, upper left). The three companies we profiled above all work hard to stay in the upper left quadrant. Another important company in this quadrant is Lego, which achieved the top ranking of Forbes' 2017 ranking of sustainable companies. Lego has always focused on community and social sustainability, with the importance of play and family at the center of the company. For example, it has long had a group that focuses on verifying the safety of raw materials, and it works closely with communities and user communities to encourage high quality play. Lego has been a WWF partner for environmental protection since 2014, and in 2017 extended the partnership to reduce CO_2 emissions and promote global action on climate change. In 2017 Lego achieved its goal of using 100 percent renewable energy three years ahead of the 2020 goal. However, in 2015, a Greenpeace video campaign highlighted Lego's partnership with oil producer Shell, showing a Lego-built Arctic landscape being destroyed by an oil spill. Lego bricks are built from plastic, which relies on petroleum products, and the Shell partnership had been important to Lego. Lego responded to the petition campaign by ending its partnership with Shell, and increasing its research and activities on substitutes for petroleum products in brick manufacturing, and on sustainable solutions for bricks "after end of use." Lego toy customers continue to benefit from the innovation and creativity of the products, the shareholders (Lego Group and the Kristiansen family) benefit from the popularity of the toys, and other stakeholders benefit from the attention paid to communities and the environment.

Going Forward: Embracing Stakeholder Theory

How should a company think about the issue of corporate sustainability? There is no simple answer to that question other than that corporations need to actively address the question in a responsible manner. The answer is not simple because the factors to be considered are complex. The answer must come from a combination of value judgments and financial analyses that executives of individual corporations will have to undertake for themselves. One framework to begin addressing the issue of corporate sustainability is stakeholder theory.

Stakeholder theory asks two questions that executives need to answer (Freeman, Wicks, and Parmar, 2004):

1. What is the purpose of the firm?
2. What responsibility do managers have to stakeholders?

Stakeholder theory rejects the separation theory, that shareholders and stakeholders are different and that one group has more rights than the other. It also believes that values are explicitly a part of management. The approach that managers choose will most likely depend on the senior executives' and board of directors' values and their view of the relationship between business and society. If they believe that society's moral or social values and business objectives are inherently in conflict, or at best totally separate domains of activity, they may favor a stance that resists doing more than the minimum. A paradigm in which business objectives and societal values are in harmony or are complementary will more likely lead to actions deemed as progressive or as leading the way.

Using the courts and the Internet, such as social media and online petitions, stakeholders can exert a lot of power today. There are many examples of this in stories from Brent Spar (Shell versus Greenpeace) to Nike (media frenzy over children working for Nike contractors). There has been a shift in expectations since Ralph Nader with *Unsafe at Any Speed* and Rachel Carson with *Silent Spring* began the trend of public outcry forcing corporate accountability in terms of what companies are expected to do and demonstrating the ability of stakeholders to enforce many of those expectations.

What is clear is that top management must set its desired course for corporate sustainability initiatives. It is also clear that there is a progression of views taking place ranging from defensive, reactive, or seeing sustainability almost as a moral issue, and from, at a minimum, a risk management view to a stance of proactive, enlightened self-interest and business opportunity that some of the leading global companies now display.

Reflection Questions

The reflection questions in this chapter are intended to increase your mindfulness about business's role in society by looking at companies and issues that are important to you personally, and your own career trajectory.

1. List some companies you admire, that work internationally. They could be drawn from the examples you identified in Chapter 8 looking at different organizational types (see p. 266). Explore these companies' approaches to corporate social responsibility. Are they part of the Global Compact? Do they report their sustainability programs and progress with the Global Reporting Initiative? Are they members of the Dow Jones Sustainability Index? What are some of the initiatives they're doing that you find interesting?

2. What is a societal or environmental issue you personally are passionate about? It could be social inequality, water access and sanitation, environmental conservation, climate change, health epidemics, education, gender, child labor, or any other issue. Identify a few companies that are addressing that issue in an international context. Which corporate initiatives do you think have the most impact? What do you think the role of companies should be in addressing this issue?

3. Think about your own values. How do you currently, in your own actions, pay attention to the impact of business on society? How important is it to you that the company you work for has a strong approach to corporate social responsibility?

Further Resources

For strong grounding on this topic, it's good to start with Andrew Savitz's *The Triple Bottom Line* (2013).

For more information on the global frameworks we reviewed, we suggest you go directly to their sources. All three sites have extensive research published, case examples, and best practice reports:

- UN Global Compact: www.unglobalcompact.org/
- Global Reporting Initiative: www.globalreporting.org/
- Dow Jones Sustainability Index: www.sustainability-indices.com/

We find that the Economist Intelligence Unit publishes well-researched reports on how companies can address business's responsibility to society. The most recent is on Global Resource Challenges, at: http://perspectives.eiu.com/sustainability/global-resource-challenges-risks-and-opportunities-strategic-management

The *Journal of Business Ethics* publishes good quality, peer-reviewed research on ethics and the social responsibility of business. A helpful recent study on the relationship between CSR and performance is Dixon-Fowler et al. (2013).

Bibliography

Accenture (2016). *UN Global Compact: Accenture Strategy Study.* Retrieved February 2018 from Accenture: www.accenture.com/us-en/strategy-index

BBC (2013). *Bangladesh Factory Collapse Toll Passes 1,000,* May 10. Retrieved from BBC News: www.bbc.com/news/world-asia-22476774

Blanchard, B. (2007). *Mattel Apologizes to China for Toy Recalls,* September 21. Retrieved April 2018 from Reuters: www.reuters.com/article/us-china-safety-mattel/mattel-apologizes-to-china-for-toy-recalls-idUSPEK10394020070921

Bowen, H. R. (1953). *Social Responsibilities of the Businessman.* Harper & Row.

Canizares, K. (2001). *Nike's Social Responsibility Rhetoric Exposed as a Lie,* May 29. Retrieved February 2013 from Organic Consumers Association: www.organicconsumers.org/old_articles/corp/nikesham.php

Carroll, A. B. (1979). A Three Dimensional Model of Corporate Performance. *Academy of Management Review,* 4, 497–505.

Carson, R. (2002). *Silent Spring.* Houghton Mifflin Harcourt.

Diermeier, D. (2012). When Do Company Boycotts Work? *Harvard Business Review,* August 6. Available at: https://hbr.org/2012/08/when-do-company-boycotts-work

Dixon-Fowler, H. R., Slater, D. J., Johnson, J. L., Elstrand, A. E., & Romi, A. M. (2013). Beyond "does it pay to be green?" A Meta-Analysis of Moderators of the CEP–CFP Relationship. *Journal of Business Ethics,* 112, 353–366.

Economist Intelligence Unit (2008). *Doing Good: Business and the Sustainability Challenge.* Retrieved February 2018 from: http://graphics.eiu.com/upload/eb/Enel_Managing_for_sustainability_WEB.pdf

Economist Intelligence Unit (2017). *Global Resource Challenges: Risks and Opportunities for Strategic Management.*

Financial Times (n.d.). *BP Draws Line Under Gulf Spill Costs.* Retrieved February 2018 from Financial Times: www.ft.com/content/ff2d8bcc-49e9-11e6-8d68-72e9211e86ab

Freeman, E. R., Wicks, A. C., & Parmar, B. (2004). Stakeholder Theory and "The Corporate Objective Revisited." *Organization Science,* 15, 364–369.

Friedman, M. (1970). The Social Responsibility of Business is to Increase its Profits. *New York Times Magazine,* September 13.

Global Compact Critics (n.d.). Retrieved January 2013, from Blogger: https://www.blogger.com/blogin.g?blogspotURL=http://globalcompactcritics.blogspot.ca/2011_01_01_archive.html&bpli=1&pli=1

Global Reporting (2018a). *About GRI.* Retrieved February 2018 from Global Reporting: www.globalreporting.org/Information/about-gri/Pages/default.aspx

Global Reporting (2018b). *Sustainability Disclosure Database.* Retrieved February 2018 from Global Reporting: http://database.globalreporting.org/

Greenhouse, S. (2013). Wal-Mart Toughens Fire Safety Rules for Suppliers After Bangladesh Blaze. *New York Times,* January 23, p. B3.

Gustavo, P. (2015). Director of Social Responsibility and Sustainability at Toks Restaurants. *International Week at IPADE.* Mexico.

KPMG & SAM (2012). *Sustainability Yearbook.* Retrieved from: https://issuu.com/sam-group.com/docs/yearbook2012.

Krauss, C. (2013). Judge Accepts BP's $4 Billion Criminal Settlement Over Gulf Oil Spill. *New York Times,* January 29.

Lazlo, C., Sherman, D., Whalen, J., & Ellison, J. (2005). Expanding the Value Horizon: How Stakeholder Value Contributes to Competitive Advantage. *Journal of Corporate Citizenship,* 20, 65–76.

Levitt, T. (1958). The Dangers of Social Responsibility. *Harvard Business Review,* 36, 41–50.

Levy, D. L., Brown, H. S., & de Jong, M. (2010). The Contested Politics of Corporate Governance: The Case of the Global Reporting Initiative. *Business & Society,* 49, 88–117.

Lewis, S. (2010, October 26). *Learning from BP's 'Sustainable' Self-Portraits: From 'Integrated Spin' to Integrated Reporting.* Retrieved February 2013 from Corporate Disclosure Alert: http://corporatedisclosurealert .blogspot.co.uk/2010/10/from-integrated-spin-to-integrated.html

Margolis, J. D., & Elfenbein, H. A. (2008). Do Well By Doing Good? Don't Count On It. *Harvard Business Review,* January. Available at: https://hbr.org/2008/01/do-well-by-doing-good-dont-count-on-it

Nader, R. (1966). *Unsafe at Any Speed: The Designed-In Dangers of the American Automobile.* Pocket Books Publishing.

Orlitzky, M., Schmidt, F., & Rynes, S. (2003). Corporate Social and Financial Performance: A Meta-Analysis. *Organizational Studies,* 24, 403–441.

Perez, G. (2015). CSR Senior VP at Toks Restaurants (Mexico). Presentation at International Week at Instituto Panamericano de Alta Dirección de Empresa (IPADE) in Mexico City.

Ramseur, J. L., & Haggerty, C. L. (2015). Deepwater Horizon Oil Spill: Recent Activities and Ongoing Developments. *Congressional Research Service,* April 17.

RobecoSAM (2017). *Measuring Intangibles: RobecoSAM's Corporate Social Sustainability Assessment Methodology.* RobecoSAM.

RobecoSAM (2018). *About Us.* Retrieved February 2018, from Sustainability Indices: http://www.sustainability-indices.com/

Savitz, A. (2013). *The Triple Bottom Line,* 2nd edn. Jossey-Bass.

Spector, B. (2008). Business Responsibilities in a Divided World: The Cold War Roots of the Corporate Social Responsibility Movement. *Enterprise & Society: The International Journal of Business History,* 9, 314–336.

Spector, B. (2013). *Implementing Organizational Change: Theory into Practice,* 3rd edn. Pearson.

Sterling, S. (2012). *How Apple's Foxconn Problem is Like Nike's Sweatshop Problem, and Why the Outcome is the Same.* Retrieved February 2013 from Digital Trends: www.how-apples-foxconn-problem-is-like-nikes-sweatshop-problem-and-why-the-outcome-is-the-same

SustainAbility (2018). *Our Story.* Retrieved 2018 from SustainAbility: http://sustainability.com/who-we-are/our-story/

Tata Group (2018). *Tata Group Profile.* Retrieved February 2018 from Tata: www.tata.com/aboutus/sub_index/Leadership-with-trust

United Nations (1987). *Report of the World Commission on Environment and Development: Our Common Future.* Retrieved from United Nations Documents: http://www.un-documents .net/our-common-future.pdf

United Nations (2017). *United Nations Global Impact Report.* United Nations Global Compact.

United Nations (2018). *The Ten Principles of the UN Global Compact.* Retrieved from United Nations Global Compact: www.unglobalcompact.org/what-is-gc/mission/principles

Valente, M. (2015). *Tata Chemicals Magadi: Confronting Poverty in Rural Africa.* Ivey Business School Publishing.

12 Conclusion

As we conclude this eighth edition of *International Management Behavior*, it is useful to reflect on how much the world has changed since the original two authors (Henry Lane and Joseph DiStefano) started their writing about international business. The first course in intercultural management was launched at the Ivey Business School in London, Canada in the early 1970s. Many business executives wondered why it was being offered; several faculty colleagues remarked that there were so few differences between doing business domestically and "going international" that they wondered what would sustain more than one or two class sessions devoted to the topic. At that time the North American Free Trade Agreement (NAFTA) wasn't on the table, China had not been recognized by then US President Richard Nixon or then Canadian Prime Minister Pierre Trudeau, and no one was anticipating the rise of the BRIC countries.

Although international business curricula had emerged in some business schools, when the first edition was published in 1988 there weren't many other books like this one, and we were not sure if a sufficient market existed to sustain sales and plan for a second edition. The intervening thirty years have seen an explosion of international activity, even involving new technology that did not exist when we started our work. And we have gone from the optimism of the "end of history," which asserted that the fundamental values of liberal democracy and market capitalism had emerged triumphant, and the election of the first multiracial, multicultural president of the United States, to the continuing pessimism of current economic turmoil, terrorism, and social disintegration in many countries.

To summarize all these changes we opened this edition with an equation that described the challenge facing global managers: Globalization equals Managing Complexity. We said that complexity was reflected in increased interdependence, variety, and ambiguity and that these were subject to constant and rapid change or "fast flux." We also said that dealing with this complexity started with developing a global mindset – understanding ourselves and our own organizations, and understanding a diverse set of other people and other organizations.

These elements of a global mindset are not different from those we faced when we wrote the first edition: but the complexity of each certainly has increased. Fortunately, the tools and technology to help us manage the increased complexity have also improved and increased. So we hope that this volume – a *very* different book than the first edition – will help our readers manage the complexity they face during their careers in international business, with increasing mindfulness about the context and the process. We have extended our original conceptions and knowledge, added our own international and cross-cultural experiences of teaching and of managing, and borrowed generously from the wisdom of our colleagues and friends.

What has not changed is our excitement about the prospects for you adding to your own rich experience during your international careers and thereby increasing your abilities to contribute to the prosperity of your organizations and society, and to the development of peace in the world. We end this eighth edition with warm and sincere wishes for success in your journey.

ⅤIVEY | Publishing

ASIS ELECTRONICS

David Wesley wrote this case under the supervision of Professor Henry W. Lane solely to provide material for class discussion. The authors do not intend to illustrate either effective or ineffective handling of a managerial situation. The authors may have disguised certain names and other identifying information to protect confidentiality.

Richard Ivey School of Business Foundation is the exclusive representative of the copyright holder and prohibits any form of reproduction, storage or transmission without its written permission. Reproduction of this material is not covered under authorization by any reproduction rights organization. To order copies or request permission to reproduce materials, contact Ivey Publishing, Richard Ivey School of Business Foundation, c/o Richard Ivey School of Business, The University of Western Ontario, London, Ontario, Canada, N6A 3K7; phone (519) 661-3208; fax (519) 661-3882; e-mail cases@ivey.uwo.ca.

Copyright © 2011, Northeastern University, College of Business Administration   Version: 2011-05-31

Peter Inge, controller for Asis Electronics, a subsidiary of a European-based corporation, reviewed the contract for an order of transmitters for the Ministry of Defense; he immediately noticed receipts totaling $6 million (approximately 20 per cent of the total contract value) that did not seem to be attached to any equipment or services provided by his company. Inge became concerned that Asis may have over-invoiced the ministry and he approached the chief financial officer (CFO) to inquire about the situation: "What plans do you have with the surplus that is in our system?" he asked. "This topic is none of my concern," the CFO replied.

Inge let the matter rest for several months until he received the annual compliance document requiring his signature. The form was part of an anti-corruption effort implemented by Asis in the 1990s after a bribery scandal resulted in the convictions of several high-level employees. The company also worked with the Organization for Economic Co-operation and Development on the "Anti-Corruption Convention," and it became a member of Transparency International, a non-profit organization devoted to reducing corruption around the world. Many considered Asis to be one of the leading companies in the fight against corruption. Asis encouraged its employees to report any irregularities to the compliance department.

The company operated under the assumption that every employee should be concerned with the good reputation of Asis in each country in which it operated. In all aspects of performing their jobs, all employees had to focus on maintaining the good reputation of – and respect for – the company.

To reduce concerns over potential repercussions for reporting irregularities, Asis established "protected communications channels" that ensured confidentiality. Attached to the compliance form was an anti-corruption handbook (see Exhibit 1). Inge reviewed the contents to see if he could find any guidance that might help him decide what to do concerning the possible overpayment.

**Exhibit 1 Asis Electronics
Anti-Corruption Handbook (Abridged)**

Table of Contents

2 Payments for routine action (prohibited)

What is this about and why is it an issue?
They are small payments made to lower-level government or private sector employees, as a personal benefit to them, to secure or speed-up the performance of a routine action to which the payer is entitled. These are sometimes known as facilitating payments. These are an issue because:

- They are a form of corruption.
- Payments for routine action are illegal in almost all countries.
- Paying for routine government action could easily open the door to more serious issues of corruption.

What is the Asis policy?
Asis prohibits payments for routine action.

What does this mean in practice?
- If you make a payment that could possibly be misunderstood as a payment to facilitate routine action, you must notify your responsible Compliance Officer and make sure that it is properly documented and posted to the correct account.
- Consult your responsible Compliance Officer when you encounter anything that looks like a request for a payment to facilitate a routine action. Such practical problems do arise in everyday business in some countries, but there are usually other ways that Asis can solve these kinds of issues.
- Never attempt to disguise such a payment as something else. The penalties for disguising such a payment are much greater than the penalties for making one!

How do I go about getting approval?
Approval will not be given.

7 Record keeping and accurate recording

What is this about and why is it an issue?
Books and records is a general term used in this guide to describe all business records. It includes accounts, correspondence, memoranda, tapes, discs, papers, books, and any other documents. It is important because the various legal codes require that we maintain accurate and complete books and records. In order to combat corruption it is important that transactions are transparent, fully documented and coded to accounts that accurately reflect their nature. Attempting to conceal a payment can create a worse violation than the payment itself.

What is the Asis policy?
- Asis books and records must be kept with reasonable detail and accuracy so that they correctly reflect all transactions.
- All controls and approval procedures must be followed.
- Asis books and records must not contain any false, misleading, or other artificial entries.

What does this mean in practice?
- Ensure that all your own transactions are fully documented, correctly approved, and coded to the correct expense description.
- If you are aware or suspect that anyone is directly or indirectly falsifying the books and records or in any other way attempting to disguise a payment, you must report your concern immediately to the "Compliance Helpdesk – Tell Us".

🛡️IVEY | Publishing    **Northeastern**
                               UNIVERSITY

RANSOM ON THE HIGH SEAS: THE CASE OF PIRACY IN SOMALIA[1]

Michael Train and Jeanne McNett wrote this case under the supervision of Professor Alvaro-Cuervo-Cazurra solely to provide material for class discussion. The authors do not intend to illustrate either effective or ineffective handling of a managerial situation. The authors may have disguised certain names and other identifying information to protect confidentiality.

Richard Ivey School of Business Foundation prohibits any form of reproduction, storage or transmission without its written permission. Reproduction of this material is not covered under authorization by any reproduction rights organization. To order copies or request permission to reproduce materials, contact Ivey Publishing, Richard Ivey School of Business Foundation, The University of Western Ontario, London, Ontario, Canada, N6A 3K7; phone (519) 661-3208; fax (519) 661-3882; e-mail cases@ivey.uwo.ca.

Copyright © 2011, Northeastern University, College of Business Administration   Version: 2012-11-26

Martin Andersen, chief operating officer (COO) of International Shipping Company (ISC), a European-owned and operated market leader in global transportation services, was looking forward to a relaxing evening. As a representative of a company that delivered cargo safely and securely to major ports, Andersen had just attended the United Nations International Maritime Organization (UNIMO) meeting in Kenya called to discuss the growing problem of piracy off the coast of Somalia. With the meeting concluded, he was going to meet colleagues from the meeting for dinner at the Tamarind Mombasa restaurant. Andersen was the first to arrive and was enjoying the view of Old Harbour when his telephone rang and he received some terrible news: one of ISC's ships, MV *Odyssey*, had been hijacked.

Background on Piracy Off the Coast of Somalia

Instances of piracy off the coast of Somalia increased dramatically in the late 2000s (see Exhibits 1 and 2). More than 100 confirmed piracy attacks had been reported, and many suspected attacks remained unreported. In 2010, Somali pirates hijacked at least 25 ships, taking more than 650 hostages. By 2011, the cost of piracy was estimated to be between US$7 billion and US$12 billion a year, including costs for fuel and security and about US$400 million in ransom payments in the period 2006-2011.[2]

One of the underlying causes of piracy in Somalia was political instability. Since the Somali Civil War began in 1991, the country lacked a stable government with effective authority. The following two decades were marred by a major rise in fighting between local groups. More than one million people – out of an original population of approximately 10 million – fled to neighboring countries such as Ethiopia.[3] The

---

[1] This case has been written on the basis of published sources only.

[2] The Economist, "Civil war, famine and piracy in Somalia: Don't aim too high," *The Economist*, October 15, 2011, p. 18.

[3] The Economist, "Somalia: Piracy and much worse," *The Economist*, October 2, 2008, www.economist.com/opinion/displaystory.cfm?story_id=12341825, accessed November 4, 2011.

Exhibit 1 Number of Reported Attacks by Pirates Worldwide

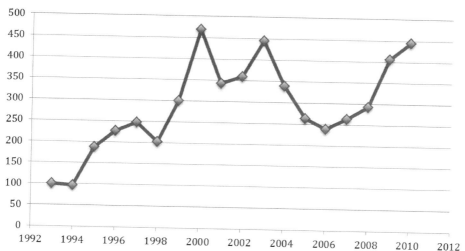

Sources: International Maritime Bureau (IMB) as reported by NATO (2009), www.nato-pa.int/Default
.asp?SHORTCUT=1770, *accessed on September 4, 2011. International Chamber of Commerce (ICC),* www.icc-ccs
.org/news/385-2009-worldwide-piracy-figures-surpass-400, *accessed September 4, 2011,* http://news.blogs.cnn
.com/2011/01/18/report-2010-was-worst-year-yet-for-piracy-on-high-seas/, *accessed September 5, 2011.*

Exhibit 2 Number of Attacks Off the Coast of Somalia

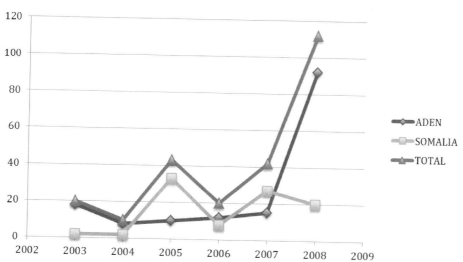

Source: International Maritime Bureau (IMB) as reported by NATO (2009), www.nato-pa.int/Default.asp?SHORTCUT=1770,
accessed September 4, 2011.

population of Somalia's capital, Mogadishu, decreased by nearly two-thirds from 1990 to 2011.[4] In 2008, the United Nations (UN) estimated that nearly 3.2 million Somalis were dependent on food aid for survival. As a failed state, Somalia was one of the poorest and most violent countries in the world. The country was also plagued by famine and over 50 per cent of the population was affected by malnutrition.[5]

The lack of stable government created an environment ripe for exploitation by many fundamentalist Islamic groups, such as al-Qaeda and Al Shabab, who successfully used fear tactics and violence to gain power. Because of the resulting political circumstances, the country became too dangerous for many foreign diplomats, charities, and journalists to enter.[6]

Various global strategies to aid Somalia were put into action. The UN and the African Union deployed about 50,000 peacekeeping troops to help reduce violence. In 2006, the United States supported an invasion by Ethiopia in the hope that the Ethiopian troops would be able to suppress the fundamentalist factions and reinstate the fallen Somali government; however, this strategy backfired in a number of ways. After nearly two years, the presence of Ethiopian troops had proved to be completely ineffective at reducing the power of fundamentalist movements or reinstating Somalia's official government; in fact, some of the insurgent groups had grown both more radical and more influential. Some fundamentalist groups had also begun to receive support

from nearby Eritrea, whose agenda was not to help Somalia but rather, to help defeat Ethiopia.[7]

Out of these difficult and traumatic circumstances, piracy emerged as one of the only alternatives to severe poverty for many unemployed youth in Somalia. Initially, the perpetrators mainly boarded the vessels of wealthy shipping companies for any money that was stored onboard; gradually, however, they began attacking ships in order to hold crew members for ransom. This highly profitable industry, along with local fundamentalist factions, proved to be a very strong attraction for Somali citizens with very few options. Pirates often worked implicitly with fundamentalist Islamic groups to provide additional on-shore security and protection for a fee.[8]

The merchant vessels that pirates typically targeted were large ships with small crews of only about 24 men. Their size and relatively slow transit speed made these boats easy targets for the small speedboats used by the pirates. Using these speedboats, pirates could approach a merchant vessel and launch hooks to climb aboard without being detected; once on board, they used small weapons, such as AK-47 assault rifles and rocket-propelled grenades, to capture the crew. Usually, the pirates then directed the captured ship to a location near the coast from which they conducted negotiations for ransom. For many years, once a ship entered

[4] The Economist, "Ahoy there!," *The Economist*, November 20, 2008, www.economist.com/node/12650244, accessed November 4, 2011.

[5] The Economist, "The world's most utterly failed state," *The Economist*, October 2, 2008, www.economist.com/node/12342212, accessed November 4, 2011.

[6] BBC News, "Somali pirates move captive ships," May 3, 2010, http://news.bbc.co.uk/2/hi/africa/8657810.stm, accessed on November 4, 2011.

[7] The Economist, "Somalia: The world's most utterly failed state," *The Economist*, October 2, 2008, www.economist.com/world/middleeast-africa/display-story.cfm?story_id=12342212, accessed November 4, 2011, Jill Dougherty, "U.S. relaxes rules governing food aid to starving Somalis," *CNNWorld*, August 2, 2011, http://articles.cnn.com/2011-08-02/world/somalia.aid.rules_1_al-shabaab-humanitarian-crisis-organizations?_s=PM:WORLD, accessed November 4, 2011.

[8] The Economist, "Anarchy in Somalia: The lawless horn, November 20, 2008, http://www.economist.com/node/12637009, accessed November 4, 2011.

Somali territory foreign navies could not pursue it;[9] however, in June 2008, the United Nations passed a resolution allowing foreign navies to enter Somali waters and use "all necessary means" to combat piracy.[10]

The crew and cargo were rarely harmed in these situations because the pirates were primarily interested in ransom money, which depended upon hostages' eventual safe release. Negotiations could take up to two months and payments tended to be between US$1 million and $3 million depending on the size of the crew and the value of the cargo. Sometimes pirates would hire a professional negotiator to obtain higher ransom prices. Once the money was received (either through informal channels, from another boat or by a drop from an airplane) the pirates would usually go ashore, leaving the captured ship and crew unharmed.

On some occasions, pirates launched their attacks from "mother ships," enabling them to reach ships even at a substantial distance from the coast (see Exhibit 3). These mother ships were usually large fishing boats that had been captured and converted into mobile bases for attacking ships. Many pirates employed fishermen or were former fishermen, so it was frequently difficult to distinguish between the two – especially from a distance.[11]

Crews on merchant ships were typically unarmed since most countries did not allow vessels with armed crews to enter port. The main defenses against pirates were water cannons, increasing speed, and maneuvering the ship to prevent pirates from boarding the ship. As piracy became an increasingly common problem, some vessels were issued non-lethal sonic weapons that could cause permanent ear damage at 300 feet (about 91 meters) in order to discourage pirates from approaching.[12]

Prevalent piracy in one of the busiest shipping lanes off the coast of Somalia had increased costs and shipping time for many shipping companies. Associated ransom costs led to higher insurance premiums. Additionally, to avoid attacks, some shipping companies decided to sail further away from shore than necessary, resulting in longer transportation times (up to four additional weeks of travel), increased costs and delays for customers. The increase in pirate attacks also led many shipping companies to employ private security firms to accompany their vessels and/or assist with on-ship defenses.

Recent Somali Hijackings

More than $100 million in ransom costs was paid to pirates in 2008.[13] For example, a Spanish fishing boat, the Playa de Bakio, was ransomed for $1.2 million. Ransoms of $800,000 and $750,000 for smaller Ukrainian and German ships were paid in the summer of 2008. By 2010, the average ransom for a captured ship had increased to $5.4 million. The highest ransom on record was $9.5 million, paid for

[9] Each coastal state may claim a territorial sea that extends seaward up to 12 nautical miles (nm) from its baselines. The coastal state exercises sovereignty over its territorial sea, the air space above it, and the seabed and subsoil beneath it. Foreign flag ships enjoy the right of innocent passage while transiting the territorial sea subject to laws and regulations adopted by the coastal State that are in conformity with the Law of the Sea Convention and other rules of international law relating to such passage.

[10] The Economist, "The Indian Ocean: The Most Dangerous Seas in the World," July 17, 2008, http://www.economist.com/node/11751360, accessed November 4, 2011.

[11] Mary Harper, "Growing Sophistication of Pirates," BBC News, April 11, 2009, http://news.bbc.co.uk/2/hi/africa/7995170.stm, accessed November 4, 2011.

[12] Frank Gardner, "Taking on Somalia's Pirates," BBC News, February 11, 2009, http://news.bbc.co.uk/2/hi/africa/7882618.stm, accessed November 4, 2011.

[13] The Economist, "The World's Most Utterly Failed State," The Economist, October 2, 2008, www.economist.com/node/12342212, accessed November 4, 2011.

Exhibit 3 Piracy Threat Map

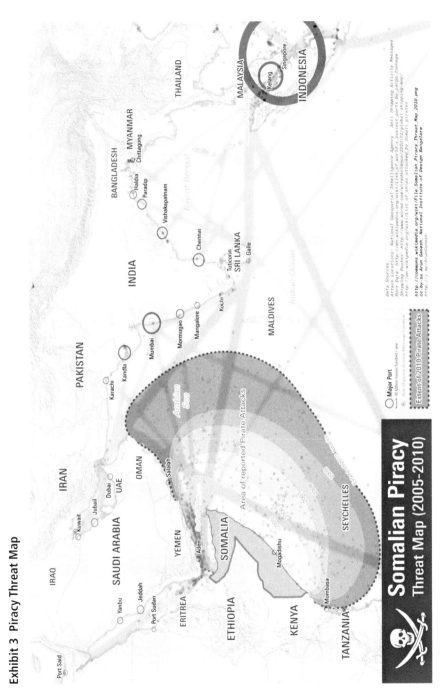

Source: CC-by-sa Arun Ganesh, National Institute of Design Bangalore. Used with permission.

the release of the Korean crude oil tanker *Samho Dream*.[14]

One of the most publicized hijackings occurred in November 2008, when Somali pirates took control of the *Sirius Star*. *Sirius Star* belonged to Vela International Marine, a Dubai-based company and a subsidiary of the Saudi Arabian state-owned oil company Saudi Aramco. The ship was registered in and flying the flag of Liberia, and home-ported in Liberia's capital, Monrovia. On November 15, 2008, Somali pirates boarded the *Sirius Star* nearly 450 nautical miles (about 833 kilometers or 517 miles) off the coast of Somalia. This was both the largest ship pirates had ever hijacked as well as the farthest offshore that they had done so. At the time of the hijacking, the tanker contained more than $100 million in oil intended for transport to the United States. The pirates docked the ship at the Somali port of Harardhere, and the international crew of 25 was reported safe.[15] Five days later, on November 20, the pirates made a ransom demand of $25 million and imposed a deadline of 10 days, threatening "disastrous" action if Vela International Marine did not comply. On November 24, the pirates reduced their demands to $15 million after the company and Saudi Arabia, with the support of several other governments,

refused to pay the ransom. Nearly two months passed before the ship and crew were finally released on January 9, 2009 – after a reported $3 million ransom was paid.[16]

If the *Sirius Star* incident provided an example of significant success for Somali pirates, the incident involving *Maersk Alabama* demonstrated that failure was adamantly possible. Despite recommendations that all ships stay beyond 600 nautical miles (about 1,112 kilometers or 690 miles) off the coast of Somalia, *Maersk Alabama* was only 240 nautical miles (about 444 kilometers or 276 miles) offshore when it was boarded by pirates on April 7, 2009. While the pirates were boarding, most of the crew members locked themselves in the engine room and disabled the bridge controls so they could maintain control of the ship. After a brief skirmish in which the crew captured the leader of the pirates, the American tanker's captain, Richard Phillips, surrendered himself in exchange for the safety of the rest of the crew. The pirates then forced Phillips into one of the cargo ship's lifeboats and sailed out to sea with the intent of holding the captain for ransom.[17] On April 9, the American destroyer USS *Bainbridge* arrived and escorted the cargo ship into harbor in Kenya. For the remainder of the day, a standoff ensued between the pirate-controlled lifeboat and *Bainbridge*. The following day, negotiations to free Phillips began while the pirates simultaneously developed plans to smuggle him onto Somali land to increase their leverage. On April 12, the captain of *Bainbridge* determined that Captain Phillips' life was in immediate danger and ordered a rescue operation. U.S. Navy SEAL snipers opened fired and killed the three

[14] The Economist, "The Indian Ocean: The Most Dangerous Seas in the World," *The Economist*, July 17, 2008, http://www.economist.com/node/11751360, accessed on November 4, 2011. Robert Wright, "Sharp Rise in Pirate Ransom Costs," *Financial Times*, January 16, 2011, www.ft.com/intl/cms/s/0/658138a6-219b-11e0-9e3b-00144feab49a.html#axzz1UvQwEEEA, accessed November 4, 2011.

[15] The Times, "Somali Pirates Hijack Saudi Oil Tanker With Britons on Board," *The Times*, November 19, 2008, www.timesonline.co.uk/tol/news/world/africa/article5172770.ece, accessed on November 4, 2011 by subscription only. The Economist, "Anarchy in Somalia: The Lawless Horn," November 20, 2008, http://www.economist.com/node/12637009, accessed November 4, 2011.

[16] BBC News, "Saudi Tanker Freed Off Somalia," *BBC News*, January 9, 2009, http://news.bbc.co.uk/2/hi/africa/7820311.stm, accessed November 4, 2011.

[17] BBC News, "U.S. Crew Seized by Somali Pirates," *BBC News*, April 8, 2009, http://news.bbc.co.uk/2/hi/africa/7989474.stm, accessed November 4, 2011.

pirates remaining on the lifeboat. A fourth pirate, who was on *Bainbridge* negotiating, was taken captive and brought to the United States to stand trial.[18]

ISC's Situation

Andersen learned that ISC's cargo ship MV *Odyssey* was carrying more than $50 million of machinery and was hijacked in the Indian Ocean, 550 nautical miles east of the coast of Somalia, by a group of 14 young men. *Odyssey* was being sailed towards the coast of Somalia and was presently 350 nautical miles from it. The ship's crew consisted of 20 men from 11 countries; the captain and the two officers of the ship were American. Because of the multinational makeup of the crew, ISC informed several national governments, including the United States, who promised to contribute any necessary resources and immediately rerouted one of its Navy's ships towards *Odyssey*'s location. The pirates had not made their demands known so far.

As COO responsible for operations-level fleet safety, and due to his relative proximity to Somalia, Andersen was asked by the company's CEO to take charge of the situation. This was the first hijacking that ISC had experienced, and as Andersen considered the issues, he remembered the discussion on initial responses at the UNIMO meeting: ISC had a policy of non-negotiation with pirates but until now, that policy had not been tested.

Andersen had some time to think – at least until the pirates contacted ISC. The company's CEO had instructed Andersen to do whatever he could to ensure the safe return of the crew, ship, and cargo. He also mentioned ready access to $3.5 million.

However, Andersen knew that negotiation was expensive in terms of both money and time: the process usually lasted around two months and cost approximately $1 million in addition to ransom costs.[19] There would also be additional costs for security to protect *Odyssey* from other pirates during negotiations, as well as lost revenues due to the ship being out of service. Nevertheless, the safety of the crew was ISC's main priority. Accordingly, one of Andersen's first ideas was simply to negotiate for as small a ransom as possible in exchange for the safe return of the crew and ship.

Andersen's second option involved the U.S. Navy ship that was fast approaching *Odyssey*. While its main priority would be to rescue the American crew members, the highly-trained SEAL team onboard would likely be successful in attacking and recapturing the ship; however, the team estimated that there was a 60 per cent chance that one or more crew members would be harmed during this operation, while damage to the ship and cargo would be minimal.[20] The approach of the U.S. Navy ship also offered Andersen the ability to negotiate with the pirates while backed by a threat of substantial force. If, however, the pirates were to kill any of *Odyssey*'s American crew members during negotiations, the Navy would attack to prevent further harm to crew members, thereby potentially proving a liability for ISC's employees and property.

Odyssey contained enough supplies to sustain the captive crew for up to two

---

[18] CNN, "Hostage Captain Rescued; Navy Snipers Kill 3 Pirates," *CNN*, April 12, 2009, www.cnn .com/2009/WORLD/africa/04/12/somalia.pirates/ index.html, accessed November 4, 2011.

[19] Mary Harper, "Life in Somali's Pirate Town," *BBC News*, September 18, 2008, http://news.bbc.co .uk/2/hi/africa/7623329.stm, accessed November 4, 2011.

[20] BBC News, "Pirates Attack Second U.S. Vessel," *BBC News*, April 15, 2009, http://news.bbc.co.uk/2/ hi/africa/7999350.stm, accessed November 4, 2011. Nick Holland, "Paying Off the Pirates," *BBC News*, April 16, 2009, http://news.bbc.co.uk/2/ hi/in_depth/7932205.stm, accessed November 4, 2011.

months but Andersen worried that the longer ISC delayed decisive action, the greater the costs to the company would be. Furthermore, if the pirates became impatient or desperate, they may take action against the crew, cargo and/or ship. Andersen knew that if the captured ship reached Somalia, it was possible that additional pirates would join the attack and the crew could be taken onshore, making the recovery of the ship by force nearly impossible without seriously endangering crew members.

Another option that occurred to Andersen was the possibility of communicating a willingness to negotiate to the pirates and requesting that a representative from the group join ISC. This representative could then be held captive in an effort to reduce the pirates' leverage, depending on the importance/rank of the captured representative to the group.

Additional Considerations

ISC's finance department reported that the company would face potentially crippling losses if the entire $50 million cargo and the $25 million ship were lost. Furthermore, ISC did not carry insurance against piracy.

The UNIMO meetings that Andersen attended had emphasized that payment of ransom encouraged further acts of piracy. They had debated U. S. Defense Secretary Robert Gates' opinion that companies paying ransoms to Somali pirates hampered efforts to deal with the problem more effectively.

Part of the problem is the number of companies – not countries, but companies – that are prepared to pay the ransoms as part of the price of doing business and clearly if they did not pay the ransoms then we would be in a stronger position ... at least it would make it a lot more dangerous and a lot tougher for these pirates and then we could address some of the longer-term problems.[21]

Any ransom payments made would increase ISC insurance premiums for future shipments. Premiums could rise as much as 20 per cent – and possibly higher should there be any problems with the crew, cargo, or ship. The death of any crew member would be a tragic loss and could cost ISC $500,000 to $1 million in payments to the deceased's family.[22]

Andersen sighed. "It is one thing to talk about these issues in a meeting at a beautiful hotel in Mombasa," he thought, "but it is a totally different thing to actually experience them." As he rushed from the restaurant back to his hotel, Andersen wondered what approach he should take in dealing with this attack against one of ISC's ships.

---

[21] Brent Lang, "Gates: Stop Paying Ransom to Pirates," *CBS News*, April 17, 2009, www.cbsnews.com/8301-503544_162-4952864-503544.html.

[22] The Economist, "The Indian Ocean: The Most Dangerous Seas in the World," July 17, 2008, http://www.economist.com/node/11751360, accessed on November 4, 2011. Kaija Hulbert, The human cost of Somali piracy, June 6, 2011, Oceansbeyondpiracy.org, oceansbeyondpiracy.org/sites/.../human_cost_of_somali_piracy.pdf

Index